Asset Allocation Considerations for Pension Insurance Funds

Christian Hertrich

Asset Allocation Considerations for Pension Insurance Funds

Theoretical Analysis and Empirical Evidence

Springer Gabler

Christian Hertrich
Fachbereich BWL
Universität Stuttgart
Stuttgart, Germany

Dissertation University of Stuttgart, 2013

D93

ISBN 978-3-658-02166-5 ISBN 978-3-658-02167-2 (eBook)
DOI 10.1007/978-3-658-02167-2

The Deutsche Nationalbibliothek lists this publication in the Deutsche Nationalbibliografie; detailed bibliographic data are available in the Internet at http://dnb.d-nb.de.

Library of Congress Control Number: 2013936080

Springer Gabler

Printed on acid-free paper

Springer Gabler is a brand of Springer DE.
Springer DE is part of Springer Science+Business Media.
www.springer-gabler.de

risk-oriented remain rare in academia to date. The present dissertation, however, pursues a strong risk emphasis. It is thereby the first research work that offers a risk-focused econometric analysis for highly regulated German Pension Insurance Funds. Christian Hertrich's research is highly innovative in terms of how SRI assets can be implemented by this type of occupational pension plan. Moreover, his dissertation implements methods and parameterisations that have been rarely used in the context of financial econometric studies applied to SRI. It is laudable that the author's studies are not limited exclusively to the existing German regulatory framework, but also includes alternative investment scenarios of occupational pension systems that pursue (partially) contrary investing philosophies, e.g. the British as well as the Dutch pension models.

The innovative approach of Christian Hertrich's dissertation is that it operates between the rigid regulations of Pension Insurance Funds in Germany and the latest findings of modern empirical capital markets theory in terms of SRI. The simulation of different asset allocation strategies combined with the calculation of adequate risk-return parameters relevant for Pension Insurance Funds offers valuable conclusions. While the dissertation is primarily focused on empirical analyses in the field of financial econometrics, it includes nonetheless practical considerations as well as regulatory aspects of Pension Insurance Funds. The author's thesis is therefore also a valuable reference for practitioners involved in the asset allocation of Pension Insurance Funds. Christian Hertrich presents hereby for the first time the options available within SRI investing by applying a risk-focused quantitative analysis. The empirical methods used as well as the results obtained in this book might not only draw the attention of academics, but also receive the recognition of practitioners.

Stuttgart, February 2013 Univ.-Prof. Dr. Henry Schäfer

Foreword

Social Responsible Investments (SRI) have benefitted in the last few years fr double-digit growth rates. In many European countries, SRIs have also reach high-digit market shares in terms of assets under management. An exception this trend is the German capital market, which lags the European growth tren Strikingly, main driver of European SRI growth are institutional investors, in pa ticular occupational pension schemes. Prevailing regulation is in many Europe an countries the predominant reason for the rapid SRI expansion (e.g. Pensio Act from 2002 in the UK). In Germany, on the other hand, occupational pensio plans remain cautious in terms of their SRI asset allocation. The lack of a compulsory regulation to include SRI strategies in the investment process, concerns with respect to underperformance in comparison to conventional asset classes as well as a perceived unfavourable risk capacity of SRI assets have impeded a more pronounced expansion so far.

This is the starting point of Christian Hertrich's dissertation. One of his fundamental research interests is to investigate the investment flexibility German Pension Insurance Funds have for SRI strategies within the prevailing regulatory as well as supervisory framework in Germany. The author uses hereby conventional SRI asset classes, e.g. equities and bonds, as well as established and common investment methods. He then expands his investment universe to include alternative investments and completes his empirical analysis by simulating new investment models that do not adhere to existing German regulation. He chooses as benchmark the British as well as Dutch pension models given their high asset allocation into equities and alternative investments as well as the flexible nature of the regulation in those countries. Furthermore, an inflation hedge model and credit risk hedging considerations are simulated and assessed for their suitability for Pension Insurance Funds. To evaluate the risk-return profiles of different risk management instruments (derivative overlays) applied and underlying investment models used, Christian Hertrich uses a set of shortfall risk measures based on Lower Partial Moments.

Empirical SRI studies exist for close to 35 years, with the majority of them focusing primarily on performance measurements. Analyses that are primarily

Preface

A few words of gratitude cannot express how much the completion of this thesis is due to the support I have received during the last few years.

Running the risk of excluding some people important to me, I owe a special thank to a small group of individuals: to my supervisor Prof. Henry Schäfer for his continuous advise and guidance during the dissertation, to my sister Isabel for her positive attitude to life and her inspirational character, to my brother Markus for our numerous discussions on econometrics as well as his strong belief in my project, to my mother for emphasising the importance of education in life and for teaching me to be the person I am today, and to my beautiful wife Ainura for the enormous support she gave me over the last few years and all the sacrifices she had to make during my studies.

This book, however, is dedicated to my little son Arman, for bringing love and joy into our lives. His birth and the first few months together during the final phase of my thesis were incredible.

London, March 2013 Christian Hertrich

Table of Content

List of Figures

List of Tables

Glossary Translated Terms

English	German
Capital Funding Principle	Kapitaldeckungsverfahren
Cash-Value Life Insurance	Kapitallebensversicherung
Certification of Retirement Pension Contracts Act	Altersvorsorgeverträge Zertifizierungsgesetz (AltZertG)
Contribution Rate	Beitragssatz
Contribution-based Defined Benefits	Beitragsorientierte Leistungszusage
Deferred Compensation	Entgeltumwandlung
Defined Benefits	Leistungszusage
Defined Contributions with Capital Guarantee	Beitragszusage mit Mindestleistung
Direct Insurance	Direktversicherung
Direct Pension Commitment	Direktzusage
Federal Agency for Financial Market Supervision	Bundesanstalt fuer Finanzdiensleistungsaufsicht (BaFin)
Federal Central Tax Office	Bundeszentralamt fuer Steuern
Federal Constitution	Grundgesetz
Federal Constitutional Court	Bundesverfassungsgericht
Federal Ministry for the Environment, Nature Conservation and Nuclear Safety	Bundesministerium fuer Umwelt, Naturschutz und Reaktorsicherheit
Federal Ministry of Finance	Bundesministerium der Finanzen
Federal Ministry of Justice	Bundesministerium der Justiz
Federal Ministry of Labour and Social Affairs	Bundesministerium fuer Arbeit und Soziales
Federal Statistical Office	Statistisches Bundesamt
German Statutory Pension Insurance Scheme	Deutsche Rentenversicherung Bund
German sustainable investment forum	Forum Nachhaltige Geldanlagen (FNG)
Guarantee Assets	Sicherungsvermoegen
Income Tax Act	Einkommenssteuergesetz (EStG)
Insurance Supervision Act	Versicherungsaufsichtsgesetz (VAG)
Investment Ordinance	Anlageverordnung (AnlV)
Law for the Improvement of the Company Pension Scheme	Gesetz zur Verbesserung der betrieblichen Altersversorgung (BetrAVG)
Occupational Pension Arrangement	Betriebliche Altersvorsorge
Pay-as-you-go System (PAYG)	Umlageverfahren
Pension Capital	Versorgungskapital
Pension Fund	Pensionsfond
Pension Insurance Fund	Pensionskasse

Pension Security Association	Pensionssicherungsverein (PSV)
Premium Reserve	Deckungsrueckstellung
Retirement Savings Act	Altersvermoegensgesetz
Social Security Code	Sozialgesetzbuch (SGB)
Social Security Contribution Ceiling	Beitragsbemessungsgrenze
Solvency Margin	Solvabilitaetsspanne
Support Fund	Unterstuetzungskasse

Glossary Abbreviations

Abbreviation	Explanation
AGM	Annual general meeting
AGTAFA	Alcohol, gambling, tobacco, armaments, firearms and adult entertainment
AltEinkG	Alterseinkuenftegesetz
AltZertG	Altersvorsorgeverträge Zertifizierungsgesetz
AnlV	Anlageverordnung
AR	Autoregressive
ARIMA	Auto regressive integrated moving average
ARMA	Autoregressive moving average
AuM	Assets under management
AVmG	Altersvermoegensgesetz
BaFin	Bundesanstalt fuer Finanzdienstleistungsaufsicht
BetrAVG	Gesetz zur Verbesserung der betrieblichen Altersversorgung
bln	billion
cc	Continously compounded
CDB	Contribution based defined benefit
CSR	Corporate social responsibility
CTA	Contractual trust agreement
DB	Defined benefit
DCCG	Defined contribution with capital guarantee
e.g.	for example
EMU	European Monetary Union
ESG	Environmental, social and governance
EStG	Einkommenssteuergesetz
et al.	and others
ETF	Exchange-traded fund
et seq.	and the following
et seqq.	and the following one or ones
FNG	Forum nachhaltige Geldanlagen
fof	Fund of funds
FRG	Federal Republic of Germany
GDP	Gross Domestic Product
GDR	German Democratic Republic

Abbreviation	**Explanation**
h	Hours
HZvNG	Huettenknappschaftliche Zusatzversicherungs Neuregelungsgesetz
i.e.	that is
k	thousand
KPI	Key performance indicator
LHS	Left-hand-side
m	Million
MA	Moving average
MAR	Minimum acceptable return
Mrd.	Milliarden
n/a	Not applicable
NGO	Non-governmental organisation
p.a.	per year
Par.	Paragraph
PAYG	Pay-as-you-go
PRI	Principle for responsible investment
PSV	Pensionssicherungsverein
RHS	Right-hand-side
RRG	Rentenreformgesetz
Sec.	Section
SET	Sequential elimination method
SGB	Sozialgesetzbuch
SRI	Social responsible investment
trn	Trillion
VAG	Versicherungsaufsichtsgesetz
VAR	Vector autoregressive
VEC	Vector error corrrection
WWI/II	World War I/II

Abstract

Executive Summary
This research dissertation provides theoretical considerations and empirical evidence that Pension Insurance Funds (Pensionskassen) in Germany should consider SRIs and alternative investments as part of their strategic asset allocation. Furthermore, derivative overlay structures appear suitable to tailor-made the risk management of pension investment portfolios without impacting average performance. Using Vector Error Correction models, combined with bootstrap simulation techniques, we are able to generate future portfolio return distributions that allow us to simulate different investment strategies.

The public pension system in Germany is facing significant challenges that are jeopardizing its pay-as-you-go (PAYG) funding principle. An aging population, low birth rates, a decreasing workforce and fundamental changes in the workspace are threatening the financing of the PAYG system. As a consequence, statutory pension benefits have decreased to 47.1% of gross salary, a level that for a considerable proportion of Germany's pensioners is insufficient to provide a satisfactory retirement pension. The German legislator has introduced a set of essential pension reforms that aim at promoting capital funded, private pension schemes. Occupational pension funds, in particular, are expected to play a more relevant role in Germany in the future as a substitute for the statutory pension system.

Pension Insurance Funds *(Pensionskassen)* are the largest external occupational pension plan in Germany, with assets under management in excess of €115bln and a market share of approximately 24%. Their asset allocation is highly regulated by the German regulator BaFin and the VAG act, resulting in a risk-conservative asset allocation that on average has 85% of total assets invested in investment grade corporate bonds and government securities.

In leading European capital funded pension systems, in particular the UK and the Netherlands, SRI (social responsible investment) strategies as well as alternative investments play a dominant role in the asset allocation of pension funds.

Approximately €1.2trn assets under management are invested by British pension funds in SRI assets, whereas up to 83% of Dutch pension funds have a SRI policy in place. In the alternative investment space, pension funds have allocated over €770bln of their investment portfolios into alternative assets globally, with European pension funds committing around €230bln into this asset class.

SRI strategies are attractive for the strategic asset management of Pension Insurance Funds for various reasons: (1) Academic research studies conclude SRIs perform at least as good as conventional assets do, with more recent studies providing evidence that SRIs outperform on average traditional securities, (2) an internal SRI policy can act as a shield against reputational risk and external stakeholder pressure groups, (3) good corporate governance by a pension fund can act as mitigant against systematic risks, (4) interpretation of fiduciary duty in Germany suggests investment managers are required to include SRI strategies as part of their asset management strategy and (5) regulatory requirements by the AltZert act and the VAG force pension fund managers to report to their beneficiaries to what extend ESG (ethical, social and governance) aspects have been considered in the asset management.

Within alternative investments, this research study focuses primarily on hedge fund assets and commodities, given their particular risk-return benefits when added to a portfolio composed of conventional assets. Hedge fund assets, for example, tend to have a low correlation to conventional assets and particular hedge fund strategies are able to generate consistently alpha returns. Commodities, on the other hand, are good inflation proxy hedges, while also offering low correlation to traditional assets. Moreover, the German regulator allows Pension Insurance Funds to add derivative overlay structures to their asset management strategy, thereby offering the flexibility of fine-tuning the risk management of the funds.

The central research objective of our dissertation is to assess the suitability of SRIs as well as alternative investments for the strategic asset allocation of German Pension Insurance Funds. Our analysis focuses on existing regulation with regard to asset allocation as well as presents alternative investment models that ignore the prevailing strict investment framework imposed in Germany.

Using the Vector Error Correction (VEC) methodology, a multivariate stochastic time series model, we estimate the data generating process of the underlying input variables. The VEC model enables us to capture long-term cointegration relationships should they exist amongst the portfolio assets selected. A bootstrap simulation on the estimated VEC models allows generating future return paths of the underlying portfolios. These return distributions will subsequently be used as input for the various asset allocation strategies we have chosen. The simulated asset allocations will include outright strategies as well as methods that combine different derivative overlay structures that facilitate portfolio managers to tailor-made their internal risk management. Due to the capital guarantee in nominal terms Pension Insurance Funds offer their beneficiaries, our performance assessment is focused primarily on downside risk mitigation.

The empirical results of our research study offer valuable conclusions for the strategic asset management of Pension Insurance Funds: (1) SRI-structured portfolios consistently perform better than conventional portfolios, (2) adding alternative investments to the asset allocation has a beneficial effect on the risk-return distribution and (3) derivative overlay structures enable pension fund managers to mitigate the downside risk exposure of their portfolio without impacting average fund performance.

In terms of alternative allocation models, (1) high-equity portfolios following the UK and Dutch average pension allocation lead to an increase in return volatility without sufficiently compensating investors with higher returns, (2) hedging against price increases by engineering a portfolio with inflation-suitable assets yields mixed results, (3) a portfolio composition that combines derivative overlay strategies for both equities and corporate bonds and uses SRI-screened assets as underlying, generates the best risk-return distributions of all strategies simulated in our study.

Zusammenfassung

Executive Summary

Die theoretischen Überlegungen sowie empirischen Ergebnisse dieser Dissertation weisen auf eine Eignung nachhaltiger Geldanlagen sowie alternativer Investments für die Vermögensanlage deutscher Pensionskassen hin. Zusätzlich wird aufgezeigt, dass sich der Einsatz von Derivateprodukten als Risikomanagementinstrumente anbietet. Mit Hilfe von Vector Error Correction Modellen sowie Bootstrap Simulationen werden zukünftige Renditepfade für die zugrundeliegenden Portfolien simuliert, welche die Bewertung von verschiedenen Anlagestrategien ermöglichen.

Die Finanzierung der gesetzlichen Rentenversicherung in Deutschland ist in den letzten Jahren zunehmend unter Druck geraten. Demographische Faktoren wie die Überalterung der Bevölkerung, die geringe Geburtenrate, der kontinuierliche Rückgang der Beschäftigten sowie der strukturelle Wandel des Arbeitsumfeldes gefährden die Finanzierbarkeit des deutschen Rentensystems im Rahmen des Umlageverfahrens. Eine Folge dieser Megatrends ist der konstante Rückgang des nominalen Rentenniveaus bis auf derzeitig 47% des letzten Bruttogehalts. Die gesetzliche Standardrente bietet demnach vielen Bundesbürgern keine ausreichende Altersfinanzierung mehr. Um dem Finanzierungsengpass des Rentensystems entgegenzusteuern, hat der deutsche Gesetzgeber eine Reihe von Rentenreformen durchgesetzt, die sowohl die betriebliche Altersvorsorge wie auch private Rentenpläne fördern sollen. Betriebliche Altersvorsorgeeinrichtungen sollen hierbei zukünftig als Substitut der gesetzlichen Rentenversicherung agieren, um dem Werteverlust der staatlichen Rente entgegen zu wirken.

Pensionskassen zählen zu den bedeutendsten externen betrieblichen Altersvorsorgeeinrichtungen Deutschlands. Mit einem Anlagevolumen von über €115Mrd. und einem Marktanteil von ungefähr 24%, nehmen sie eine Schlüsselfunktion in der betrieblichen Altersvorsorge ein. Die Rahmenbedingungen der Kapitalanlage von Pensionskassen sowie die erlaubten Leistungszusagen sind durch die Aufsicht der BaFin sowie den gesetzlichen Bestimmungen des

Versicherungsaufsichtsgesetzes (VAG) hochgradig reguliert. Dies hat unter anderem zur Folge, dass Pensionskassen im Durchschnitt 85% ihres Anlagevermögens in festverzinsliche Unternehmens- und Staatsanleihen investieren.

In europäischen Ländern, in denen die Altersrenten hauptsächlich über das Kapitaldeckungsverfahren finanziert werden und in denen betriebliche Altersvorsorgeeinrichtungen eine hohen Marktanteil haben, spielen nachhaltige Geldanlagen sowie alternative Investments bereits eine wichtige Rolle in der Kapitalanlage. Vor allem die betrieblichen Rentensysteme Großbritanniens sowie der Niederlande sind hierbei federführend. Zirka €1,2Bln an Vermögenswerten sind bereits von britischen Pensionsfonds in SRI angelegt worden. Bis zu 83% der niederländischen Fonds haben ihre Kapitalanlage nach nachhaltigen Gesichtspunkten aufgestellt. Desweiteren haben Pensionseinrichtungen weltweit über €770Mrd. in alternative Geldanlagen investiert, davon allein €230Mrd. durch europäische Pensionsfonds.

Nachhaltige Geldanlagen bieten Pensionskassen eine Reihe von wesentlichen Vorteilen: (1) wissenschaftliche Studien belegen, dass nachhaltige Geldanlagen eine ähnliche oder sogar höhere Performance erzielen können als konventionelle Investments. (2) Eine nachhaltige Ausrichtung der Vermögensverwaltung einer Pensionskasse kann als eine Art Schutzschild gegen externe Stakeholder Gruppierungen agieren. (3) Eine gute Unternehmensführung kann die Vorsorgeeinrichtung vor Systemrisiken schützen. (4) Die Auslegung von treuhänderischer Pflicht in Deutschland suggeriert, dass unter bestimmten Bedingungen der Portfolioverwalter in nachhaltige Geldanlagen investieren sollte. (5) Der Gesetzgeber hat eine Berichtspflicht über die Einhaltung von ESG Faktoren (ethische, soziale sowie Governance Aspekte) in der Vermögensverwaltung von Pensionskassen im Rahmen des Altersvorsorgeverträge Zertifizierungsgesetzes (AltZertG) eingeführt.

Die empirische Analyse der Dissertation befasst sich innerhalb der alternativen Investments hauptsächlich mit Hedgefondstrategien sowie Rohstoffen. Diese Einschränkung ist mit den besonderen Merkmalen dieser speziellen Asset Klassen im Rahmen der Portfoliorisikominimierung gerechtfertigt. Hedgefonds weisen einerseits geringe Korrelationen mit herkömmlichen Anlageklassen auf. Zusätzlich erzielen bestimmte Hedgefonds Strategien auf beständige Weise Alpharenditen. Rohstoffe hingegen bieten Fondmanagers eine Absicherung gegen inflationäre Tendenzen sowie geringe Korrelationen zu konventionellen Vermögenswerten. Des weiteren lassen die gesetzlichen Anlagebestimmungen den Einsatz von Derivaten zu, die den Pensionskassen eine Kalibrierung des internen Risikomanagements ermöglichen.

Die zentrale Forschungsfrage der Dissertation ist in diesem Kontext, ob sich nachhaltige Geldanlagen sowie alternative Investments für die strategische Asset Allokation deutscher Pensionskassen eignen. Dabei werden Investmentmodelle analysiert, die die derzeitige Gesetzgebung für das Anlagevermögen berücksichtigen, sowie alternative Anlageansätze betrachtet, die den gesetzlichen Rahmen ignorieren.

Die Methodik der empirischen Untersuchung beruht auf dem *Vector Error Correction (VEC)* Modell, einem stochastischen Zeitreihenmodell, das für die jeweiligen Geldanlagen die statistischen Eigenschaften der zugrundeliegenden Zeitreihen schätzen kann. Ein wesentlicher Vorteil des VEC Modells ist die Möglichkeit, bestehende Kointegrationsbeziehungen festzustellen. Mit Hilfe von *Bootstrap* Simulationstechniken werden anschließend zukünftige Renditeverlaufspfade der jeweiligen Portfolien berechnet. Diese Renditeverteilungen dienen daraufhin als Input für die verschiedenen Anlagestrategien, die im Rahmen dieser Dissertation simuliert werden. Dabei werden einfachere Strategien, sogenannte *Outright-Modelle*, wie auch komplexere Anlageansätze berücksichtigt, die den Einsatz von Derivaten ermöglichen. Aufgrund der Kapitalgarantie, die über die Beitragszusage mit Mindestleistung den Leistungsempfängern von Pensionskassen angeboten wird, müssen die Ergebnisse der simulierten Strategien mit Blick auf Risikominimierung bewertet werden. Dabei spielt die Unterschreitung des nominalen Anfangsvermögens der Pensionskassen eine zentrale Rolle.

Die empirischen Ergebnisse sowie Erkenntnisse, die im Rahmen dieser Dissertation gewonnen werden konnten, bieten bedeutende Forschungsbeiträge: (1) Portfolien, die in nachhaltige Geldanlagen investieren, erzielen durchgehend bessere Ergebnisse als Fonds, die lediglich in konventionelle Vermögenswerte anlegen. (2) Die Hinzunahme von alternativen Investments führt zu einer optimaleren Risiko-Rendite Verteilung der Portfoliorenditen. (3) Derivateoverlays ermöglichen es Pensionskassen, das Downside Risiko der Portfolien zu minimieren, ohne dabei die durchschnittliche Performance zu beeinträchtigen.

Die Ergebnisse der simulierten Alternativszenarien ermöglichen folgende Schlussfolgerungen: (1) Portfolien mit einem hohen Aktienanteil, die den britischen sowie niederländischen Pensionsmodellen nachempfunden sind, weisen eine hohe Renditevolatilität auf. Dieses hohe Portfoliorisiko wird jedoch nicht durch eine höhere Durchschnittsrendite kompensiert. (2) Die Absicherung von Inflationsrisiken mit Hilfe von Geldanlagen, die vor Preissteigerungen schützen sollen, führt zu uneinheitlichen Ergebnissen. (3) Die Verbindung aus Derivateoverlays sowohl für Aktieninvestments wie auch Unternehmensanleihen, kombiniert mit nachhaltigen Geldanlagen, führt zu den besten Performanceergebnissen der empirischen Studie in Bezug auf die Anlageziele von Pensionskassen.

1. Introduction

1.1 Research Framework[1]

1.1.1 Relevance of Pension Insurance Funds

The occupational pension system in Germany has its origins in the 19th century, when industrial companies like Krupp, Siemens, BASF and Hoechst implemented the first pension schemes for their employees to protect them against the financial effects of disability or death.[2] These early forms of pension benefits were introduced prior to the acclaimed German statutory pension system, which came into effect in 1889 under Reich Chancellor Otto von Bismarck.[3] While occupational pension plans were initially voluntary services offered by a small group of entrepreneurs with a distinguished sense of paternalistic responsibility towards their employees, nowadays 51% of all German companies and 97% of all large corporations offer some form of occupational pension scheme. With 12.3m pension members, 15.1% of Germany's total population is currently covered by an occupational pension plan.[4]

There are five occupational pension alternatives that can be offered by law to employees in Germany. Amongst those, *Pensionskassen* (subsequently referred to as Pension Insurance Funds) represent the largest external occupational pension scheme available with more than 4.5m[5] pension members and €115.8bln[6] assets under management (AuM). Pension Insurance Funds obtain approximately 23.6%[7] of market share in terms of AuM amongst occupational pension plans in Germany and have benefited from the largest growth of pen-

1 This dissertation is based on the corresponding PhD research proposal document published by the same author in November 2011. Some sections of that report are reflected in this thesis. See Hertrich (2011) for more details.
2 See Sabrowski (2007), p. 11. Retirement benefits were introduced at a later stage. See Gieg (2008), p. 19.
3 See Uebelhack (2011), p. 12 or Sabrowski (2007), p. 11. The founding dates for the first pension funds are hereby: Krupp (1858), Siemens (1872), BASF (1879) and Hoechst (1882).
4 See Bundesministerium fuer Arbeit und Soziales (2008), p. 11, p. 22 and p. 32. Large corporations are defined as companies with more than 1,000 employees. For the current population, we have used the 2010 figure of 81.5m inhabitants as reported by Statistisches Bundesamt (2011, a).
5 See Bundesministerium fuer Arbeit und Soziales (2008), p. 110.
6 See BaFin (2012, b).
7 See Schwind (2011), p. 476.

sion members in the last years.[8] Regulated as a life insurance company under the German Insurance Supervision Act (VAG), Pension Insurance Funds also represent a 9.6% market share amongst German insurers.[9]

1.1.2 Future Challenges

The importance of Pension Insurance Funds is expected to change fundamentally in coming years, as Germany's society is facing significant challenges that will impact the role capital-funded occupational pension plans will play in the future. An aging population as well as a decreasing workforce (-34.4% forecasted until 2060)[10] is jeopardizing the funding of the pay-as-you-go (PAYG) statutory pension system. Moreover, in the next 20 years, the ratio of pensioners to contribution payers in Germany is expected to increase drastically from currently 65:100 to 110:100, making a PAYG funding system unviable.[11] As a consequence of these forecasted funding issues, the state pension levels have been decreasing steadily (from 57.3% of gross salary in 1957 to 47.1% in 2010), whereas the contribution rates have increased concurrently from 14.0% to 19.9% as of today.[12] In addition, the German legislator has reduced future state pension levels even further: by 2020 and 2030, the pension levels are expected to drop to 46.0% and 43.0% of gross salary, respectively.[13]

Capital funded pension schemes, both occupational as well as individual private plans, are expected to counterbalance the funding gap of the state pension system. To date, nonetheless, the relevance of occupational pension schemes in Germany remains low: despite the 51% of market share amongst German employees, the pension benefits originated from occupational pension schemes represent only 5% of total pension benefits[14] and 3% of pension income.[15] In other European countries, however, the shift towards occupational and private pension plan solutions has already occurred. In the Netherlands, for example, occupational pension schemes already represent 40% of pension benefits,

8 See Bundesministerium fuer Arbeit und Soziales (2008), p. 110.
9 See BaFin (2012, b).
10 See Statistisches Bundesamt (2009), p. 39.
11 See Braueninger (2010), p. 2.
12 See Deutsche Rentenversicherung Bund (2011), p. 15 and p. 27.
13 See Sec. 154 Par. 3 No. 2 SGB VI.
14 See FAZ (2005).
15 See Statistisches Bundesamt (2007), p. 594.

while in the UK and in Switzerland the market share is 25% and 32%, correspondingly.[16]

The German legislator has reacted to the funding threat of the statutory pension system and has implemented a series of measures to promote private sector pension solutions. Since 1999, a series of law reforms have been passed that have positioned occupational pension plans as an enforceable right by employees (deferred compensation contributions), have introduced beneficial tax treatments (deferred taxation of contributions), have implemented the Pension Fund as fifth pension alternative and instituted the first form of defined contribution payments in the German pension system (Defined Contributions with Capital Guarantee).[17]

1.1.3 Investment Allocation Aspects

The asset allocation of Pension Insurance Funds has a very conservative profile from a risk-return perspective. On average, 86.6% of assets under management are invested in highly rated corporate or risk-free government bonds, whereas 5.2% are allocated towards real estate assets and only 4.6% into equities.[18] This portfolio allocation by asset category has been relatively constant in the last 5 years, independently of prevailing market conditions.[19]

The investment management of Pension Insurance Funds is highly regulated by the German regulator BaFin and the respective legislation. The investment strategy is subject to strict asset class allocation restrictions, diversification requirements, counterparty exposure limitations as well as liquidity rules, as defined in the corresponding sections of the VAG, the AnlV ordinance and the various circular letters of the BaFin (in particular R4/2011). The prevailing investment restrictions and the capital guarantee in nominal terms pension members of Pension Insurance Funds benefit from, may explain the current conservative investment profile of this occupational pension type.

---

16 See FAZ (2005).

17 Major reforms have been the RRG act in 1999, the AltZertG in 2001, the AVmG in 2002, the HZvNG in 2002, the 'RV-Nachhaltigkeitsgesetz' in 2004, the AltEinkG in 2005, the 'Gesetz zur Foerderung der zusaetzlichen Altersvorsorge' in 2007 and the 'RV-Altersanpassungsgesetz' in 2008. For more details, see appendix A.

18 See Bafin (2012, b).

19 See BaFin (2012, d).

Recent regulatory amendments, nonetheless, have introduced more flexibility into the asset allocation, especially in terms of alternative assets. Circular R7/2004 and R4/2011 have provided details on alternative asset classes, in particular hedge fund and commodity investments. While the inclusion of both asset classes has been capped at 5% each of the total investment portfolio, the mere fact of allowing Pension Insurance Funds to consider alternative asset classes can be deemed a confession by the regulator that future asset allocations require a different asset mix to enable German pension plans to maintain or increase their benefit levels.[20] Moreover, Pension Insurance Funds have the possibility to add derivative overlay structures to their investment portfolios, as defined in derivate circular letter R3/2000.[21]

1.1.4 SRIs and Alternative Investments in the Pension Fund Sector

A. Social Responsible Investments

SRI (social responsible investment) is an umbrella term for investments and investing strategies that include ESG factors (environmental, social and/or governance) into the investment process.[22] Pension funds are the leading institutional investor group for SRI assets. To date, 65.3% of total European SRI assets belong to European pension funds.[23] In some European countries with large private-sector pension fund structures, like the Netherlands or the UK, the significance of SRI assets is even more pronounced: in the UK, a total of £939bln assets under management[24] of pension funds are allocated into some form of SRI strategy, a figure that represents approximately 69% of the total size of the German asset management industry.[25] Dutch pension funds, on the other hand, accumulate up to €396bln of SRI assets, equivalent to 53.3% of the pension assets in Netherlands.[26] To date, up to 83% of Dutch pension funds claim to have already some form of SRI policy in place.[27]

---

20 See circular R7/2004, section A.2.C and R4/2011, section B.6.1.C.
21 See circular R3/2000.
22 See Fung et al. (2010), p. 1.
23 See Eurosif (2010), p. 16.
24 See Eurosif (2010), p. 53.
25 Eurosif (2010), p. 35. Based on a total size of the German asset management industry of €1,710bln.
26 See Eurosif (2010), p. 41 et seq.
27 See VBDO (2011), p. 7.

In Germany, on the other hand, SRIs by occupational pension schemes have historically been an asset class of marginal relevance. While there are no official data available on the actual volume of SRI assets under management, some indicators suggest that the involvement by German pension funds is considerably below that of neighbouring countries. Germany, for example, has to date only 8 German signatories[28] for the UN PRI (Principles for Responsible Investment), whereas the UK has 28 and the Netherlands 27 signatories. From these 8 signatories, there is no single occupational pension scheme represented. In the UK, on the other hand, 20 out of 28 signatories are occupational pension plans.[29]

There are nonetheless various trends and drivers that may potentially lead to a change in investment attitude by German pension funds in connection to SRI assets. First, non-monetary factors or non-tangible drivers like reputational risk, ethical reasons or good corporate governance aspects may lead a pension manager to consider SRI strategies. Second, recent interpretation of fiduciary duty suggests pension fund managers may have to include SRI strategies into their portfolios to fulfil their obligations as trustees.[30] Third, legal and regulatory requirements implemented in the last few years in Germany are expected to promote a more 'SRI-friendly' investment environment.[31] German pension schemes are now obliged, for example, to publish how ESG factors have been considered in their investment process,[32] a regulation that is stricter than in the majority of other European countries.[33] Fourth, numerous academic research studies have provided robust statistical evidence that SRIs achieve at least a similar financial performance than equivalent conventional assets do.[34] Furthermore, the increasing product range of SRIs across different asset classes, the more sophisticated screening methods available, combined with a growing number of related consulting and rating services by private-sector advisory firms, is expected to facilitate a broader expansion of SRIs within the German

[28] This number refers to asset owners only. We have excluded investment managers and professional service partners.
[29] See PRI (2012).
[30] See Freshfields (2005), p. 13.
[31] See Preu, Richardson (2011), p. 884.
[32] See Sec. 7 Par. 7 AltZertG and Sec. 115 Par. 5 VAG.
[33] See Preu, Richardson (2011), pp. 882.
[34] For European (ex-UK) performance studies, see Weber et al. (2011), p. 84, Renneboog et al. (2008), p. 304, Schroeder (2007), p. 343, Van de Velde (2005), p. 136 et seq., Kreander et al. (2005), p. 1481, Bauer et al. (2005), p. 1765 and Schroeder (2004), p. 125.

pension fund sector. The importance of SRI assets in leading European pension fund markets will undoubtedly also have an impact on the growth prospects of SRI investing in Germany in general.

B. Alternative Investments

Pension funds are also important investors in alternative investments. European pension funds, for example, have more than $294bln assets under management in the alternative investment space.[35] Given the investment flexibility the German regulator allows Pension Insurance Funds with regard to hedge fund and commodity assets, portfolio managers should consider including them in their asset allocation. The rationale for adding alternative investments, in particular hedge fund assets and commodity investing, to the traditional asset allocation mix can be manifold: (1) research findings suggest large hedge funds may generate alpha returns due to managerial skills and obtain investment returns that are uncorrelated to market movements,[36] (2) commodities tend to have a low/negative correlation to traditional asset classes and therefore have a positive risk diversification effect on the overall investment portfolio of pension funds as well as being a suitable inflation hedge.[37]

1.2 Problem Definition

The prevailing regulatory investment framework in Germany for Pension Insurance Funds imposes strict conditions on investing possibilities for pension fund managers. Moreover, the figures on the actual asset allocation of Pension Insurance Funds reveal that the average investment portfolio is predominantly invested in highly-rated corporate and government bonds, while equities or real estate assets play only a minor role to date. The overall risk-return profile is therefore considerably risk-averse, focused primarily on capital preservation.

In addition, we have identified that social responsible investments are already playing an important role for pension funds in other European countries, in particular the UK and the Netherlands. Expected growth rates for the SRI as-

35 See Towers Watson, Financial Times (2011), p. 51 et seq.
36 See Sun el al. (2012), p. 137 et seq., Jagannathan et al. (2010), p. 253, Agarwal et al. (2009), p. 2249, Ding et al. (2009), p. 891, Kosowski et al. (2007), p. 262 et seq.
37 See Belousova, Dorfleitner (2012), p. 2463-2471, Woodard et al. (2011), p. 264 et seq., Conover et al. (2010), p. 17, Fuertes et al. (2010), p. 2545 et seq., Smimou (2010), p. 54, Marshall et al. (2008), p. 1818 and Gorton, Rouwenhorst (2004), p. 27 et seq.

set class as well as the increasing number of UN PRI signatories from the pension fund sector indicate that the significance of SRIs will increase in coming years for pension schemes. In Germany, conversely, SRIs remain rather a niche asset class, for traditional asset managers[38] in general and for occupational pensions schemes in particular. The outlook, nonetheless, appears promising: growth rates for SRIs in Germany have been considerably higher than for traditional asset categories, even during the current financial crisis, and the growth forecasts are encouraging.[39] The intrinsic motivation to invest in SRI by a pension fund manager, the interpretation of fiduciary duty for trustees operating in Germany, as well as legal and regulatory requirements specific for German pension funds support the view that occupational pension schemes should reconsider their current investment practise and include SRI investing strategies into their asset allocation mix. Furthermore, recent empirical research findings indicate that SRI assets perform from a mean-variance perspective at least as well as traditional asset classes do.

Based on the large allocation by Pension Insurance Funds into fixed-income assets, any viable SRI strategy has to include bond securities. The interest by finance practitioners to include ESG criteria into the investment process for fixed-income securities has risen substantially in the past couple of years, both in the European financial markets as well as in Germany. European SRI mutual funds, for example, already have approximately 38% of their fund strategies in sustainable fixed-income portfolios,[40] whereas 52% of the German total SRI assets are invested in bond securities.[41] This trend will also play an essential role for the strategic asset management of Pension Insurance Funds, given their traditionally large exposure into this asset class. Academic research on the suitability of SRI fixed-income investment strategies for occupational pension schemes in general, and German Pension Insurance Funds specifically, does to our knowledge not exist to date.

---

38 Here we refer primarily to the mutual fund industry. As we will discuss in the main section of the dissertation, the actual SRI market in Germany is larger when additional market segments are included in the calculation.

39 Eurosif expects SRI volumes in Germany to grow by 56% between 2010-2012. The growth rate between 2007-2010 has been 16%, despite the turmoil in financial markets during this time period. See Eurosif (2010), p. 35 et seq.

40 See Vigeo (2010), p. 23.

41 See Eurosif (2010), p. 36.

We have also determined that Pension Insurance Funds have by law certain flexibility in including alternative investments into their asset portfolios, in particular commodities and hedge fund assets.[42] While their allowable allocation is capped at 5% respectively and therefore rather small, their potential risk diversifying effect as well as inflation hedge characteristics could potentially be beneficial for the investment management of pension schemes in Germany. In addition, portfolio managers may consider the investment possibilities derivative overlay structures can offer them as part of a modern risk management tool.[43]

Any modification of the asset allocation of German Pension Insurance Funds needs to ensure that the strategic investment objectives, as defined by the prevailing regulation worded in VAG, AnlV and the circulars of the BaFin, remain unaffected. Downside risk minimisation, liquidity, risk diversification and profitability have to be central drivers of a viable portfolio management policy that attempts to include SRI strategies or alternative investments (or both). From an academic standpoint, it would be nonetheless interesting to analyse the impact of ignoring current investment regulation and simulate alternative investment models that may be more suitable to face the major challenges posed to the German pension system: tail-risk, inflation impact, failure to meet the embedded capital-guarantee of Pension Insurance Funds, default risk within the corporate bond allocation, a severe reduction of the formerly highly-rated government bond investment universe in the context of the European sovereign debt crisis as well as the currently record-low interest rate environment in the majority of large economies globally.

1.3 Research Objectives and Contributions

1.3.1 Research Objectives

Our research dissertation will analyse the following core aspects:

1. The suitability of SRIs across asset classes, with special emphasis on corporate and government bonds, for the strategic asset management of German Pension Insurance Funds.

---

[42] See circular R7/2004, section A.2.C and R4/2011, section B.6.1.C.
[43] See circular R3/2000.

2. The adequacy of alternative investments, in particular commodities and hedge funds.

The overall focus of our study will be of a quantitative nature. The principal empirical method will be based on stochastic time series simulations and dynamic asset allocation strategies.

We define the following main research questions for our thesis:

A. Should German Pension Insurance Funds invest in Social Responsible Investments (SRIs) as part of their strategic asset management?

We have provided evidence that European pension funds are allocating considerable proportions of their investment portfolio into SRI assets. In addition, SRIs are already playing an increasingly important role for German mutual funds. In our study, we will analyse if and how German Pension Insurance Funds should invest into SRI assets.

A shift away from traditional asset classes into SRI strategies, however, can only be justified if similar mean-variance distributions are attained. Should the empirical evidence suggest otherwise, we conclude that SRIs may not be appropriate assets for Pension Insurance Funds, as under existing regulation capital preservation is a determinant factor of the strategic investment management. For the purpose of our analysis, we will first determine an adequate econometric time-series model that captures the data generating process of the underlying assets and allows to run bootstrap simulations to obtain risk-return distributions for the Standard, SRI and Alternative portfolios, which will subsequently be used as inputs for the respective dynamic allocation strategies.

Existing empirical research studies in the context of SRIs focus primarily on equity investments. Given the high allocation Pension Insurance Funds have into fixed-income securities, however, a new investment management method will have to be defined as one that enables the inclusion of corporate and government bonds into the empirical analysis. This aspect of our research includes considerations on suitable asset classes as well as adequate investment strategies.

B. Are alternative investments a suitable asset class for German Pension Insurance Funds?

As we have already discussed, the German regulator allows Pension Insurance Funds to invest a certain proportion of their regulated investment portfolio into alternative asset classes. To date, nonetheless, the funds allocated into alternative assets remain negligibly low. Our research study will investigate whether alternative investments should be added to the portfolio mix of Pension Insurance Funds and how the resulting asset composition may impact expected risk-return distributions, in particular in terms of downside risk mitigation. We will hereby focus primarily on commodity and hedge fund assets given their peculiar risk diversification potential and inflation proxy hedge.

A topic that will also be debated in our dissertation is how alternative investments may be replicated in a socially responsible manner, therefore adding on the advantages that SRI assets may offer to occupational pension schemes in general.

C. Should Pension Insurance Funds consider derivative overlays as part of their strategic asset allocation?

German regulation allows Pension Insurance Funds to add derivative overlays to the investment portfolios, as defined in circular R3/2000.[44] Our simulation study will test how different available derivative structures may enable portfolio managers to operate a tailor-made risk management and achieve better risk-return results.

D. What alternative asset allocation models may be suitable for Pension Insurance Funds?

We will consider alternative portfolio allocations that ignore the strict regulatory investment framework of Pension Insurance Funds currently present in Germany. The challenges to the funding of the German pension system we will discuss in our research, i.e. the long-term investment effects caused by aging and forecasted decline of the German population as well as more imminent risks due to inflation, corporate default risk, portfolio tail-risk, the accelerating reduction of the government bond investment universe since the outbreak of the

---

[44] See circular R3/2000.

European sovereign debt crisis as well as the low interest rate environment, may enforce a reconsideration of existing investment conceptions. This could be specifically relevant for German Pension Insurance Funds given their inflexible investment framework enforced by law and the regulator and that has ultimately led to the prevailing high allocation into fixed-income securities. This section of our research study will include portfolios with different equity allocations (higher yield focus), portfolios with an overweight allocation in real estate assets as well as commodities as a form of a (potential) inflation hedge and portfolios for which credit risk on the corporate bond allocation is hedged. Moreover, we will analyse how suitable credit hedging strategies work when a large proportion of the overall investment portfolio is hedged against corporate default risk (both equity and corporate bond allocations).

1.3.2 Research Contributions

To our knowledge, no academic study has been published to date that concentrates on our research proposal. We expect therefore our research results to represent a considerable contribution to the research community as well as to finance practitioners. Our dissertation is expected to provide a number of valuable contributions in the following areas:

1. Determine if SRIs are a suitable asset class for the strategic asset management of German Pension Insurance Funds, primarily from an empirical and risk management point of view.

2. Establish a methodology on how to invest in fixed-income securities (corporates and government bonds) in a SRI-friendly way.

3. Offer empirical evidence on whether alternative investments, in particular hedge funds and commodity assets, are appropriate assets for the investment management of Pension Insurance Funds.

4. Analyse if Pension Insurance Funds should include derivative overlays as part of their risk management.

5. Compute alternative investment scenarios that ignore existing regulation. These new investment models will have a special focus on (1) high equi-

ty allocations, (2) inflation hedging as well as (3) assess the suitability of credit hedging strategies.

1.4 Methodology

Our research methodology is composed of a multistep process, as depicted in figure 1.

Figure 1: Step-by-Step Process Empirical Analysis

Source: Own figure.

In step 1, once the individual asset classes for both the Standard Portfolio as well as the SRI Portfolio have been determined, we will use a multivariate Vector-Error-Correction model (VECM) to capture the data generation process of the underlying time series. The main advantages of the VECM technique are that (1) it allows for the inclusion of long-term cointegration relationships, (2) it has a high degree of forecasting precision and (3) enables researchers to consider dynamic, inter-temporal features that may be present amongst the target variables chosen.

Subsequently (step 2), we will use the estimated VECM to simulate future return distributions of the underlying assets using the bootstrap simulation method. The obtained return paths will permit to analyse the riskiness of the simulated asset class using the entire return distribution (expected mean, variance, skewness and kurtosis). In step 3, the return distributions will be employed as input for the different investment strategies we have selected for Pension Insurance Funds. The two underlying benchmark investment styles are hereby outright Buy-and-Hold strategies as well as Constant-Mix investing approaches. Within the more sophisticated investment techniques, we will include derivative overlay structures that are allowed under BaFin circular R3/2000: put option strategies, collars, yield enhancement methods and bond-call option methods.

The resulting portfolio value distributions will be analysed with special focus on downside risk (step 4), as Pension Insurance Funds offer their members capital guarantee at nominal terms via defined contributions with capital guarantee. We suggest to assess downside risk by calculating specific downside risk measures based on Lower Partial Moments (LPM), as the resulting portfolio distributions of the various strategies may not be normally distributed and therefore standard variance or standard deviation techniques may not apply. We have identified the Downside Deviation, Omega, the Sortino Ratio and the Kappa 3 as suitable risk measures for our research purposes, in addition to standard indicators of skewness and kurtosis.

1.5 Existing Research Studies and Delimitation

1.5.1 Existing Research Studies

Our research project relies on existing empirical methodologies and research findings. Both for our theoretical considerations on why Pension Insurance Funds should consider SRIs and alternative assets as part of their strategic asset allocation process as well as for the quantitative analysis of our research, we have benefited from existing research results and techniques. Theoretical as well as empirical studies have also contributed to the definition of our own research proposal. We have adequately referenced in our dissertation any external contribution we have considered or included. The most relevant studies are summarised in table 1.

Table 1: Summary of Empirical Research Studies

Author(s)	Title	Year	Format	Contributions for our Research Project
Schroeder	Die Eignung nachhaltiger Geldanlagen fuer die Vermoegensanlage von Stiftungen	2010	HBL	• Research study that analyses the suitability of SRI assets for the portfolio management of German foundations • Applies time series models (VECM), bootstrap simulation as well as portfolio allocation techniques to obtain risk-return distributions and determine optimal asset allocation • SRIs focused exclusively on equity assets
Schaefer, Mayer	Nachhaltige Geldanlagen fuer betriebliche Altersvorsorge-ein-richtungen	2010	RP	• SRIs offer occupational pension schemes in Germany the possibility to fulfil their fiduciary duty • Almost any asset class is in theory replicable in SRI-friendly

Author(s)	Title	Year	Format	Contributions for our Research Project
				manner • Demand by German occupational pension schemes for SRIs expected to grow in coming years • Need for further studies in this context highlighted, in particular with respect to SRI-structured fixed-income portfolios given their relevance within the German occupational pension system
Frere et al.	Asset Liability Management in Pensionskassen – Einfluss aktueller Problemstellungen und Auswahl von geeigneten Assetklassen	2009	RP	• ALM model for German Pension Insurance Funds based on conventional asset classes • Portfolio composition applies simple weighted average returns and simple portfolio variance calculations • Quantitative analysis uses exclusively historical data for risk return distributions, no advanced econometric methodology or simulation study is considered • SRI asset considerations are not part of the research paper
UNEP, Mercer	Demystifying Responsible Investment Performance	2007	RP	• Summary of 20 major research studies that assess the performance of SRIs in comparison to traditional asset classes • Major conclusion is that the relationship between ESG factors and asset performance is at least neutral, suggesting there is no performance disadvantage for investing in SRI assets
Ohlms	Aktives Investmentportfolio Management – Optimierung von Portfolios aus derivatebasierten dynamischen Investmentstrategien	2006	PHD	• Optimization of investment portfolios applying a multi-period econometric investment model • Inclusion of derivatives as part of the optimization process
Reinschmidt	Dynamische Steuerung von Portfoliorisiken	2005	PHD	• Econometric analysis to determine portfolio optimization strategies • Focus on volatility-varying time-series methodologies
Freshfields	A legal framework for the integration of environmental, social and governance issues into institutional investment	2005	RP	• Asset managers have a legal obligation in their role as trustees to invest in SRIs to fulfil their fiduciary duty • This obligation also applies to German asset managers, therefore suggesting also German pension funds should invest in

Author(s)	Title	Year	Format	Contributions for our Research Project
				SRIs
Schumacher-Hummel	Die Rolle von Pensionskassen im Bereich Socially Responsible Investments	2005	PHD	• Research study focused on determining if there are internal or external factors that may influence pension funds to invest in SRI • Survey-based analysis for Swiss pension funds
Skaanes	Einflussfaktoren auf die strategische Asset Allocation Schweizer Pensionskassen	2005	PHD	• Analyses the factors that determine the asset allocation of Swiss pension funds • Empirical analysis uses simple mean-variance calculations based on historical data as well as survey-based information
Eberts	Strategische stochastische Investmentmodelle fuer den deutschen Kapitalmarkt	2002	PHD	• Applies stochastic investment models, in particular time series methodologies, to run simulations on various asset classes • Includes cointegrated model approaches as well as VARs
Juselius, MacDonald	International parity relationships between the USA and Japan	2002	RP	• Research paper that explains in detail how to implement a VEC regression in the context of macroeconomic variables
Scherer	Anlagestrategien fuer Schweizer Pensionskassen	1995	PHD	• Time-series based simulation analysis to determine optimal portfolio allocation for Swiss pension funds • Mean-variance-based approach, using stochastic dominance
Stephan	Strategische Asset Allocation in Lebensversicherungsunternehmen	1995	PHD	• Early-stage research study combining time series analysis and portfolio optimization for the asset management of German insurance businesses • Applies VEC regression models

Abbreviations used: 'RP'=research paper, 'HBL'=habilitation thesis, 'PHD'=doctoral dissertation.

1.5.2 Delimitations

There are several restrictions that will be imposed on our research project. These constraints will be necessary to guarantee that our methodology and research results remain representative, replicable by interested researchers and implementable by practitioners. The principal delimitations are hereby:

1. The benchmark portfolios used for our empirical analysis will imitate the average allocation of German Pension Insurance Funds as published by the BaFin (see also section 2.5.2). As such, our portfolios will be repre-

sentative for all German Pension Insurance Funds currently approved by the German regulator.

2. The respective asset classes used in our empirical analysis will be replicated using suitable indices of leading index providers. This applies to equities, corporate bonds, government bonds, real estate as well as alternative investments. Also for the corresponding SRI assets, we will use indices where available. In general, using indices has the advantage they represent a transparent methodology to select a portfolio of assets following known index calculation rules. Using particular indices provided by a selected group of index providers represents obviously a limitation of our study, as there are alternative methods offered by other large index providers available in the market that could have also been chosen for the empirical analysis. Nonetheless, we have attempted to use those indices and providers that apply methodologies and investment themes that represent a so-called 'commonly-' or 'widely-accepted' understanding by either the academic society or practitioners of a particular investment strategy or SRI screening methodology.

3. An essential prerequisite for any empirical analysis is the availability of time series data, as econometric models like the VECM require long historical data series to be able to capture long-term cointegration effects. As a consequence, the historical time period of 10 years we have fixed has been predetermined by the availability of time-series data from the different index providers.[45]

4. The validity of our research results is conditioned upon the precision of the VECM estimation exercise as well as the subsequent bootstrap simulation. Both techniques are extensively used in research studies and therefore suitable for our research purposes. Nonetheless, we acknowledge that any econometric regression analysis or stochastic simulation is never able to fully capture all dynamics of the underlying data. Moreover, historical performances and statistical patterns of financial

[45] For SRI indices, in particular, no time periods longer than 10 years are currently available. This restriction applies primarily to fixed-income indices.

securities may change in the future due to new regulations or regime shifts.

5. Our quantitative analysis will focus primarily on the asset side of German Pension Insurance Funds. Pension liability aspects will not be considered in this study. Nevertheless, no asset management simulation for a capital-funded pension plan can be computed ignoring completely existing liabilities. Our empirical analysis is therefore targeted at determining an asset allocation mix that yields portfolio returns that are sufficient to match the pension liabilities incurred by pension funds offering defined contributions with capital guarantee. Moreover, we will pursue a risk management analysis that is predominantly focused on downside risk minimisation.

1.6 Thesis Outline

Chapter 2 positions the Pension Insurance Fund within the overall German pension system as well as the occupational pension scheme. After a historic review of the German pension system and the origins of the occupational pension plans (subsection 2.2), a benchmarking analysis is presented to compare the main features of the Pension Insurance Fund versus the other four occupational pension alternatives available in Germany (2.3). In addition, benefit and contribution alternatives are discussed with the aim to choose the appropriate option that the empirical analysis will be based on. Moreover, a detailed explanation of the legal, regulatory and economic investment management aspects are provided, which will allow us to tailor the econometric analysis with regard to required asset allocation and appropriate portfolio strategies (2.4, 2.5)

In chapter 3, the suitability of SRIs (3.1) as well as alternative asset classes (3.2) for the strategic asset management of Pension Insurance Funds is discussed. Our assumption will be that any implementation of a new asset class or investment strategy can only be justified if no financial disadvantage is caused to pension beneficiaries, as this would breach fiduciary duty.

The theoretical foundation of our empirical analysis is worded in chapter 4. The econometric model applied in our study and the bootstrap simulation technique are explained in detail in subsections 4.2 and 4.3. Furthermore, the respective portfolio strategies that will be used in the simulation are described (4.4). This section includes also the derivative overlay structures contemplated. Besides, the specific portfolio performance measures are defined that emphasise downside risk assessment (4.5).

The results of the empirical analysis are presented in chapter 5. The section starts with the statistical description of the investment portfolios that will be simulated in the analysis (5.2) as well as the VEC model estimation process itself (5.3). Subsequently, the results of the simulation exercise for the various investment strategies are presented in 5.4, followed by considerations on alternative investment models in 5.5.

The main conclusions of our research dissertation are discussed in detail in section 6.1. Furthermore, the methodological delimitations and shortcomings of our study are debated in 6.2, whereas section 6.3 refers to the research outlook and outstanding issues.

2. Insight into the German Pension Insurance Fund

2.1 Objectives

The main objectives of chapter 2 are to illustrate the role and relevance of the occupational pension scheme within the three-pillar pension system in Germany. The emphasis of this section will be centred on the expected or future role occupational pension funds may play given the funding issues the statutory pension system is facing. Demographic shifts in the society as well as radical changes in the labour environment are forcing legislators as well as regulators to position occupational pension solutions as a fundamental element of any pension mix, rather than a mere 'add-on' as they used to be perceived in the past.

Amongst the five different occupational pension alternatives available in Germany, our research study will focus primarily on German Pension Insurance Funds given their historic role, relative importance in terms of size as well as market share amongst Germany's private sector corporations. The analysis we will conduct on the investment restrictions Pension Insurance Funds are subject to by prevailing regulation in Germany will provide valuable information for the portfolio composition of the empirical analysis. In addition, we will explore the average asset allocation mix Pension Insurance Funds have historically pursued and how they are invested today in times of economic uncertainty and financial distress. This information will determine our input parameters for the simulation study. Moreover, it is essential to understand pension benefit and contribution options these funds can offer to their members, as these components will have a crucial influence on the asset allocation strategy of the respective pension fund.

The structure of chapter 2 is as follows: first, a brief overview of the German pension system is given, with particular emphasis on the funding issues the statutory pension system is confronted with and the role played by the occupational pension scheme. Second, we will discuss the economic importance of Pension Insurance Funds within the occupational pension system and provide details on pension benefits as well as the scope of insured risk events covered by this pension fund type. Subsequently, we will focus in section 2.5 on all relevant investment management considerations of Pension Insurance Funds that will be required to realise our research study.

2.2 Overview of the German Pension System

2.2.1 Historical Context

In this section, we will give a brief overview of the major historical developments and events that have shaped today's pension system in Germany. This review will enable us to understand the rationale for the creation of the occupational pension system, how it has evolved over time and how Pension Insurance Funds are positioned in an historical context.

A. From the 19th Century to the Foundation of the Federal Republic of Germany (FRG) in 1949

Although occupational pensions schemes have played historically a minor role in terms of economic relevance in Germany in comparison to the public pension system, they were founded first. Large industrial corporations[46] already created in the middle of the 19th century insurance institutions that offered to their employees and family members protection against the financial effects of death and disability.[47] Retirement insurance, nonetheless, which is nowadays the preeminent component of occupational pension schemes, was introduced at a later stage. The effort and rationale by the companies to offer occupational pension benefits to their workforce was purely voluntary, driven in the majority of the cases by a sort of paternalistic and caring sense of responsibility by the founder of the firm.[48]

The origins of the German public pension system date back to the era of Reich Chancellor Otto von Bismarck,[49] who introduced in 1889 a (compulsory) pension law for German workers. In its initial form, the pension system would cover retirement (with a retirement age of 70 years) and disability risks for em-

---

46 See Sabrowski (2007), p. 11 or Uebelhack (2011), p. 12.
47 See Sabrowski (2007), p. 11.
48 See Gieg (2008), p. 19.
49 Otto von Bismarck (1815-1898) was German Reich Chancellor from 1871-1890. See Deutsche Nationalbibliothek (2012).

ployed blue-collar workers only.[50] As stated by the law, the pension contributions would be paid half by the employer and half by the worker.[51] The legislator established the capital funding methodology as the funding principle of the pension system.

Bismarck's motivation for implementing a social system in Germany is a highly debated topic in the academic world. Without doubts, important demographic and social changes in Germany's population seem to have been one of the major reasons. Within the working class, industrial workers started playing an increasingly dominant role, while the previously dominating agricultural segment of the population was decreasing rapidly. Connected to this overthrow of structural elements within the society was a significant migration into urban areas. The new urban life, however, could not provide the same sort of social protection as people used to have within their families in rural zones. Poverty and social imbalances created a real threat to Germany's fast growing cities, making the implementation of a social welfare system necessary. Many historians, however, argue that the real motivation of Bismarck's reforms was the fast spreading ideology of social democracy amongst Germany's blue-collar workers. This political movement was perceived as a danger to the monarchy and to the ruling elites of the country at that time. Bismarck's pension system promise was thereby targeted to act as an incentive for the working class to stay loyal to prevailing powers.[52]

Germany's white-collar employees did not have any pension insurance coverage until 1911, when a separate social insurance to the prevailing scheme of 1889 was introduced. This differentiation of the German workforce, though intentional, created a two-class system, as white-collar employees benefited from higher pension benefits and longer entitlement periods than workers did. Furthermore, employees could already benefit from pension benefits from the age of 65 years onwards, therefore 5 years earlier than their blue-collar counterparts.[53] Self-employed citizens, on the other side, did not have any access to

[50] Disability risk coverage played a predominant role in that time in comparison to retirement pension. Just before WWI, pension contributions would be allocated to 90% for disability benefits and only 10% for retirement payments. See Henning (1995), p. 273.
[51] See Doering (2000), p. 169.
[52] See Schmidt (1998), pp. 28-30.
[53] See Kohlmeier (2008), p. 7.

pension insurance until 1922, when some form of self-employment was included in the pension system.[54] Nonetheless, until today, a vast range of self-employment practises does not give any access to Germany's statutory social insurance coverage.[55]

Bismarck's statutory pension scheme defaulted in 1922/23, when hyperinflation destroyed the value of the asset base of the capital funded system,[56] thereby forcing the government to introduce a Pay-as-you-go (PAYG) arrangement, in which current contributions would be used to pay current benefits. During the economic boom of the early years of the Third Reich, low unemployment and an important capital injection by the government into the pension system led to a substantial increase in pension contributions and a surplus in the pension budget. The healthy state of the pension system persuaded the German administration to switch back to the capital funded system.[57] Unfortunately, the funding sustainability of the pension system was destroyed by the Nazi regime from 1938 onwards, as the underlying capital funds were used to finance the enormous rearmament that took place in Germany prior to the outbreak of WWII.[58]

B. From the Foundation of the FRG in 1949 to the Reunification in 1989

The German pension system went into default after WWII, as a large proportion of the asset base had been invested into German government bonds and real estate, two asset classes that (almost) completely devalued due to the devastating effects of the war.[59] The allied forces that occupied Germany, nevertheless, decided to maintain the social system in place, although the level of contributions the system could afford to pay to its members remained at a very low level until the 1950s, when the economic boom in Germany led to a stabilization of pension finances.[60] In 1949, the first amendments were implemented

---

54 Predominantly domestic work.

55 Today's social insurance system continues to be focused around the concept of employment. As stated in Sec. 2 Par. 2 SGB VI, every employer is forced to be insured in the statutory pension insurance, health insurance scheme, long-term care insurance, accident insurance and unemployment insurance plan. A large number of self-employed activities, on the other hand, remain essentially uncovered by the statutory social insurance system under Sec. 2 SGB VI. See Kohlmeier (2008), p. 7 et seq. and p. 11 et seq.

56 By the time of the monetary reform in 1924, the asset base of the pension system had decreased to just 10% of the value it had in 1910. See Doering (2000), p. 177.

57 See May (2010), p. 89.

58 See Doering (2000), p. 27 et seq.

59 See Frerich, Frey (1993), p. 5 et seq.

60 See Hockerts (1980), p. 67.

by the allies, which were aimed at introducing some level of dynamic adjustment of pension benefits to the price level in the economy.[61] Despite these modifications, pensioners in the post-war period represented the largest segment of the impoverished German population.[62]

In 1957, major pension reforms were introduced. First, the level of benefit entitlement after retirement was increased considerably to enable pensioners to maintain a living standard similar to the one pre-retiring. Second, pension calculations became dynamic by adjusting for changing living conditions, in particular price inflation and changes in gross salaries, thereby enabling pension members to benefit from the economic growth of the country in the post-war period.[63] In addition, independent pension systems for self-employed farmers, public service employees and craftsmen were introduced.[64] The 1957 reform ended basically the static pension system of the Bismarck era and established the pension framework that is still in place in Germany today.[65] 1972 marked a crucial moment in the history of Germany's public pension system, as important changes were implemented that led to the vastest expansion of pension benefits after WWII. Early retirement at the age of 63 years was introduced, more than 10 million beneficiaries received a 14.4% benefit increase with further increments in subsequent years and pension entitlements for minimum wages were announced.[66]

The German occupational pension system, in the meantime, lost economic significance as a form of salary substitution upon retirement, in particular after the 1957 pension reforms. Benefit entitlements provided by occupational pension solutions became mere remuneration instruments and played a rather complementary role in the retirement finances of pensioners.[67] Despite the decreasing economic importance of occupational pension plans, their market share continued to expand in the 1960s and 1970s. Direct Pension Commitments, in particular, were the predominant alternative offered by companies to

---

61 The act is called 'Sozialversicherungs-Anpassungsgesetz' from 1949.
62 See May (2010), p. 90.
63 See Schmaehl (2007), p. 12 et seqq.
64 See May (2010), p. 93.
65 See Ruerup (2002), p. 137.
66 See Hermann (1990), p. 120 et seq.
67 See Gieg (2008), p. 19.

their employees.[68] In 1974, the institution of the BetrAVG (Law for the Improvement of the Company Pension Scheme) was a milestone for the occupational pension scheme, as this act created the first legal framework for the second pillar of the German pension system.[69]

The decade of the 80s represented a period of consolidation for both the public and the occupational pension systems. The economic downturn, combined with the option of early retirement introduced in the 1972 reform, put considerable pressure on the funding of the public pension system, leading to important cutbacks in 1983/1984 and 1989, respectively.[70] The pessimistic economic outlook of the period also had a negative impact on the occupational pension system. As a consequence, the number of members and pension plans stagnated during the entire decade. In addition the high unemployment rate led many skilled employees to accept job contracts without pension plan.[71]

C. From the German Reunification in 1989 To Date

The reunification of the FRG with the socialist-dominated German Democratic Republic (GDR) posed a real threat to the pension system of a unified Germany given the very different living standards in both countries. At the time of reunification, the ratio of average income in the East to the average income in the West had expanded to 1:28.[72] Hegelich (2004), for example, criticises the integration of both welfare systems into one single scheme "resulted in disintegration".[73] The German legislator was subsequently forced to finance the significant funding gap created by the merger of both pension systems and the attempt to offer similar benefit levels in the Eastern part of Germany to those prevailing in the wealthier West. As Merten (2000) argues, the adjustment of both systems made Eastern pensioners the "true winners of the reunification".[74] Oc-

---

68 See Sabrowski (2007), p. 11 et seq.

69 See May (2010), p. 97.

70 The major elements were the increase of the social security contributions to 18.5% of gross salary in 1983/84 and the increase of the minimum age for retirement to 65 years. See May (2010), p. 98.

71 See Sabrowski (2007), p. 12 et seq. Historically, occupational pensions plan were offered almost exclusively to employees with a high position as some form of additional remuneration component.

72 See Merten (2000), p. 317. This number takes into account the then prevailing exchange rate.

73 Hegelich (2004), p. 82.

74 Merten (2000), p. 317.

cupational pension structures lost further importance during these times, even suffering a decrease in number and membership.[75]

The costs and financial implications of the German reunification, combined with the high number of repatriates from Eastern Europe, who also benefited from pension entitlements, as well as the increasing aging of the German population put the pension system in jeopardy. The pension reforms introduced between 1999-2002 (for more details see appendix A) were intended to cause a paradigm shift in the German pension systems. The objective of the German legislator was to promote the second and third pillar of the pension system so as to disburden the statutory pension scheme from its long-term financing challenges. Capital-funded pension plans were sponsored, in particular with the AltZertG (2001) and AVmG (2002) law bills. As part of theses developments, the 'Riester-Rente' for private pension plans and the Pension Fund for occupational pension schemes were introduced.[76] Overall, the reforms emphasized the expansion of the second and third pillar with the objective of incentivising citizens to take responsibility of their pension financings as well as reducing the role of state pensions.[77]

2.2.2 Institutional Structure

A. Overview of the German Pension System

The German pension system is structured similarly to most pension schemes in developed countries. The system is composed of three elements ('three-pillar-system'): (1) a statutory (basic) public pension scheme (first tier), (2) occupational pension schemes (second tier) and (3) individual private pension plans (third tier). The overall pension system has mandatory as well as voluntary components, while there are also aspects that are regulated and administered by the public service or the private sector.[78]

A.1 Statutory Pension System (First Tier)

The statutory public pension system represents the largest pension insurance component in Germany, with almost 80% of all pension benefits paid out

---

[75] See Sabrowski (2007), p. 12.
[76] See May (2010), p. 102 et seq.
[77] See Busemeyer (2005), p. 573.
[78] See Schmaehl (2005), p. 119.

to pensioners originated from this source. Approximately 80% of German employees are member of the first tier pillar. The state pension scheme has such an economic importance in Germany that approximately 10% of the countries gross domestic product (GDP) runs through this system.[79]

A.2 Occupational Pension System (Second Tier)

Occupational pension schemes have been introduced in both the public and the private sector. Within the public sector, in general all employees are covered by some form of supplementary pension plan, which comes usually in the form of collective agreements and offer defined benefit structures to its members. These pension arrangements are normally integrated within the German social pension insurance. In the private sector, approximately 51%[80] of companies offer occupational pension schemes, although the distribution is unequal between male and female employees and also depends on the respective industry sector. Collective agreements on occupational pension schemes in the private sector have historically played a minor role, although they have gained significance after the 2001 pension reform.[81]

A.3 Individual Private Pension Schemes (Third Tier)

Retirement plans within in the third tier have many different investment alternatives. Common instruments in Germany are savings plans, real estate objects and investments into equity or investment funds. Not all of these investments an employee may decide to undertake are allocated exclusively for retirement provisions, so that a clear distinction of funds assigned to the third tier is a difficult task. In addition, there are pension plans that are subsidised by the legislator and which have been introduced in recent years (e.g. the 'Riester-Rente' in 2001).[82]

B. Economic Importance of the Pension System

B.1 The German Pension System in the European Context

Figure 2 compares the distribution of pension benefits amongst the three pension tiers in the European context. As the chart illustrates, the public pen-

---

79 See Duenn, Fasshauer (2009), p. 112.
80 See Bundesministerium fuer Arbeit und Soziales (2008), p. 11.
81 See Schmaehl (2005), pp. 119-121.
82 See Duenn, Fasshauer (2009), p. 113.

sion system plays a predominant role in all industrialised countries, although at different penetration levels. While in Germany (85% market share), Spain (92%) and Italy (74%) the public pension scheme is doubtlessly the major source of pension benefits, in some developed countries the second tier and third tier achieve similar market shares. In Switzerland, for example, public pensions represent only 42% of total average pension benefits, while occupational pension schemes obtain 32% and private pension plans 26% of market share. The US is also a peculiar market, as the first tier embodies 45% of all pension benefits, the second tier 13% and individual private pension solutions up to 42%. These numbers are also a reflection on the role social security systems play in the respective countries. While in some countries private sector and individual pension plans are necessary to guarantee an adequate pension benefit level upon retirement (i.e. US, Switzerland, Netherlands, France, UK), some countries rely primarily on statutory pension schemes (i.e. Germany, Spain, Italy).

Figure 2: Origin of Pension Benefits in Europe and the US (2005, in % of a Two-Person Household)

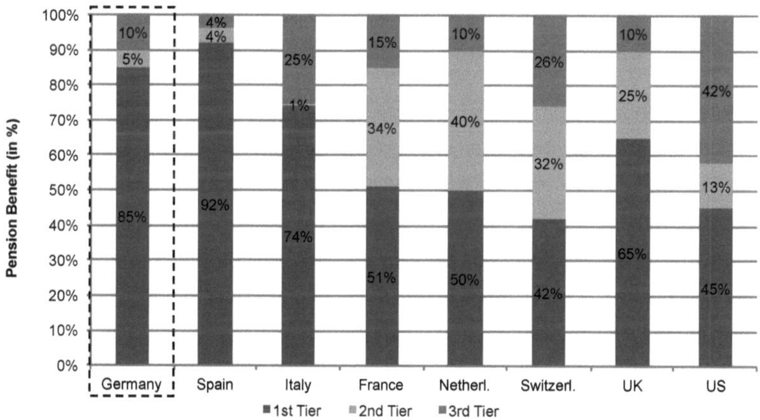

Source: FAZ (2005), p. 24.

B.2 Pension Income Distribution in Germany

Furthermore, we have analysed how the gross income of an average German pensioner is originated. This figure goes beyond the sources of pension benefits discussed in the previous section as also non-pension income is considered. The German Federal Statistical Office has published empirical data for the years 1998 and 2003 that show the income distributions of a one-person pensioner household. Figure 3 summarises the main findings. Public pension plans remain hereby the main source of income for Germany's pensioners with more than 70% of weight, followed by real estate ownership[83] with 15% and benefits sourced from private pension solutions. Occupational pension schemes remain with 2.9% relatively unimportant as income stream for today's pensioners.[84]

Figure 3: Gross Income Distribution of German Pensioners (1998 vs. 2003)

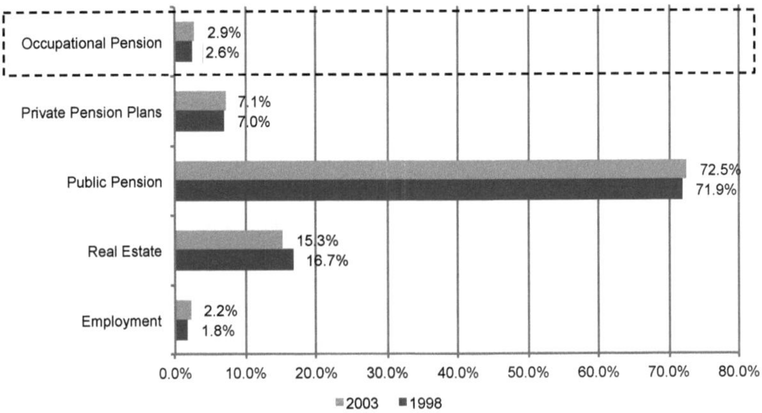

Source: Own figure, based on Statistisches Bundesamt (2007), p. 594. Note: Data shows distribution of gross income of German pensioners in 1998 and 2003, respectively, for a one-person pensioner household. Numbers are an average for Western and Eastern Germany.

An analysis of Germany's three-tier system by Deutsche Rentenversicherung Bund (2005) comes to interesting conclusions in connection to the relevance of the second and third tier of the pension system. While the authors of the study state that the public pension system will remain the predominant source of pension benefit income in the foreseeable future, they also conclude that both the second and third tier will have to play a much more dominant role than they than currently in order to provide sufficient supplementary retirement benefits to pensioners. Moreover, the report analyses the distribution of the potential pension entitlement of all three pension tiers amongst employees of the age range 40-60 years to get a better insight into the potential future distribution of Germany's pensions.[85] Figure 4 summarises the breakdown of two different target

83 For real estate assets, the Federal Statistical Office includes income generated through rent but also outright real estate ownership.

84 See Statistisches Bundesamt (2007), p. 594.

85 See Deutsche Rentenversicherung Bund (2005), pp. 12-15.

groups[86] and distinguishes between male and female employees as well as Western and Eastern Germany.

Figure 4: Expected Pension Entitlement in Germany (2005)

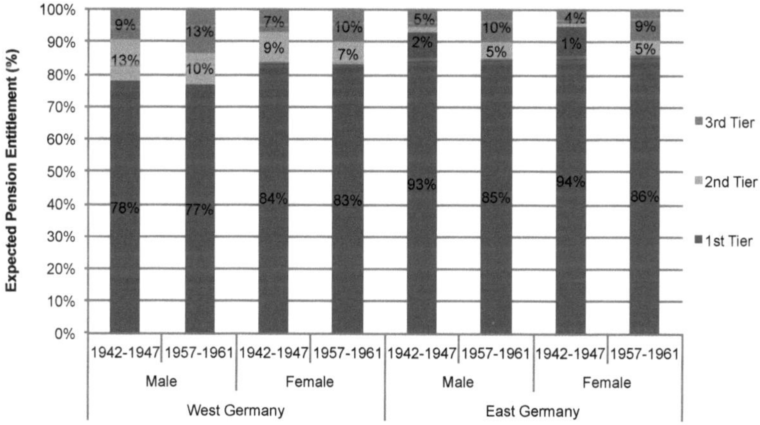

Source: Deutsche Rentenversicherung Bund (2005), p. 7.

This statistics provides four interesting observations: (1) the importance of the tier one pension benefits for the younger generation is decreasing for both male and female employees and (2) the growth of tier two and tier three pension alternatives is considerably higher in the Eastern part of Germany than in the West. The latter observation can be explained by the lack of pension financing alternatives during the communist era in the GDR and a current urge by employees to obtain complementary pension benefits upon retirement. Moreover, (3) occupational pension schemes (tier two) are primarily expanding in Eastern Germany, while in Western Germany the penetration rates are actually slightly declining within these age groups, and (4) tier three alternatives achieve the highest growth rates within the generation of 1957-1961 of Germans, who will retire in the next 10-15 years.

2.2.3 Major Challenges and Outlook

A. Demographic Transformations

The reforms of the German pension system after 1999 were a reaction of politicians, pension experts and regulators to the underfunding of retirement

[86] Group 1: date of birth between 1942-1947 and group 2: 1957-1961.

benefits in the public pension system. Principal causes of the funding gap were at the time of the reforms considerable demographic shifts in Germany's population, a high base unemployment rate, fundamental changes in the workspace as well as a transformation of the socio-economic relevance of family structures. Driving factors within the demographic challenges were a decreasing birth rate, higher life expectancies, access to a healthier lifestyle as well as the increasing possibility of early-retirement. The rising gap between birth rate and death rate was thereby highlighted as one of the largest threats to the funding prospects of the German pension scheme.[87]

More than ten years after the first major pension reform took place in 1999, these inherent risks remain central: the German Federal Statistical Office reports that currently more people aged 65 or above live in Germany than aged 15 or below. Moreover, the population forecasts for the next decades remain challenging from a pension financing standpoint: from 81.5m citizens in Germany in 2010, it is expected that by 2030 this number will decrease to 77.4m and by 2060 down to 64.6m people (-20.7%).[88] Simultaneously, the number of people between 20-65 years, an age range representative for the working population, will drop from 49.7m in 2008 to 32.6m by 2060 (-34.4%).[89]

Figure 5: Forecasted Aging of the German Population from 2008 to 2060

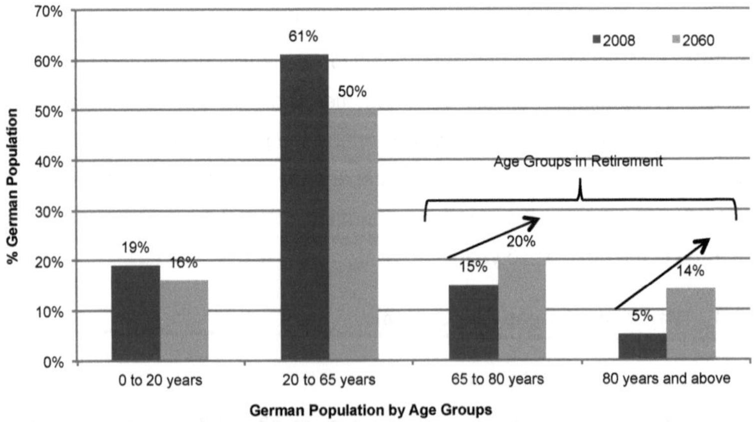

Source: Own figure, on the basis of Statistisches Bundesamt (2009), p.16.

87 See Klatt (2003), p. 2.
88 See Statistisches Bundesamt (2011, a).
89 See Statistisches Bundesamt (2009), p. 39 and p. 44.

Figure 5 illustrates how the age groups in retirement will increase from 20% of the German population for 2008 to up to 34% by 2060 (+70%), based on the demographic forecasts of the German Federal Statistical Office. The age group from 20 to 65 years, which represents the largest proportion of Germany's population, will suffer a decline from 61% to 50% in the same time period. The most dramatic change nonetheless is expected for the age group that is older than 80 years. This part of Germany's society will encounter a significant expansion from 5% as of today to 14% by 2060, what represents the highest growth rate of all age groups considered in the statistic.[90]

During the same time period, the life expectancy of women is supposed to go from 82.4 years in 2008 to 89.2 years (+8.3%) in 2060 and for the male population from 77.2 years to 85.5 years (+10.8%). With an average of 1.4 children per woman in Germany, a number that has remained almost constant over the last 30 years, each new generation is in comparison to the previous one smaller by approximately 1/3. The assumed immigration into Germany is not expected to be able to balance out this population deficit, as forecasts of the German Federal Statistical Office indicate.[91]

As a consequence of such significant demographic shifts, the difference between the number of newly born and the number of people passing away has been negative since the beginning of the 1970s and is forecasted to widen considerably in the next 50 years. In 2008, this gap was 161k people p.a., whereby the predictions for 2060 estimate that the difference will widen to 553k p.a., an increase of more than 3.4 times.[92]

B. Workspace Changes

Profound transformations in the workspace have led to additional pressure on the statutory pension system. Flexible working hours, an increase in low-paid jobs, part-time employment, the growing relevance of contract workers as well as a higher number of free-lance employees have led to considerably lower contributions to the state pension system and simultaneously longer periods of absence from employment. As a consequence of these new employment struc-

---

[90] See Statistisches Bundesamt, (2009), p. 16.
[91] See Statistisches Bundesamt, (2011, b).
[92] See Statistisches Bundesamt, (2009), p. 13.

tures, a considerable proportion of low-paid employees have insufficient funding means to finance private or occupational pension scheme alternatives.[93]

C. Decreasing Pension Levels of the Statutory System

The statutory pension levels have been decreasing steadily in Germany, from 57.3% of gross salary in 1957 to 47.1% in 2010, leading thereby to lower living standards for pensioners. For a substantial proportion of today's pensioners, pension benefits are insufficient to provide a satisfactory retirement funding. Concurrently, the contribution rates (as % of gross salary) have experienced a steady rise in the last 60 years, from 14.0% in 1957 to currently 19.9%.[94] The future pension levels are forecasted to decline further. For 2020 and 2030, the German legislator has already fixed the minimum levels at 46.0% and 43.0% of gross salary, respectively.[95]

Figure 6: Contribution Rates and Pension Levels in Germany (Since 1957)

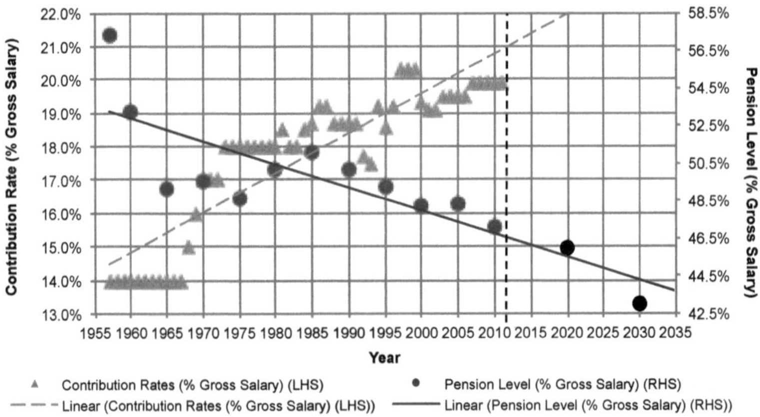

Source: Own figure, on the basis of Deutsche Rentenversicherung Bund (2011), p. 15 and p. 27. Note: The minimum pension levels for 2020 and 2030 have been fixed by the legislator.

On the back of the funding threats posed by demographic shifts, labour market dysfunctions and decreasing pension levels, the German legislators reacted and from 1999 onwards introduced a set of essential pension reforms with the prime objective to close the widening funding gap of the pay-as-you-go (PAYG) state pension system and promote capital funded pension schemes. In this con-

---

[93] See Krupp (2002), p. 500.
[94] See Deutsche Rentenversicherung Bund (2011), p. 15 and p. 27.
[95] See Sec. 154 Par. 3 No. 2 SGB VI.

text, the respective regulations for both the German occupational and individual private pension systems were reviewed. It is important to highlight that the promoted expansion of the private sector (occupational and private) pension alternatives was intended to be almost entirely on a voluntary basis by the involved parties. The rationale behind this voluntariness from the viewpoint of the German legislator was that employees should take responsibility for their own pension finances to prevent any funding gap related to low public pension benefit entitlements, while at the same time corporations should be reminded of their socio-political responsibility *vis-a-vis* their employees.[96]

C. Outlook

The statutory pension reforms and the demographic shifts expected over the next decades have caused a significant paradigm change in Germany's welfare system, especially with regard to the future funding structure of pensions. Lamping, Rueb (2010) describe these changes as "less generosity, more market-based private provision and more activation of citizens to behave like consumers on welfare markets [.]"[97] As Hinrichs, Kangas (2003) highlight, there is a large time lag until such reforms usually become effective, as the majority of pension modifications do not have an immediate impact, but may take years or even decades until they materialise to a measurable change.[98]

Pension experts agree that private sector solutions have to compensate for the funding issues the public pension system will face in the future. Both individual private pension plans as well as occupational pension schemes have to mitigate the decreasing pension levels in Germany.[99] Advocates of funded pensions argue that a capital funded pension system would guarantee higher asset returns and therefore offer a better funding when retirement age is reached. Moreover, encouraging employees to have in addition to their public pension either a private pension scheme or a company pension plan (or a combination of both) would lead to a more effective risk diversification of the entire pension system in Germany.[100]

---

96 See Klatt (2003), p. 4.
97 Lamping, Rueb (2010), p. 50.
98 See Hinrichs, Kangas (2003), p. 575.
99 See Bulmahn (2003), p. 30.
100 See Ribhegge (2004), p.128.

These pension reforms, however, will have important social repercussions that go beyond just pension financing issues. German welfare systems have been historically based on the principle of social equality and accessibility for all citizens in need. Promoting private pension planning, though, may lead to social imbalances, as only well-educated citizens with above-average earnings power may be able to get access to private pension solutions.[101] The effect of this trend could be greater social imbalances in the earnings distribution of Germany's pensioners.[102] Moreover, the European integration of national welfare systems may require opening up national social security schemes, a trend that could in theory in the future lead to a single-market pension system, with all the funding issues for statutory schemes associated with such a radical reform.[103]

2.2.4 Conclusions

The German pension system has a long history, dating back more than 180 years in case of occupational pension plans and almost 125 years for the public pension scheme. While occupational pension plans used to have at inception a strong complimentary and in some instances substitutionary role, their economic role declined rapidly since then to become some form of salary incentive scheme for employees.

The German PAYG statutory system, while still important in terms of members and coverage, is suffering from considerable demographic changes Germany's society is experiencing, which, based on government forecasts, will further deteriorate in the next 50 years. Moreover, unprecedented transformations of the workspace environment are putting additional pressure on the public pension system. The impact of these changes is jeopardizing the funding viability of statutory pensions, as fewer contributors are financing an increasing number of beneficiaries. The German legislator has implemented various important pension reforms to counterbalance the decreasing funding level of the pension scheme. This has resulted in steadily decreasing pension levels and constantly rising contribution rates (for both employees and employers). Nonetheless,

[101] See Bulmahn (2003), p. 33 et seq.
[102] See Lamping, Rueb (2010), p. 51.
[103] See Guardiancich (2011), p. 33 et seq.

forecasted pension levels are expected to be insufficient to offer pensioners an acceptable financial position upon retirement.

Since the major pension reforms introduced by the German legislator in 1999 (see also appendix A for more details), capital-funded solutions originated in the private sector (occupational pension plans and individual private pension plans) have been promoted by the Government to counterbalance the decreasing pension levels of the state system. Germany is hereby following common practise in many other European countries and the US, where private sector pension solutions play already a crucial role (e.g. in France 49% of pension benefits, the Netherlands 50%, UK 35%, Switzerland 58% and 55% in the US).[104] The evidence provided in this section suggests that the demographic megatrends Germany's society is facing as well as the inter-linked funding issues of the state pension system are unsustainable to guarantee the viability of the pension system and may require profound reforms to ensure future generations receive adequate pension levels to ensure a minimum acceptable living standard. The promotion of capital-funded pension solutions, in particular occupational pension schemes, as well as the assessment of new asset classes and investment strategies appear as an adequate approach to reposition and prepare the German pension system for the future. Our research study will attempt to provide some recommendations and empirical evidence to the potential repositioning of the German occupational pension system, with special emphasis on Pension Insurance Funds.

Subsequent section 2.3 will provide insight into the German occupational pension system. Apart from the legal definition for an occupational pension plan, the five pension alternatives will be discussed as well as the rationale for the sponsoring company to offer such pension provisions. Overall, the rationale for section 2.3 is to position the Pension Insurance Fund within the occupational pension alternatives the German regulator as well as the law allows and thereby highlight the major differences existent between the Pension Insurance Fund and the other four pension schemes in terms of funding responsibility, insolvency protection and pension obligations.

---

[104] See FAZ (2005), p. 24.

2.3 Pension Insurance Funds as Integral Part of the Occupational Pension Scheme

2.3.1 Definition Occupational Pension Scheme

Sec. 1 Par. 1 No. 1 BertrAVG provides the legal definition for occupational pension scheme under German law. Based on the lawful wording, an occupational pension plan is an arrangement by an employer to his employees to offer benefits that protect them against financial shortfalls caused by retirement[105], disability or death risks.[106] Entitlement to these claims will only be conceded once one of the insured risk events occurs and the affected employee is unable to pursue his labour duties.[107] Pension benefits have to include at least longevity risk and can optionally include death or disability risks.[108] A further legal requirement is that the claim base of the insured person has to be linked to either a current or a past employment contract between employee and employer (employee-employer relationship).[109]

Once the employer commits to contribute pension benefits for his employees via an occupational pension arrangement, he is obliged by law to satisfy any claims originated from that commitment.[110] The pension promise can be based on different methods of calculation. These are either defined benefits, contribution-based defined benefits or defined contributions with capital guarantee (see also section 2.4.4 for more details).[111] Pension claims originated from earnings conversion via the deferred compensation method as well as voluntary direct payments[112] by employees into their occupational pension schemes are also under the protection of the BetrAVG.[113]

---

[105] The term longevity risk is often used instead.

[106] In the case of death, the beneficiaries will be the surviving dependents of the employee. All three risk categories (retirement, disability, death) are also classified as biometric or biological risks.

[107] See Foerster, Rechtenwald (2008), p. 138. In case of retirement, the 'inaptness' is caused by the legal enforcement to retire.

[108] See Doetsch et al. (2010), p. 33.

[109] See Klatt (2003), p. 21. For the lawful definition of 'employee', see Sec. 17 BetrAVG.

[110] See Sec. 1 Par. 1 No. 3 BetrAVG.

[111] See Sec. 1 Par. 2 No. 1, 2 BetrAVG.

[112] These payments can only be directed towards Pension Funds schemes, Pension Insurance Funds or Direct Insurance schemes as defined by Sec. 1 Par. 2 No. 4 BetrAVG.

[113] See Schumann (2003), p. 22 et seq. Deferred compensation payments are allowed since the 1999 and 2001/2002 pension reforms that introduced the new right of earnings conversion.

BetrAVG offers employers five implementation alternatives for an occupational pension scheme: the Direct Pension Commitment ('Direktzusage'), Support Fund ('Unterstuetzungskasse'), Direct Insurance ('Direktversicherung'), the Pension Insurance Fund ('Pensionskasse') and the Pension Fund ('Pensionsfond').[114] It is important to highlight that any implementation of an occupational pension arrangement occurs at the sole discretion of the employer, with the only exception of the deferred compensation pension benefits that an employee can enforce by law (see section 2.4.4, D for more details). The company will consider economic, legal and tax aspects to decide which pension structure is the most adequate one.

Further relevant distinctions are the various periods into which occupational pension plan commitments can be subdivided, in particular in terms of the investment phase and the period of pension benefit pay-out. Figure 7 illustrates these phases graphically for a capital funded pension plan.[115].

Figure 7: Investment and Pay-out Periods of an Occupational Pension Plan

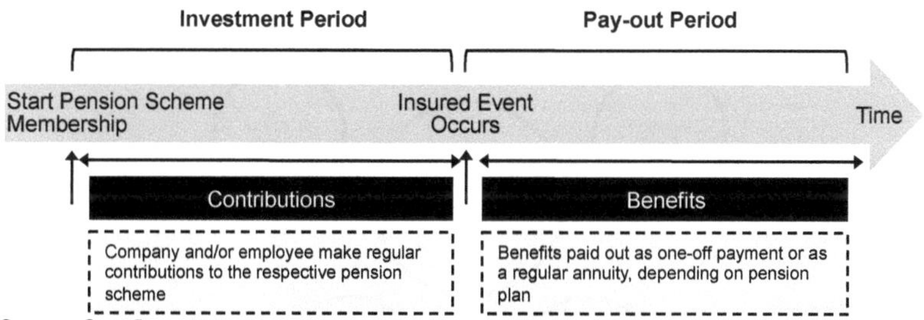

Source: Own figure.

2.3.2 Types of Occupational Pension Plans

A. Introduction

The five occupational pension scheme alternatives under BetrAVG differ in terms of supervision by the German regulator, tax and legal treatment, contributions as well as benefit payments.[116] The pension plans can be further divided into an external and an internal system. The Direct Pension Commitment and

---

For more details on deferred compensation payments and direct payments by employees, see Sec. 1 Par. 2 No. 3, 4 BetrAVG.

114 See Rohde, Kuesters (2007), p. 18 et seq.

115 For defined benefit schemes, however, there would be no contribution payments into the pension scheme during the investment period. See section 2.4.4, A for more details.

116 See Doetsch et al. (2010), p. 15.

the Support Fund represent the internal pension schemes of the BetrAVG, for which there is a direct legal relationship for pension benefits and contributions between employer and employee. In the external alternatives, i.e. the Pension Insurance Fund, the Direct Insurance and the Pension Fund, on the contrary, the employer interconnects an external, independent third party that is responsible for all pension-related aspects of the company. In this scenario, the employer has a direct claim for his pension benefits to the third party provider, while the employer remains subsidiary liable only.[117] Rather than being a bilateral legal relationship between company and employee, we obtain a 'triangle' of legal as well as commercial relationships between the sponsoring company, the employee and the external pension provider.[118] Figure 8 summarises the different alternatives and their differences with respect to external versus internal pension plan.

Figure 8: Overview of the German Occupational Pension Scheme

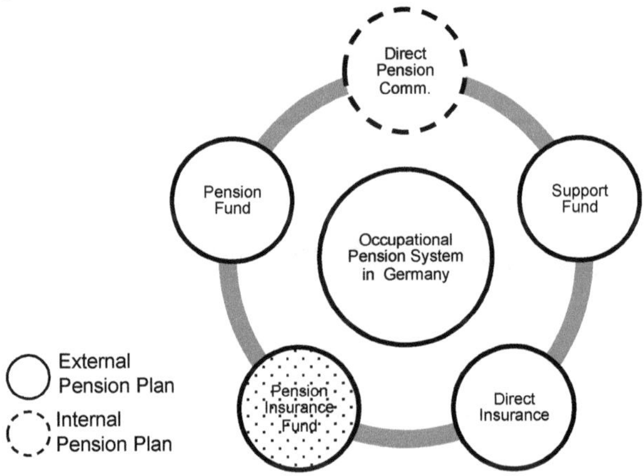

Source: Own figure.

The main purpose of this section is to obtain an overview and better understanding of how the different types of pensions schemes are integrated into the German occupational pension system, where their main differences but also similarities are in terms of legal claims of the beneficiaries, protection by the PSV and the terms of the different pension benefits it can offer to its members.

[117] Sec. 1 Par. 1 No. 3 BetrAVG regulates the subsidiary role of the employer.
[118] See Campen (2009), p. 154.

Moreover, the information presented here will enable us to draw comparisons to the Pension Insurance Fund that will be discussed in more detail in section 2.4.

B. Direct Pension Commitment ('Direktzusage')

In the Direct Pension Commitment, it is the company itself that fulfils all pension obligations, both during the investing phase of the pension scheme and subsequently once pension benefits are paid out. No external third party provider is involved.[119] The company bears hereby the full investment responsibility of the underlying pension provisions and any hedging of the biometric risks associated with the pension liabilities, unless it has decided to re-insure its pension commitments with an external insurer.[120] Alternatively, the company can also externalise the pension management into a CTA (contractual trust agreement) investment vehicle.[121] To mitigate the company default risk an employee is exposed to in a Direct Pension Commitment pension plan, the company is obliged to insure any vested benefit entitlements via the PSV,[122] a private sector insolvency solution for occupational pensions schemes.

The company can create pension provisions that are tax deductible under German income law (Sec. 6a EStG) for the respective pension commitments.[123] The funds related to these pension provisions are available to the company and represent an internal form of funding from a financing standpoint. The company, therefore, benefits from lower tax burdens resulting from tax deductions while any payment to the beneficiaries are only made once an insured event actually occurs.[124] Langohr-Plato (2007) estimates that in Germany due to tax deferral effects originated from pension provisions, up to 60% of pension underlying funds remain in the company form of cash liquidity.[125]

---

119 See Uebelhack (2011), p. 106 et seq.
120 See Klatt (2003), p. 28.
121 See Uebelhack (2011), p. 107. For more details on risks and benefits of CTAs for Direct Pension Commitments, see Prangenberg, Liesebach (2004) or Misterek (2012).
122 'Pensions-Sicherungs-Verein auf Gegenseitigkeit'.
123 See Klatt (2003), p. 28 et seq. See Sec. 6a EStG on the corresponding lawful wording.
124 See Bissels (2009), p. 14.
125 See Langohr-Plato (2007), p. 23.

Figure 9: Involved Parties in a Direct Pension Commitment

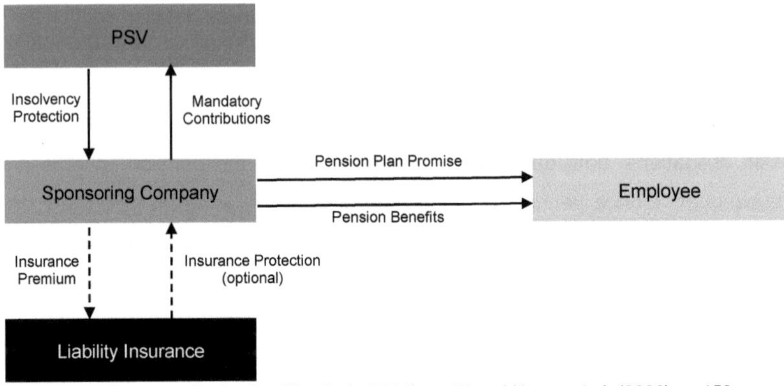

Source: Own figure, on the basis of Doetsch (2010), p. 16 and Hanau et al. (2006), p. 152.

C. Support Fund ('Unterstuetzungskasse')

The Support Fund is also part of the internal pension alternative within the occupational pension system. In comparison to the Direct Pension Commitment, however, beneficiaries of a Support Fund do not have a legal claim to any guaranteed pension plan payment (either in form of a guaranteed return or absolute amount).[126] The employer is fully responsible for the funding of the Support Fund. This can occur either via regular pension contributions into the fund or one-off payments. Excess returns achieved with the investments of these contributions scheme are the third source of financing.[127] The sponsoring company, nonetheless, has the option to re-insure its pension commitments with an external reinsurance provider, similar to the Direct Pension Commitment scheme.[128]

From an investment management perspective, the Support Fund is independent in its asset allocation and is even allowed to provide financing in form of a loan to the sponsoring company for any excess cash funds it may have at any given point in time. This form of reallocating funds back to the sponsoring company permits the employer to mitigate the financing effort it faces by com-

[126] See Sec. 1b Par. 4 BetrAVG. Nonetheless, the German Federal Labout Court ('BAG') has *de facto* given employees a legal claim on pension entitlements from Support Funds. See Uebelhack (2011), p. 111.
[127] See Klatt (2003), p. 30.
[128] See Rohde, Kuesters (2007), p. 58.

mitting to a Support Fund.[129] Pension plan members in Support Funds also benefit from default protection via the PSV.[130]

Figure 10: Involved Parties in a Support Fund

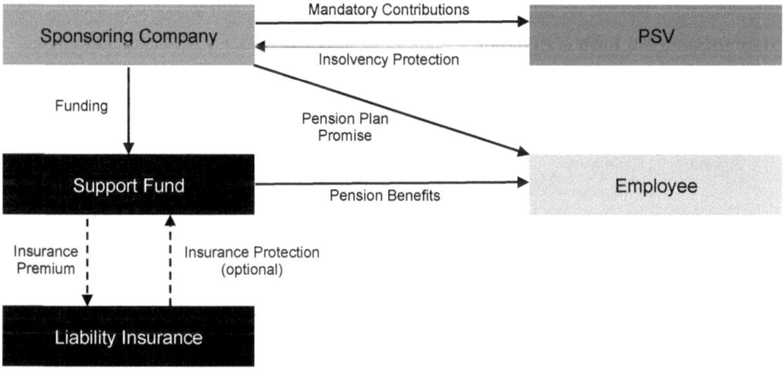

Source: Own figure, on the basis of Doetsch (2010), p. 17 and Hanau et al. (2006), p. 153.

D. Direct Insurance ('Direktversicherung')

In a Direct Insurance scheme, as defined in Sec. 1 Par. 2 No. 1 and Sec. 1b Par. 2 BetrAVG, the employer offers his employees a life insurance contract. Insurance premiums are paid directly by the company to an external life insurance provider. The beneficiary of the insurance policy is the employee directly and his surviving dependents indirectly. The policyholder, nonetheless, is the employer.[131] The premium paid to the insurer can either be paid entirely by the company or by the employer via deferred compensation or direct payments.[132] All investment risk related to the insurance contract are transferred entirely to the insurance company.

The insurance company will fulfil its legal obligations under the insurance contract by paying out benefits to the employee as soon as an insured risk event occurs, while also satisfying its contractual responsibility versus the company. The company, on the other hand, will only be discharged from its commitments as soon as the insurer commences paying benefits to the employee.[133] Even if the employee pays part (or the entirety) of the insurance premi-

129 See Bissels (2009), p. 19.
130 See Hanau et al. (2006), p. 154.
131 See Uebelhack (2011), p. 110.
132 See Braun (2010), p.31.
133 See Braun (2010), p.30 et seq.

ums himself, via deferred compensation schemes or direct payments, the legal relationship between company and insurer remains unchanged.[134]

The insolvency protection for beneficiaries in a Direct Insurance is provided through the regulation of the insurance sector in Germany via the BaFin (see also section 2.4.5 for more details).[135]

Figure 11: Involved Parties in a Direct Insurance

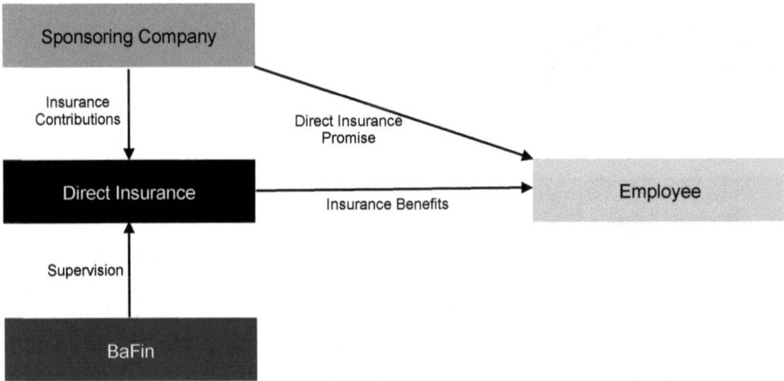

Source: Own figure, on the basis of Doetsch (2010), p. 19 and Hanau et al. (2006), p. 158.

F. Pension Fund ('Pensionsfond')

The Pension Fund was introduced in Jan-2002 by the AVmG act as the 'fifth pillar' of the German occupational pension system. It is defined in Sec. 112 Par. 1 VAG (German Insurance Supervision Act) as an independent pension institution that offers insurance coverage for retirement, death and disability, similar therefore to the Pension Insurance Fund and the Direct Insurance Fund. Despite certain similarities and regulations in the VAG, a Pension Fund is not an insurance institution in a traditional sense as specified in Sec. 1 Par. 1 VAG.[136] The BetrAVG, on the other hand, positions the Pension Fund on par with the Pension Insurance Fund.[137] As an independent entity, the Pension Fund is legally separated from the sponsoring company. Similar to the Direct Pension

[134] See Bissels (2009), p.15.
[135] See Uebelhack (2011), p. 110.
[136] See Melchiors (2004), p. 581.
[137] See Sec. 1b Par. 3 No. 1 BetrAVG.

Commitment, the Direct Insurance and the Pension Insurance Fund, beneficiaries in a Pension Fund have a *de jure* enforceable claim on benefit payments.[138]

Although Pension Funds can offer their members all benefit alternatives available under Sec. 1 Par. 2 BetrAVG,[139] their competitive advantage lies in practise in pension plans that provide defined contributions with capital guarantee (DCCG).[140] The objective of the German legislator with the introduction of the DCCG was actually to enable Pension Funds to invest to a higher degree in riskier growth assets, particularly equities, and obtain therefore a different risk-return profile versus the other occupational pension schemes available in Germany.[141]

Pension Fund schemes are under the protective umbrella of the PSV, analogous to the Support Fund and the Direct Pension Commitment. Pension Fund plans that offer Defined Contributions with Capital Guarantee also have to be under the supervision of the BaFin.[142]

Figure 12: Involved Parties in a Pension Fund

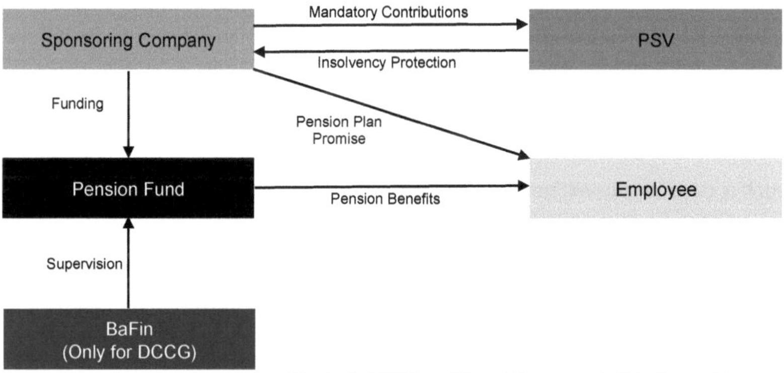

Source: Own figure, on the basis of Doetsch (2010), p. 22 and Hanau et al. (2006), p. 161.

[138] See Sec. 112 Par. 1 No. 3 VAG.
[139] Defined benefits, contribution-based defined benefits or defined contributions with capital guarantee.
[140] See Klatt (2003), p. 31.
[141] See Hanau et al. (2006), p. 160.
[142] See Beckstette, Schmidt (2002), p. 57.

2.3.3 Rationale for the Sponsoring Company

A. Human Resource Management Aspects

The role of occupational pension plans as part of the overall human resource management strategy of a firm is an area of interest well covered in academic research. For Europe, the majority of research studies are UK-market focused; the main conclusions do, nonetheless, also apply to occupational pension plans in Germany. Our main point of interest is hereby to understand what specific role occupational pension schemes can have in terms of employee motivation, retention or recruiting.

In an early study by Terry, White (1997), the authors conclude that pensions schemes do not play a key role in motivating employees. On the contrary, pension plans can actually be demotivating if they are removed or adjusted, rather than acting as motivators if the scheme remains unchanged.[143] In a broad employee survey conducted by Loretto et al. (2000), more than 80% of the respondents state occupational pension plans are essential or have been very important as part of their job search process.[144] Taylor (2000), in-line with Terry, White (1997), suggests pension schemes are an ineffective mean to reduce employee turnover, unless the respective employee is close to retirement.[145] Hales, Gough (2003), on the other hand, emphasize it is imperative for a company to use a pension plan not as a simple employee remuneration deal, as in such a case loyalty will not be achieved, but rather convey the message that the company takes responsibility for its employees.[146] Gough, Hick (2009), in one of the more recent research studies, determine that occupational pension plans offer a strong retention function for existing employees, whereas the recruitment function to attract new workers is rather limited.[147]

The evidence for the German occupational pension system remains rare. Two recent studies, nevertheless, enable us to draw similar conclusions than those we have obtained for the UK pension market. The FAZ Institute (2008), for example, conducted a survey amongst HR managers of large German cor-

[143] See Terry, White (1997), p. 168 and p. 174.
[144] See Loretto et al. (2000), p. 265.
[145] See Taylor (2000), p. 257 et seq.
[146] See Hales, Gough (2003), p. 337 et seq.
[147] See Gough, Hick (2009), p. 165.

porations with respect to the utility of occupational pension plans. 79% of respondents believe employees in management positions can be retained with an attractive pension plan model, whereas 77% of the managers opine pension schemes facilitate the recruitment of future talent.[148] Towers Watson (2010) infer from their survey results that HR management in Germany needs to make the internal pension plan policy more transparent for it to be a powerful HR instrument.[149]

B. Reduction in Social Security Costs

Pension contributions a sponsoring company pays for its employees are social security tax-exempt under Sec. 3 No. 63 EStG.[150] These tax benefits reduce overall remuneration costs for a company, as for every €1 paid in salary an employer has to contribute currently 19.62% to the social security system. A €1 contribution to a pension plan, therefore, would reduce the social security costs of the company by €0.196.[151] Using pension contributions as a form of remuneration to employees can consequently have a measurable impact on the overall social security costs of a company.

C. Social Commitment and Responsibility

A company that offers its employees occupational pension schemes demonstrates to its stakeholders its social responsible function. This commitment will also influence positively on the reputation of the company, an effect that might have monetary value.[152]

2.3.4 Conclusions

German legislation allows companies to offer their employees five different occupational pension plan alternatives. Each of these pension schemes has particular financial, regulatory and legal risks for the sponsoring company. A key aspect for our research study is to understand which involved party bears the overall investment risk of the pension plan, how this risk is defined and

---

[148] See FAZ Institute (2008) and FAZ (2008).
[149] See Towers Watson (2010), p. 3.
[150] The full tax-exemption applies to Direct Pension Commitments and Support Funds only. For Pension Insurance Funds, Pension Funds and Direct Insurance schemes, the tax exemption is capped at 4% of the Social Security Contribution Ceiling for the respective year. See Uebelhack (2011), p. 199.
[151] See Braueninger (2010), p. 5.
[152] See Braueninger (2010), p. 5 et seq.

quantified. Based on prevailing legislation, it is the decision of company management and ultimately shareholders to decide what type of occupational pension scheme shall be offered to employees. The German legislator, meanwhile, has introduced a mandatory element to the previously voluntary occupational pension system with the implementation of deferred compensation payments.

For a corporation, offering occupational pension schemes may have substantial economic and reputational advantages: (1) pension plans can be a powerful HR management tool to attract new employees and motivate or retain existing staff, a factor that can be crucial in times of scarcity of highly skilled workers, (2) the advantageous tax treatment of pension contributions allows companies to reduce their social security costs and (3) offering pension plans demonstrates a certain degree of social responsibility by a company towards its workforce that may ultimately contribute to enhance the firm's reputation.

In section 2.4, we will discuss essential elements of the German Pension Insurance Fund we deem relevant for the purposes of our research study. We will focus in particular on the economic relevance of Pension Insurance Funds within the German occupational pension system, their legal definition, the insured risk categories they cover, the different forms of pension contributions and benefits allowed by law and the regulatory environment under which they operate.

2.4 Principal Elements of the Pension Insurance Fund

2.4.1 Economic Relevance

German corporations are increasingly offering their employees occupational pension plans. While at the end of 2001 only 31% of companies had a pension plan in place, by the end of 2007 already 51% of corporations did so. For large corporations (>1,000 employees) this rate was as high as 97%.[153] Figure 13 depicts the historical development of the market share of occupational pension schemes in Germany.

---

[153] See Bundesministerium fuer Arbeit und Soziales (2008), p. 32.

Figure 13: Market Share of Occupational Pension Schemes in the German Corporate Sector

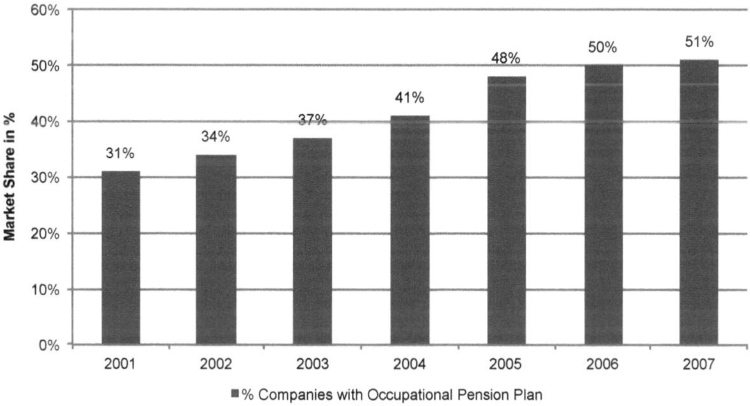

Source: Own figure, on the basis of Bundesministerium für Arbeit und Soziales (2008), p. 11.

Using as reference official statistics published by the BaFin, there are currently 150 regulated Pension Insurance Funds active in Germany.[154] Using underlying covering funds (assets under management) as a reference, Pension Insurance Funds have a total asset base of € 115.8bln under management. Within insurance companies, Pension Insurance Funds obtain 9.7% of total market share, behind life insurers (62.5% or €742.7bln), health insurance companies (16.0% or €189.6bln) and accident insurance corporations (11.6% or €138.0bln).[155]

Based on figures by Schwind (2011) on the relative size of occupational pension schemes, Pension Insurance Funds achieve the second largest market share in Germany with 23.6% of total AuM in occupational pension plans invested, after Direct Pension Commitments with 54.0%. Pension Insurance Funds are therefore the largest external occupational pension plan. Table 2 illustrates the split of total AuM within German occupational pension schemes.[156]

---

[154] See BaFin (2012, a).

[155] See BaFin (2012, b), p. 3.

[156] See Schwind (2011), p. 476. Due to the time difference between the data provided by the BaFin (2012, b) on Pension Insurance Funds and the publication of Schwind (2011) (with data for 2009), which is the latest and only available update to date on assets under management for all five occupational pensions schemes, the AuM numbers for Pension Insurance Funds refer on this page to two different time periods.

Table 2: Market Share of German Occupational Pension Schemes (2009, in €bln)

Pension Scheme	Assets under Management	
	In % of Total	In €bln
Direct Pension Commitment	54.0%	245.1
Pension Insurance Fund	23.6%	107.1
Direct Insurance	11.0%	49.9
Support Fund	8.2%	37.2
Pension Fund	3.2%	14.5
Total	100.0%	453.8

Source: Own representation, on the basis of Schwind (2011), p. 476.

Chart 14 illustrates how the relative market share of occupational pension schemes has evolved in the last 20 years. The Pension Insurance Fund, in particular, maintained its role as largest external pension alternative in Germany throughout this time period. Moreover, the overall increase in assets under management in the time period 2000-2008 reflects the increasing importance of occupational pension solutions in Germany.

Figure 14: Asset Base Evolution for Occupational Pension Schemes (Since 1990, in €bln)

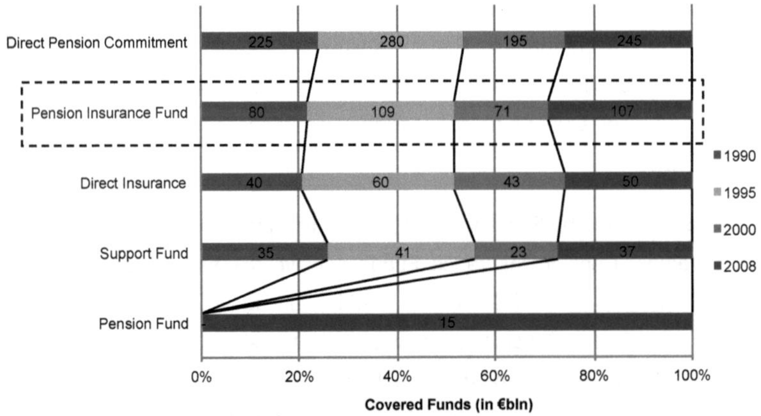

Source: Own figure, on the basis of aba (2011) and Schwind (2011), p.476. Note: Due to the introduction of the Pension Fund in 2002, there is no prior pension data available for this pension alternative.

Using the number of pension members released by the Federal Ministry of Labour and Social Affairs, Pension Insurance Funds have benefited from the highest increase in terms of pension members between the end of 2002 and the end of 2007, more than doubling the number of contributors from 2.1m members to 4.5m (increase of 114.9%).[157]

Figure 15: Pension Members by Occupational Pension Scheme (Dec-2002 to Dec-2007, in million people)

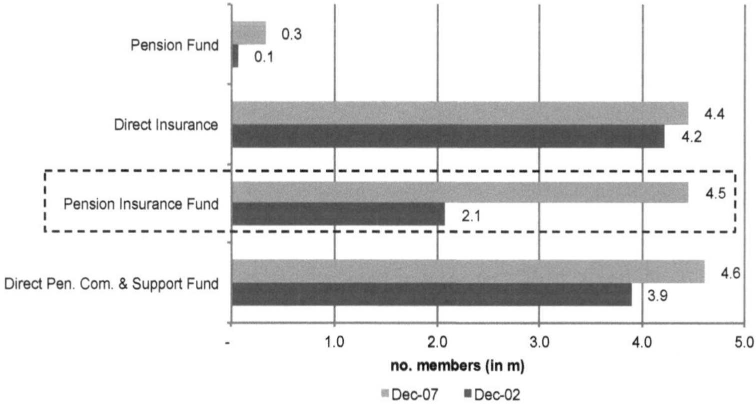

Source: Own figure, on the basis of Bundesministerium fuer Arbeit und Soziales (2008), p. 110.
Note: Data for Direct Pension Commitments and Support Funds is available as a single figure only.

2.4.2 Definition

The BertrAVG defines a Pension Insurance Fund as an independent pension institution that offers employees and their surviving dependent a legal claim for benefits originated from an occupational pension arrangement.[158] The German Insurance Supervision Act (VAG), on the other hand, states that a Pension Insurance Fund is a life insurance company, which offers his members insurance coverage for any potential shortfall an insured employee or his surviving dependents may suffer due to retirement, disability or death. Moreover, the Pension Insurance Fund shall execute its insurance business via a capital funded system. The VAG also indicates that insurance claims are only legally binding as soon as one of the insured risk events occurs and the affected pension member is unable to continue with his contractual labour obligations.[159]

---

[157] See Bundesministerium fuer Arbeit und Soziales (2008), p. 110.
[158] See Sec. 1b Par. 3 BetrAVG.
[159] See Sec. 118a VAG. Retirement is hereby understood as the 'inability' to continue with the work obligations due to reaching retirement age.

As it is the case for the Direct Pension Commitment and the Support Fund pension schemes, the Pension Insurance Fund involves the company as the contribution payer, the employee as the insured counterparty of the contract as well as member of the pension fund and the pension fund itself as the insurance provider.[160] Employees have also the flexibility to contribute additional funds to their pension plans via deferred compensation payments or direct payments (see also sections 2.4.4, D and E).[161]

Figure 16: Involved Parties in a Pension Insurance Fund

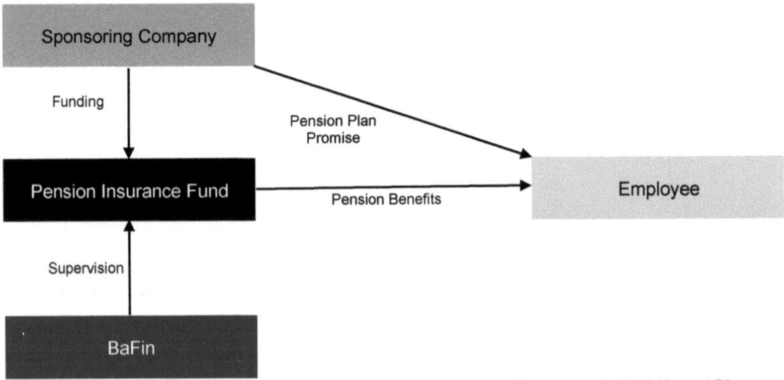

Source: Own figure, on the basis of Doetsch (2010), p. 21 and Hanau et al. (2006), p. 159.

In principal, the VAG allows two forms of Pension Insurance Funds: (1) the traditional pension plan associated with a particular sponsoring company and founded for the sole purpose to offer to its members occupational pension services as part of a broader remuneration package, and (2) Pension Insurance Funds created by life insurance companies that offer pension services similar to those Direct Insurance schemes do (as discussed in section 2.3.1, D).[162] Our research study will focus exclusively on the former, traditional pension alternative.

Moreover, there are Pension Insurance Funds linked to specific collective labour agreements or that act as occupational pension provider on behalf of cer-

[160] See Doetsch et al. (2010), p. 20.
[161] See Braun (2010), p. 32.
[162] See Dresp (2011, a), p. 27. See also Sec. 118a and Sec. 118b No. 3 VAG for the respective legal wording.

tain segments of the public sector[163] or ecclesiastic institutions. Additionally, there are Group Pension Insurance Funds founded for a specific industry sector or that are sector-independent.[164]

2.4.3 Insured Risk Categories

A member of a Pension Insurance Fund is entitled to receive benefits only in case that one of the insured risk events actually occurs. These events are retirement, death or disability. A particular pension plan can offer protection against all three risks or a combination of them, although any alternative has to include at least retirement insurance if it wants to benefit from tax subsidies.[165]

A. Retirement

The concept of 'retirement risk' or 'longevity risk' as well as 'retirement age', after which the beneficiary is entitled to receive pension benefits, can be determined and defined at the discretion of the parties involved. There is no clear definition or wording in the BetrAVG act. The retirement age, however, is usually fixed at 65 years of age. The earliest age that should be contemplated is 60 years.[166] With the increase of the public pension retirement age from 65 years to 67 years in Germany, the earliest retirement age for occupational pension scheme is expected to gradually adjust to 62 years in the coming years. While it has been common practise to pay benefits as soon as an employee retires, it is also feasible to agree to a part-time model, in which the worker reduces the workload (and correspondingly his salary) and starts receiving occupational pension plan benefits earlier.[167] In general, should an employee benefit from an early retirement pension based on the public pension system, he has also a right for an early payment of his occupational pension benefits.[168]

---

163 The largest being the 'Versorgungsanstalt des Bundes und der Laender' (VBL) with over 4.2m insured members and 4.1m beneficiaries. See VBL (2012).

164 See Schmitz, Laurich (2004), p. 547 et seq.

165 See Kerschbaumer, Perreng (2005), p. 19 et seq. See also Sec. 118a VAG on the corresponding legal wording. The details on the respective taxation benefits are defined in Sec. 82 EStG.

166 Individual working groups have managed to contractually agree even younger age levels. Examples in Germany are flight crews from airlines, which can receive benefits from occupational pension plans from the age of 55 years onwards. See Veit (2009), p. 424.

167 See Foerster, Rechtenwald (2008), p. 141 et seq.

168 See Dresp (2011, b), p. 91.

B. Disability

Disability risk is also not defined in detail in the BetrAVG. Therefore, the counterparts themselves define terms and conditions that are covered in the pension plan in case of disability of the affected worker. It is common practise though to adhere to the disability regulation of the public pension system. Pension claims are normally fulfilled under the condition that the disabled pension member also receives disability benefits from the social insurance agencies. Since 2001, the public pension system draws a distinction between full- or partial disability,[169] a concept that also has been implemented afterwards in many occupational pension plans.[170]

C. Death

The pension contract may also include benefits for surviving dependents. Benefits are paid out when either the active or already retired pension scheme member passes away. Beneficiaries can be widows, widowers or orphans or a combination of them.[171] The pension level for widows is usually fixed at 50-70% of the respective pension entitlement of the deceased pension member and at 10-40% for any orphan. The total pension payout is usually capped at 100% of the pension entitlement across widow(s) and orphans.[172]

2.4.4 Pension Benefits and Contribution Alternatives

In this section we will describe the benefit alternatives that are relevant for Pension Insurance Funds. The respective characteristics of the chosen benefit structure will have a significant impact on the strategic asset allocation of the fund as the contributions will have to be reinvested pursuing different investment objectives.

---

169 See Sec. 43 Par. 1 and Par. 2 SGB VI. Partial disability is given when a worker can do at least 6h per day of his normal workload. Full disability implies that the affected employee is unable in the foreseeable future to do at least 3 working hours per day.

170 See Foerster, Rechtenwald (2008), p. 142.

171 See Schumann (2003), p. 25 et seq.

172 See Dresp (2011, b), pp. 94-96.

Figure 17: Benefit Alternatives as defined by BetrAVG

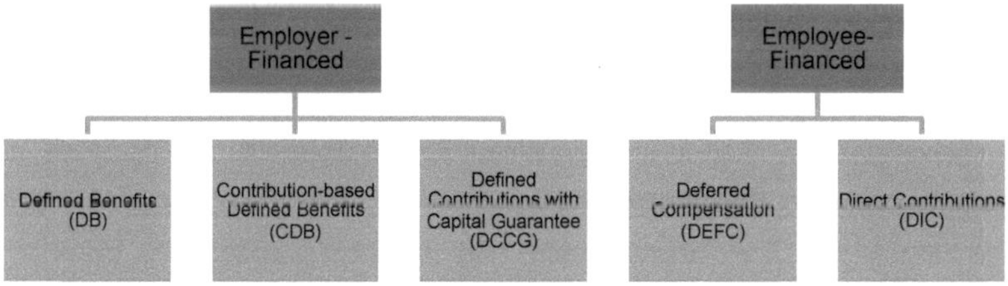

Source: Own figure.

As figure 17 illustrates, there are two major distinctions for pension benefits: either benefits are financed by the sponsoring company or benefits are originated directly by the employees. Combinations of both alternatives are feasible and common practise. Moreover, benefits can be paid to the beneficiary either as a one-off amount as soon as an insured event occurs or as an annuity.[173] Pension Insurance Funds can offer all three employer-financed benefit alternatives.

A. Defined Benefits (DB)

Defined benefit plans represent the basic form of pension scheme for employees in Germany.[174] Regulated in Sec. 1 Par. 1 BetrAVG, defined benefit plans guarantee pension fund members a certain benefit level once one of the insured risk events occurs. The benefits are typically paid out as a percentage of the last salary received or as a fixed amount. There are no contribution payments during the investment period for this form of scheme. DB plans are feasible for all five occupational pension plan alternatives of the BetrAVG.[175]

There are primarily three different approaches of defined benefit payments that can be included in DB pension plans: (1) Fixed nominal amount which can be adjusted by the years of company affiliation, (2) for each year of affiliation, a fixed amount times a multiple that includes individual factors (e.g. salary) or generic features (e.g. the social security contribution ceiling) and (3) benefits that are calculated on the basis of the number of years of affiliation times a fixed

[173] See Veit (2009), p. 423.
[174] See Roth (2009), p. 22.
[175] See Sec. 1 Par. 1 and Sec. 1b Par. 2-4 BetrAVG.

percentage of the last salary (e.g. 0.75% of the last salary times number of years employed at the company).[176]

From a financial risk perspective, the committed benefits in DB plans by the employer are not linked to any investment performance over the life of the insurance coverage. Beneficiaries know at inception of the pension plan coverage the calculation of their future benefits they will receive once a risk event occurs.[177] All the financing risk of the DB plan remains therefore with the pension scheme sponsor (i.e. the company).[178] Defined benefits pension schemes can be illustrated as follows:

Figure 18: Overview of Defined Benefit Pension Schemes (DB)

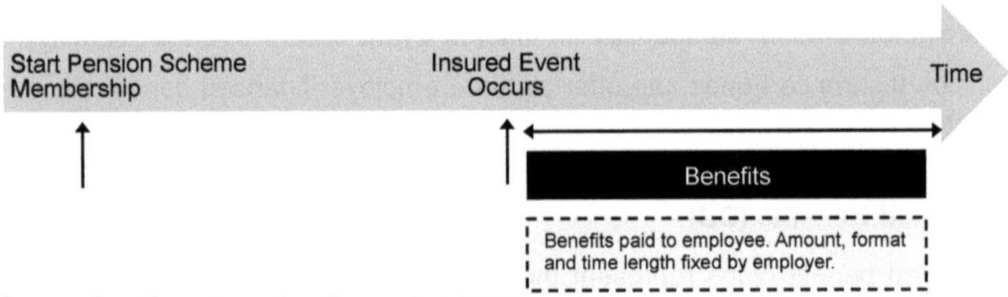

Source: Own figure, based on Hanau et al. (2006), p. 162.

B. Contribution-based Defined Benefits Schemes (CDB)

In a contribution-based defined benefit scheme, the employer promises to contribute fixed contribution payments to the pension scheme.[179] These contributions are then reinvested via one of the occupational pension alternatives. The benefits for the claimant, thereby, are the result of applying an actuarial formula to these regular employer contributions. The calculation of this actuarial formula is fixed at inception and remains unchanged over the investing period. This formula also enables the employer to determine the required contributions he needs to pay into the pension scheme so as to obtain the agreed pension contributions once an insured risk event emerges.[180]

Administrative costs for either running a pension plan in-house or using the services of an external provider as well as the costs associated with the insur-

[176] See Foerster, Rechtenwald (2008), p. 147.
[177] See Veit (2009), p. 435.
[178] See Klatt (2003), p. 116.
[179] See Sec. 1 Par. 2 No. 1 BetrAVG.
[180] See Veit (2009), p. 439.

ance of death and/or disability risks are deducted from the gross benefit entitlements the invested capital will have generated until that point.[181] CDB schemes can be offered in any of the five occupational pension alternatives.[182]

Figure 19: Overview of Contribution-based Defined Benefits Schemes (CDB)

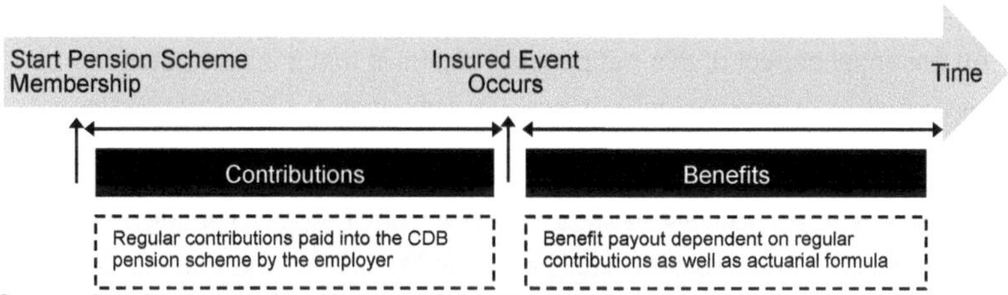

Source: Own figure, based on Hanau et al. (2006), p. 164.

C. Defined Contributions with Capital Guarantee (DCCG)

Defined contributions with capital guarantee plans were introduced in the BetrAVG in Jan-2002, when the AVmG law act came into effect. Main motivation for this new benefit structure was the demand by pension plan providers as well as sponsoring companies to introduce pure defined contribution plans, which back then were already in place in some European countries (especially the UK). Traditional benefit structures in use in Germany (DBs and CDBs) had proven to be highly unpredictable from a financing point of view for the respective sponsors. The German legislator, however, decided to implement DCCGs as a compromise to these external demands.[183]

Following the legal definition in the BetrAVG, in a DCCG pension plan the employer commits to pay regular contributions to either a Pension Fund, Pension Insurance Fund or Direct Insurance scheme.[184] Once an insured event materializes, the claimant is entitled to receive the sum of all contributions accumulated until that point plus any excess returns the invested capital may have generated during the investment period. The potential expenses associated with the hedging of biometric risks will be deducted from this gross pension capital. The net amount (net pension capital) represents the capital entitlement of the claimant. This capital needs to be guaranteed by the employer. The

[181] See Klatt (2003), p. 118 et seq.
[182] See Hanau et al. (2006), p. 163.
[183] See Hanau et al. (2006), p. 168.
[184] See Sec. 1 Par. 2 No. 2 BetrAVG.

BetrAVG consequently obliges an employer to pay the pension contributions and to guarantee the net pension capital.[185] Given the specific characteristics of DCCG schemes, pension beneficiaries will therefore only be able to determine their exact pension entitlements once the insured risk event actually happens.[186]

An essential aspect of this net pension capital is that it is understood to be in nominal terms, so that employees assume full inflation risk on all contributions paid into the scheme over the investing period. Furthermore, should there be any investment shortfall between guaranteed net pension capital and actual capital available, the employer would be forced to finance the funding gap.[187] In summary, from an investment risk perspective, a pension plan member bears all investment risk exposure down to the guaranteed 'backstop' by the employer, which is the net pension capital (also called minimum capital). Any shortfall below that level is absorbed completely by the sponsoring company.[188] As the company does not provide a guaranteed return on the contributions made over time, DCCG plans are also called 'zero-return-guarantee' plans.[189]

Figure 20: Overview of Defined Contributions with Capital Guarantee (DCCG)

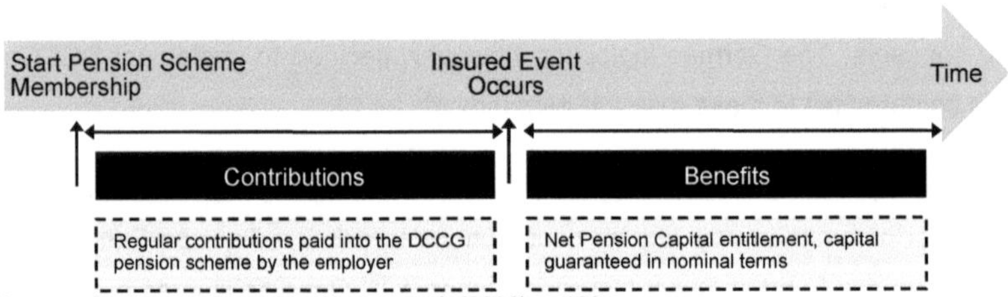

Source: Own figure, based on Hanau et al. (2006), p.169.

D. Deferred Compensation Contributions (DEFC)

The introduction of deferred compensation contributions paid directly by employees denotes a substantial change in the German occupational pension system. While the implementation of occupational pension schemes used to be a voluntary service by the company to its employees, the deferred compensation

[185] See Foerster, Rechtenwald (2008), p. 148.
[186] See Veit (2009), p. 440.
[187] See Hanau et al. (2006), pp. 168-170.
[188] See Braun (2010), p. 43 et seq.
[189] See Langohr-Plato, Teslau (2003), p. 661.

concept introduced an element of enforceability to the second pillar of the German pension system. Furthermore, the clear separation that existed previously between occupational and individual pension systems became blurred, as deferred compensation payments are allocated within the occupational pension system but are paid by the employee directly.[190]

Deferred compensation payments are defined in Sec. 1a of the BetrAVG. They became legally enforceable on Jan-2002 with the AVmG reform bill. Since then, employees can force an employer to offer occupational pension plans through deferred compensation payments,[191] even for companies that do not have any occupational plan in place at all.[192] The maximum amount that can be allocated from the gross salary of an employee towards deferred compensation contributions is capped at 4% of the social security contribution ceiling of the public pension system.[193] Deferred compensation contributions are a form of tax efficient pension planning, as contributions are not taxed during the investment period (deferred taxation).[194]

Employer and employee have hereby full flexibility in deciding what pension scheme to use and what type of benefit to offer for DEFC payments.[195] In case no agreement is reached, though, the BetrAVG defines the following procedure: (1) The employer can enforce that DEFC contributions are paid into either an company-internal pension scheme or into an external Pension Fund or a Pension Insurance Fund, and it is also at his discretion to choose which external provider to use (in case no internal solution is available).[196] (2) Should the company neither offer a Pension Fund nor a Pension Insurance Fund solution, the employee can request that the company transfers the DEFCs contributions into a Direct Insurance scheme. Again, it is the right of the employer to decide which external direct insurance plan to use.[197]

---

[190] See Schumann (2003), p. 82.
[191] See Sec. 1a Par. 1 No. 1 BetrAVG.
[192] See Hanau et al. (2006), p. 5.
[193] For 2012, that ceiling has been fixed at €67,200 per year or €5,600 per month for West-Germany, and €57,600 per year or €4,800 per month for Eastern-Germany. This means that for an employee in West-Germany, the maximum amount that can be contributed for deferred compensation payments is €224 per month. See Deutsche Rentenversicherung Bund (2012).
[194] See Uebelhack (2011), p. 58 et seq.
[195] See Hanau et al. (2006), pp. 32-34.
[196] See Sec. 1a Par. 1 No. 3 BetrAVG.
[197] See Foerster, Rechtenwald (2008), p. 150.

Figure 21: Overview of Deferred Compensation Payments

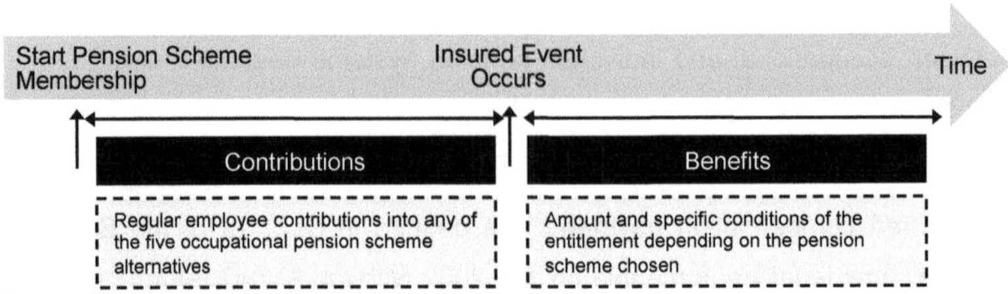

Source: Own figure.

E. Direct Contributions

Direct pension contributions by the employee within the framework of the BetrAVG are feasible under Sec. 1 Par. 2 No. 4 BetrAVG. The contributions have to be originated from the employee's post-tax net salary. The German legislator determines that these contributions have to be allocated to a Pension Fund, Pension Insurance Fund or Direct Insurance pension scheme.[198] Which alternative the claimant can choose depends on the pension scheme the company already has in place for its employees.[199] Direct contributions also benefit from deferred taxation, as defined in Sec. 82 Par. 2 No. 1 EStG.

Figure 22: Overview of Direct Contributions

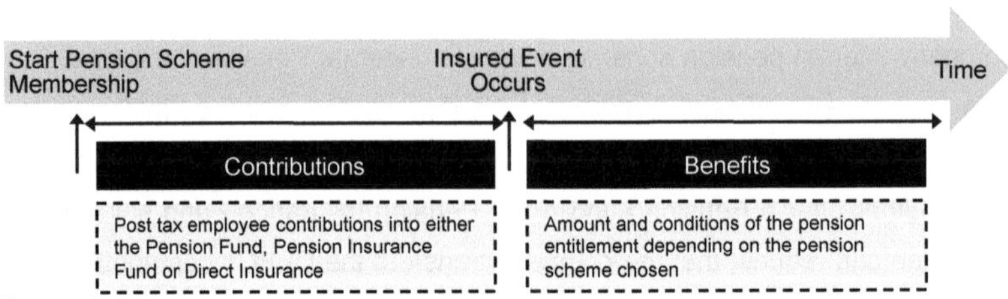

Source: Own figure.

Table 3 summarises the various combinations of pension plan schemes and benefit options within the framework of the BetrAVG that have been presented in this section.

[198] See Rohde, Kuesters (2007), p. 17 et seq.
[199] See Veit (2009), p. 446.

Table 3: Benefit Alternatives by Pension Plan Scheme and Type of Contribution

	Defined Benefits			Contribution-based Defined Benefits			Defined Contributions with Capital Guarantee		
	EFB	*DEC*	*DIC*	*EFB*	*DEC*	*DIC*	*EFB*	*DEC*	*DIC*
Direct Pension Commit-ment	X	X		X	X				
Support Fund	X	X		X	X				
Direct Insurance	X	X	X	X	X	X	X	X	X
Pension Insurance Fund	X	X	X	X	X	X	X	X	X
Pension Fund	X	X	X	X	X	X	X	X	X

Source: Own representation, based on Hanau et al (2006), p. 172, Veit (2009), p. 441 and Rohde, Kuesters (2007), p. 17. Abbreviations used: 'EFB'= employer-financed benefits, 'DEC'= deferred compensation financed benefits, 'DIC'= direct contributions by pension plan members.

2.4.5 Regulatory Supervision

A. Regulatory Supervision by the BaFin

Pension Insurance Funds are under the supervision of the German regulator BaFin. The legal framework for the supervision is the German Insurance Supervision Act VAG.[200] The principal responsibilities of the BaFin are hereby (1) to grant the permission for new Pension Insurance Funds to initiate their business activities, (2) to control and approve on a regular basis the business plans for all regulated schemes in Germany and (3) to assess the mandatory reporting on asset allocation and management changes.[201] (4) Moreover, the regulator has the power to enforce his representatives to be present at Supervisory Board meetings or AGMs.[202] (5) The BaFin is also point of contact for any complaints or disputes pension members may have with their respective occupational pen-

[200] Sec. 83 VAG, in particular, describes all the powers the German regulator has in the insurance sector.
[201] See Gieg (2008), p. 56.
[202] See Sec. 83 Par. 1 No. 5 VAG.

sion schemes.[203] Another important responsibility is the regular supervision of the reporting requirements Pension Insurance Funds are subject to.[204]

The BaFin puts significant emphasise on capital requirements as well as solvency considerations, as both factors are decisive for the viability of pension funds. A constant control ensures that the risk of financial distress is minimised. Solvency considerations, especially, are closely watched and strict guidelines impose a disciplined regime on pension fund managers. In extreme cases of breaching solvency requirements, the BaFin can intervene and either reduce benefit payments (Sec. 89 VAG) or, *ultima ratio,* enforce closure of all business activities of a fund (Sec. 87 VAG).[205]

2.4.6 Conclusions

Occupational pension schemes have benefited from strong growth amongst private sector corporations in Germany in the last years. Within the five occupational alternatives feasible under BetrAVG, Pension Insurance Funds are the largest external pension scheme available in terms of assets under management and membership growth.

Insured pension members benefit from retirement, death or disability provisions via three different pension benefit structures: defined benefits (DB), which are historically the eldest and most relevant option, contribution-based defined benefits (CDB) and defined contributions with capital guarantee (DCCG), the most recent benefit innovation introduced by the German legislator. Our empirical study will focus exclusively on DCCG benefits as they have been implemented explicitly to enable pension fund managers to better risk-manage pension plans, minimise the financing risk associated with defined benefit pension schemes and participate in return rates of capital-funded investment funds. While the German regulator did not go as far as allowing pure capital-funded defined contribution plans, DCCG schemes facilitate a better strategic asset management as beneficiaries bear all investment risk above the capital guarantee at nominal terms of the contributions paid into the pension plan.

---

[203] Circular letter R1/2006 describes the process of complaint for affected pension members. See BaFin (2006).
[204] See Dresp (2011, c), pp. 177-182.
[205] See Klatt (2003), p. 80 et seq.

The tight regulatory supervision by the BaFin guarantees a high level of solvency in the German Pension Insurance Fund sector. Considering the emergency measures the BaFin could in theory undertake, Pension Insurance Funds appear a low-risk occupational pension scheme alternative.

In following section 2.5 we it will provide details on the investment framework imposed by law and the regulator in Germany on Pension Insurance Funds and that will ultimately determine how the strategic portfolio allocation is restricted, both in terms of asset allocation and investment strategies. Furthermore, we will present data on the actual asset allocation pursued by Pension Insurance Fund as well as discuss the potential implications the introduction of Solvency II may have on the strategic asset management.

2.5 Investment Management Considerations

2.5.1 Regulatory Investment Framework

A. Overview

The legal and regulatory framework for the investment management of German Pension Insurance Funds is primarily defined in the Insurance Supervision Act VAG, the Investment Ordinance (AnlV or 'Anlageverordnung')[206] and the various circular letters of the BaFin (in particular R 4/2011[207]).[208]

The prime objective of these regulations is to ensure that pension promises by companies made to their pension scheme beneficiaries will be fulfilled when benefits are claimed in the future. For that purpose, the asset-liability-management of Pension Insurance Funds requires to be monitored and regulated. As stated by the BaFin, "insurance undertakings must invest the guarantee assets and the other restricted assets in a way that ensures maximum security and profitability, while maintaining the insurance undertaking's liquidity at all times, maintaining an adequate diversification and spread".[209] For so-called primary insurers, to which Pension insurance Funds belong, the Investment Ordinance AnlV defines allowable assets for investing, diversification require-

---

206 See BaFin (2011, a).
207 See BaFin (2011, b).
208 See Frere et al. (2009), p. 64.
209 Bafin (2012, c). Citation refers to Sec. 54 Par. 1 VAG.

ments for the investment portfolio, "spread thresholds, matching and location requirements" as well as a qualitative framework of how the internal investment management has to be implemented.[210]

Rules and regulations for the investment management of Pension Insurance Funds can be grouped into 3 categories: (1) Balance sheet aspects, (2) qualitative investment management guidance and (3) quantitative asset class specifications and limitations. While Sec. 54-54d VAG define the requirements for the fund allocation in generic terms, Sec. 65-79 VAG refer to balance sheet aspects (in particular terms and conditions of the Guarantee Assets), the Investment Ordinance AnlV and BaFin's circular letters specify concrete asset allocation limitations as well as investment standards with respect to diversification and risk spreading.

B. Balance Sheet Aspects

The key balance sheet item for any investment strategy of Pension Insurance Fund is the Guarantee Asset position as defined by Sec. 66 VAG. Its amount must be at least equivalent to the sum of the balance sheet values of the unearned premiums, the premium reserve (as defined in Sec. 65 VAG), provisions for outstanding claims, rebates and unused premiums, creditors from the direct insurance business and received premiums that may have to be repaid in case of cancellation or rescission of an insurance contract.[211] For the Guarantee Asset portfolio, specific investment rules and principles have to be fulfilled, as worded in Sec. 54 of the VAG act, the AnlV ordinance and BaFin circular letters.[212]

The German regulator also determines the minimum capital adequacy requirements a Pension Insurance Fund has to fulfil to be allowed to run its operational business. The applied rules are hereby summarised in the VAG (Sec. 53c VAG) as well as the KapAusstV guideline ('Kapitalausstattungs-Verordnung').[213] The so-called solvency margin is hereby required to be at least

---

[210] Bafin (2012, c).
[211] See Sec. 66 Par. 1a VAG.
[212] See Fath (2011), p. 164 et seq.
[213] See BaFin (2009, a).

4% of the premium reserve plus 0.3% of risk capital.[214] Figure 23 summarises all relevant balance sheet aspects of Pension Insurance Funds.

Figure 23: Balance Sheet Considerations based on VAG

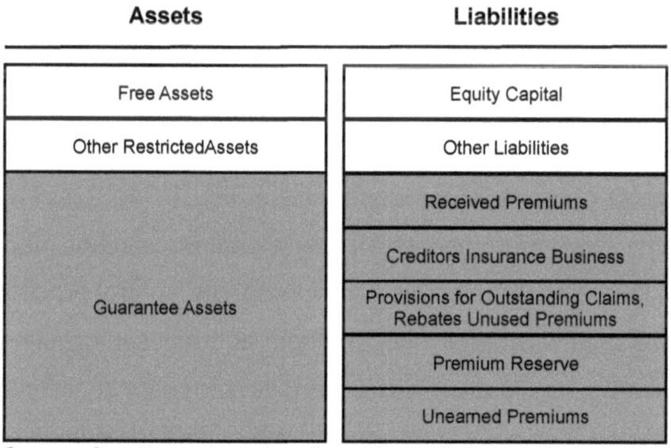

Source: Own figure, based on Sec. 65, 66 VAG.

C. Investment Management Principles

C.1 VAG Act

The VAG requires the asset selection for the Guarantee Asset Base of a Pension Insurance Fund to be guided by prudence, profitability, liquidity, diversification and risk spreading.[215] The prudence principle is hereby the predominating factor that guarantees that the pension scheme can fulfil its contractual obligations towards its members. Assets selected should provide profitability, although the VAG does require that a specific asset should achieve a guaranteed or minimum return. Moreover, the entire asset side of the pension fund shall offer sufficient liquidity to be able to comply with its on-going and regular benefit obligations. Adequate asset diversification, a basic principle in modern portfolio theory, should provide risk reduction for the unsystematic risk exposure of the portfolio. Within risk spreading, a conservative investment approach has to limit the exposure to single counterparties to avoid default risk.[216] Sec. 54 Par. 2 VAG also enlists asset class categories into which Pension Insurance Funds can in principle invest. A greater detail on the allowed asset categories

[214] See Sec. 4 Par. 1 KapAusstV. Risk capital is defined in Sec. 4 Par. 1 No. b KapAusstV.
[215] See Franz (2011), p. 1027 and Sec. 54 Par. 1 VAG.
[216] See Klatt (2003), pp. 87-89.

can be found in the AnlV guidelines as well as BaFin circulars R3/2009[217] and R4/2011[218].

C.2 AnlV Regulation

The AnlV regulation describes in Sec. 2 in more detail into what asset classes Pension Insurance Funds can invest in.[219] In addition, the guidelines define quantitative restrictions (Sec. 3 AnlV), diversification considerations (Sec. 4 AnlV) as well as foreign exchange matching principles (Sec. 5 AnlV). The most relevant aspects of the AnlV are nonetheless Sec. 1 Par. 2,3 in which the regulator highlights the importance of a professional investment management, defines capital investment principles and appropriate control procedures in place. Also, insurers shall word their own strategic and tactical investing policy. Internal risk monitoring has to allow asset managers to react appropriately to changing economic and financial conditions that may affect the overall performance of the asset portfolio.

C.3 BaFin Circulars R3/2009 and R4/2011

Recent BaFin circulars R3/2009 as well as R4/2011 specify how the daily operations of the asset management of Pension Insurance Funds have to be structured. Additionally, both circulars also clarify definitions provided by the AnlV or VAG or suggest practical rules for the implementation in an investment management context. In general, R4/2011 provides more detailed specifications than R3/2009. The investment guidelines of the AnlV regulation do nonetheless apply as an overriding principle for the respective BaFin circulars.

With regards to internal risk management, R4/2011 names five principal risk categories for the pension contributions invested within the Guarantee Asset base: (1) market risk (primarily fluctuations in price levels as well as volatility of market prices), (2) credit risk (default or downgrades of debt assets), (3) concentration risk (risk associated with correlated assets), (4) liquidity risk (fund unable to meet obligations as assets are not fungible) and (5) legal risk (complex contractual terms or exposure to foreign legal systems). The board of the

[217] See BaFin (2009, b).
[218] See BaFin (2011, b).
[219] The main investment forms are: (secured) debt, loans, advance payments, mortgage bonds, receivables due from subordinated liabilities, asset backed securities, government or supranational debt, equity, real estate in the form of developed shares in REITS or closed-end funds, investment funds in general and cash deposits. See Sec. 2 AnlV.

pension fund has to define a precise strategic and tactical asset management policy that takes into account these portfolio risks. Moreover, one board member has to be made responsible for all risk management aspects of the portfolio (following the so-called 'prudent-person principle') and an appropriate front and back office has to be put in place to execute the investment guidance of the board.[220]

All relevant asset management rules and recommendations have to be written down in an internal asset management policy book.[221] Furthermore, as part of a satisfactory risk management system, the Pension Insurance Fund has to run stress tests on his portfolio on a quarterly basis.[222] Based on R4/2011, section B.2.3, however, the pension plan has the possibility to outsource all risk management aspects of the fund to an external counterparty. Also, the pension scheme is obliged to provide BaFin on an annual basis a description of (1) the expected or targeted asset allocation for the coming year, (2) the internal asset-liability system in place and (3) the risk exposures of the current asset portfolio.[223]

C.4 Derivative Overlay Structures as Defined in R3/2000

Circular R3/2000 defines what derivative overlay structures German direct insurance companies are allowed to invest in. The circular describes precise requirements in terms of maximum sizes allowed as well as specific terms of the derivative transactions, in particular strike levels of the underlying options. R3/2000 will be our main reference act for the derivative overlay strategies we are considering in our empirical analysis, as they have to comply with existing regulation.

---

220 See R4/2011, section B.2.1.
221 See R4/2011, section B.2.2.
222 See R4/2011, section B.2.3.
223 See R4/2011, section B.2.5.

D. Quantitative Asset Class Specifications and Limitations

For the purpose of our empirical analysis, the quantitative rules and regulations for the asset management of Pension Insurance Fund are of fundamental importance.

Table 4 summarises all investible asset classes, the allocation caps imposed by the regulator as well as particular requirements for risk diversification and risk spreading based on the specifications of VAG, AnlV and R4/2011. It is important to highlight that these investment restrictions refer exclusively to the Guarantee Asset pool of insurers and Pension Insurance Funds.

Table 4: Summary of Investment Restrictions as Defined by VAG, AnlV and R4/2011

Asset Class	Max. Allocation	Law Reference	Comments
1. Asset Classes			
Risk Capital	35%	Sec. 3 Par. 3 VAG	Includes shares, subordinated debt, participation rights, loans backed by shares or cash, investment funds
Real Estate	25%	Sec. 3 Par. 5 VAG	Direct or indirect investments allowed (e.g. REITs or real estate funds)
Bonds/Mort-gages/Loans	50% each	B.3.4.D R4/2011	Investment grade with rating, two ratings per bond recommended Maximum 12 years to maturity and NPV of at least 50% of par value. If maturity is longer than 12 years, then minimum return of current actuarial interest rate (1.75%) or minimum coupon at the same level is required For assets that drop below a B- or B3 rating: if the direct investment or fund participation is more than 3% of the total fund volume, a disposal or swap into risk-free assets needs to occur within 6 months; if the assets represent less than 3%, the fund has 6 months to observe if the respective rating improves and then additional 6 months for the disposal or swap into risk-free assets
Indirect Investments	1%	Sec. 4 Par. 4 VAG	Indirect investments, e.g. private equity funds or venture capital, into one single entity cannot exceed 1% of the Guarantee Assets
ABS, CLN	7.5%	Sec. 3 Par. 2 No. 1	Maximum maturity of 12 years, NPV of the capital guarantee of at

		VAG	least 50% of par value, as for bonds Stricter rules than for bonds/mortgages/loans: requires investment grade rating, in case of downgrade there is no possibility to allocate bonds into high yield. Disposal threshold is already reached at rating of BB+ or Ba1
High Yield	5%	Sec. 3 Par. 2 No. 3 VAG	If at least B- / B3, then allocation to Guarantee Assets possible
Commodities	5%	Sec. 3 Par. 2 No. 3 VAG	No physical delivery of underlying commodities allowed
Low-Risk Loans	30%	Sec. 4 Par. 2 VAG	Loans issued by governments, supranational and regional entities that are considered (quasi) risk-free
Subordinate Debt	1%	Sec. 4 Par. 4 VAG	For same issuer
Equity	1%	Sec. 4 Par. 4 VAG	For same issuer
Hedge Funds	5%	Sec. 3 Par. 2 No. 2 VAG	Either via fund-of-funds or direct investments
Exchange Rates	70%	Sec. 5 AnlV, Annex C No. 6 VAG	Up to 30% of the Guarantee Assets can be invested in a currency that is not the currency of the liabilities of the pension plan Real estate is denominated in the currency of the respective country in which the object is located, for shares the reference point is the stock exchange of the main listing
Maximum Allocation Single Asset Class	50%	B.3.4.B R4/2011	50%, unless specified otherwise for asset classes within the Guarantee Assets
Minimum Return Assets	> 0%	B.3.1.A R4/2011	Minimum return not required, although assets that contractually offer zero return are not allowed
2. Counterparty Exposure			
Maximum Exposure Single Counterparty	5%	Sec. 4 Par. 1 VAG	Exposure to any counterparty is limited to 5% of the Guarantee Assets
Secured Debt Instrument by Single Financial Institutions	15%	Sec. 4 Par. 2 VAG	Refers to plain-vanilla secured bonds, covered bonds, for which there is protection on the collateral via law or regulation
Single Portfolio Manager	20%	B.3.5.B R4/2011	If Guarantee Assets are managed by one single portfolio manager only Manager can invest into a single company only 1% of the assets
Sponsoring Company	5% / 15%	Sec. 4 Par.	Limit for one sponsoring company

		6 VAG	5% Sum of all existing companies (if 3 or more) cannot exceed 15%
Exemption Clause	5% / 10%	Sec. 3 Par. 2 No. 4 VAG	Assets under the exemption clause can only represent up to 5% of the Guarantee Assets. The BaFin can allow an increase to up to 10% under special circumstances

Source: Own representation, based on the respective law acts as referenced in the table.

The main conclusions that can be drawn from these asset allocation restrictions are that they will lead to a relatively fixed-income dominated investment portfolio, as in theory it is possible to allocate up to 100% into corporate bonds, government or supranational securities. Even for risk-seeking fund managers, a portfolio could not have more than 35% in risky capital, what in practise would potentially be replicated via equities or subordinated debt investments. Moreover, the usage of alternative investments is also restricted to 5% for hedge fund assets and commodities, respectively. Illiquid investing strategies, e.g. private equity or venture capital, cannot exceed more than 1% of the Guarantee Asset portfolio. The actual asset allocation profile of German Pension Insurance Funds (see subsequent section 2.5.2 for more details) confirm these assumptions, as up to 86% of the portfolios are invested in bond securities and only around 5% in equities.

2.5.2 Asset Allocation in Practise

While section 2.5.1 summarises the legal and regulatory requirements that Pension Insurance Funds have to fulfil within their Guarantee Assets, figure 24 illustrates how German Pension Insurance Funds are actually invested. This asset allocation represents the average allocation of all 150 regulated Pension Insurance Funds in Germany that are under the supervision of the BaFin.

Figure 24: Asset Allocation for German Pension Insurance Funds (Q4 2011, in €m)

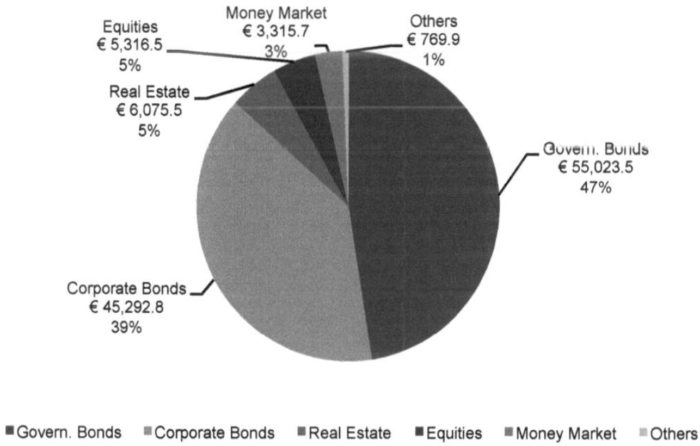

Source: Own figure, on the basis of BaFin (2012, b).

As figure 24 highlights, fixed-income securities represent approximately 86% of the total asset allocation of Pension Insurance Funds, whereas riskier equity assets obtain only 5% of the asset pool. Bonds issued by governments and supranational institutions are the most relevant asset category with €55.0bln (47.5% market share) of investments, followed by corporate bonds with €45.3bln (39.1% market share). Alternative investments, hedge funds and commodities in particular, are not yet meaningfully represented, although by law asset allocation for each asset could be up to 5% each. Also high-yield debt does not seem to be too relevant for the portfolio managers. While pension funds are considered to be important investors in the real estate sector due to the long-term investment horizon of the underlying assets and the steady cash flows, real estate investments do currently play only a minor role in the asset allocation (5% of AuM).

To ensure that our allocation analysis remains representative and uses time-persistent data, we have plotted the average sector asset allocation for German Pension Insurance Funds for the last 5 years.

Figure 25: Historic Asset Allocation of German Pension Insurance Funds (Last 5 Years, Using as Reference Respective Year-End (Q4) numbers)

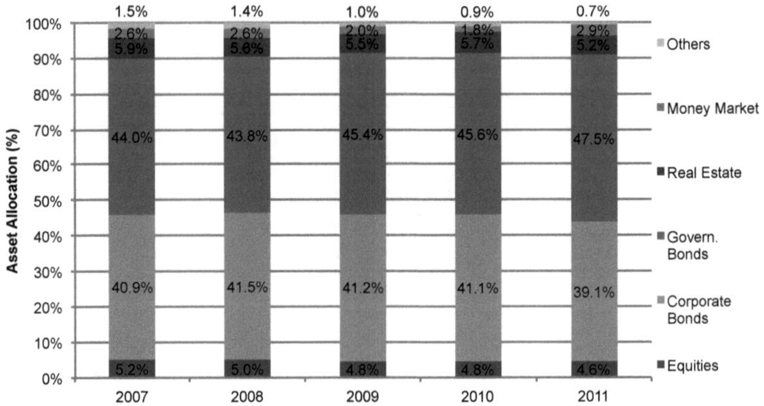

Source: Own figure, on the basis of BaFin (2012, d).

As chart 25 shows, the asset allocation of Pension Insurance Funds has experienced only minor changes in the past 5 years amid the turmoil caused by both the credit crisis post the Lehman collapse in September 2008 and the impact of the European sovereign credit crisis on financial markets since its outbreak in autumn 2009.[224] Government bonds, which should be per definition the safest investment class available within a financial system, have increased from 44.0% of the average asset allocation as of 2007, and therefore just before the beginning of the financial crisis, to 47.5% as of Q4 2011. The asset classes that concurrently decreased were equities, real estate and corporate bonds. These average allocation changes are most probably a reflection of a general trend seen during the 2008-2012 time period during which investors shifted out of risky asset classes into so-called 'safe-haven'. Nevertheless, these allocation changes are not large in magnitude. Actually, the time-consistency of the average asset allocation figures for German Pension Insurance Funds allows us to run our stochastic simulation models with consistent and representative input parameters, therefore turning our outputs into universally valid results.

[224] We will assume for the remainder of our research study that the European sovereign debt crisis unfolded in autumn 2009 when the Greek fiscal crisis became public. See Featherstone (2011), p. 194 et seq.

Due to the relevance of fixed-income securities within the portfolios of Pension Insurance Funds, we have provided a more detailed breakdown of this asset category in figure 26:

Figure 26: Investments in Fixed-Income Instruments by German Pension Insurance Funds (Q4 2011, in €m)

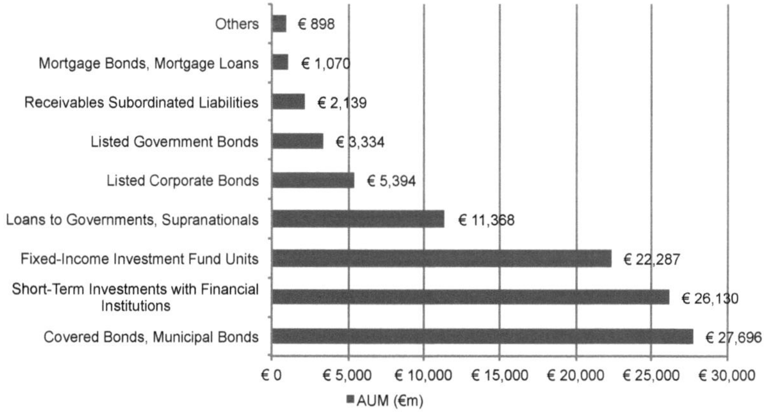

Source: Own figure, on the basis of BaFin (2012, b).

Covered bonds and municipal bonds represent the largest asset group with €27,696m (or 23.9% of total asset allocation), whereas deposits at financial institutions with €26,130m (22.6%) and fixed-income investment funds with €22,287m (19.2%) represent the second and third largest asset category, respectively. In terms of issuer type of covered bonds and municipal bonds, the BaFin statistics indicate a 77.6% market share for public or government entities and a 22.4% stake for private-sector financial institutions.[225] For fixed-income investment funds, we assume an equal 50% / 50% split, as Pension Insurance Funds will invest in both (highly-rated) credit funds and government portfolios. With respect to deposits with central banks and financial institutions, the BaFin statistics determines a 69.0% (€18,020m) split of private-sector assets and 31.0% (€8,110m) of short-term government securities.[226]

[225] The covered bond segment with €12,360m is assumed to be split equally between public / private sector issuers, as public sector issuance volumes reached in the last 3 years consistently a 50% market share. See Verband Deutscher Pfandbriefbanken (2012), p. 22.

[226] See BaFin (2012, b).

2.5.3 Considerations on Solvency II

Solvency II is considered to be one of the major projects for the future supervision of the financial services industry in the European Union.[227] The objective of the rulebook is to set stronger requirements on capital adequacy as well as risk management for insurance companies to better protect insurance clients. The implementation of the Solvency II rules is thereby expected to reduce the likelihood of losses caused by severe market disruptions that would ultimately affect policyholders. Moreover, the new standards should also facilitate insurers to pursue business across the EU.[228] The directive will be implemented for supervisors and the European Insurance and Occupational Pensions Authority (EIOPA) on 01-Jan-2013 (transposition phase), whereas the requirements are expected to become effective for the daily business operations of insurers from 01-Jan-2014 onwards.[229]

The Solvency II directive is based on three main pillars: (1) capital adequacy, (2) governance rules and (3) reporting requirements. Capital adequacy includes quantitative aspects, especially rules for the valuation of assets and liabilities as well as minimum capital requirements. The second pillar refers to adequate organisational and operational structures for insurers and appropriate internal management and control systems. New reporting requirements will put an increased emphasize on aspects like corporate strategy, risk management and the application of standardised or internal models. Moreover, insurers will also be forced to publish their quantitative requirements for solvency capital.[230]

The implementation of Solvency II is expected to have an impact on the investment management of German insurers and occupational pension schemes. Both the asset structure as well as the investment strategy could be transformed, as riskier assets will have to be backed by more capital, probably making riskier investment strategies overall more punitive from a cost of capital perspective for Pension Insurance Funds. Additionally, the valuation of assets and liabilities may be modified. While VAG, AnlV and circular R4/2011 offer a de-

[227] The Solvency II set of rules and measures were adopted in the Directive 2009/138/EC of the European Parliament and of the Council, published on 25-Nov-2009. See European Parliament and the Council of the European Union (2009).
[228] See FSA (2012).
[229] See EIOPIA (2012).
[230] See BaFin (2012, e).

tailed and rigid set of rules for the asset management of insurers, Solvency II will focus more on qualitative requirements of an adequate investment management. Furthermore, assets will be classified depending on their intrinsic risk that will subsequently determine the capital requirements of the respective insurer or pension fund.[231]

The actual implementation of Solvency II for occupational pension schemes in Europe in general, and in Germany in particular, is still open for debate. While the directive is supposed to apply to both insurers and occupational pension funds simultaneously, recent opposition from politicians as well as pension experts has led to a delay, so that details and wording on the respective rules that will apply to pension schemes are not available yet.[232] Critics highlight the significant additional capital requirement triggered by Solvency II of approximately €40-50bln for Pension Insurance Funds, what represents around 8x the prevailing capital position.[233] Pension experts also criticise that the EU Commission does not sufficiently consider the control and safety mechanisms already in place for the German occupational pension sector, in particular the obligation by the sponsoring company to cover any funding shortfalls at the pension scheme and the default protections offered by the PSV.[234] Moreover, Pension Insurance Funds have weathered the turmoil of the financial crisis rather well in comparison to other financial institutions.[235]

Assuming Solvency II will be implemented for occupational pension schemes at some point in the next 2 years, there may be a change in how the investment management for Pension Insurance Funds will be managed. The current debate amongst politicians and regulators may nonetheless lead to a tailor-made solution that is more appropriate for the particular business needs of occupational pension schemes, especially considering the existing regulatory framework in Germany under which Pension Insurance Funds already operate. More

---

231 See Franz (2011), p. 1031.

232 On 01-Jun-2012, the European Commissioner for Internal Market and Services, Michel Barnier, announced a delay to the timetable of the Solvency II implementation for occupational pension schemes. Revisions to the Institutions of Retirement Provision Directive will not be concluded, as initially scheduled, by the end of 2012, but during summer 2013 instead. The implementation is currently planned for 01-Jan-2014. See European Commission (2012).

233 See Bolzen, Eder (2012).

234 See Rezmer, Drost (2012).

235 See Krueger (2011).

clarity by policy-makers in the next 1-2 years will be required to enable us to assess the potential impact of Solvency II on the investment management of Germany's Pension Insurance Funds.

2.5.4 Conclusions

The investment management of Pension Insurance Funds is highly regulated in the VAG act, the AnlV ordinance and the circular R4/2011. The prime objective of the prevailing regulatory framework is to ensure the asset allocation offers beneficiaries maximum security and profitability and to guarantee an appropriate level of liquidity and risk diversification. The flexibility in terms of using derivative overlays as part of a risk management is also restricted via circular R3/2000.

The rigorous set of asset rules worded in circular R4/2011 leads to a rather risk-averse investment profile, as the allocation into risk capital is relatively low, whereas the possibilities for highly rated fixed-income securities are ample. Nonetheless, given the capital guarantee defined contributions with capital guarantee offer, such a conservative strategy seems plausible. As a consequence, both current and historic asset allocation by Pension Insurance Funds in Germany are predominantly fixed-income dominated.

The average portfolio for the Guarantee Assets has approximately 86% of its allocation invested in either highly rated or risk-free fixed-income bonds and only 4.9% in equities. Real estate assets cover 5.6% of the investment portfolio.[236] As statistics by the BaFin indicate, the allocation of Pension Insurance Funds is very constant over the years, independently of the prevailing market conditions.

The potential introduction of Solvency II in the next couple of years may have an impact on the operational business of Pension Insurance Funds, in particular in terms of capital adequacy. Under rules currently debated for Solvency II, Pension Insurance Funds would have to increase their capital base by a massive factor of 8, what would turn their business model unsustainable. The current debate amongst politicians and regulators may lead to a solution that is

---

[236] Average of the last 5 years based on the statistics by BaFin (2012, d).

specific to occupational pension schemes, rather than one that applies a single rulebook for insurers and pension funds alike.

2.6 Summary

Forecasted demographic changes over the next 50 years pose a real threat to the funding and viability of the state pension system in Germany. Under the assumption that by 2060 the German population will decrease by approximately 20.7% to 64.6m inhabitants[237] and that the working population will decline by 34.4% to 32.6m people[238] in the same time period, the ratio of German pensioners to contributors for the statutory pension system will shift dramatically in the next 20 years from 65:100 nowadays to 110:100.[239] These dramatic demographic changes, combined with decreasing pension levels for state pensions, are threatening the capacity of the first pillar of the German pension system to provide an adequate retirement income for pensioners, as the funding of the system is based on the PAYG principle. Recent reforms by the German legislator are focusing on promoting private sector solutions to counter-balance the decline in state pensions. Occupational pension schemes, in particular capital funded plans, are expected to play a major role in the future. Market share of occupational pension schemes in Germany's private sector companies over the last five years are indicating that private pension plans have already gained importance within the German pension system.

In addition, occupational pension plans represent a powerful human resource management instrument. Research studies have provided evidence that occupational pension schemes can increase employee retention and may be an incentive for the recruitment of future talent. Moreover, the German legislator offers beneficial tax treatments on pension contributions that enable corporations to reduce their overall social security costs.

Pension Insurance Funds, the largest external pension scheme in Germany, have experienced the largest growth in terms of pension plan members

[237] See Statistisches Bundesamt (2011, a).
[238] See Statistisches Bundesamt (2009), p. 39 and p. 44.
[239] See Braeuninger (2010), p. 2.

amongst all five pension alternatives.[240] In addition, they can offer their members defined contributions with capital guarantee benefit structures, an alternative introduced by the German legislator in 2002 with the AVmG act. This benefit structure is the nearest form available in Germany to a purely capital funded, defined contribution based pension scheme. Its implementation was supposed to expand the market share of occupational pension plans in Germany.

The actual investment management of Pension Insurance Funds is highly regulated by the BaFin in the respective sections of the VAG act, the AnlV ordinance and the various BaFin circulars. The regulation attempts to guarantee that the asset management of Pension Insurance Funds offers maximum security, profitability, risk diversification, sufficient liquidity and an adequate asset mix. To fulfil these investment targets, a restrictive set of rules is in place that imposes maximum asset allocation caps, minimum diversification requirements as well as defines concentration specifications.

The benefit structures Pension Insurance Funds can offer to their members as well as the investment framework they operate in leads to a conservative asset allocation that is highly dominated by low-risk fixed-income securities. Growth capital in the form of listed equity, which plays a major role in other European pension fund systems like in the UK or the Netherlands, has for the German Pension Insurance Fund sector a minor relevance. An interesting aspect of the asset allocation is its consistency in time, independently of prevailing market conditions. While this supports the validity of our stochastic simulation study, as the input parameters are time-independent, it appears rather surprising that pension fund managers maintain their asset allocation constant. Current strict and inflexible investment regulation in Germany may undoubtedly play a crucial role. Our empirical results may give some clarification if such investment behaviour is justified.

After the most relevant aspects for our research objectives of the German Pension Insurance Funds have been elaborated in chapter 2, we will focus in chapter 3 on Social Responsible Investments (SRIs) and alternative investments, highlighting their performance versus conventional asset classes, the

[240] Growth in the number of pension plan members of 114.3% for the time period 2002-2007. See Bundesministerium fuer Arbeit und Soziales (2008), p. 110.

different screening and investment methodologies available to date, their potential risk-return benefits in connection with portfolio construction considerations as well as the rationale and suitability for their inclusion in the investment allocation of German Pension Insurance Funds.

3. SRIs and Alternative Investments: Expanding the Efficient Frontier?

3.1 Objectives

In the first part of this chapter, we will provide a definition for the broad term 'sustainable' or 'SRI' investments and discuss the differences amongst the various understandings that exist for the same concept. In addition, we will describe the investment strategies SRI investors can pursue and assess which ones are more suitable for Pension Insurance Funds committed to implement SRI methods. An important aspect for any investment diversification into new asset categories is their relative performance in comparison to conventional assets. Should the mean-variance profile be considerable worse, a change in the strategic asset allocation for a pension fund would not be implementable, as it would contradict fiduciary duty. Another relevant aspect we analyse in this chapter is for which different asset classes SRI methods can be contemplated. While historically the SRI space has been predominantly equity-focused, recent developments have noticeably changed the investable universe.

Besides, we provide statistics on the actual size of the SRI market in Europe and in Germany, to better understand how realistic a meaningful shift by German Pension Insurance Fund into the SRI segment may be. We also will investigate how relevant sustainable investing already is for European pension funds to determine if any trend can be detected that could potentially influence the investor behaviour of German pension funds. We will conclude the section on SRI investing by debating what the main justifying factors may be for pension fund managers to consider allocating assets into this particular asset class.

Furthermore, we will debate the suitability for the strategic asset allocation of Pension Insurance Funds of alternative investments, with a particular emphasize on hedge fund assets as well as commodities. The diversification potential of this asset class, combined with its unique features in terms of asset structure and investing possibilities, make alternative assets an appealing asset category for our purposes. In this context, we will discuss empirical evidence in connection with risk-return benefits alternative investments may offer their investors. In addition, we will measure the mean-variance effect the inclusion of alternative investments may have for conventional investment portfolios by using historical time series data. Finally, we will discuss if alternative investment approaches and SRI methodologies can be combined in one single portfolio.

3.2 Social Responsible Investments (SRI)

3.2.1 Definition

A. Conceptual Framework

A precise definition of social responsible investments (SRI) remains a challenging task, as the concept of 'sustainability' or 'social responsibility' cannot be measured or captured by purely quantitative methods or parameters. In academic circles, traditional finance concepts continue to be dominated by a purely neo-classical understanding and remain consequently an ethical value-free domain.[241] A widely accepted academic classification for SRI does therefore not exist to date, rather various valid definitions and methodologies in parallel.[242] In the Anglo-Saxon academic literature, for example, the terminology includes, amongst others, the notations of 'socially responsible investing', 'social responsible investment', 'ethical investment' and 'social investment' for similar underlying concepts.[243]

In common terms, SRIs can be considered an umbrella terminology for investments and investment strategies that include considerations "to create positive social change, minimise environmental damage and incorporate religious or ethical beliefs."[244] Environmental, social and/or governance standards (also denominated 'ESG factors') will thereby influence the investment decisions of the investor.[245] For Schaefer (2009), all those asset classes that in addition to traditional investment criteria (risk, return, liquidity) include ethical or moral principles can be generally considered social responsible investments.[246] Renneboog et al. (2008) emphasize not only the integration of social, environmental and corporate governance or ethical criteria into the investment process, but also the

---

[241] See Schaefer (2012), p. 12.
[242] See Dittrich (2009), p. 22.
[243] See Loew (2002), p. 11.
[244] Fung et al. (2010), p. 1.
[245] See Fung et al. (2010) p. 4.
[246] See Schaefer (2009), p. 64.

range of different investment screens in use to select or exclude certain assets. In some instances, such ESG considerations can also include shareholder activism aspects as part of a broader SRI investing approval as well as for example engagement activities by an investor in local communities.[247]

A.1 Classical Definition: Ethical Investments

Early definitions of SRI referred primarily to so-called 'ethical investments'. As specified by Sparkes, Cowton (2004) an ethical investment "describes the process in which value-based organisations apply internal ethical principles to an investment strategy."[248] Dittrich (2009), on the other hand, refer to ethical investments as investments that include ESG values with the objective of contributing to sustainable development.[249] Sustainable development is hereby generally understood as an inter-generational economic activity that emphasizes the conservation of the environment as an important element of economic activity rather than having a focus exclusively on profit maximization.[250] For these early definitions of SRI or ethical investment strategies, SRI-accordant methods are more norm- and value-centred investment strategies, for which the achievement of sustainability targets is super-ordinated to a classical shareholder value orientation.[251]

In a historical context, ethical investments go back to the 18th century, when religious investors actively avoided investing in so-called 'sin' stocks, which refer to business activities that involve alcohol, tobacco, weapons and gambling. Church groups like the Methodists and the Society of Friends (Quakers), in particular, were dominant US-based investor groups in this context. The concept has been evolving constantly in recent times, from the influence of the political motivated movements triggered by the Vietnam War and Apartheid in South Africa to civil rights movements and environmental protestors in the 1970s and 1980s,[252] in what Entine (2003) defines as the "concurrent movement known as green or ethical consumerism".[253] Institutional investors, such as pension funds

247 See Renneboog et al. (2008), p. 1723.
248 Sparkes, Cowton (2004), p. 46.
249 Sustainable development is a term originated and defined during the UN-conference in Rio de Janeiro in 1992.
250 See Dittrich (2009), p. 22.
251 See Schaefer (2009), p. 65 et seq.
252 See Louche (2009), p. 214 et seq.
253 Entine (2003), p. 2.

and insurance companies, seeking investment opportunities that were in accordance with social and/or environmental aspects were the main drivers of mainstreaming responsible investments at the beginning of the 20th century to what is nowadays known as social responsible investments (SRI).[254]

In conclusion, the history of early SRI investing or ethical investing is rooted primarily in moral principles promoted by religious organizations as well as social as well as environmental issues denounced by different interest groups.[255] As a consequence, the classical definition of ethical investments encompasses predominantly an early form of negative screening or exclusionary investment methodology, which we will discuss in more detail in subsequent section 3.2.3, B.[256]

A.2 Modern Definition: Social Responsible Investments (SRIs)

In recent years, the concept of SRI has changed substantially, as it is considered a practice of increasingly integrating ESG factors into the financial investment process. Conventional financial criteria and social or environmental objectives play a role in the decision process over the acquisition or disposal of an investment.[257] This definition puts an equal weight between return optimization on the one side and social/environmental objectives on the other.

Under the modern definition of SRI, these assets include commonly investments in companies that have strong ESG policies in place and avoid investments in assets that are involved in 'undesirable' business activities, e.g. alcohol or weapons production.[258] Negative screenings as well as positive screening methods (Best-in-Class, thematic approaches) are typically associated with this form of investments.[259] In-line with this definition, Schoenheit (2005) describes SRIs as investments that are targeted at companies that exhibit particular ecological and/or social characteristics or behaviours in the view of the investor.[260]

---

[254] See Osthoff (2008), p. 16.
[255] See Louche, Lydenberg (2006), p. 5 et seq.
[256] See Schaefer (2012), p. 13, quoted after Cowton (1994).
[257] See Sandberg (2010), p. 143.
[258] See JP Morgan Global Research (2010), p. 79.
[259] See Eurosif (2010), p. 8.
[260] See Schoenheit (2005), p. 77.

While in the earlier understanding of SRI a subnormal return was acceptable and in some circumstances even desired, nowadays the expected return of an SRI should be comparable or even higher to conventional market investment opportunities.[261] As Eccles (2011) describes it: "In this mainstream-able form of SRI, ESG issues could be considered only in so far as they might be financially material and no further. There was no room in this for constraining individual greed…[.]"[262] As Knoll (2002) clarifies, SRIs are not charitable assets, as a conventional return on the investment is targeted. Furthermore, investment decisions are not based exclusively on financial criteria, but combined with ESG factors to finally form a view on whether to invest in an asset or not.[263] This definition clearly differentiates from the early SRI definitions that were predominantly ethically driven. The modern SRI concept emphasises how a corporation approaches ESG issues and how these factors may impact the investment performance of an investor. Extra-financial factors are assumed to have important financial long-term impact on the business environment of a corporation and a failure to address these threats might lead to an underperformance of that particular asset. On the other hand, corporations that have positioned their ESG policy appropriately may have a competitive advantage that ultimately might lead to an outperformance for their shareholders.[264]

B. Categories of SRI Investing

In the context of investing in SRI assets, academics as well as practitioners use different terminologies and definitions interchangeably. We therefore present a clearer differentiation to avoid any misunderstandings in the subsequent sections of our research study.

B.1 Sustainable Investing

Sustainable investing is understood to integrate long-term ESG criteria into the investment process with the objective of achieving "superior risk-adjusted financial returns" in comparison to conventional benchmarks or investment methods for the same asset class. ESG criteria are used in the decision process alongside traditional financial aspects (for example cash flow analysis or

---

[261] See Sparkes (2001), p. 195.
[262] Eccles (2011), p. 26.
[263] See Nilsson (2009), p. 6, quoted after Knoll (2002).
[264] Allianz Global Investors (2010), p. 5.

relative valuation matrices). The focus on obtaining superior risk-adjusted returns is a clear differentiating factor to the notions of 'ethical investing', 'socially directed investments' or 'impact investing', in which lower financial returns may be tolerated for achieving ESG objectives.[265] In our understanding and for the purposes of our research study, Social Responsible Investments (SRIs) will follow a sustainable investing approach with the aim to obtain returns that are comparable or higher to yields generated by conventional asset classes.[266] Moreover, we will use 'sustainable investing' and 'SRI investing' interchangeably.

B.2 Ethical Investing

The main differentiating factor between sustainable and ethical investing is the emphasis on financial return generation. While for sustainable investing methods the fulfilment of ESG factors and the generation of financial returns are equally important in the asset selection process and rank *pari-passu*, ethical investing methods select securities primarily based on ethical factors and less on financial parameters. Ethical investors are willed to waive financial returns for the fulfilment of their ethical beliefs and values.[267]

B.3 Socially Directed Investing (SDI)

Socially Directed Investing (SDI) differs from sustainable investing as in the former approach investors are willed to accept lower than standard market returns for the purpose of pursuing a social activity or development. Frequently, this method refers to an 'ethical' banking model in which clients forego part of their interest rates on their bank deposits to fund social projects.[268] SDI concepts are usually some form of banking-driven social investment form, whereas SRIs are predominantly equity driven investments by institutional investors.[269]

---

[265] See World Economic Forum (2011), p. 10.

[266] The superior risk-adjusted returns as defined by the World Economic Forum (2011) are compared to conventional benchmarks and investment approaches for the same asset class.

[267] See Kreander et al. (2005), p. 1466.

[268] See Sparkes (2001), p. 195. A good representative example is the Triodos Bank in the UK, which pays below-market rates on deposits in return for committing financial resources to sustainable projects in the area of microfinance, energy and climate, arts and culture as well as organic food and agriculture. See Triodos Bank (2012).

[269] SRIs in the early days were predominantly equity investments. Their scope is expanding rapidly into other asset classes, like corporate bonds, government bonds, private equity or commodities. See also section 3.2.4.

B.4 Impact Investing

Impact investing has emerged more recently as a proper alternative asset class. Impact investments are investments that aim at creating a positive impact beyond pure financial returns by improving the "lives of poor and vulnerable people or to provide environmental benefits at large. ... Impact investments can deliver positive social outcomes by expanding access to basic services for people in need or through production processes that benefit society".[270]

B.5 Shareholder Activism

Shareholder activism includes a range of different alternatives available to dissatisfied shareholders to respond to disappointing corporate actions and pressure company management to improve performance, which could eventually lead to an enhanced shareholder value.[271] Active shareholders seek corporate changes primarily by entering into negotiations with management behind the scenes (informal activism), or though a formal process by submitting proxy proposals for shareholder vote at AGMs.[272]

While many research studies conclude that the primary motivation for institutional investors, in particular pension funds, to pursue activism activity is to impact or improve the financial performance of a corporation as well as address corporate governance issues,[273] in the last 10 years there has been a noticeable change in shareholder engagement as more attention is being paid to the social performance of the firm as well. Recent research suggests that both financial and 'moral legitimacy' of corporations are now being challenged by shareholder activism.[274] Activism targeting social and environmental objectives is increasingly becoming an integral part of SRI, as institutional investors are legally bound by their fiduciary duty to obtain the best results on their investments and activism is perceived as a method to increase financial performance. [275] This form of socially motivated activism has to be distinguished from advocacy campaigning, which is not focused on financial returns but rather seeks

[270] JP Morgan Global Research (2010), p. 8.
[271] See Gillan, Starks (2000), p. 276.
[272] See Renneboog, Szilagyi (2009) p. 4.
[273] See Del Guercio, Hawkins (1999), p. 298 et seq.
[274] See Judge et al. (2010), p. 259, quoted after Sullivan, R. and Mackenzie, C. (2008).
[275] Based on estimates by Judge el al. (2010), p. 269 et seq., approximately 40% of shareholder activism via shareholder resolutions is sociallly-motivated, in particular in the US.

public attention to complain about a certain activity of a company that is allegedly non-social.[276]

C. SRI Definition by Leading Social Investment Forums

Leading social investment forums have worded their own respective definitions for social responsible investments or strategies.

C.1 US Social Investment Forum (USSIF)

The USSIF defines SRIs as an investment process that considers "both the investor's financial needs and an investment's impact on society". SRI investing assumes that "corporate responsibility and societal concerns are valid parts of investment decisions. SRI investors encourage corporations to improve their practices on environmental, social and governance issues".[277]

C.2 UK Social Investment Forum (UKSIF)

The UK counterpart, UKSIF, sees social responsible investments as "motivated by both a social or environmental purpose and a financial objective, i.e. a mixed motive rather than purely a philanthropic one. Social investment includes but extends wider than investment in social businesses. In addition, demand for investment in social businesses includes but goes beyond equity or equity-like investment".[278]

C.3 European Sustainable Investment Forum (Eurosif)

Eurosif states that "sustainable and responsible investing (SRI) is a generic term covering any type of investment process that combines investors' financial objectives with their concerns about Environmental, Social and Governance (ESG) issues."[279] The forum identifies two common factors that are involved in all the different forms of SRI investing: (1) investors have a long-term investing horizon and (2) ESG issues have a meaningful impact on long-term investment performance.[280]

---

[276] See Sparkes (2001), p. 202 et seq.
[277] USSIF (2011).
[278] UKSIF (2011).
[279] Eurosif (2010), p. 8.
[280] See Eurosif (2010), p. 8.

C.4 Forum Nachhaltige Geldanlagen (FNG)

The German sustainable investment forum, FNG, declares: "Sustainable investments supplement the traditional criteria of profitability, liquidity and security with environmental, social and ethical evaluation criteria. Sustainable investment is the umbrella term for sustainable, responsible, ethical, social and environmental investment and all other investment processes that take the influence of ESG (environmental, social and governance) criteria into account in their financial analyses."[281]

3.2.2 SRI Investors Types and Investment Motivations

A. Differentiation between SRI Investors and the Neoclassical Understanding of Rational Investors

Neoclassical finance is based on the fundamental concept of 'rational investors' who, as described by Merton, Modigliani (1961), "always prefer more wealth to less and are indifferent as to whether a given increment to their wealth takes the form of cash payments or an increase in the market value of their holdings in shares".[282] A rational investor therefore only considers risk and expected return to evaluate the performance of his investment portfolios.[283] Traditional finance theory does not allow for any influencing factor on the investment process other than maximizing portfolio return given the investor's individual risk aversion. Additional considerations, such as ESG criteria, cannot be included in this theoretical framework unless they provide an equivalent return at lower volatility or yield higher returns for the same risk as classical assets do.[284]

The gap between the 'rational investor' and a SRI-minded investor could be bridged by the notion of 'normal investor', who based on Statman (2005) is influenced in his investment decision process by cognitive biases and emotions.[285] This investor type could therefore include in addition to risk-reward aspects, ESG considerations into his investment process. As Etzioni (1991) clarifies in this context, economics has also a moral dimension that diverges from

---

[281] FNG (2012).
[282] Merton, Modigliani (1961), p. 412.
[283] See Statman (2005), p. 32.
[284] See Beal et al. (2005), p. 66 et seq.
[285] See Statman (2005), p. 36.

the neoclassical understanding.[286] This would imply that investors consider in their decision-making process rational factors as well as "what is right".[287] Bollen (2007) concludes that some investors may derive utility from owning shares in their investment portfolio that comply with certain individual values or societal concerns, thereby deriving a multi-attribute utility function that incorporates an additional aspect to the investing process of the neoclassical optimization framework. An investment into SRI assets would thereby fulfil or consume the SRI attribute of that particular investor.[288]

In conclusion, a new component might be added to the neoclassical utility function, which will lead to an indifference-space rather than the utility curves commonly used in traditional finance. While in the conventional model indifference is provided for any point on the respective utility curve, in the multi-attribute utility framework an investor is indifferent between any points on the indifference plane.[289] In this context, Beal et al. (2005) use the categorizations of 'consumption-investors' and 'investment-investors' defined by Cullis et al. (1992) earlier. A 'consumption-investor' would thereby obtain direct utility from investing in an ethical manner, whereas 'investment-investors' would receive their utility in an indirect way through the social outcome of the underlying investments.[290]

B. Categorization of Institutional SRI Investors

While the previous subsection A provided the definition of the 'typical' SRI investor from a theoretical standpoint, we will focus in this part on a categorization of different types of institutional SRI investors. Given the wide range of financial intermediaries involved in the SRI market as well as the product innovation existing in this area, there are various angles for categorizing SRI investors. Due to the focus of our research study on institutional Pension Insurance Funds, a thorough analysis of retail investors is not envisaged.

---

286 See Etzioni (1991), p. 355.
287 Webley et al. (2001), p. 28.
288 See Bollen (2007), p. 685.
289 See Beal et al. (2005), p. 73.
290 See Cullis et al. (1992), p. 9.

B.1 Institutional Investors and per se SRI Investors

Based on Schoenheit (2005), investors can be subdivided into *per se* SRI investors and institutional investors that invest in SRI. The first group is usually associated with clerical institutions or the church, political parties, foundations, trade unions or NGOs.[291] For these investor types, SRI principles can be statutory and therefore reflection of the norms and principles that define the respective institution or organization.[292] Institutional investors that may also invest into SRI but that do not have statutory obligations are primarily banks, insurance companies, pension funds or corporations.[293] There are mainly three alternative paths how institutional and per-se SRI investors can get exposure to SRI: allocating funds into existing SRI mutual funds, invest into SRI special funds (with a tailor-made SRI mandate) or have either an in-house SRI research team or hire external asset managers responsible for the entire investment process.[294]

B.2 SRI Investors, Rators and Connectors

Louche (2009) differentiates amongst three different actors involved in SRI: investors, rators and connectors. Within SRI investors, the author distinguishes between retail and institutional investors, with institutions ranging from investment companies, mutual funds, brokerage firms, insurers, foundations and investment banks. Rators, on the other hand, can be subdivided into rating organisations and SRI index providers. While rating agencies screen companies or governments using ESG criteria and publish recommendations and rating valuations to investors, index providers offer index calculations and pricings based on a predefined SRI methodology. The third group established by the author are so-called connectors, which encompass venues offering networking, exchange and meeting. More precisely, this group comprehends membership associations and academic SRI initiatives focused on advancing public knowledge of SRIs in general.[295]

B.3 Universal Owners

Universal owners are defined as large, long-term focused institutional investors, (primarily insurance companies, pension funds or large foundations) that

[291] See Schoenheit (2005), p. 121.
[292] See Gascoigne (1999), p. 5.
[293] See imug (2002), p. 7.
[294] See Schoenheit (2005), p. 122.
[295] See Louche (2009), p. 217 et seq.

have become so large and broadly invested across asset classes and regions that they are understood to own a share of the global economy. Both on an individual basis and as a group, they share a common interest in improving economic, social and environmental conditions that will impact their investment universe.[296] Their long-term financial success will be linked to the ability of the global economy to generate economic growth on a sustainable basis.[297]

As these investors own a portfolio that reflects fundamentally the structure of the global economy, their portfolios will internalise both positive and negative external factors. As Hawley, Williams (2007) conclude, universal owners should therefore have a strong economic interest in any reform that might lead to an improvement of the functioning of the global economic system.[298] To avoid therefore negative externalities impacting the long-term financial performance of the funds, their investment decisions should involve an adequate risk management through asset allocations and active ownership that are perceptive to ESG factors.[299]

B.4 Sustainability Index Investors

Many large investment funds belonging to pension funds or insurers belong to the universal owner investor categorisation. The size of their asset base, their investment focus across regions, sectors and asset classes expose them to the overall macroeconomic environment. As we stated earlier, this investor type "owns the market". As a consequence, their portfolios follow broad market indices, a fact that turns them therefore to index or quasi-index trackers. This is also the underlying assumption we will use for our empirical analysis.

For SRI index investors, an investor type relevant for the purposes of our research study, a further differentiation can be identified that includes four main investor types: (1) SRI investors, (2) ESG tilt investors, (3) sustainability premium investors and (4) environmental opportunity investors. These investors will differentiate primarily in terms of the emphasis they put on sustainability aspects versus financial performance considerations. Table 5 outlines these index

[296] See Kiernan (2007), p. 478.
[297] See Briand et al. (2011), p. 3.
[298] See Hawley, Williams (2007), p. 415 et seq.
[299] See Briand et al. (2011), p. 3.

investors by types of investment sought, performance expectations as well as the respective ESG factors they focus on.

Table 5: Types of Sustainability Index Investors

	Ethical Considerations Dominant			Financial Considerations Dominant
	SRI Investors	**ESG Tilt Investors**	**Sustainability Premium Investors**	**Environmental Opportunity Investors**
Description Investment Objectives:	• Index is selected primarily based on social performance aspects rather than financial aspects	• Benchmarking the market, but sustainability tilt is included in investment strategy	• Investment in companies with strong ESG performance that are expected to generate financial outperformance	• Investment focus on particular environmental sectors supposed to outperform
Investment Strategies Targeted:	• Underlying ESG screening approach aligned with ESG understanding of the investor • Negative screening techniques very common selection criteria	• Index should follow the market closely in terms of sector and country allocation weights • Underlying securities are selected based on ESG factors	• Indices with alpha-return potential • Outperformance achieved by investing in assets with a strong ESG performance	• Indices with a clear investment focus on emerging technologies or leading companies
Performance Expectation:	• Willingness to forgo performance for achieving social objectives	• Market performance with sustainability emphasis	• Outperformance versus benchmark ('alpha-focus') via investments in strong ESG-performers	• Predominantly outperformance-focused
ESG Factors Emphasized:	• Primarily negative screening investment approach, focusing on social and governance factors	• ESG factors are all emphasized in the investment process	• Environmental factors will outweigh, whereas social or governance elements might play a subordinated role	• Environmental upside opportunities predominate

Source: Own representation, based on ECPI (2011, a), p. 7.

C. Interaction Amongst Parties in the SRI Market

Figure 27 summarises graphically the interconnection and relationships amongst the various players in the SRI market. This overview includes investors (institutional and retail), rating agencies, corporations as well as the connectors previously discussed. Following the theory of financial intermediation, intermediaries create specialised financial commodities that are demanded by individuals. These individuals derive their utility from consuming these financial commodities. In this theoretical framework, the existence of financial intermediaries, and consequently the whole financial industry, is based exclusively on the presence of market imperfections that will lead to transaction and information costs for the individual.[300] In the context of figure 27 for the SRI market, financial commodities are represented by SRI funds or indices, whereas rators reduce information costs by providing research services. Investors that demand SRI product knowledge define the individuals within the transaction cost approach.

Figure 27: Interconnected Parties in the SRI Market

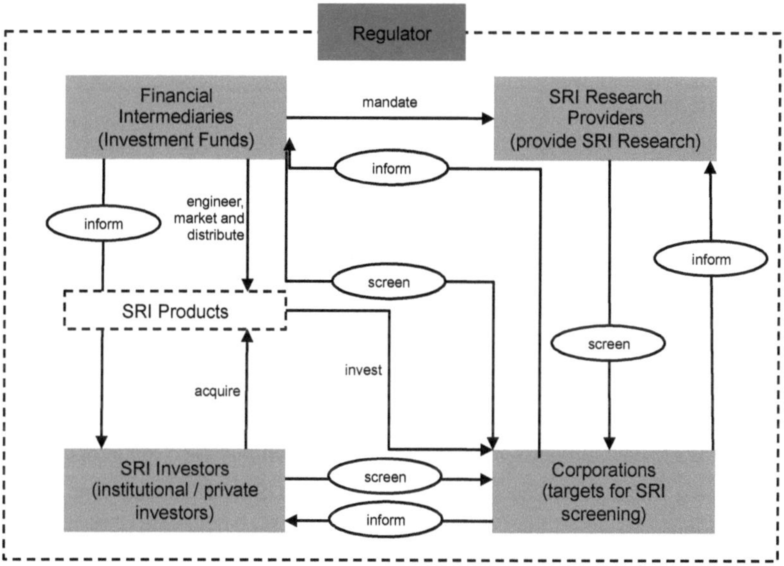

Source: Own representation, based on Schoenheit (2005), p. 112.

D. Investor Motivation

As we have seen in section B, there exist a range of different SRI intermediaries with their individual investment preferences and motivations. Consequently, it is not possible to determine a unique set of motivations to invest in SRI assets for a single investor, but rather a combination of different factors. The most common ones are summarised below. While this section focuses on institutional investors in general, we will discuss in 3.2.8 investment motivations to invest in SRI for Pension Insurance Funds in particular.

300 See Benston, Smith (1976), pp. 215-217.

D.1 Institutional Investors

Reputational Risk

Financial institutions are under increasing scrutiny by external stakeholders, e.g. NGOs or the media, in terms of the impact their investments might have. Such attention can pose a reputational risk for the respective investor.[301] To avoid exposure to public criticism and minimise the potential costs associated to it, investors may be incentivised to include social, ethical or environmental considerations into their investment or business activities.[302] On the opposite side, an intact reputation may offer institutions advantages with respect to attracting new funds or employees.[303]

Ethical Reasons

For certain institutional investors, adopting SRI techniques or applying responsible financing policies has become part of their business strategy, as management feels responsible to contribute to sustainable development. Ethical values become hereby paramount to the individual investor and are reflected in business principles.[304] For this investor type, it is almost irrelevant whether the inclusion of SRI considerations has any impact (positive or negative) on fund performance or not. Large government funds, for example the Norwegian Government Pension Fund or the French Fonds de Reserve pour les Retraites, adhere to ethical values as reflected in their own charta. Also insurance companies, e.g. Storebrand Life Insurance, and many US or UK ethical funds subscribe to this vision.[305]

For investors with a well-defined ethical mission, for example foundations, endowments or financial institutions belonging to churches, a so-called 'mission-driven' investment approach attempts to avoid any conflict with the in-house objectives or principles as well as to use the investments to support the work of the organization.[306]

---

301 See Eurosif (2011), p. 9.
302 See Scholtens (2006), p. 26.
303 See Allianz Global Investors (2010), p. 9.
304 See Eurosif (2011), p. 9.
305 See UNEP (2006), p. 4.
306 See inrate (2010), p. 6.

Corporate Governance Aspects

Good corporate governance can be a competitive advantage for a financial institution or an investor. Implementing CSR competences at the fund itself or shifting the underlying investment funds into SRI assets can be perceived as good governance by external stakeholders, as such policies might potentially mitigate systematic and mega-risks that could negatively impact long-term performance. An open and critical dialogue with the stakeholders of the institutions, for example, could be an efficient and promising method of weak-point analysis.[307]

Engagement-driven Investing

For those investors seeking changes in a company via shareholder engagement activities, SRI strategies offer a wide range of potential activism instruments. By engaging in a direct dialogue with company management, investors seek a change in behaviour and corporate policies in sustainable matters. While in the past avoidance strategies were used predominantly as engagement methodology (negative screening), nowadays a mix of approaches is usually followed, with shareholder activism gaining more relevance. Although social issues do not tend to obtain majority votes at AGMs, shareholder engagement often leads to a dialogue with management that ultimately may trigger a change in policies.[308]

Fiduciary Duty

An important topic we will discuss in more detail in subsequent section 3.2.8, D relates to fiduciary duty of an asset manager to include SRI considerations into his investment process. This duty is deducted from the 'Freshfields Report'[309] published in 2005 and the follow-up study by UNEP[310] in 2009 that concluded that asset holders are obliged under certain circumstances to include ESG factors in their investment management business.

Financial Performance and Risk Management

Section 3.2.5 focuses entirely on the performance comparison of SRI investments versus conventional asset classes. Anticipating at this stage our

[307] See Schaefer (2009), p. 75 et seq.
[308] See Louche (2009), p. 224 et seq.
[309] See Freshfields (2005).
[310] See UNEP (2009).

conclusions, research studies on this topic do not provide statistical evidence that investing in SRI assets leads to any risk-adjusted return disadvantage versus conventional investments. More recent academic studies based on more sophisticated econometric models even provide empirical evidence that SRI investments may outperform equivalent conventional assets.[311]

As a recent research study by Weber et al. (2008) concluded, credit risk analysis could be considerably improved by the inclusion of sustainability criteria into the conventional assessment process, therefore mitigating the default risk and potential performance impact for the investor. Considering SRI factors might lead to an overall improved risk prediction as well as better risk management. For those investors that have a large exposure to credit risk either via corporate bonds or swap instruments, considering sustainability aspects would therefore be appropriate.[312]

D.2 Retail Investors

While retail investors are not the main focus of our research study, it is nonetheless relevant to understand motivations to pursue SRI as an investment strategy by individual investors. Ultimately, for both SRI investment houses as well as pension funds, retail investors represent a client group that decides how to allocate excess funds for investing purposes or retirement planning. Consequently, at least some considerations with regards to the investment behaviour of retail clients seem justified.

Overall, research findings with respect to investor behaviour and motivations to pursue SRIs remain in general mixed. In one of the latest research studies on this topic, Nilsson (2009) analyses the behaviour of private retail investors when investing in SRI mutual funds. The main conclusion of the survey is that private retail investors can be categorised into two groups, with the first group regarding financial returns more relevant than the social responsibility aspect of the fund, whereas the second retail group does not perceive financial returns as the first objective when making SRIs decisions. These findings suggest that (1) SRI

---

[311] See Weber et al. (2011), p. 84 for recent comparison analyses.
[312] See Weber et al. (2008), p. 47.

investors cannot be a priori assumed to be socially concerned and (2) some SRI investors put social responsibility before any financial return achievable.[313]

These results are in-line with conclusions drawn in a study on UK retail investors conducted by Lewis, Mackenzie (2000). The key takeaway of this research paper is that retail investors investing into SRI are willed to forego financial returns.[314] In another study by the same authors, the results suggest institutional fund managers already invested in SRI commonly have a certain, fixed proportion of their funds in SRIs, but at the same time maintain large holdings in 'unethical' funds. On their SRI funds, the managers are more tolerant to generate lower returns than on their conventional assets, which are regarded as the core segment of the fund.[315]

Early studies in the UK, on the other hand, indicate that institutional investors are very price-elastic with respect to ethical investments, i.e. they will add ethical funds into their portfolios only as long as the expected returns can match returns on conventional funds.[316] The acclaimed research study by Anand, Cowton (1993) infers complex non-financial dimensions of utility functions for ethical investors that are difficult to predict, reason why it remains a challenging task to find a common denominator to the behaviour of ethical investors.[317]

For our empirical analysis, we will assume that SRI assets target competitive returns similar to those expected to be achieved by traditional asset classes both in the short and long term. Simultaneously, corporate social responsibility as well as ESG concerns will play a valid part in the investment decision process.[318] In terms of fiduciary duty the asset manager is committed to in his role as trustee of a Pension Insurance Fund, only SRI assets that achieve comparable risk-adjusted returns to conventional asset allocations can be justified.

---

313 See Nilsson (2009), p. 25 et seq.
314 See Lewis, Mackenzie (2000), p. 187.
315 See Webley et al. (2001), p. 28, quoted after Mackenzie, Lewis (1999).
316 See Webley et al. (2001), p. 28, quoted after Lewis, Cullis (1990), Cullis et al. (1992) and Lewis, Webley (1994).
317 See Anand, Cowton (1993), p. 377 and p. 382 et seq.
318 See Fung et al. (2010), p. 6.

3.2.3 Investment Strategies

A. Overview

SRI objectives can be divided into two excluding categories. The investor can either be (1) predominantly orientated towards generating the highest return for his portfolio while obtaining additional benefits from investing into ESG-compliant assets or (2) his prime investment objectives are to acquire assets with the aim of influencing the underlying business operations of the company with respect to its ESG policy.[319]

Engineering SRI-accordant portfolios requires the same standards of practise than the construction of conventional asset portfolios, namely defining an investment policy, fixing short-term and long-term goals and estimating adequate and observable risk parameters. In the classical process of asset selection, the investors' investment objectives can be thought of as a well-balanced system of risk, return and investment horizon. For SRI-investments, however, a fourth element, sustainability, is included.[320] Schaefer, Lindenmayer (2007, b) describe hereby the SRI process as a 'magic rectangle' that includes risk, return, liquidity as well as sustainability.[321]

In academic research, there are primarily two opposing philosophies of SRI methods: active and passive SRI strategies. Within the active methodologies, investors use their voting rights (also called 'voice-option') to achieve social, ecological or economic impact at the company level, whereas passive SRI strategies are characterised by the absence of any such active involvement. A further distinction can be drawn between pre- and post-phase SRI strategies. In the pre-phase, investors decide on certain screening or filter criteria (positive and/or negative screening) or the inclusion of ESG methods as part of the investment process (integration), which are then applied to select a target pool of assets out of the total universe of available investments. In the post-investment period, once the target portfolio has been allocated, investors have the option to

[319] See Schaefer (2001), p. 28, quoted after Schaefer, Guelle (2000).
[320] See Fung et al. (2010), p. 27.
[321] See Schaefer, Lindenmayer (2007, b), p. 8.

pursue shareholder activism strategies.[322] For passive investment strategies, should the target company not comply with the ESG objectives of the investor, he will simply exit his position and sell the stake in the market (exit option).[323] Investor strategies employed in the pre-investment period can be classified as either exclusionary (negative screening) or inclusionary (positive screening, best-in-class).[324] It is common that investors combine several strategies in their investment management process. An important aspect to consider is that funds that follow negative/positive screening or shareholder activism strategies reduce their investment universe, as their selection process assumes that certain single assets or entire industry sectors are entirely excluded. For best-in-class or integration investment policies, on the other hand, such a reduction in the investable space does not occur.[325] Figure 28 illustrates the different SRI possibilities over the time horizon of an investment process.

Figure 28: SRI Management over the Lifetime of an Investment Process

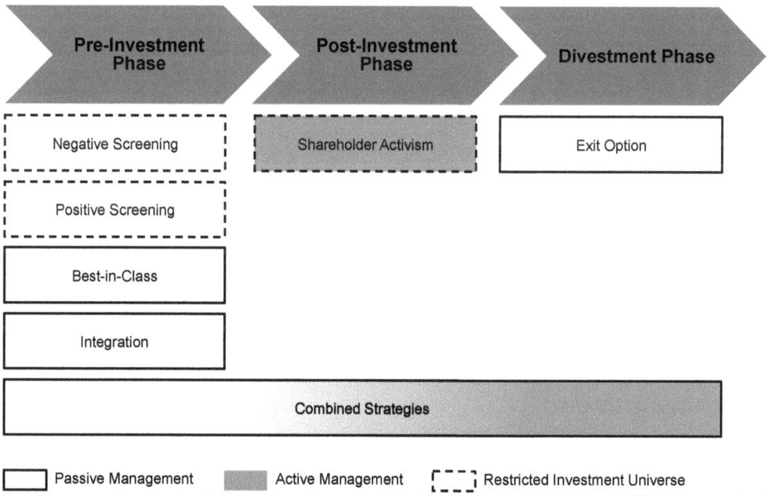

Own figure, on the basis of Schaefer, Lindenmayer (2007, a) p. 1083, Eurosif (2010), pp. 13-15 and Eurosif (2005), p. 18.

---

[322] Academic research on this topic is predominantly equities focused, as the first asset class considered for SRIs has been historically shares. Moreover, only equity capital enables investors to actively participate in AGMs and vote.

[323] See Schaefer, Lindenmayer (2007, a), p. 1083.

[324] See McLachlan, Gardner (2004), p. 13.

[325] See Schaefer, Lindenmayer (2007, a), p. 1083 et seq.

For the purpose of our research project, we will focus primarily on combined strategies in the pre-investment period (BiC combined with negative screening) as they are the most frequently used by both practitioners and academics. Also, best-in-class, in particular, leads to no reduction of the investing universe and a subsequent negative screening overlay ensures that undesired sectors do not enter the target portfolio. For government bonds, however, we will pursue a positive screening method as for European governments, in particular, a BiC plus negative screening approach does not appear appropriate.

Figure 29 summarises the market share of different screening strategies employed in Europe by institutional investors.[326]

Figure 29: Core (LHS) and Broad (RHS) SRI Strategies in Europe (2010, in €bln)

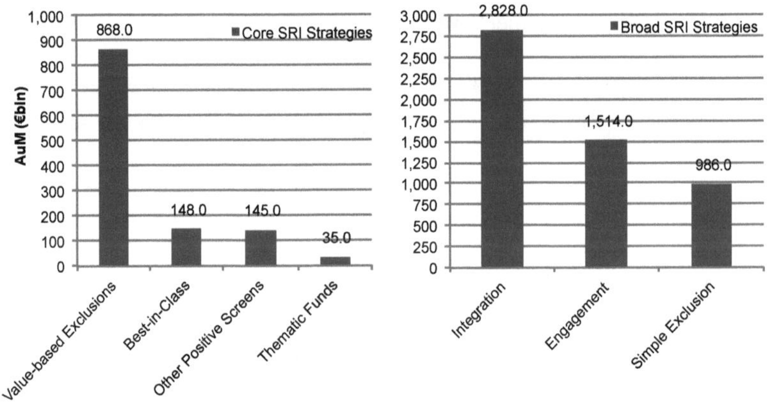

Own figure, on the basis of Eurosif (2010), p. 13.

B. Negative Screening

Negative screening is one of the most frequently used screening methodologies by institutional investors.[327] Based on research estimates by Eurosif, approximately 72.6% (or €868bln AuM) of Core SRI strategies in Europe are managed via negative screening selection mechanisms.[328] Within this ap-

326 Eurosif defines Core SRI as strategies that include value-based exclusions (with more than two negative criteria for exclusion) and different forms of positive screening. Broad SRI, on the other side, encompasses simple explusion methods, engagement (shareholder activism) and integration strategies. See Eurosif (2010), pp. 13-15.

327 See Renneboog et al. (2008), p. 1728.

328 See Eurosif (2010), p. 13.

proach, companies, industry sectors or sovereign issuers (governments) are analysed to determine whether they fulfil certain criteria for social responsibility as defined by the investor. Usual exclusion criteria include, *inter alia,* companies involved in business activities such as alcohol production, tobacco, gambling, defence industries, pornography, abortion, poor workplace conditions or violation of human rights. Common practise amongst fund investors is to perform first a screening from a broad pool of securities[329] and then create the investment portfolio based on financial and quantitative metrics.[330] The respective screening processes are in practise usually conducted by specialised rating agencies. Based on Schaefer et al. (2006), there are globally more than 70 rating agencies focused on this type of rating service.[331]

Negative screening is considered the most basic form of SRI screening, as investors often simply exclude entire industry sectors from the portfolio selection process. Issues arise hereby for larger conglomerates that operate in different business areas and can therefore not be screened by the simple form of negative screening. In such instances, a precise allocation mechanism needs to be established and thresholds defined, so that an objective assignment is possible.[332] Historically, negative screening methods have been popular investment strategies, in particular amongst pension funds as well as charities and churches. As a reference point, in the Netherlands, one of the largest European pension fund systems in terms of size and scale, around 42% of all pension fund assets are managed by some form of negative screening methodologies.[333] A widely used alternative refers to norms-based screening approaches that can be part of negative screening techniques. The norms-based philosophy is to exclude companies that do not comply with internationally accepted norms like the UN Global Compact measures,[334] the OECD Guidelines for Multinational Enterprises[335] or the Millennium Development Goals[336].[337]

---

329 For a European based pension fund with a high allocation into European equities, an adequate pool could be a broad equity benchmark index, for example the Stoxx 600 index.
330 See Renneboog et al. (2008), p. 1728.
331 See Schaefer et al. (2006), appendix, table 2.
332 See Fung et al. (2010), p. 28.
333 See Eurosif (2005), p. 19.
334 See United Nations (2012, a) on The Ten Principles in the areas of human rights, labour, environment and anti-corruption.
335 See OECD (2012).
336 See United Nations (2012, b).

C. Positive Screening

Positive screening is an inclusionary strategy, as investors select actively assets that meet certain SRI-accordant investment criteria. These criteria ensure that a company is managed and acts in a social-responsible or sustainable way.[338] The investment assets chosen tend to be from companies that are regarded as innovators in their respective sector for social and/or ecological achievements.[339] The most popular screening categories or topics applied by investors in their selection processes are usually related to corporate governance topics, labour relations, environmental factors, sustainability, certain community involvements by the company or exemplary renewable energy usage.[340] Due to the particular profile of European government bonds (EMU only), a positive screening method for these securities in our study seems the most suitable approach.

Moreover, positive screening is considered a more difficult exercise than negative screening, as some social or ecological criteria are difficult to quantify in a financial model. As a consequence, positive screening has a certain degree of subjectivity by the rating agency or the respective investors that define the criteria for asset selection.[341] Nonetheless, due to its systematic approach, institutional investors consider positive screening a more explainable and defendable methodology than for example shareholder activism practises.[342]

D. Best-in-Class (BiC)

Best-in-class (BiC) represents a special form of positive screening, in which a company's environmental and ecological performance is rated and measured against an industry standard. Only the best companies in their respective industry qualify for the target portfolio.[343] This concept differs therefore from the negative as well as positive screening methodology, as no security or sector is excluded/included *a priori* from the investment process. Using a set of predefined key financial indicators (KPIs), which attempt to quantify the degree of sustain-

---

337 See Eurosif (2005), p. 18.
338 See Fung et al. (2010), p. 28.
339 Also denominated 'pioneers' or 'innovators', while the activity itself can be called 'pioneer-screening'. See Schaefer, Lindenmayer (2007, a), p. 1083.
340 See Renneboog et al. (2010), p. 402.
341 See Fung et al. (2010), p. 28.
342 See Eurosif (2005), p. 19.
343 See Schmidt, Weistroffer (2010, b), p. 10.

ability of an investment asset, companies are rated and ranked relative to their peers within the same industry sector, so that the best-performing corporations can be determined and included in the investment process.[344]

The best-in-class technique is a useful tool for investment targets that cannot be categorised into either positive or negative screening criteria *per se*. It is in particular suitable for investment decisions that entail corporations with multiple business lines corresponding to different industry sectors.[345] With €148bln AuM invested in best-in-class strategies, it is one of the less frequently used methods in Europe (in particular in comparison to negative screening), what is partially explained by the higher research capabilities required to follow BiC methods (see also figure 29).

In practise, BiC strategies are frequently combined with negative screening criteria. As data in figure 29 (Europe) as well as in figure 32 (for Germany) indicate, the BiC and negative screening combination is actually the most popular SRI strategy followed by institutional SRI investors. The rationale hereby is that (1) the BiC investment filter ensures that only best-performing companies or assets are selected based on a predetermined set of KPIs, (2) the negative screening overlay allows the investor to exclude undesired industry sectors or business activities from his investment portfolio and (3) the negative screening method can act as 'risk-shield' against external stakeholder pressure groups, as certain unacceptable or unethical sectors will be immediately excluded from the investment process.

The investment methods underlying our SRI assets for both equities as well as corporate bonds in the empirical simulation study will follow a combined BiC and negative screening approach as it reflects the most popular approach by practitioners as well as enables to consider generally assumed normative perceptions by society in terms of exclusion criteria.

E. Shareholder Activism

The implementation of shareholder activism as an active SRI management strategy can be divided into three phases. Phase one refers to the simple exer-

---

[344] See Schaefer (2009), p. 66.

[345] See Fung et al. (2010), p. 29.

cise of voting rights by an investor at the AGM of a targeted company. In phase two, on the other hand, the investor would seek an active dialogue with management to discuss specific social responsible aspects of the business operations of the company. Finally, phase three is centred on the concept of shareholder advocacy, in which investors remain in constant dialogue with management. Shareholder advocacy is exercised in particular by large pension funds in the US and the UK.[346] In an extensive research study conducted by Judge et al. (2010), the authors suggest socially motivated shareholder activism tend to target large-sized companies with low ownership concentration and that operate in countries of high economic inequality. Moreover, engagement activities tend to be positively related to prior profitability of the target company.[347]

Despite the rather recent history of shareholder activism in Europe (with the exception of the UK market), there are nonetheless currently €1,514bln AuM in Europe following some form of shareholder activism method within broader SRI strategies. (see also figure 29).

F. Integration

Integration is defined as the "explicit inclusion by asset managers of ESG risk factors into the traditional financial analysis".[348] In the guidelines of asset managers or asset owners, integration of ESG factors will thereby become part of the investment process, *pari passu* to traditional financial investing metrics. ESG considerations are considered an inseparable part of the entire investment process.[349] For the integration methodology to be applicable and successful, it is essential to have policies in place that define how the causal link between the consideration on environmental and social aspects and the impact on economic value are interconnected.[350] In practise, the implementation of ESG factors occurs via the key performance indicators (KPIs) mentioned beforehand. [351]

One of the major points of criticism against integration is the fact that despite many asset funds having a formal integration policy document in place, for out-

[346] See Schaefer, Lindenmayer (2007, a), p. 1084.
[347] See Judge et al. (2010), p. 270.
[348] Eurosif (2010), p. 15.
[349] See Schumacher-Hummel (2005), p. 100 et seq.
[350] See Schaltegger, Figge (2008), p. 7.
[351] See Schmidt, Weistroffer (2010), p. 11.

siders it remains unclear how these ESG criteria are integrated in the investment process.[352] Nonetheless, integration strategies have become one of the most popular methods for European fund managers, with more than €2,828bln AuM invested (see figure 29).

3.2.4 Asset Class Considerations

SRI investment strategies discussed in section 3.2.3 have been predominantly equity focused. The reason for this is that equity investments have historically been the first asset class in the SRI space, in particular due to the voting rights associated with share ownership and the possibility to exercise influence on company management. As a consequence, the vast majority of SRI research studies to date have an equity component.

Nonetheless, various combinations of different SRI strategies elaborated in 3.2.3 can also be implemented across other asset classes. Fixed-income securities, in particular corporate debt, are nowadays already a popular SRI asset class for pension funds (see also section 3.2.6, A on the European SRI market size).

In this section we will contemplate other asset types that can be structured to be SRI-compliant and that will be replicated in our empirical study. A recent research paper by PRI (2011) indicates that the degree of implementation of ESG considerations for certain asset classes has already reached significant levels. In particular for conventional asset classes (equities, corporate and government bonds as well as real estate) the depth of sustainable investments by PRI signatories is considerable.

---

352 See Eurosif (2010), p. 15.

Table 6: ESG Integration by PRI Signatories Across Asset Classes (2009 and 2010, Global)

	2010		2009	
	% / $bln with ESG Integration	**% of Total Market Share**	**% / $bln with ESG Integration**	**% of Total Market Share**
Listed Equities (DM)	74% / $3,679bln	9%	69% / $2,525bln	7%
Listed Equities (EM)	75% / $729bln	5%	68% / $478bln	5%
Sovereign Bonds	46% / $2,815bln	8%	30% / $1,579bln	5%
Corporate Bonds	67% / $2,275bln	29%	56% / $1,373bln	19%
Private Equity	69% / $209bln	8%	61% / $122bln	5%
Listed Real Estate	70% / $171bln	21%	58% / $172bln	24%
Non-listed Real Estate	86% / $711bln	7%	84% / $418bln	4%
Hedge Funds	18% / $33bln	2%	19% / $36bln	2%
Infrastructure	87% / $105bln	0%	89% / $63bln	0%
Total	**63% / $10,727bln**	**7%**	**51% / $6,766bln**	**6%**

Source: Own representation, based on PRI (2011), p. 16. Abbreviations used: 'DM'=Developed Markets, 'EM'=Emerging Markets. Note: The second and fourth columns indicate the assets with ESG integration (in % and $bln) that PRI signatories have invested relative to their own total AuM. Column three and five show what percentage these ESG integrated assets represent of the global AuM invested in the respective asset class by institutional investors (i.e. total market size).

A. Cash and Cash Equivalents

Cash and cash equivalents refer primarily to interest-bearing savings accounts or money market investments. Pursuing a SRI-accordant policy with cash investments for a pension fund is feasible via choosing banking societies that advocate corporate social responsibility or have signed international agreements, which promote responsible management for the banking industry.[353] While there are several SRI money market funds operating in Europe with more than €3.3bln of AuM, it is still challenging to practise a structured asset management approach in the money-market segment.[354]

B. Fixed-Income Securities

Fixed-income securities are the most important public asset class in international capital markets in terms of market size and liquidity. Bond securities are

[353] See EIRIS, UKSIF (2006), p. 6 et seq. The authors also refer to the EIRIS Guide to Ethical Banking as a reference policy.

[354] See Garz, Volk (2010), p. 40. As of 2010, there were 15 European listed funds in totat offering SRI money market investments. See p. 76 on the exact names of these funds.

the core holdings for well-diversified investment portfolios, both for institutional investors as well as high net worth individuals. We distinguish between the two main categories, government bond securities and corporate debt.

B.1 Government and Supranational Bonds

Pension fund investors should have a region- or country-wide ESG screening analysis in place to choose securities from governments that comply with international accords, treaties and conventions. Common agreements considered in the screening process might include corporate governance regulatory practises, environmental policies, ratifications of labour rights conventions, human rights as well as treaties on civil liberties and political rights.[355]

Fund managers can also select bond instruments from governments that commit to the creation of public goods, e.g. state schools, the development of alternative energy sources or required infrastructure projects.[356] Moreover, supranational as well as government institutions have issued thematic bonds in the past that offer an interesting investment opportunity for pension fund managers. The World Bank and the European Investment Bank (EIB), for example, have placed so-called 'green bonds' to institutional investors and used the proceeds raised to finance environmental projects in the area of renewable energy, climate change or energy-efficient real estate.[357]

In general, the majority of investors seeking SRI exposure in government bonds have traditionally followed a negative screening approach; nonetheless investors' investment behaviour is gradually changing towards more thematic orientated bond investing strategies.[358] In addition, SRI methods for government bonds tend to be less developed than those for corporate bonds. Many investors also follow an overweight/underweight strategy on certain issuers rather than excluding them all together. Engagement activities still remain rare for this type of investment.[359]

---

355 See ECPI (2010), p. 2.
356 See Wood, Hoff (2007), p. 25.
357 See Garz, Volk (2010), p. 36 for issue details on some of the bonds issued by the World Bank or the EIB.
358 See Eurosif (2011), p. 12.
359 See EIRIS, UKSIF (2006), p. 8 et seq.

B.2 Corporate Bonds

The screening process for corporate bonds is very similar to the methods we have described for public equity investments in section 3.2.3. The main difference lies in the stronger ownership entitlement of equities, as bondholders do not have shareholder-voting rights at AGMs, so that any form of shareholder activism is limited in scope. Some companies, however, may listen to important bondholders, in particular for issuers with no listed equity (see our previous World Bank or EIB example). Best-in-class and negative screening are the most frequently applied screening strategies.[360]

C. Real Estate Investments

As we discussed in section 2.5.2, German Pension Insurance Funds have approximately 5-6% of total AuM allocation in real estate investments.

EIRIS, UKSIF (2006) consider sustainability aspects in relation to real estate objects as primarily associated with energy efficiency and its contribution to climate change: (1) real estate buildings consume around 40% of global energy and up to 70% of all electricity in the US, (2) circa 30% of operating costs of a building are energy-related and (3) 30% of carbon dioxide emissions can be tracked back to real estate objects. The development of sustainable real estate investments seems therefore a logic consequence. Apart from the ecological benefits of environmental-friendly real estate assets, sustainable buildings tend to generate higher rental yields, therefore offering investors also economic incentives to invest.[361]

Wood, Hoff (2007), on the other hand, identify six key factors for sustainable real estate investments that will enable investors to shape the economic, social and environment performance of their assets: (1) invest in housing projects that support low-income homeownership or rental, (2) acquire assets in need for rehabilitation that could create economic development, (3) develop mixed-use communities and/or mixed-income communities that will support tenant satisfaction and subsidise economic activity, (4) built or acquire environmentally efficient buildings ('green buildings'), (5) ensure that sustainable building materials are used for construction projects and (6) guarantee that the workforce em-

[360] See EIRIS, UKSIF (2006), p. 7 et seq.
[361] See Schaefer et al. (2010), p. 35 et seq.

ployed in building and maintenance of real estate assets are treated with fair labour practises.[362]

For pension funds, investing in real estate can occur in many ways. Most property investments involve usually the outright purchase of commercial property and subsequent rental of the asset. The property can be acquired directly or via pooled funds (in case of listed funds, investors commonly buy shares in tax-efficient REIT structures). Also direct (listed) equity investments are a viable alternative.[363] Based on research estimates by PRI (2011), approximately $826bln assets by PRI signatories are invested in non-listed real estate or property globally, out of which $711bln (or 86% equivalent) are subject to ESG integration (see table 6). This figure implies that 7% of the total non-listed real estate market is already subject to ESG integration by PRI signatory investors. For the overall listed real estate assets, the ESG integration is considerably higher: with $171bln of assets with ESG integration, around 21% of the global available investment pool is subject to ESG criteria.[364]

Despite such apparently large investment possibilities in sustainable real estate assets, the supply for German real estate in form of listed REIT vehicles, real estate funds or outright investments remains very low.[365] Furthermore, the market for sustainable real estate property in Germany is not expected to grow more than the overall German real estate market, as a survey by Schaefer et al. (2012) revealed. In addition, pension fund managers have little knowledge about socially responsible property investments in general, so that at current there are no clear indications that their involvement will increase in the future.[366]

3.2.5 Performance vs. Conventional Asset Classes

The inclusion of SRI screening techniques as part of the strategic asset allocation of a pension fund, at the expense of more conventional asset classes, needs to be justified to current contributors as well as beneficiaries. One of the obvious drivers for stakeholders is undoubtedly fund and asset performance. The performance of SRIs in comparison to conventional asset classes or in-

[362] See Wood, Hoff (2007), p. 57 et seq.
[363] See Garz, Volker (2011), p. 71 et seq.
[364] See PRI (2011), p. 16.
[365] See Schaefer et al. (2010), p. 36.
[366] See Schaefer et al. (2012), p. 15 et seq.

vestment strategies is an extensively covered topic in academic literature. In this section, we will summarise the latest research findings relevant for our own research study. The majority of research papers published on this topic is US-market specific, in particular earlier analysis. Due to the focus of our empirical analysis on European financial markets, we will highlight academic studies that analyse European SRI performance only.[367]

A. Equities Performance Studies

A.1 UK-Market Performance Studies

Earlier European studies are predominantly UK-market specific. This dominance is explained by the long history of capital markets and related institutions based in the financial centre of London as well as the considerable size of the local pension fund market and its early involvement in SRI activities. The first relevant research paper published on the UK market is by authors Luther el al. (1992), who analyse the fund performance of 15 ethical funds and come to the conclusion that they show weak evidence of a small outperformance versus the UK (FTSE-all-share index) and global stock markets (MSCI Global index). Nonetheless, the authors admit their target-investing universe is too diverse in comparison to the benchmark indices to allow a representative analysis.[368] In a follow-up study by Luther, Matatko (1994), the small-cap bias is eliminated by simply including a small-cap index and a large benchmark index. The results show SRI funds do not yield any outperformance versus those indices.[369]

The first study that uses fund structures as benchmark reference instead of indices, is the study by Mallin et al. (1995), which compares the returns of 29 SRI funds to the performance of 29 non-ethical funds that share similar portfolio compositions and fund sizes. The authors show weak evidence of an outperformance of SRI funds on a risk-adjusted basis versus non-SRI funds, while the overall UK market underperformed.[370] Gregory et al. (1997) redefine the target

[367] This literature review is not intended to be exhaustive; its main objective is to represent the most relevant research papers for our own research study.
[368] See Luther et al. (1992), p. 64 and p. 68 et seq. The asset allocation into small-cap stocks, in particular, distortions the comparison to both benchmark indices. See p. 65.
[369] See Luther, Matatko (1994), p. 87. The authors apply Jensen's Alpha as a measure of fund outperformance versus the indices.
[370] See Mallin et al. (1995), p. 495. The researchers suggest the outperformance may be a temporary phenomenon caused by the increased interest in ethical investments and investors' awareness of the new asset class.

universe of Mallin et al. (1995) by matching pairs of ethical to non-ethical funds that are similar in fund investment style, regional focus, age of fund and size of the fund at the end of the formation year.[371] The researchers conclude that the performance difference between ethical and non-ethical unit trusts is statistically not different from zero.[372]

A.2 European Market Performance Studies (Non-UK)

One of the first European empirical analyses in the context of SRIs is Schroeder (2004), who analyses 16 German and Swiss funds, 30 US funds as well as 10 SRI indices.[373] The conclusion of the study, which employs a number of different factor-regression analyses to estimate fund performance, is that German, Swiss and US SRI funds do not underperform their respective benchmarks. Most SRI indices, on the other hand, exhibit a positive, yet statistically insignificant Jensen's alpha. In summary, Schroeder provides empirical evidence that SRI assets yield on average similar risk-adjusted returns than conventional assets do.[374] In a study conducted by Bauer et al. (2005), the researchers apply a multi-factor model to overcome the benchmark problem many previous studies suffered from. 103 ethical mutual funds in total from Germany, UK and the US are considered.[375] Their results indicate there is no evidence of significant differences in risk-adjusted returns between ethical and conventional mutual funds after controlling for common factors like size, book-to-market and momentum factors. Moreover, UK and German ethical funds, in particular, appear to be heavily exposed to small cap stocks, whereas US funds invest to a higher degree into large cap companies.[376]

The first purely European-focused empirical study on SRI performance is Kreander et al. (2005), which contemplates the performance of 30 European ethical funds from the UK, the Netherlands, Germany and Sweden. The authors apply a matched pair approach for fund evaluation that includes fund age, size, country and investment universe as factors and use a multi-factor regression

---

371 See Gregory et al. (1997), p. 707.
372 See Gregory et al. (1997), p. 723.
373 See Schroeder (2004), p. 125.
374 See Schroeder (2004), p. 131.
375 See Bauer et al. (2005), p. 1753.
376 See Bauer et al. (2005), p. 1765.

model to estimate fund performance.[377] On a risk-adjusted basis, the analysis shows there is no difference between ethical and non-ethical fund performance.[378] Van de Velde et al. (2005) published a European-focused research study, in which portfolios with different levels of corporate social responsibility scores are created and compared to each other.[379] Their results indicate that high-rated sustainable companies outperform the market (between 0-21bps per month), whereas the funds with the lowest sustainability ratings underperform the benchmark by 19-34bps per month. For all funds, however, the spread to the benchmark return is statistically not significant.[380]

In a research paper published by Schroeder (2007), the author compares SRI indices to conventional benchmark indices using single- and multi-factor models. 29 international SRI equity indices in total, out of which 10 are European and 7 have a global reach, form the database for his study.[381] Schroeder concludes that SRI indices do neither yield an out- nor under-performance compared to their respective equity benchmarks. Another important conclusion from this paper is that the reduced investment universe for SRI indices does not lead to a risk-adjusted yield reduction based on classical portfolio theory.[382] The analysis by Renneboog et al. (2008) concentrates on SRI and conventional funds from 17 countries from Europe, North America and Asia-Pacific. Employing the Carhart four-factor model for performance calculation, the researchers determine that (1) average SRI fund in the US, UK and most part of Continental Europe strongly underperform domestic benchmark indices, implying SRI funds may be overpriced by the market, (2) conventional funds achieve similar returns than SRI funds do and (3) funds having in-house SRI departments generate better returns than funds without their own investment process policies. Furthermore, the results verify there is no size effect for SRI funds, whereas for conventional funds a larger AuM base implies return erosion.[383]

---

[377] See Kreander et al. (2005), pp. 1470-1473.
[378] See Kreander et al. (2005), p. 1481.
[379] See Van de Velde et al. (2005), p. 131. For the sustainability score, the authors used the data provided by Vigeo, an independent corporate social responsibility agency.
[380] See Van de Velde (2005), p. 136 et seq.
[381] See Schroeder (2007), p. 334.
[382] See Schroeder (2007), p. 343.
[383] See Renneboog et al. (2008), p. 304.

The most recent study with a European perspective is by Weber et al. (2011), who uses 151 SRI mutual fund performances for the time period 2001-2009 to consider whether there are performance differences for SRIs in 'bear' or 'bull' market periods. The respective fund performances are compared to the MSCI World index as benchmark reference. The fund sample includes SRI portfolios from Europe, North America, Asia Pacific, South Africa and Latin America.[384] The research study suggests the sample universe of SRI funds outperforms the benchmark during the entire observation period, i.e. including missing stock market environments as well as periods of declining equity prices. [385]

B. Fixed-Income Performance Studies

B.1 Government Bonds

Analysing SRI performance in the context of government bonds is a rather recent research field and therefore covered by few academic studies only. In one of the first analysis for the European government bond markets, Scholtens (2010) develops a methodology to assess the environmental performance of government bond funds using a set of different indicators.[386] The author concludes in his work that sustainability factors can be suitable for fund managers to track their progress towards more sustainable investing. In addition, allocating funds into government bonds with an above-average SRI performance yields slightly superior returns. This outperformance, nonetheless, is not applicable to all screening methodologies considered in this study.[387]

Drut (2010), on the other hand, published the first article that combines different sovereign bond markets in a wider SRI framework. Applying a selected set of criteria based on internationally recognized codes and norms,[388] countries and governments are rated applying a rating system developed by rating agency Vigeo.[389] Drut's results suggest that investment managers can add SRI-

---

384 See Weber et al. (2011), p. 76 et seq.
385 See Weber et al. (2011), p. 84.
386 The World Bank's Adjusted Net Savings (ANS), the Ecological Footprint (ECF) promoted by the World Wildlife Fund, the Environmental Sustainability Index (ESI) and the Environmental Performance Index (EPI) developed by the Yale Centre for Environmental Law and Policy. See Scholtens (2010), p. 119 and p. 128.
387 See Scholtens (2010), p. 128 et seq.
388 Drut uses the millennium Development Goals, Agenda 21, the International Labor Organizations conventions (ILO), the United Nations Charters and Treaties as well as the OECD Guiding Principles. See Drut (2010), p. 132.
389 Vigeo Sustainable Country Rating. See Vigeo (2012).

compliant sovereign bonds to their asset portfolios without significantly losing diversification. The analysis indicates that the overall portfolio ratings of a government bond portfolio can be improved in terms of SRI-considerations without displacing meaningfully the efficient frontier.[390]

Both Scholtens (2010) and Drut (2010) obtain results for SRI government bond investments that will play an essential role in our simulation study, as German Pension Insurance Funds have a significant proportion of their assets invested in government securities.

B.2 Corporate Bonds

The two most relevant research publications in the context for SRI corporate bond performance are the studies by Hutton et al. (1998) and the recent academic paper by Derwall, Koedijk (2009).

Hutton et al.'s (1998) research study compares the performance of the Lehman Corporate Bond index with a tailor-made index of corporate bonds that attempts to replicate the performance of debt issued by companies included in the KLD Domini 400 Social index.[391] The results obtained for the time period 1990-1996 indicate that the SRI index performed better than the conventional bond index by approximately 4bps per month, albeit at the cost of a higher volatility of 14bps on average. Nonetheless, on a risk/return basis, the SRI portfolio performed similarly to the conventional index.[392]

The most recent corporate bond study that includes a benchmarking analysis between SRI and conventional assets is Derwall, Koedijk (2009). The authors' research focuses on evaluating the performance of SRI fixed-income mutual funds in the US relative to similarly structured conventional bond funds. For all funds included in the analysis, the underlying bond instruments are exclusively corporate bonds with a medium- to long-term duration. Applying a multi-factor model to perform the comparison and ensuring similarity amongst the funds benchmarked in terms of fund size, fund management fees, fund age as well as turnover,[393] the results indicate that for the time period 1987-2003 SRI corpo-

[390] See Drut (2010), p. 143.
[391] See Hutton et al. (1998), p. 296 et seq.
[392] See Hutton et al. (1998), p. 300 et seq.
[393] See Derwall, Koedijk (2009), p. 215.

rate bond funds generated total returns similar to those achieved by conventional bond funds. For fund structures that in addition to corporate bonds also allocated a certain proportion of their assets into equities (mixed portfolios), SRI portfolios outperformed conventional funds by 1.3% per year.[394] The researchers conclude that "as (in the original in capital letters; comment by author) we do not find any indication that socially motivated constraints are binding on fund performance, our evidence supports the idea that SRI in the fixed-income industry is a financially viable investment approach."[395]

The conclusions drawn by the authors of both research studies contemplated in this section are essential for our research objectives, as they indicate that SRI corporate bond portfolios perform at least as well as similarly structured conventional portfolios do. Corporate bonds will have a considerable weight in the overall asset allocation of German Pension Insurance Funds, as they represent together with government bonds the largest segment of the average portfolio. Thus research findings support our proposal to replicate conventional bond assets by SRI securities.

C. Concluding Remarks on Empirical SRI Studies

In general, the majority of research studies for equity portfolios present empirical evidence that European SRI equity funds perform in-line with conventional funds. The same conclusion applies to studies focused on SRI indices. When comparing fund performance to the corresponding domestic benchmarks, research studies draw mixed conclusions. Moreover, it appears that many SRI equity funds have a biased towards small-cap stocks, in particular European based portfolios. The literature review also reveals that a large number of studies use either single- or multi-factor regression models as econometrical technique. More recent studies have considerably improved the scope of the analysis, as more matching variables have been applied, so that the comparability to conventional funds or benchmark indices has improved meaningfully. In summary, there is no statistical evidence that investing in SRI equity assets should cause any risk-adjusted return disadvantage versus conventional investment assets.

394 See Derwall, Koedijk (2009), p. 227.
395 Derwall, Koedijk (2009), p. 227.

For research on bond portfolios, the same rationale applies, as for both corporate and government bond assets corresponding SRI portfolios achieve similar total returns than traditional bond funds do. The existence of a very recent study provides certainty that the latest econometric methodology has been used to run the empirical analysis, so that potential biases of earlier studies are avoided.

Overall, equities and fixed-income SRI performance studies available to date support our research proposal of structuring the asset portfolios of German Pension Insurance Funds applying SRI screening approaches.

3.2.6 SRI Market Size

A. European SRI Market

A.1 Overall European SRI Market

The European SRI market continues to grow, despite the adverse economic effects since the start of the credit crisis in 2007/2008 and the subsequent European sovereign debt crisis since 2009. At the end of 2009, assets worth almost €5trn were invested in SRIs, up from €2.7trn in 2007 (including core and broad SRI strategies). Adjusting for the EU expansion to 14 countries during this time period, this represents an 87% growth rate over two years and a CAGR of 37%. Out of these €5trn, €1.2trn (24%) are invested in core SRI and €3.8trn (76%) in broad SRI.[396] Based on estimates by EFAMA, the core SRI segment therefore represents approximately 10% of the total European fund management industry.[397]

[396] See Eurosif (2010), p. 11.

[397] Using as reference €12.4trn of assets under management at the end of 2009, as reported by EFAMA (2010), p. 2.

Figure 30: The European SRI Market in Perspective (AuM in 2010, in €bln)

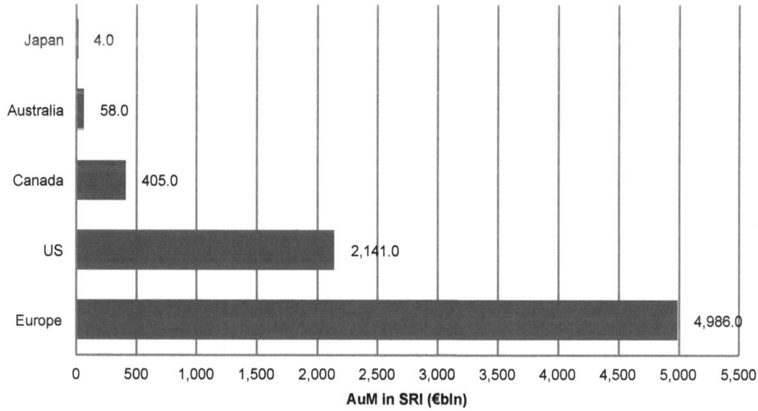

Source: Own figure, on the basis of Eurosif (2010), p. 59.

Comparing the combined European market by AuM to the US market, which is the largest single SRI market in the world to date, it becomes apparent why SRIs play such a relevant role for European investors. European SRI assets are by now 2.3 times the asset base currently invested by US investors (see also figure 30).

The overall European SRI market remains predominantly an institutional market, with 92% of AuM in the hands of professional investors. A split by assets classes shows an overweight allocation into fixed-income instruments (53% of total SRI assets), while equities cover 33% of the asset pool.[398] Recent trends suggest that fixed-income securities as well as monetary funds are becoming more relevant in the SRI space (33% and 114% AuM growth rate respectively between 2007 – 2009), while equities have declined by 7% in the same time period. These numbers compare to lower growth rates for bonds and monetary funds in the traditional asset management space (-5% for fixed-income funds, +4% for monetary funds, -14% for equities).[399] The geographic allocation for European SRI assets is predominantly European (85% of AuM,

[398] See Eurosif (2010) p. 7.
[399] See Eurosif (2010), p. 11.

out of which only 10% in the respective domestic market), 6% North American and 3% Asian (Asia-Pacific and Japan combined).[400]

A.2 European Sustainable Mutual Fund Market

Focusing exclusively on the European sustainable mutual fund market, table 6 depicts the robust growth SRI funds[401] have enjoyed in the last years. With over 897 funds licensed for distribution in Europe at the end of 2010, the investment volume reached €75.3bln, an increase of 41.3% versus the 2009 asset base.

Table 7: Growth of the SRI Mutual Fund Industry in Europe (Since 2006)

Year	Number of Funds	AuM (€mln)	Annual Growth Rate (%)
2010	879	75,265	+41.3%
2009	683	53,276	+9.4%
2008	537	48,720	0.0%
2007	437	48,735	+43.3%
2006	388	34,009	+41.0%

Source: Own representation, based on Vigeo (2010), p. 7 and p. 10.

The regional distribution[402] of the European sustainable mutual fund market is nonetheless highly skewed: the four largest markets, Belgium (227 funds in 2010), France (215), the UK (98) and Switzerland (91) together account already for approximately 72% of the funds included in the study. France confirms its leading position as largest European SRI market for mutual funds. An insightful reference in this context is the corresponding asset class distribution. Based on the data provided by Vigeo (2010), fixed-income funds are increasing their market share in the SRI mutual fund sector. In 2010, approximately 38% of SRI mutual funds had an explicit fixed-income investment strategy, up from 20% five years before. These figures highlight the overall importance of fixed-income securities within the European SRI segment.[403] Figure 31 illustrates the increasing market share of sustainable fixed-income funds.

400 See Eurosif (2010), p. 18.
401 Vigeo (2010) refers hereby to 'green', 'social' and 'ethical' funds without providing a detailed definition what is included in each of these categories.
402 Regional distribution refers to the domicile of the respective fund.
403 See Vigeo (2010).

Figure 31: SRI Fund Type in the European Mutual Fund Market (2006-2010)

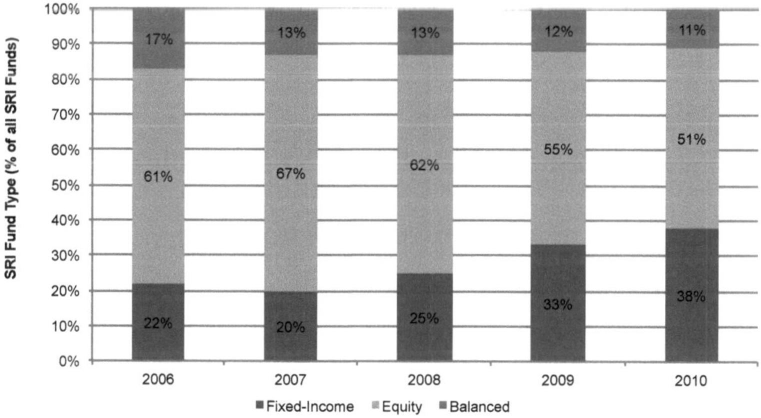

Source: Vigeo (2010), p. 23.

B. German SRI Market

B.1 German Sustainable Mutual Fund Market

The precise size of the German SRI market is difficult to determine, as assets are invested across various asset categories and fund types (in mutual funds, thematic or specialised funds, certificates, account deposits at cooperative banks or social, ecological financial institutions). As a consequence, depending on the source used and the precise definition of SRI market applied, the respective market size may vary considerably.

Based on Eurosif estimates, for example, by the end of 2009, approximately €12.9bln SRI AuM were invested in Germany via mutual funds, out of which 94% were allocated towards core SRI strategies. With €1,706bln total AuM invested in the German asset management industry, SRI assets represent 0.8% of the domestic mutual fund industry, considerably below the European average market share of 10%. Nonetheless, the German SRI fund market has expanded by 16% since the 2007 pre-crisis levels and is expected to grow by 56% between 2010-2013.[404] As figure 32 illustrates, the investment strategies used by investors in the German SRI mutual fund space have been dominated by value-based exclusion strategies (€8.8bln AuM) and best-in-class methods (€7.9bln).

[404] See Eurosif (2010), p. 35 et seq.

Figure 32: Investment Strategies by SRI Mutual Funds in Germany (2009, in €bln)

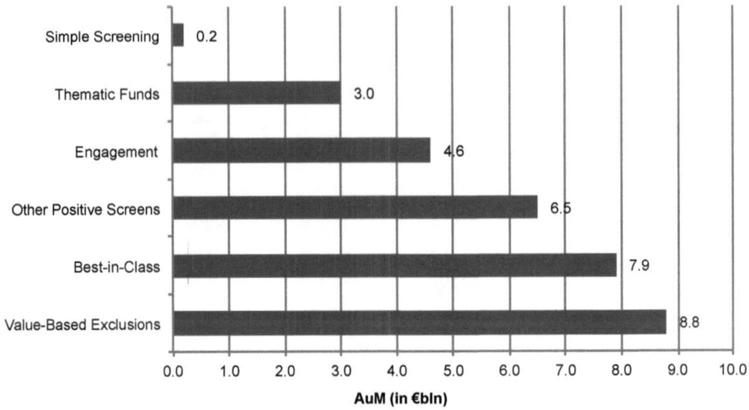

Source: Own figure, on the basis of Eurosif (2010), p. 35. Note: Double-counting possible, therefore the sum of all strategies exceeds €12.9bln of the total German SRI mutual fund industry.

The investor structure of the German SRI market for mutual fund investments also differs from the average European allocation: by the end of 2009, 55% of AuM were in the possession of institutional investors (down from 63% in 2007), with the remaining 45% of assets held by retail investors. Religious institutions as well as charities represent the most important investor groups, followed by NGOs foundations and occupational pension schemes.[405]

The average asset structure allocated into SRI in Germany reflects the European average, as bonds represent more than half of the allocation (52%), with equities 38% of AuM. 66% of all SRI assets are allocated towards SME companies and 34% to large cap targets.[406] Figure 33 summarises German asset allocation by asset classes and regions.

[405] See Eurosif (2010), p. 36.
[406] See FNG (2010), p. 20.

Figure 33: German SRI Asset Allocation by Asset Class and Region (2009, mutual funds only)

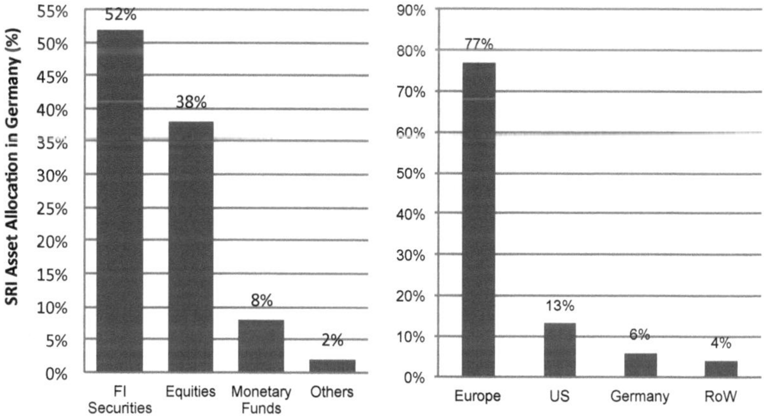

Source: Own figure, on the basis Eurosif (2010), p. 35 and p. 20. Abbreviations used: 'FI'=fixed-income, 'RoW'=rest of world.

The product range for SRI mutual fund investments has expanded considerably in the last few years: at the end of 2009, 313 ethical funds across different asset classes (primarily equities, fixed-income, fund of funds, microfinance funds and ETFs) were approved for distribution in German speaking countries (Germany, Austria, Switzerland), up from 112 funds in 2004 (+180% growth).[407] Based on Oekom (2011), investors could choose amongst 304 licensed funds that pursuit investment strategies related to sustainability, ethics or renewable energies only (+9.0% versus 2009 number of 279 funds).[408]

Taking into consideration sustainable investments owned outside the German mutual fund sector, the actual size of the SRI market is considerably larger. Based on estimates by strategy consulting firm Funds@Work, the total asset base of social responsible investments in Germany could be as large as €250bln, or 19x the size of the current German SRI mutual fund market.[409] While this number is based on a survey of asset managers and does therefore

[407] See Schmidt, Weistroffer (2010), p. 5.
[408] See Oekom (2011), p. 9, quoted after ECOreporter (2011).
[409] See Funds@Work (2010), p. 1. This sum includes fund investments into mutual funds as well as the sum of SRI assets in specialised funds in Germany. The €250bln are calculated as follows: assuming a total asset base of €736bln AuM for all investors that participated in the survey conducted by Funds@Work in 2010, 69% were invested in Germany, 29% in Switzerland and 2% in Austria. The sum of assets reported to be managed using some sustainable criteria was approximately €360bln in total. The €250bln for German SRI assets are calculated as 69% out of €360bln. For the survey, a total of 120 institutional investors in Germany participated, with a total asset under management base of €736bln.

reflect only part of the German investment universe, it indicates that the commonly used market size of €12.9bln is most probably too low.[410] A recent study by Union Investment (2011), for example, suggests the actual SRI market size in Germany reaches a few hundred billion Euros.[411] An important amount of these additional funds is invested in direct investment mandates and special funds and is therefore not publicly accessible to external investors. Apart from mutual and special funds discussed so far, there are additional SRI market segments in Germany that are significant in size and enjoy robust growth rates.

B.2 Certificates

Certificates replicating sustainable investment strategies account for approximately €8.7bln of sustainable investments in Germany. Historically, certificates have been a relatively popular investment class for German retail clients. Investors can to date choose amongst almost 250 different sustainable certificates from 30 issuers, primarily investment banks and investment funds.[412]

B.3 Social and Ecological Banks

Social and ecological banks in Germany have benefited in the last couple of years from solid growth. Their business objectives include, amongst others, the commitment to reinvest clients' deposits to finance exclusively sustainable projects. Approximately €3bln of sustainable financing are currently committed by German social and ecological banks.[413]

B.4 Clerical Banks

Similar to Germany's social and ecological financial institutions, clerical banks have strict ESG policies in place for any loans that are conceded to their clients. By 2010, there were a total of €15.3bln deposits placed at these institutions.[414]

---

[410] Based on the scope of the study conducted by Funds@Work, it can be considered representative for our purposes.

[411] See Union Investment (2011), p. 2. The survey includes investors with a total AUM base of €1,030bln. 64% of these investors indicated they consider some form of sustainable criteria as part of their investment process.

[412] See Deutscher Derivate Verband (2009), pp. 6-8.

[413] See Schneeweiss (2010), p. 13.

[414] See Schneeweiss (2010), p. 14.

B.5 Microfinance Investments

Another pool of SRIs outside the range of traditional mutual fund investments is microfinance. Whilst this asset class is currently still in a developing stage in Germany, up to €300-400m of investments are already committed.[415]

3.2.7 Relevance of SRIs for European Capital-Funded Pension Schemes

A. Overview

65.3% of European SRI assets are in the hands of pension funds, although 98.1% (or €3,161bln equivalent) of these investments are held by public pension funds and only 1.9% (€61bln) by occupational pension schemes. There are, however, clear signs that corporate pension funds are intending to expand their SRI commitment within their investment portfolios.[416] The significance of pension funds in the SRI space also becomes evident when the global composition of the 253 signatories (asset owners only)[417] of the UN Principles for Responsible Investment (PRI) is analysed: approximately 50% are institutional investors categorised as 'non-corporate' pension funds, while 24% of signatories are corporate pension schemes.[418] Using as reference 138 European asset owners that appear as signatories and applying the same percentages, there are to date a total of 102 institutional pension scheme investors in Europe committed to various degrees to SRI, with 33 funds belonging to occupational pension schemes only. The distribution by country of these 138 asset owners is nevertheless skewed towards three countries: in the UK, there are 28 (20.3%) asset owners registered as PRI signatories, 27 (19.6%) in the Netherlands and 17 (12.3%) in Denmark.[419]

---

415 See Schneeweiss (2010), p. 17. These assets under management refer exclusively to the investments made by German investors. To date, there are only two foreign providers of microfinance investments in Germany: Dutch clerical bank Oikocredit and Swiss special bank ResponsAbility.

416 See Eurosif (2010), p. 16.

417 See PRI (2012). Data as of 25-Jun-2012.

418 See PRI (2011), p. 56. Based on a representative survey amongst asset owners that are also PRI signatories.

419 See PRI (2012). Here we have applied the percentages of the PRI (2011) report on the current numbers of PRI signatories, as the 2012 disclosure on the asset split by investor type is not available to date.

Figure 34: Role of Pension Funds in the European SRI Sector

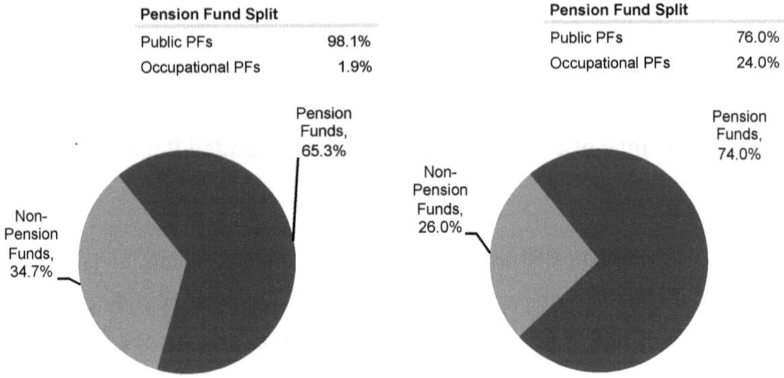

Source: Own figure, on the basis of Eurosif (2010), p. 16, PRI (2011), p. 56 and PRI (2012).
Note: LHS pie chart shows the market share of European pension funds as % of all European SRI assets, whereas the RHS chart represents the share of pension funds as % of all European asset owners that are also PRI signatories.

A more detailed analysis of the two leading countries in terms of SRI involvement by pension funds, the UK and the Netherlands, provides evidence that Germany remains at a relatively early stage of sustainable investing by pension schemes.

B. United Kingdom

The UK is "acknowledged as a global leader in sustainable and responsible finance".[420] With more than £939bln assets invested in SRIs (84x the total size of the German mutual fund SRI market) at the end of 2009, occupational pension schemes are undoubtedly a driving force of sustainable investing. In addition, the UK is the first country in the world to introduce in 2000 disclosure requirements regarding SRI policies for occupational pension schemes.[421] Furthermore, already 20 out of 28 (71%) British signatories of the UN PRI are pension funds.[422]

[420] Eurosif (2010), p. 53.
[421] See Eurosif (2010), p. 53.
[422] See PRI (2012). These numbers refer to asset owners only.

C. Netherlands

The Dutch SRI market has a total SRI asset base of €396bln and more than €743bln of pension assets.[423] The two largest pension funds in the country, APG and PGGM, represent almost 50% of pension fund assets and are regarded as *avant-garde* for SRIs and sustainability initiatives in the country and worldwide.[424] Based on a study by VBDO, 83% of Dutch Pension Funds have already SRI policies in place. Out of these funds, 65% apply exclusion strategies and 33% integrate ESG criteria into their investment process.[425]

D. Germany

Obtaining reliable data on the actual SRI involvement by German pension schemes remains a difficult task. As we have identified so far, pension funds in neighbouring European countries tend to have significant investments in SRI assets and they also represent the largest group of UN PRI signatories. Germany, on the other hand, has only 8 signatories (5.8% of all European signatories, asset owners only) and is therefore considerably underrepresented, particularly taking into account its leading economic position in Europe. Moreover, there is only one public entity that is involved in pension fund management (the 'Bayerische Versorgungskammer'), whereas there is no single private-sector occupational pension scheme represented to date.[426]

In this context, Schaefer (2005) states that although occupational pension schemes are supposed to be the precursors of SRI investing in Germany, they have so far disappointed, primarily due to a limited product range for non-equity products and the restrictive investment rules set by the German regulator.[427] Nevertheless, recent events are indicating that the low involvement of German pension funds in the SRI space is potentially changing. A representative survey-based study by the Bundesministerium fuer Umwelt, Naturschutz und Reaktorsicherheit, Fortis Investment (2008) suggests that in the long-term ESG considerations in the strategic investment management of German occupational

---

[423] Data as of end 2009.
[424] See Eurosif (2010), p. 41 et seq.
[425] See VBDO (2011), p. 7.
[426] See PRI (2012).
[427] See Schaefer (2005), p. 560.

pension schemes will improve the risk-adjusted performance of the funds and promote overall sustainable development.[428]

3.2.8 Motivation for German Pension Insurance Funds

A crucial question in the context of our research study is to understand what the drivers and rationale for pension schemes in general and Pension Insurance Funds in particular could be to consider sustainable investments. In this section we summarise the most important aspects that might lead to a major involvement of German pension funds in the SRI space in the foreseeable future. Some arguments are conclusions from previously discussed aspects, some points however are new perspectives and contributions.

A. Intrinsic Motivation

We discussed in section 3.2.8 that for certain types of institutional investors an intrinsic motivation can lead to an involvement in sustainable investing. Ethical beliefs reflected in the business principles, for example, or mission-related investing activities by some institutions (e.g. churches, foundations or endowments) can lead to a SRI commitment.

The same thought-process can be applied to Pension Insurance Funds. In particular ESG considerations in the business philosophy or strategy of the sponsoring company can be a reason for the pension fund to adhere to sustainable investing activities. In this case, the occupational pension scheme would adopt the ESG principles the company is committed to. The intrinsic motivation for sustainability becomes thereby part of the overall group that includes the company itself and its associated pension fund. In addition, for those pension funds pursuing an impact at the underlying companies invested, some form of shareholder engagement can be part of their SRI investment activity. The activism effort might support the transfer of the funds own internal ESG understanding to the invested company.

---

[428] Bundesministerium fuer Umwelt, Naturschutz und Reaktorsicherheit, Fortis Investment (2008), p. 5.

B. Corporate Governance Aspects

Benefitting from good corporate governance can be a competitive advantage for a Pension Insurance Fund. Apart from shielding the fund from external pressure groups (see also subsequent section), high governance standards can act as a suitable risk management instrument, protecting the institution from systematic and mega-risks that could negatively impact the long-term performance of the fund.

C. Reputational Risk and External Stakeholder Pressure

Based on research findings by Garz, Volk (2010), large listed corporations in Germany are getting under increasing pressure to include sustainability considerations into the investment management process of their respective occupational pension schemes. The authors imply that while sustainability has been often implemented on the operational side of the businesses, pension investing has been neglected so far.[429]

Furthermore, a study commissioned by the German Federal Environmental Ministry and Fortis Investments establishes that "although the Germans are seen internationally to be leaders in the area of environmental protection and 86% of occupational pension clients request that their pension schemes do not invest in companies making environmentally damaging products, German occupational pension schemes are deemed unprogressive when it comes to comprehensive integration of sustainability aspects. The largest barrier cited was the lack of active, sustainability leaders among institutional investors. The fiduciary duties in Germany do not represent a barrier."[430] To avoid therefore any reputational risks related to external stakeholder pressure groups, a Pension Insurance Funds could envisage including sustainable investing principles as part of the strategic investment management.

As previously alluded to in section 3.2.3, negative screening methods are a suitable SRI approach to avoid any form of activism or external criticism by external stakeholders, thereby mitigating reputational risk. As in practise it is not feasible to approach all stakeholders of a Pension Insurance Fund to determine

---

[429] See Garz, Volk (2010), p. 3.

[430] Bundesministerium fuer Umwelt, Naturschutz und Reaktorsicherheit, Fortis Investment (2008), p. 8.

their individual investment preferences, simply implementing negative screening criteria can be a suitable approach. The specific set of exclusion criteria chosen should ideally cover aspects or topics that are commonly perceived by society ('common-sense' approach) as repulsive or unacceptable.

The negative screening criteria underlying the SRI indices used for our empirical analysis attempts to follow this principle, as business practises in the area of alcohol, gambling, tobacco, armaments, firearms and adult entertainment ('ex-AGTAFA') are rejected.

D. Fiduciary Duty [431]

One of the most impactful documents to justify the obligation by institutional investment managers, in particular pension fund managers, to include ESG considerations into their asset allocation process is the 'Freshfields Report' published in 2005. This study, commissioned to the law firm Freshfields Bruckhaus Deringer, analyses whether the integration of ESG factors by asset owners for a total of nine jurisdictions,[432] including Germany, is "voluntary permitted, legally required or hampered by law and regulation; primarily as regards public and private pension funds, secondarily as regards insurance company reserves and mutual funds."[433] The central concept underlying the analysis is to determine for different jurisdictions whether fiduciary duty is solely related to maximizing financial returns for an investment fund or whether the law would require incorporating other investment objectives. Particular emphasis was given to objectives that could create beneficial institutional or societal conditions, which in the long term would lead to benefits for the investor.[434]

The conclusions of the study are unambiguous: "integrating ESG considerations into an investment analysis so as to more reliably predict financial perfor-

---

[431] Fiduciary duties are defined as duties that trustees, for example a pension fund, have towards their beneficiaries. While this term is legally defined only for common law jurisdictions, there is sufficient evidence that civil law jurisdictions require from investors a similar set of core responsibilities. The two core fiduciary duties for the trustee hereby include (1) manage funds in the interest of the ultimate beneficiery and (2) excercise due care and prudence when managing the beneficiery's funds ('prudent man rule'). See Sandberg (2010), p. 145 et seq.

[432] Australia, Canada, France, Germany, Italy, Japan, Spain, UK and US.

[433] Freshfields (2005), p. 6.

[434] See Freshfields (2005), p. 6. The authors use as an example the protection of the environment that for long-term investors, in particular pension funds, would eliminate a potential threat to investment returns.

mance is clearly permissible and is arguably required in all jurisdictions."[435] This deduction, however, is based on a set of assumptions that need to be fulfilled before a fiduciary obligation for the portfolio manager can be concluded. In summary, the authors imply that either (1) the ESG considerations are integrated into the investment decision process of the fund and there is consensus (expressed or in some instances implied) amongst beneficiaries that mandates a particular investment strategy or (2) including ESG considerations into the investing process is expected to have a material impact on returns for the fund. Should neither point (1) nor (2) be sufficiently evidenced, ESG considerations may still be taken into account (but not compulsory) if including them offers a point of differentiation between equally attractive investment opportunities.[436] As stated in a follow-up study by UNEP (2009), the results of the Freshfields study have enabled institutional investors in the respective jurisdictions to "clarify the legality behind the considerations of ESG issues with respect to pension funds, insurance company reserves and mutual funds, as well as foundations".[437]

Nevertheless, the wording and the conclusions drawn from the Freshfields (2005) study have received considerable attention post publication. Thornton (2008), referring to the report, states: "There has been a tendency in recent years for those pushing for greater social responsibility in trustee investment to seek to undermine ... the paramount principle of financial best interests...[.]"[438] Eccles (2011) argues that the two pre-conditions established by Freshfields represent two considerable obstacles to mainstreaming SRI, in particular as aspect (1) will be rarely given and empirical evidence for point (2) on the performance advantage of SRI's over conventional assets yields mixed results.[439] Sandberg (2010) claims legal reform is needed to overcome the contingent support SRIs have received from the Freshfields report. First, the proposal by Freshfields to expressly allow trustees to take ESG considerations into account should be encoded in law to be effective and convince institutional investors to take the suggestion seriously.[440] Moreover, the author proposes institutional investors

---

[435] Freshfields (2005), p. 13.
[436] See Freshfields (2005), p. 14.
[437] UNEP (2009), p. 18.
[438] Thornton (2008), p. 408.
[439] See Eccles (2011), p. 23 et seq.
[440] See Sandberg (2010), p. 156.

should be obliged by law to meet certain sustainability benchmarks or indicators as part of their overall investment management process.[441]

E. Regulatory Requirements

There are currently eight European countries that have specific national SRI regulations in place for their pension systems: UK (implemented in 2000), Germany (2001), Sweden (2001), Belgium (2004), Norway (2004), Austria (2005), Italy (2005) and Spain (in process).[442]

Recent German legislation relating to the disclosure of investment strategies and non-financial information is expected to encourage more SRI engagement by occupational pension schemes in the future.[443] The two most relevant legal acts in this context are the Certification of Retirement Pension Contracts Act (AltZertG) and the VAG. The AltZertG requires from any institution offering pension plan products a mandatory reporting duty to communicate on an annual basis how ESG issues have been considered in the allocation process.[444] The VAG specifies in similar manner that German occupational pension schemes, in particular Pension Insurance Funds, Pension Funds and Direct Insurance Schemes, shall inform their beneficiaries if and to what extend ESG considerations have been incorporated in the investment management process.[445] On this aspect, prevailing German legislation goes beyond the precedent set in the UK, which requires UK pension plans simply to publish if SRI policies are in place, but not to specify to what degree such policy has been implemented.[446]

Moreover, the German legislator also forces large corporations to include non-financial performance indicators (i.e. related to environmental and corporate governance issues) into their regular management reports.[447] Major driver of German legislative implementations has been the EU via Directive 2003/51/EC that for the first time included sustainability considerations in com-

[441] See Sandberg (2010), p. 156, quoted after Richardson (2009).
[442] See Eurosif (2010), p. 19.
[443] See Preu, Richardson (2011), p. 884.
[444] See Sec. 7 Par. 7 AltZertG.
[445] See Sec. 115 Par. 4 VAG.
[446] See Preu, Richardson (2011), p. 882.
[447] See Sec. 289 Par. 3 HGB.

pany reporting.[448] These measures may also encourage more SRI investing in Germany by facilitating pension fund managers an easier evaluation of corporate environmental performance.[449]

F. SRI Performance

Financial performance of SRIs is an essential factor for mainstreaming SRI in general and increasing their relevance for the investment management of Pension Insurance Funds in particular. As discussed in section 3.2.5, most recent empirical results suggest SRI assets generate returns that are as good as those achieved by conventional asset classes. While earlier studies conclude SRI assets underperform traditional assets, better econometrical techniques have enabled academics to improve the comparability of performances across asset types and to obtain empirical results that favour SRIs. We have provided evidence from existing academic studies that the in-line or outperformance of SRI strategies do not apply exclusively to equities, but also corporate and government bonds. This point is crucial for our empirical study, as a significant proportion of the average asset allocation of German Pension Insurance Funds will be invested in fixed-income securities. The SRI results across asset classes support our research objectives, as there appears to be sufficient evidence that including SRI strategies as part of the strategic asset allocation of Pension Insurance Funds should not cause any performance disadvantage to beneficiaries.

G. German Market Share in SRIs, Product Innovation and Increase in Related Services

Under the assumption of more than €250bln of SRI AuM invested in Germany, the SRI market has already reached a critical size to catch the attention of a larger number of institutional investors.[450] While the numbers are still considerably behind the largest European markets for SRI, the growth rate for German SRI assets remain promising.

Moreover, new product knowledge may lead to a more rapid expansion of SRI in the German pension fund space, especially due to historically high allo-

[448] See Sec. 78 Par.1 No. 1 Directive 78/660/EWG, after amendment by Sec. 1 Par. 14 Directive 2003/51/EG.
[449] See Bundesministerium fuer Umwelt, Naturschutz und Reaktorsicherheit (2009), p. 10.
[450] See Funds@Work (2010), p. 1 or Union Investment (2011), p. 2.

cation into fixed-income securities and constant investments into real estate. The expansion of SRI screening techniques to corporate and government bonds as well as considerations on sustainable real estate investments offer Pension Insurance Funds a wide range of product coverage for their investment portfolios. Concurrent to the increasing product supply available to investors, a growing number of SRI-related financial services are being offered to the investor community: research services at major investment banks, consulting firms specialising in SRI advisory services, rating firms offering ESG ratings,[451] law firms with dedicated SRI specialists, the lobbying effort by forums like FNG in Germany and an increasing number of ESG indices that replicate different investment themes,[452] amongst others.

H. Best Practise in Leading Pension Fund Markets

Leading capital-funded pension systems in Europe, in particular in the UK and Netherlands, are considered SRI-pioneers. As we have previously seen, a significant proportion of the asset base of pension funds in these countries is invested following a SRI screening method. Provided that the market share of German occupational pension schemes will increase over the next years to compensate for the funding insufficiencies the public pension system is facing and the advantages SRI investing has for long-term orientated pension fund investing, we can expect the SRI allocation of German pension fund schemes to grow. As Preu, Richardson (2011) conclude, the implementation and influence of SRIs in Germany may be more effective in the future than what SRI investors have achieved in other European countries so far, despite the currently relatively small market size of sustainable investments.[453]

3.2.9 Conclusions

Sustainable investing is a broad term that encompasses a wide range of different categories, so that a precise and single definition is difficult to obtain. Nonetheless, we have presented different aspects of the term that include social responsible investing, ethical investing, socially directed investment, impact

[451] See Schaefer (2003) on the rising demand since the 90s for a new type of rating category that includes ESG considerations.

[452] See Schaefer, Engelhardt (2008) on a summary on the rising supply of ESG indices, their main screening methodologies as well as their thematic coverage.

[453] See Preu, Richardson (2011), p. 900.

investing and shareholder activism. Moreover, we have discussed that institutional investors have a multitude of investment strategies available to pursue sustainable investing, which include the most common methods of negative and positive screening as well as best-in-class methodologies, but also newer concepts in the context of SRI investing, like integration and shareholder activism.

These strategies enable investors to pursue more versatile SRI-orientated portfolio management policies. We have provided evidence that a combination of BiC and negative screening is one of the most popular investment approaches used in practise. We have also discussed the various advantages this combined strategy may have for institutional investors in general and pension funds specifically, namely choosing the best performers based on a set of KPIs under the BiC method, whereas the negative screening overlay allows eliminating commonly perceived undesired industries or business practises. The negative screening element also serves as risk-shield against public scrutiny or criticism by eternal stakeholder pressure groups.

SRI performance studies for the UK and US market have a relatively long history. Nonetheless, we have been able to present recent European academic research studies that suggest SRI assets perform in-line with conventional asset classes. These results are essential, as in the past one of the major disadvantages of SRIs were the apparent underperformance versus traditional assets. As we have highlighted, new econometrical techniques in the last few years have facilitated a much more precise comparison of SRI return data and evidenced that SRIs do not yield worse results than conventional assets do. While SRI performance studies tend to be predominantly equities-focused, we have been able to provide empirical evidence for corporate as well as government bond SRI performance. The conclusions drawn for equity funds and indices are also valid for fixed-income assets: on average, SRI strategies perform at least as well as traditional asset classes. These results are essential for our research objectives, as they support our initial research proposal for this dissertation.

For German Pension Insurance Funds to consider SRI assets at larger scale, portfolio managers must be able to invest in sustainable assets across various asset classes, not just equities (as the first asset class for which SRI strategies were considered). Section 3.2.4 has summarised the alternatives already available for different asset categories to invest in a sustainable manner: corporate and government bonds, listed and unlisted real estate, cash and money market and alternative investments (more details in chapter 3.3.5). In comparison to the US or leading European SRI markets (in particular the UK and the Netherlands), Germany remains at an early stage of market development. However, growth rates recorded in the last few years as well as growth forecasts are promising. In addition, there are robust indications that the German SRI market may be larger than the directly invested assets within the mutual fund industry suggest, which are usually used as main reference to estimate market size.

Pension funds are the largest player in the SRI space in Europe with around 2/3 market share in the SRI market. While it remains difficult to estimate with precision the SRI investing activity by German pension fund schemes, there are indications that the current asset base invested is still very low. There are for example no private German pension funds as PRI signatories, whereas numerous British and Dutch pension funds are committed to the PRIs. Nevertheless, we believe there are solid and justifiable reasons why SRI investing may play a major role in the future for German Pension Insurance Funds. First, some occupational pension schemes will have an intrinsic motivation to invest in SRI. Ethical values or ESG-orientated business principles may be part of the 'DNA' of the sponsoring company and are transferred and adopted by the pension fund. Moreover, fiduciary duty seems to imply that trustees are legally obliged to invest in SRI, even more so since empirical evidence for the performance of sustainable assets across asset categories suggests SRI techniques generate returns that are in-line with conventional assets. Second, German corporates are increasingly being targeted by discontent stakeholders for not including SRI considerations into the asset management of their pension fund schemes. Third, the German legislator has introduced new regulations (within the VAG and AltZertG frameworks) that enforce pension funds to disclose their SRI activity and commitment. Moreover, product innovation enables pension fund managers to expand the product range away from equities into fixed-income securities and real estate. Given the high allocation by German Pension Insurance Funds into fixed-income asset classes, this innovation could be a catalyst for more SRI growth.

In subsequent section 3.3, we will focus on the suitability of alternative investments for the strategic asset allocation of Pension Insurance Funds. Hedge fund strategies and commodity investments, in particular, will be discussed from a theoretical and empirical standpoint to ultimately assess their potential fit for the purpose of our research study. While risk management aspects like inflation hedge and portfolio diversification effects are the predominant drivers for considering alternative investments, we will also attempt to include SRI aspects.

3.3 Alternative Investments

3.3.1 Definition

Alternative investments include traditionally hedge funds, private equity, venture capital and commodity assets. Some investors also consider more 'exotic' investments like timber or farmland, oil and gas programs and illiquid, private (distressed) debt as part of the alternative investment space.[454] The overall investment objectives of alternative investments are thereby relatively similar: (1) capital preservation, (2) appropriate risk and volatility management, (3) levered returns, (4) low correlation with conventional asset classes[455] and consequently higher portfolio diversification and (5) access to investing strategies unavailable to portfolio managers of traditional long-only funds.[456] While these aims do not apply to all types of alternative investments simultaneously, they are commonly present as a combined mix. An important remark by Anson et al. (2011) and Lhabitant (2004) in this context is that alternative investments are in most cases not a separate asset class *per se*, but rather a subset of an existing asset category. By applying different or new investment strategies to an existing asset class, alternative investments can expand their investment opportunity set.[457]

[454] See Schneeweiss et al. (2002), p. 2.

[455] In our understanding, conventional assets include cash and cash equivalents, equities, corporate and government bonds as well as (listed and non-listed) real estate objects.

[456] See Hedges (2005), p. 2.

[457] See Anson et al. (2011), p. 18. or Lhabitant (2004), p. 273. Good examples are long/short equity strategies that many hedge funds pursue. Given their investment flexibility versus long-only mutual funds, for example, hedge funds can replicate market-neutral strategies by going long an underlying and shorting simultaneously other securities of the same sector. With his technique, they expand the investment opportunity set by simply applying a new strategy to an existing asset category.

While some authors include real estate assets into the alternative instrument category,[458] due to the rather long history of real estate involvement by German Pension Insurance Funds, we will assign them to the conventional asset classes. Moreover, for the purpose of our research study, we will concentrate on hedge fund and commodities investments only, given their relevance in the alternative investment space, their high liquidity (versus illiquid assets like private equity or infrastructure assets), the explicit wording of the German law for these two investment categories for German Pension Insurance Funds (in particular AnlV and R4/2011) and the unique benefits they offer to the investment opportunity set when added to a conventional investment portolio. Moreover, for both asset classes, there are sufficient long-term historical time series available that will enable us to run econometric models.[459]

3.3.2 Strategic Asset Allocation Considerations

A. Hedge Fund Investing

A.1 Definition

Hedge funds tend to be loosely regulated investment companies that seek to generate returns that are not highly correlated to returns on stocks or bond securities. In general, hedge funds use considerable leverage on their investment positions to enhance portfolio returns.[460] Investing in hedge funds, implies usually creating exposure to a broad and well-diversified portfolio of different hedge fund portfolios. For pension funds, this usually occurs via a fund-of-funds (fof) investment, as a proper investing approach into hedge funds requires intensive research resources for regularly reviewing, selecting and monitoring the portfolio of different hedge fund strategies. For many pension funds, such resources are simply not affordable given the small allocation they tend to have into hedge fund assets. An alternative methodology could also be to hire external specialised consultants and externalise the whole investment process. [461]

---

[458] See Amenc, Le Sourd (2003), p. 5.

[459] For many alternative investments, such long historical time series do not exist to date, making empirical analysis based on econometric techniques difficult to perform.

[460] See McCrary (2005), p. 1 and p. 4.

[461] See Lhabitant (2006), p. 517.

A.2 Main Benefits vs. Conventional Assets

Including hedge fund assets into the investment portfolio can offer many benefits to pension fund managers. First and probably most importantly, robust empirical evidence suggests hedge funds achieve superior performances versus conventional asset classes. Historically, hedge funds have generated higher absolute returns, better risk-adjusted returns and obtained lower downside risk (see also 3.3.4 within this chapter on hedge fund performance).[462] Also, hedge funds tend to have lower correlations to conventional assets. While traditional asset classes have experienced a rising correlation across markets and asset categories due to the globalization of international capital markets and more frequent herd behaviour by investors on a global scale, hedge funds offer low to medium correlation to conventional asset returns.[463] Adding the fund-of-funds (fof) overlay structure to a conventional hedge fund investment offers additional advantages: apart from the diversification effect of investing in several funds at once and the higher professional due diligence offered by the fund-of-funds manager, these-structures are generally also more cost-efficient.[464]

A.3 Key Risk Differences versus Conventional Assets

Table 8 summarises the major risk differences that exist between conventional assets and hedge fund strategies. Risk management considerations will play a crucial role for pension fund managers that are contemplating to diversify their portfolios using alternative investment assets.

---

[462] See Lhabitant (2006), pp. 518-520. The researcher analysed the performance of hedge fund assets using the CS/Tremont index (which is the same as we are using for our empirical analysis), for the time period 1994-2005. In terms of absolute returns, the hedge fund index yielded 10.7% vs. 8.6% and 7.9% for the S&P 500 and the Euro Stoxx 50, respectively. The annualized volatility for the same time period was 8.0% for hedge funds, 16.2% for the S&P 500 and 22.1% for the Euro Stoxx 50. Analyzing the maximum drawdown of assets, i.e. the largest amount of capital invested that would have been lost from the peak to the lowest trough in the observation period, an investor invested in the S&P 500 would have lost -46.3%, in the Euro Stoxx 50 -61.6% and in hedge fund assets only -13.8%. In terms of Sharpe ratios, hedge funds achieved 0.80 vs. the 0.26 for the S&P500 and the 0.16 for the Euro Stoxx 50.

[463] See Lhabitant (2006), pp. 521-523. Correlation coefficients of 0.48 and 0.51 to the S&P 500 and Euro Stoxx 50, correspondingly, 0.11 to the 1m USD-Libor and -0.08 versus global government bonds.

[464] See Nicholas (2004), pp. 66-75.

Table 8: Risk Management Considerations for Hedge Fund Investments

Category	Hedge Fund Portfolio	Conventional Portfolio[465]	Risk Management Implications[466]
Investment Objective	Absolute return	Relative return versus benchmark	• Independently of market conditions, hedge funds focus on generating alpha
Market Exposure	Potential multiple of -1 to +1 due to debt leverage	Majority sector and/or investment style indices have beta-factors close to 1 for broad, well-diversified portfolios	• Individual skill-set of portfolio manager becomes more relevant • Execution risk in changing markets important
Investment Styles	Vary significantly across funds (defining characteristic of individual portfolio managers)	Due to investment strategy restrictions, investment style varies rarely (long-only approach)	• Aggregating different investment styles and manager skills make overall risk assessment difficult
Risk Profile	Depending on fund strategy, differs significantly	More homogenous and well-defined risk profile	• Fund manager needs to allocate risk adequately based on the underlying investment strategy of the hedge fund
Liquidity Risk	Illiquid investments and excessive leverage can cause severe liquidity risks	Liquid assets and low/zero leverage considerable risk mitigators	• Liquidity squeeze for hedge funds is considerable, as seen during the 2008 credit crisis • Quantification of liquidity risk essential
Business Relationships	Portfolio manager as well as clients invest as partners in the fund	Portfolio manager acts as agent for the client	• Only hedge funds in which portfolio managers are coinvested should be considered
Risk Interplay	Significant risk exposure due to greater risk variety as well as interdependency of risk categories	Primarily market risk (equity, interest rate, foreign exchange and credit risk)	• Risk assessment should consider risk aggregation of different inherent risk classes

Source: Own representation, based on Hedges (2005), p. XVI et seq. and Jaeger (2003), p. 2.

While hedge fund investments offer attractive attributes to a pension fund manager, it is essential to understand the inherent risks this asset class has. While some of the risk categories discussed in table 7 are constrained in a fund-of-fund investment format, some are market risks that could also severely affect a fof investment.

---

[465] The conventional portfolio refers to a broad, well-diversified portfolio of a large long-only investor, for example a pension or mutual fund.

[466] Denotes risk management implications hedge fund investments may have for a traditional pension fund manager.

B. Commodities Investing

B.1 Definition

Commodities are a peculiar asset class in that they are real assets that have an intrinsic value and usually provide their owners a certain utility. Commodities can be used for example as input factor in a manufacturing process or serve as a consumption good. Commodities supply is constrained as for the majority of products there is limited availability, either due to production limitations or shortage of resources. Another essential characteristic is their heterogeneity as an asset class, as the product quality is not standardised and each good has its own particular features. Further distinctions can be drawn between hard commodities (e.g. metals and energy-related products) and soft commodities (e.g. livestock and agriculture), storability[467], availability and renewability of the product.[468] Also, commodity assets can be acquired either in physical form, via derivatives (mostly commodity futures), through investments in productive assets (farmland, forests, mines) or by purchasing the equity of a publicly listed company that manages commodity assets (e.g. listed mining companies, oil producers).[469]

B.2 Main Benefits vs. Conventional Assets

The essential benefit of commodity investments is their low correlation with conventional asset classes. Several long-term research studies have provided robust empirical evidence that the correlation relationship between commodities, shares and bonds is negative. Moreover, commodity assets are an excellent inflation hedge instrument, as they tend to be highly positively correlated with changes in inflation and interest rates.[470] The overall inflation rate, actually, is largely dependent on prices of physical commodities, so that commodities futures act as an excellent inflation proxy.[471]

---

[467] Storability refers to the characteristic that some products require very specific storage conditions (e.g. agricultural products, livestock), whereas other commodities are easier to store (e.g. metals, coal).

[468] See Anson et al. (2011), pp. 29-31.

[469] See Knoepfel (2011), p. 3.

[470] See Greer (2000), p. 50 or Jensen et al. (2002), p. 110.

[471] See Jensen et al (2000), p. 490.

B.3 Characteristics of Commodities Investing

The most common way for investors to get exposure to commodities is via derivatives, in particular commodities futures. The majority of investments are pooled in index funds, which acquire futures positions in the underlying commodities on a rolling basis without physical delivery (positions are closed out before expiry).[472] A direct investment, on the other hand, is inconvenient and costly for financial investors, as high transactions costs, insurance expenses and storage charges are necessary to get exposure to the asset.[473] As investors typically do not acquire the physical product directly, commodity trading has a negligible effect on production levels of the commodities in the long term. In the short term, nonetheless, trading activity may impact physical demand and significantly influence price movements (see also subsection E in this chapter).[474]

The introduction of exchange-traded-funds (etfs) for commodities in recent years, as well as the increasing product offer in mutual funds, has enabled a wide range of investors (including retail investors) to get exposure to commodity investments in a cost-efficient and convenient manner.[475] Prior to these product innovations, asset allocations by mutual or pension funds directly into commodity assets were rare. The majority of investments occurred as indirect investments in either the equity capital of a commodity producer or the corresponding debt securities. Many of the commodity producers, however, tend to hedge their exposure to commodity price fluctuations, so that investing into the shares of a producer will not generate the same return distribution than direct commodity investments.[476]

3.3.3 Pension Funds in the Alternative Investment Sector

A. Market Share in Global Alternative Investments

In the last 10 years, large institutional investors have diversified away from traditional, liquid assets, like bonds and equities, into alternative asset classes,

---

[472] See Knoepfel (2011), p. 4 et seq.
[473] See Jensen et al. (2002), p. 101 or Jensen et al. (2000), p. 490.
[474] See Knoepfel (2011), p. 4 et seq.
[475] See Conover et al. (2010), p. 10.
[476] See Georgiev (2001), p. 40. See p. 46 et seq. on the empirical evidence on the return difference between direct commodity investments and equity investments in a producer's share capital.

particularly hedge funds, real estate assets, commodities and infrastructure. New risk-return constellations as well as a wider product range have been the predominant drivers of this investment shift.[477]

Based on a representative survey Thomson Watson and the Financial Times compute on an annual basis, detailed data for the investment pattern of pension funds in the alternative investment space is available.[478] A total of 197 of the largest asset managers in the world that manage assets on behalf of pension funds participate in the survey, with an asset base in alternative investments of $2,311.5bln AuM in total and $1,089.9bln on behalf of pension funds.[479] Details on the distribution of the underlying alternative assets managed on behalf of pension funds are summarised in figure 35.

Figure 35: Distribution of Alternative Investments by Asset Class (LHS) and Domicile of the Asset Manager (RHS) (in $bln, 2010)

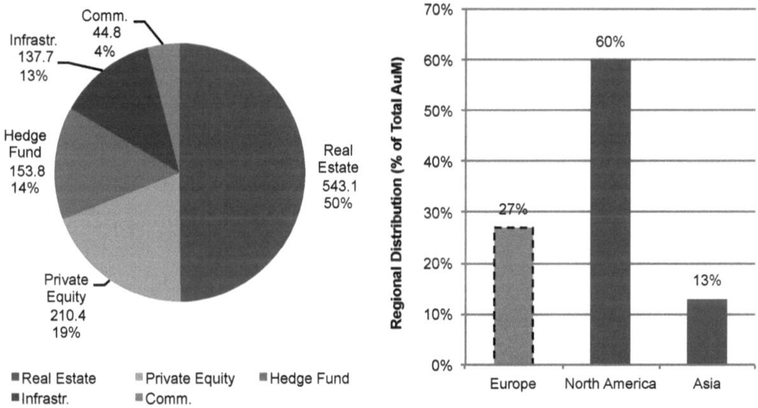

Source: Own figure, on the basis of Towers Watson, Financial Times (2011), p. 52. Abbreviations used: 'LHS'=left hand side, 'RHS'=right hand side, 'Comm.'=commodities, 'Infrastr.'=infrastructure.

Real Estate investments are the predominant asset class within alternative investments with 50% (or $543.1bln AuM) of all assets, followed by Private Equity (19% or $210.4bln) and Hedge Funds (14% or $153.8bln). Assuming a Eu-

[477] See Garz, Volk (2011), p. 33.

[478] See Towers Watson, Financial Times (2011). The survey comprehends a total universe of 197 asset managers globally that manage assets on behalf of pension funds. These investors are chosen by AuM managed and represent therefore the largest asset managers for pension funds in the world. The data of the survey is as of 31-Dec-2010.

[479] See Towers Watson, Financial Times (2011), p. 2.

ropean market share of 27%, the total European alternative asset base for pension funds is structured as follows:[480]

Table 9: Alternative Investments by European Pension Funds (in $bln, 2010)

Asset Class	AuM in $bln		Country	In %	AuM in $bln
Real Estate	146.6		United Kingdom	50%	147.1
Private Equity	56.8		Switzerland	24%	70.6
Hedge Fund	41.5		France	12%	35.3
Infrastructure	37.2		Others	14%	41.2
Commodities	12.1				
Total	**294.3**				**294.3**

Source: Own representation, based on Towers Watson, Financial Times (2011), p. 51 et seq.

Using the total global market size of alternative investment assets, we can compare the assets invested by pension funds in relation to the entire market size. For private equity, the results suggest that 8.4% of total alternative assets are invested in pension fund portfolios, for real estate the corresponding figure is 4.8%, for hedge funds 8.0%, for infrastructure funds 0.5% and 11.8% for commodities.[481] The large proportion of real estate and private equity assets is not surprising given their long-term investment horizon these investments offer. The allocations into hedge fund assets (14% of total alternative AuM) as well as commodities (4%) remain moderately low to date. This can be partly explained by the rather recent product offering into commodities in form of ETFs and futures indices.

While the data used in this section does not represent the entire universe of pension fund investments in the alternative investment space, we have to assume that a significant proportion of pension funds mandate external portfolio managers to take fiduciary responsibility over the underlying assets. Consequently, the conclusions we can draw from this data gives us a representative insight into how and to which extend pension funds invest in the alternative investment space.

[480] We implicitely assume that the country of origine of the pension fund corresponds to the domicile of the asset manager. We acknowledge this may not always be the case.

[481] Using as reference for the total market size for 2010: $2,517bln for private equity, $11,310bln for real estate, $1,920bln for hedge funds, $28,900bln for infrastructure investments and $380bln for commodities. See PRI (2011), p. 16 for all alternative investments except commodities and TheCityUK (2011), p. 1 for the AuM for the commodities market.

3.3.4 Performance, Portfolio Diversification and Inflation Hedging

A. Performance Considerations

A.1 Hedge Fund Performance

Hedge fund performance analyses are a popular research field in finance given the growing role hedge fund investments are playing in capital markets nowadays. The objective of this section is to summarise the most relevant academic studies on hedge fund performance, with particular emphasize on those papers that compare risk-return constellations across asset classes. Table 10 summarises the major conclusions from our literature review.

Table 10: Literature Review: Hedge Fund Performance

Author(s)	Year of Publication	Time Period Considered	Summary
Sun et al.	2012	1996-2009	• Robust evidence that skilled hedge fund managers are more likely to pursue unique investment strategies that will ultimately generate superior performance • Strong persistency in the results obtained[482]
Dichev, Yu	2011	1980-2008	• Compares dollar-weighted returns (similar to IRR calculations) to corresponding buy-and-hold fund returns and reveals that alpha of hedge funds is close to 0 • Dollar-weighted returns on average 3-7% below fund returns and lower than returns on broad indices like the S&P 500[483]
Jagannathan et al.	2010	1996-2005	• Strong empirical evidence of performance persistency amongst top hedge funds suggests superior managerial investment talent • Results adjusted for survival-bias, option-like features in hedge fund strategies and serial return correlation caused by illiquid investments[484]
Sadka	2010	1994-2008	• Funds that incur in high liquidity risk generate high future returns, indicating that the outperformance of hedge funds during the observation period could be due to beta risk and not alpha[485]
Agarwal et al.	2009	1994-2002	• Hedge funds that have better managerial incentives achieve better performance re-

[482] See Sun et al. (2012), p. 137 et seq.
[483] See Dichev, Yu (2011), p. 261.
[484] See Jagannathan et al. (2010), p. 253.
[485] See Sadka (2010), p. 69 et seq.

Author(s)	Year of Publication	Time Period Considered	Summary
			turns • Moreover, funds with higher managerial discretion (e.g. longer lock-up and restriction periods) obtain higher returns[486]
Ding et al.	2009	1994-2005	• On a risk-adjusted basis, large hedge funds perform better than small funds • Large funds tend to have more often illiquid assets[487]
Eling	2009	1996-2005	• Empirical analysis provides evidence of short-term persistency in hedge fund returns (up to 6 months) • Indication that long-term persistence is not existent • Survivorship bias and return smoothing cast doubts on short-term persistency • Convertible arbitrage and emerging market hedge funds tend to have highest short-term performance persistency[488]
Griffin, Xu	2009	1980-2004	• Weak evidence of long-term persistency of hedge fund performances • Hedge funds are not superior stock-pickers than mutual funds[489]
Boyson	2008	1994-2004	• Young, small hedge funds with strong past performances outperform mature, large and underperforming funds by almost 10% per year • Fund selection based on age, size and past performance more likely to generate persistent superior returns[490]
Kosowski et al.	2007	1990-2002	• Statistical evidence of long-term return persistency • Abnormal hedge fund performance cannot be attributed to luck but to portfolio manager ability[491]

Source: Own representation, based on the respective research references.

In summary, recent research studies on hedge fund performance obtain mixed results in terms of alpha generation. While the majority of studies suggest there is statistical evidence that large hedge funds can generate persistent portfolio performances and are able to generate alpha due to managerial skills, there are numerous studies that contradict these findings. Moreover, including illiquid assets into the investment portfolio can skew fund performance, as they tend to yield higher returns.

486 See Agarwal et al. (2009), p. 2249.
487 See Ding et al. (2009), p. 891.
488 See Eling (2009), p. 396.
489 See Griffin, Xu (2009), p. 2566 et seq.
490 See Boyson (2008), p. 41 et seq.
491 See Kosowski et al. (2007), p. 262 et seq.

For Pension Insurance Fund managers that are considering adding hedge fund portfolios to their asset mix, a few risk mitigating factors can be deducted from these academic research findings: funds with low allocations into illiquid assets, with large overall investment portfolios, long track records and with a high ownership in the fund by the portfolio managers might outperform the overall hedge fund market and provide attractive risk-return constellations versus conventional asset classes.

A.2 Commodities Performance

We have summarised the most relevant empirical studies for commodity assets to determine if recent research findings can give us an indication of the suitability of this asset class for the portfolio management of pension funds.

Table 11: Literature Review: Commodities Performance

Author(s)	Year of Publication	Time Period Considered	Summary
Belousova, Dorfleitner	2012	1995-2010	• Energy and precious metals generate the highest added value as they enhance performance and diversify risk • Agriculture, livestock and industrial metals provide the highest portfolio risk reduction and are thus recommendable for risk-averse investors[492]
Daskaladi, Skiadopoulos	2011	1989-2009	• Diversification benefits from adding commodities to traditional portfolios is limited, independently of the underlying utility function, commodity instrument used and performance measure applied • Increasing financialization of commodities has deteriorated previously existing diversification effect[493]
Woodard et al.	2011	1994-2006	• A selective use of commodity investments can generate significant portfolio improvements from a mean-variance perspective • Crude oil is the single most relevant commodity in terms of adding to portfolio performance, followed by copper, cattle and silver[494]
Conover et al.	2010	1970-2007	• Strong evidence that commodities offer diversification to equity portfolios • Risk reduction independently of underlying investment style of the portfolio[495]
Fuertes et al.	2010	1979-2007	• Commodities should be tactically added

[492] See Belousova, Dorfleitner (2012), p. 2464 et seq.
[493] See Daskaladi, Skiadopoulos (2011), p. 2624 et seq.
[494] See Woodard et al. (2011), p. 264 et seq.
[495] See Conover et al. (2010), p. 17.

Author(s)	Year of Publication	Time Period Considered	Summary
			to conventional portfolios as they yield abnormal returns and reduce overall risk • Active commodity strategies can earn considerable alpha[496]
Smimou	2010	1985-2007	• European investors can obtain considerable gains by investing in US or Canadian agricultural commodities • The low correlation coefficient of commodity futures and international equity portfolios leads to a significant risk reduction[497]
Marshall et al.	2008	1984-2005	• Commodities can be very effective in adding diversification to a stock and bond portfolio, partially due to their robust performance in time periods of high inflation • Technical trading strategies with commodities futures do not lead to any significant alpha generation[498]
Erb, Harvey	2006	1969-2004	• The authors contradict a number of studies that suggest commodity futures have equity-like returns • Results indicate that equity-like returns are only achieved under very specific conditions: primarily futures that may have positive roll or spot returns in the future[499]
Gorton, Rouwenhorst	2004	1959-2004	• For the chosen investment horizon, commodity futures significantly outperform spot commodity investments • Negative correlation of commodity futures with stocks and bonds is stronger over longer investment periods[500]
Jensen et al.	2002	1973-1999	• Adding commodity futures to a diversified portfolio invested in conventional asset classes leads to higher investment returns • For unmanaged (passive) futures investments, performance increases by 100bps p.a., whereas for managed (dynamic) futures the increase is approximately 300bps p.a.[501]

Source: Own representation, based on the respective research references.

The research studies we have summarized for commodities are relatively consistent with respect to the benefits of adding commodity assets to the asset mix of conventional portfolios. In general, due to their low or even negative cor-

[496] See Fuertes et al. (2010), p. 2545 et seq.
[497] See Smimou (2010), p. 54.
[498] See Marshall et al. (2008), p. 1818.
[499] See Erb, Harvey (2006), p. 94.
[500] See Gorton, Rouwenhorst (2004), p. 27 et seq.
[501] See Jensen et al. (2002), p. 110.

relation, commodity investments offer a high degree of risk diversification when mixed with conventional assets like stocks and bonds. The positive risk mitigating effect is more pronounced for longer investment periods, a fact that favours especially Pension Insurance Funds given their long-term investing perspective.

B. Portfolio Diversification Effect

As discussed in section 2.5.1, German Pension Insurance Funds have the flexibility to allocate a proportion of their total investment portfolio into alternative asset classes. The limits, as defined by the regulator for the relevant asset categories, are thereby 25% for real estate assets[502] and 5% for hedge fund and commodity investments, respectively. In addition, section 2.5.2 enabled us to determine that to date German Pension Insurance Funds have very low investments into alternative asset classes, as the portfolios are characterised by a substantial allocation into traditional assets, with a considerable overweight into fixed-income securities.

In this section we want to determine whether the benefits of adding alternative asset classes into the classical portfolio allocation may in fact lead to a risk reduction and an overall performance improvement. By using the actual historical time series data for the two largest asset classes Pension Insurance Funds currently invest in (corporate and government bonds), we will calculate the corresponding correlation matrix of the four asset categories. We will hereby apply the same time series indices we will also include in our empirical analysis in chapter 5.

Table 12: Correlation Matrix of European Corporate Bonds, European Government Bonds, Hedge Funds and Commodities (Monthly Returns, Dec-02 until Dec-11)

	Europ. Corp. Bonds	Europ. Gov. Bonds	Hedge Funds	Commodities
Europ. Corp. Bonds	*1.00*	0.50	0.44	0.14
Europ. Gov. Bonds		*1.00*	-0.26	-0.23
Hedge Funds			*1.00*	0.48
Commodities				*1.00*

Source: Own representation, data provided by VWD Data Provider. Underlined numbers indicate correlation coefficients of <0.50.

502 As mentioned earlier, given the long history of Pension Insurance Funds investing in real estate objects, we consider these assets as part of the conventional asset pool.

As table 12 shows, European government bonds exhibit a negative correlation with respect to international hedge funds as well as commodities futures (-0.26 and -0.23 respectively). While the correlation between European corporate bonds and hedge funds is with 0.44 considerably larger, the coefficient is nonetheless lower than the correlation between corporate and government bonds (0.50). With a correlation coefficient of 0.14, returns of European corporate bonds tend to move almost independently from commodities.

Grouping traditional asset classes with corresponding alternative assets and calculating the resulting portfolio volatility as well as performance is a suitable indicator as to what extend alternative assets contribute to risk diversification in the Markowitz portfolio context.[503] Table 13 summarises the resulting portfolio returns and volatilities for changing portfolio weights among European corporate bonds, government bonds and a fixed allocation of 5% in hedge funds and commodities, respectively.

Table 13: Mean-Variance Effect of Adding Hedge Funds and Commodity Investments to European Corporate and Government Bonds (Monthly Returns, Dec-02 until Dec-11)

% Corp. Bonds	% Gov. Bonds	% Hedge Funds	% Comm.	Portfolio Return	Portfolio Volatility
0.0%	90.0%	5.0%	5.0%	3.99%	3.28%
10.0%	80.0%	5.0%	5.0%	4.01%	3.17%
20.0%	70.0%	5.0%	5.0%	4.03%	3.11%
30.0%	60.0%	5.0%	5.0%	4.05%	3.10%
40.0%	50.0%	5.0%	5.0%	4.07%	3.14%
50.0%	40.0%	5.0%	5.0%	4.09%	3.22%
60.0%	30.0%	5.0%	5.0%	4.11%	3.35%
70.0%	20.0%	5.0%	5.0%	4.13%	3.51%
80.0%	10.0%	5.0%	5.0%	4.15%	3.71%
90.0%	0.0%	5.0%	5.0%	4.16%	3.94%

Source: Own representation. European corporate bonds are represented by the Iboxx EUR Corporates index, European government bonds by the Iboxx EUR Eurozone index, hedge funds by the DJCS Hedge Fund index and commodities by the DJ UBS Commodity index. Note: Time period: Dec-02 until Dec-2011.

[503] Based on the variance of a portfolio P as defined by $Var(P)=a^2Var(X)+b^2Var(Y)+2abr_{xy}\sigma_x\sigma_y$ with r_{xy} as correlation coefficients between 2 assets. For correlation coefficients lower than 1, the resulting variance of a portfolio will be lower than the simple weighted average variances of the two assets. Correlation coefficients of 0 indicate that the two assets move independently to each other (no structure recognizable), while negative correlation coefficients indicate that assets are moving in inverse directions. From a risk reduction perspective, correlation of 0 or less are desirable. See Copeland et al. (2005), pp. 115-121.

Plotting the efficient frontier of different investment scenarios (conventional portfolio standalone, with 5% hedge fund weight, 5% commodities proportion and a 10% combined alternative investment allocation). We obtain the following mean-variance distributions:

Figure 36: Efficient Frontiers Amongst European Corporate and Government Bonds and Alternative Investments
(Based on Monthly Returns, Dec-02 until Dec-11)

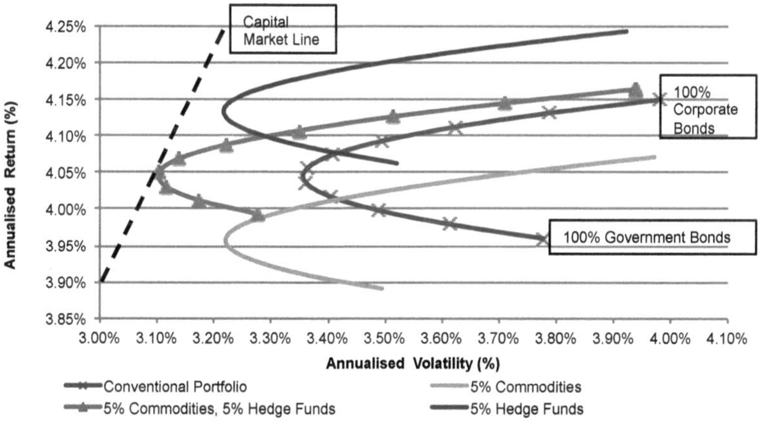

Source: Own figure, data provided by VWD Data Provider. Note: Using the mean-variance calculations in the Markowitz portfolio context, we obtain for changing weights between European corporate bonds and European government bonds the efficient frontier of the conventional portfolio. For the three additional portfolios, we maintain the initial weight of the alternative investment constant and vary only the weights between the corporate bonds and government bonds. The risk-free rate has been fixed at 3.90% for illustrative purposes only. We acknowledge that at the time of our research study, the deposit facility fixed by the ECB was at 0.25% and the fixed-rate for main refinancing operations at 1.00%. See ECB (2012, e).

The results obtained in the graph are compelling: Allocating first a small proportion of alternative investments to an otherwise conventional portfolio of corporate and government bond assets can lead to a meaningful improvement of the mean-variance profile. The portfolio with the highest improvement is thereby the fund with both hedge funds and commodity assets. As our examples have shown, a rationally behaving investor would not choose any combination of the conventional portfolio, but rather invest in a mixed portfolio that also considers alternative investments.[504] We therefore conclude that alternative investments should be considered as part of our stochastic simulation study.

---

[504] A rationally behaving investor would in our example choose the mixed portfolio with 5% commodities and 5% hedge fund assets.

C. Inflation Hedge Considerations

As our literature summary in table 11 concludes, commodity investments are a suitable inflation hedge for investors. As commodities are real assets, they possess an intrinsic value that will reflect changes of price levels. Moreover, commodity prices tend to be correlated with the overall state of the economy and therefore vary in periods of expansion or contraction.[505] Research findings by Belousova, Dorfleitner (2012),[506] Woodard et al. (2011),[507] Jensen et al. (2002),[508] Greer (2000),[509] Bird (1984)[510] and Bodie, Rosansky (1980)[511] confirm that commodities can be used as part of a strategic asset allocation strategy to obtain partial of full inflation hedge.

3.3.5 SRI Considerations in the Alternative Investment Space

A. Overview

So far we have examined alternative investments exclusively from a conventional angle, without contemplating any sustainability aspects. Recent developments, both in academia as well as by finance practitioners, have contributed to a relatively broad range of alternative investments that include sustainability considerations. So far, sustainable alternative investments can be obtained for private equity (including venture capital) type assets, microfinance structures, hedge funds and commodities.[512] As we will consider only hedge fund and commodity assets in our empirical analysis, we will focus exclusively on those two securities in this section.

B. Sustainable Hedge Fund Investments

Hedge fund investments are generally not considered appropriate for sustainable investors as their investing horizon is focused on short-term investments to exploit market inefficiencies. Some people argue, nonetheless, that hedge fund investing activities might improve market efficiency and enable fund

---

505 See Belousova, Dorfleitner (2012), p. 2456.
506 See Belousova, Dorfleitner (2012), p. 2463.
507 See Woodard et al. (2011), p. 15.
508 See Jensen et al. (2002), p. 110.
509 See Greer (2000), p. 50.
510 See Bird (1984), p. 866.
511 See Bodie, Rosansky (1980), p. 27.
512 For more details on sustainability aspects on private equity assets, see EIRIS, UKSIF (2006), p. 9, for venture capital Eurosif (2007), p. 2 et seq. and for microfinance Garz, Volk (2011), p. 87 et seq.

managers to apply SRI principles and thereby cause the target company to change its corporate behaviour.[513] Based on statistics by Garz, Volk (2011), approximately 20% of the current asset base of hedge funds is in principle eligible for sustainable investing activities.[514]

In principle, hedge funds can apply the same ESG techniques we defined in section 3.2.3 for long-only investment funds. Fund managers may for example pursue engagement opportunities based on their ownership of both public and private companies within their investment portfolios. Moreover, they could implement ESG strategies by shorting companies that are underperforming in ESG-related aspects and take long positions in those stocks they believe are strong ESG representatives. The implicit assumption for such a shorting strategy is, however, that there is a direct financial impact triggered by a specific ESG issue in the short term.[515] The suitability of hedge fund techniques for sustainable-minded pension fund managers relates primarily to strategies based on fundamental analysis. Investment approaches linked to technical trading algorithms are thereby not appropriate, as the asset managers of such funds generally do not have a thorough knowledge about the underlying business.[516]

C. Sustainable Commodity Assets

Conventional commodities are at current a highly debated and controversial asset class as financial trading in those assets appears to have a destabilising effect in the real economy (see also section E in this chapter with more details). ESG factors can therefore play a crucial role in any commodity investment process, as the underlying assets can create several issues that a pension fund manager needs to consider. First, long-term environmental and social trends (e.g. climate change, scarcity of natural resources, population growth) will have a meaningful price impact on affected commodities. Also, many ESG issues are directly linked to the production exploration of commodities, e.g. pollution of the environment or exploitation of workers. [517]

---

[513] See EIRIS, UKSIF (2006), p. 12.
[514] See Garz, Volk (2011), p. 81.
[515] See Wood, Hoff (2007), pp. 70-73. No empirical data was provided by the authors to substantiate their suggestion.
[516] See Garz, Volk (2011), p. 82.
[517] See Knoepfel (2011), p. 2.

Suitable ESG approaches in the context of commodity investments can be to focus on either the commodity directly or on the source of the asset. Within the underlying asset itself, investors can apply negative/positive screening techniques to either eliminate commodity products that have a negative impact or overweigh those that have beneficial characteristics.[518] Investors considering rather the original source of the asset can scrutinize environmental regulations, human rights infringements or corruption at the regional level from which the commodity is originated from.[519] Here the emphasis lies on the conditions under which the respective commodity assets are extracted or processed. The screening process becomes more cumbersome for standardised commodity products, like cocoa or oil, for which tracing back of the original production site is not feasible.[520]

A further option for sustainability minded investors could also be to acquire directly the stock or corporate bonds of the producing or exploring company. Certain commodity-related topics can be selected based on positive screening methods (e.g. renewable energy) or best-in-class approaches. However, given the negative external effects frequently caused by commodities, commodity investments tend to get eliminated frequently via traditional negative screening methods.[521]

D. Sustainable Alternative Investments by PRI Signatories

D.1 PRI Signatories

The investment activity of PRI signatories is a good indicator of how committed ESG-minded institutional investors are towards alternative investments. Based on statistics by PRI, approximately 1.0% of total AuM of PRI signatories are currently invested in hedge funds and commodities respectively, 0.7% in infrastructure, 1.8% in private equity and up to 6.3% in real estate (sum of listed and non-listed real estate investments).[522] The respective dollar amount invest-

---

518 As an example, investors could favor natural gas over crude oil within the energy assets or eliminate resource-intensive commodities like live cattle and invest in timber instead.

519 See Wood, Hoff (2007), pp. 81-83.

520 See Oekom (2011), p. 16. For standardized commodity products, the authors recommend traceability methods already applied in the timber industry or in the Kimberley Process for diamonds.

521 See Garz, Volk (2010), p. 27.

522 For the commodities number, we have used the PRI (2010), p. 7 figure, as no disclosure was made in the PRI (2011) document.

ed would therefore represent around $1,841.5bln in total in alternative investments by PRI signatories. Assuming that 50.6% of signatories are from Europe and 73.1% of them represent pension fund schemes (public and private), up to $494.2bln of sustainable alternative assets are allocated to the investment portfolios of European pension funds.[523] Focusing exclusively on occupational pension schemes (24% of European signatories), the alternative investment allocation into sustainable assets would be approximately $162.5bln.[524]

D.2 Eurosif Estimates

Eurosif (2010) estimates that to date approximately 5.6% (or €95.7bln) of all European SRI assets are invested in sustainable hedge funds, around 3.1% in real estate (€53.1bln), 1.6% (€27.3bln) in private equity/venture capital and 0.5% (€8.5bln) in commodities assets. Approximately €1bln are allocated to microfinance funds. A significant proportion of these funds have been acquired by large pension funds from Nordic countries.[525]

E. Alternative Investments: Controversial Debate

E.1 Commodity Assets

The presence of institutional investors in the commodity markets has increased dramatically in the last 20 years. While in 1990 professional investors represented only 25% of all market participants in the commodity markets, their market share is nowadays close to 85%. For the commodity futures market segment, their share reaches almost 100%.[526] For this investor type, commodities are simply an investment class like equities, corporate bonds or money market instruments. In general, these investors do not trade on the fundamental relationship of demand and supply in a particular commodity product, therefore leading to distortions in the price discovery process of the asset. As institutional investors hold the largest positions in commodity markets, their trading flows and patterns will undoubtedly have an influence on price movements.[527]

---

[523] For this calculation we have used the proportion of ESG investments PRI signatories have in the respective asset class, as reported in PRI (2011), p. 16.
[524] Data for the calculation from PRI (2010), p. 6 et seq. and PRI (2011), p. 16.
[525] See Eurosif (2010), p. 17.
[526] See UNCTAD (2012), p. 2, quoted after Masters (2008).
[527] See UNCTAD (2012), pp. 2-4.

Several acclaimed recent research studies conclude that financial speculation is one of the major drivers of price volatility in commodity markets. Baffes, Haniotis (2010), for example, analyse the role played by speculation, increased demand for food in emerging markets as well as biofuel[528] in the recent soft commodity boom. The researchers provide evidence that speculation is the predominant factor, with biofuel playing some role too, but to a lower degree than initially expected. Stronger food demand by emerging markets, on the other hand, has no meaningful impact on market prices.[529] McPail et al. (2012), on the other hand, state that in the short-run, speculation is the driving force of soft commodity price bubbles, whereas in the long-run, energy price shocks, in particular crude oil price volatility, are the determinant factor.[530]

Regulators have increased their scrutiny in relation to the role played by some commodity speculators in recent commodity price bubbles[531] that have led to serious and far-reaching shortages for end-users in some commodities.[532] In particular for soft commodities, extreme price volatility can have severe economic and social consequences. While dramatic food price changes have an impact on hedging costs at commodity futures exchanges, they also lead to food price inflation by increasing input costs for livestock producers and food processors. For developed markets, on the other hand, higher input costs are less relevant, as they represent only a small proportion of overall agricultural input costs, whereas for emerging markets that are import-dependent, food price volatility can be highly problematic.[533]

---

528 For the US, biofuels are primarily maize-based ethanol and for Europe oilseed-based biodiesel production. See Baffes, Haniotis (2010), p. 11.

529 See Baffes, Haniotis (2010), p. 18.

530 See McPhail et al. (2012), p. 409. High crude oil prices will impact corn demand and supply in cash soft commodity markets and lead to an increase in demand for ethanol products. Ethanol production, on the other hand, uses corn as main input factor.

531 In 2003-2008, nominal prices for energy and metals rose by 230%, for food and precious metals doubled and fertilizers increased by factor 4. In 2008, rice prices doubled within a short time period of just 5 months from $375 per ton in January to $757 per ton in summer. See Baffes, Haniotis (2010), p. 3.

532 See Garz, Volk (2010), p. 26. For some very specific commodities, the implication of high speculation and the related external effects could even lead to the elimination of an ESG-set target. Garz and Volk mention as an example the speculation in rare earth minerals that are used as crucial input material for the new generation of energy-efficient car batteries. A price bubble caused by speculative traders may ultimately lead to a considerable delay or reduction in the production of electronic cars by carmakers due to excessive input costs.

533 See McPhail et al. (2012), p. 401 et seq. The authors analyze cause and effect of the record prices for crops (corn, wheat, rice, soybeans) in the time period from mid-2007 to mid-2011.

Misleading price signals in soft commodity markets based on speculation can trigger serious negative social and environmental effects for commodity producers and end-consumers. Producers could for example change their agricultural production based on a perceived increase in demand for a specific underlying or open new mines for natural resources, what could cause severe interruptions of the food supply for poor countries or vast environmental damages by the additional exploration.[534] As highlighted in a research study by Dartanto, Usman (2011), fluctuations in global soft commodity prices can also lead to increasing poverty in emerging economies.[535]

In this context, the suitability of commodity assets for SRI investing purposes, in particular those assets related to agricultural products, remains doubtful. While we discussed some SRI techniques before that could be imposed on commodity investments, the negative external effects caused by commodity speculation require a careful and critical debate. A large number of governments, supranational governance institutions and international organisations have come up in the last few years with a list of governance proposals to respond to soft commodity bubbles. These measures range from providing emergency aid and loans to meet food demand in the short-term, enhancing commodity supply levels through an increase in agricultural investments in developing countries, controlling demand by reconsidering biofuel policies and improving the mechanism of international food trade to avoiding future supply bottlenecks.[536] However, as criticised by Clapp (2009), these governance proposals do not address properly the main issue of commodity bubbles, namely speculation in financial markets.[537]

E.2 Hedge Funds

Hedge fund investment behaviour in the past has lead to criticism by policy makers and academics. This becomes even more relevant when SRI-minded investors consider hedge fund strategies. As empirical evidence by Brunnermeier, Nagel (2004) suggests, hedge funds are unable to prevent price bub-

---

[534] See Oekom (2011), p. 16.

[535] See Dartanto, Usman (2011), p. 169. This research study focuses on the impact caused by the soybean price increases during 2007-2009 and the interlinked increase in poverty in Indonesia.

[536] See Clapp (2009), p. 1191.

[537] See Clapp (2009), p. 1193.

bles and measures such as short-selling constraints are insufficient to explain the investment failure of this 'sophisticated' investor group.[538]

Harmes (2002) highlights the increasing heard-behaviour in financial markets caused by hedge funds in their role as market leaders and the systematic risks they represent due to the high leverage their trading positions usually have. Moreover, hedge funds have been accused by regulators of increasing volatility across asset classes, also in commodity markets. The involvement of hedge funds in recent currency crises, in particular, has caused widespread criticism and questioned their legitimacy as market participants.[539]

E.3 Suitability of Alternative Investments for SRI Purposes?

We have provided substantiated evidence that speculation remains the major driver of price volatility in commodity prices. In accordance with Clapp (2009), we believe that only a better regulated market will lead to a functioning global commodity market that is driven primarily by fundamental factors and enables non-commercial participants to pursue hedging activities as well as allow for an efficient allocation of demand and supply. Apart from regulating commodity markets, we believe that soft commodities, in particular, are a challenging asset class to reconcile with a SRI investment philosophy. While we discussed in the previous section some techniques that may at least add some SRI considerations to the investing process, for some 'fundamental' SRI investors, especially ethical investors, commodity investments may simply not be a suitable asset class. At this point, we do nonetheless not see major obstacles to include commodity investments as part of the strategic asset allocation of Pension Insurance Funds, as long as the allocation represents only a minor proportion of the overall portfolio. Moreover, we encourage as an internal 'best practise' guide to follow the SRI practises we discussed in subsection C. We believe that the benefits commodity assets offer in terms of inflation proxy hedging as well as risk diversification effect make them an attractive asset class for a well-diversified portfolio.

---

[538] See Brunnermeier, Nagel (2004), p. 2038.

[539] See Harmes (2002), pp. 161-167. In terms of currency crises, the author refers primarily to the Sterling crisis in 1992 that forced Britain to leave the European Exchange Rate Mechanism (ERM) and the devaluation of the Thai baht and the contagion to other Asian currencies in 1997-98.

Also the inclusion of hedge fund investments needs to be considered with care, in particular in the context of a suitable SRI strategy. While the risk diversification effect of including hedge fund assets into a conventional portfolio is quantifiable and in general undeniable, we acknowledge the negative repercussions hedge fund investing can have on the well-functioning of financial markets. We would thereby recommend following the SRI approach we have elaborated in subsection B in this chapter to enable pension funds to benefit from hedge fund assets.

3.3.6 Conclusions

Alternative investments offer portfolio managers attractive characteristics due to their peculiar risk-return profile. Given that pension funds are the largest investors in the alternative investment space, assessing their potential inclusion in the strategic portfolio management of German Pension Insurance Funds is justified. As the German regulator explicitly allows up to 10% of total assets to be invested in hedge fund and commodity assets, we will focus in our empirical analysis primarily on the effects these two asset categories may have on the risk-return performance of conventional portfolios.

Academic evidence for hedge fund investing is rather mixed. A pension fund manager needs to screen closely the respective funds and strategies he wants to invest in. Large funds with a long track record, a sizeable allocation into illiquid assets and a large ownership by the corresponding portfolio managers tend to lead to alpha generation due to managerial skills. Given the rather opaque structure of hedge funds and the difficulty pension fund managers might face when choosing their hedge fund portfolio, a fund-of-fund type of structure appears as the most suitable investing method. Contrary to our hedge fund conclusions, research findings for commodities are more uniform. Due to their low or negative correlation to conventional asset classes, they offer investors a clear advantage with regard to portfolio risk diversification. In addition, commodities behave as appropriate inflation proxy hedges.

We have analysed the interaction among hedge fund, commodities indices as well as corporate and government bond indices using the same historical time series data of our empirical analysis in chapter 5. The results indicate that the inclusion of both hedge fund and commodity assets leads to a better mean-variance distribution than without alternative investments, so that considering both asset categories in our stochastic simulation study is justified based on empirical evidence.

Researchers as well as practitioners have considered sustainability aspects in connection with alternative investments. While the challenges are higher in comparison to conventional assets, there are nonetheless suitable investing strategies Pension Insurance Funds might consider as part of their strategic asset allocation policy. We acknowledge however that alternative investments represent a controversial asset category in terms of sustainability considerations.

Due to the lack of adequate historical time series data for sustainable alternative investment methods, our stochastic simulation study can only include conventional alternative hedge fund and commodities assets. We see nevertheless substantial potential for future research on this aspect of pension fund investing.

3.4 Summary

SRIs have reached a strong presence in European capital markets. With close to €5trn AuM, approximately 10% of the total European fund base is invested in sustainable investments. The assets invested in the German fund market remain relatively low in comparison to the activity in other European countries. Nonetheless, we have highlighted the difficulty in estimating precisely the actual size of the German SRI market given its presence outside the mutual fund sector. Within capital-funded pension systems in Europe, SRI methodologies have already found numerous advocates. Almost 2/3 of European SRI assets are invested in pension fund portfolios. Also the role of pension schemes within the PRI signatories indicates how committed European pension funds are towards SRI investing strategies.

While obtaining precise figures for the AuM base by German pension funds into sustainable assets is challenging, it is fair to say that German pension schemes lag their European counterparts in terms of depth and sophistication of their SRI asset base. We have nonetheless provided convincing arguments why occupational pension plans should either consider SRI investments in the near future or increase an existing commitment. First, pension schemes are under increasing pressure by stakeholders of their sponsoring companies with respect to the apparent discrepancy between sustainability understanding and implementation of ESG considerations within the corporate business and lack of commitment in the corresponding strategic investment policy of the pension scheme. Moreover, fiduciary duty under German law seems to suggest that under specific conditions, the consideration of ESG factors in the investment process as mandatory. Recent German legislation with regard to disclosure of SRI activity by occupational pension schemes is supposed to accelerate the implementation of corresponding ESG considerations in the investment management of pension plans. Also, for many investors investing into SRI is driven by an intrinsic motivation based on ethical reasons or mission-related beliefs of the respective fund. The pursuit of good corporate governance or the avoidance of reputational risks might also justify an engagement into SRI. In addition, recent product innovation in the SRI space and the increasing number of related services by rating agencies and index providers in Germany may indicate a higher engagement by pension funds. Finally, best practises in the SRI sector by leading pension funds in capital-funded system, e.g. the Netherlands and the UK, could lead to a higher involvement by German pension schemes.

We have discussed in detail various academic research studies that have analysed the performance of SRI assets in comparison to conventional asset categories. In summary, the results imply that sustainable assets, including equities, corporate as well as government bonds, perform in-line with traditional assets, so that beneficiaries of a pension fund should not suffer any disadvantage should the fund swap into SRI investing methodologies. The actual realisation of SRI investing can occur across asset classes. The product range of ESG investments has expanded significantly in the past years, so that pension fund managers have the choice to overlay SRI techniques on basically all asset classes they are invested in. This is an essential advantage given the high engagement Pension Insurance Funds have in fixed-income securities.

Apart from the benefits SRI assets may offer Pension Insurance Funds, we have analysed in detail the benefits alternative investment could provide when included in the asset management of pension schemes. More precisely, we have focused on hedge fund and commodity investments given their role the German legislator has conceded to both asset classes when allowing Pension Insurance Funds to allocate up to 5% in each of these categories. Our portfolio modelling exercise in the Markowitz mean-variance context has yielded valuable results: using the same time series data we are including in our stochastic simulation study, we provide empirical evidence that even minor allocations into alternative investments can have a beneficial effect on overall risk diversification and portfolio performance. While academic studies are supportive of the economic benefits commodity investments can add to a conventional portfolio due to low correlation and inflation hedging characteristics, the conclusions for hedge funds are rather mixed. Nonetheless, we will consider in our empirical analysis both commodity as well as hedge fund investments as a potential extension of the prevailing, predominantly conventional asset allocation mix of German Pension Insurance Funds.

ESG considerations in the context of alternative investments are a much-debated and recent topic in the academic community. There are sufficient reasons to apply SRI methods to alternative investments with caution, as various research studies provide evidence of the negative external effects these assets can cause on the real economy. This topic will remain undoubtedly a controversial area of SRI investing and we believe that for some SRI investors, alternative investments may not a suitable asset class.

4. Theoretical Foundation

4.1 Objectives

The main objective of chapter 4 is to define the theoretical concepts we require to run our empirical analysis, which will yield results that will enable us to answer our research questions.

1. First, we need to define a suitable stochastic time series model that fits the underlying historical data and captures the dynamics of the assets that we want to include in our regression. An adequate model should allow for the inclusion of short-term dynamics and long-term interactions, if present, as well as provide parameter stability and satisfactory forecasting precision.
2. Once a regression model has been fitted that captures the data generating process of the underlying assets, we will run bootstrap simulations on the estimated model to simulate potential future return paths of the target portfolios. A large number of simulated data points per time period and a long-enough forecasting time horizon will yield a return distribution that will be subsequently used as input variable for the strategic asset allocation strategies we have chosen for German Pension Insurance Funds.
3. The aim of these strategies is to replicate current market practise in terms of long-only investment strategies by pension funds but also to explore the possibilities the German regulator allows insurers and Pension Insurance Funds with respect to derivative overlay structures. We will simulate various investment strategies that offer pension fund managers a wide range of asset allocations, e.g, classic outright investing, hedging, yield enhancement as well as bond-call option methods.
4. Furthermore, our research study will assess new asset allocation models that ignore prevailing regulation in Germany and determine whether Pension Insurance Funds would benefit from regulatory frameworks currently in place in other European countries with sizeable pension fund industries. Figure 37 summarises all the major steps of our empirical analysis.

Figure 37: Summary Empirical Analysis

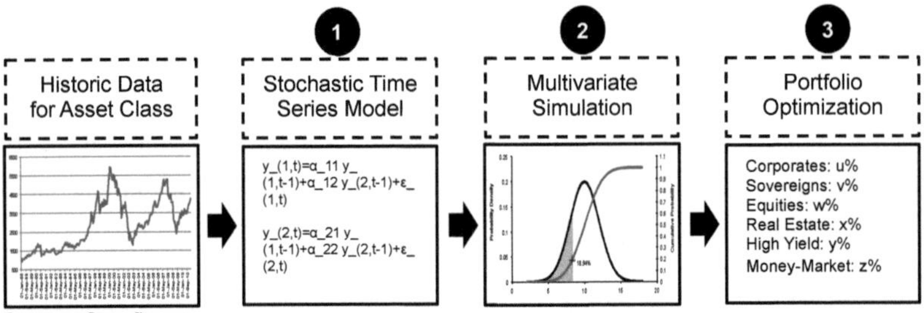

Source: Own figure.

Given the risk-averse investment behaviour German Pension Insurance Funds have shown in the past and the capital preservation character defined contributions with capital guarantee have, adequate performance measures need to be defined that emphasize the downside risk of a particular investment strategy and portfolio allocation. We will introduce numerous risk-return measures based on Lower Partial Moments (LPM) that seem suitable for the investment objectives of Pension Insurance Funds.

Next section 4.2 focuses on describing in detail the VEC modelling technique we will apply to capture the data generating process of our underlying data. In part 4.3, we will discuss the bootstrap simulation that will enable us to generate the return distributions we need for our performance analysis, whereas 4.4 describes the investment strategies we will use in our analysis, both outright methods as well as derivative overlay structures. The downside-risk performance measures we will compute are described in detail in section 4.5.

4.2 Vector Error Correction Modelling Technique

4.2.1 Stochastic Time-Series Model Selection

A. Overview

In this section we will define an appropriate stochastic time series model that will enable us to approximate the true data generating process (DGP) of the underlying historical data of the investment portfolios we are contemplating. The chosen model should fit the data well and be robust in terms of parameter stability and precise with respect to forecasting predictions. Only a model able to fulfil these requirements will be suitable for our simulation study. Our aim is to obtain a parsimonious model structure that replicates properly the dynamics that exist among the asset classes that are included in our target portfolios.

For those portfolios that have cointegrated assets, we will fit a Vector Error Correction model (VECM), whereas for assets that have only short-term interactions, a Vector Autoregressive Model (VAR) is more appropriate. Assets that are independent of the price movements of other securities in the portfolio will be fitted with an ARMA(p,q) model.

B. ARMA(p,q) Models

ARMA models are one of the most important classes of modern time series models. The technique was first introduced in 1970 and has become widely used in research studies, in particular thanks to the increasing computational possibilities of software applications.[540] Box and Jenkins, who are associated with pioneering the academic application of ARMA models,[541] developed a three-stage modelling approach for such models that has become the standard methodology for time series analysis.[542] In essence, ARMA-type models comprehend MA(q) (moving average) elements, AR(p) (auto regressive) models and the ARMA(p,q) models themselves, which are combinations of AR(p) and MA(q) components.[543]

MA(q) models are the simplest time series models available as they are merely a linear combination of q white noise innovations.[544] Y_t depends thereby exclusively on the current as well as previous values of these innovations:

$$Y_t = \varepsilon_t + \alpha_1\varepsilon_{t-1} + \alpha_2\varepsilon_{t-2} + \ldots + \alpha_q\varepsilon_{t-q} \quad (1)$$

[540] See Brooks (2008), p. 206.
[541] See Box, Jenkins (1970). Box and Jenkins' seminal book 'Time Series Analysis: Forecasting and Control' is considered by many academics the cornerstone of modern time series analysis.
[542] See De Gooijer, Hyndman (2006), p. 447. The Box-Jenkins three-stage methodology includes the identification, estimation and verification phases. This structure of building an adequate time series model has become a frequently used approach. For our analysis, we have followed a similar method.
[543] See Chatfield (2004), p. 46.
[544] White noise terms have an expected mean of zero and constant variance. Each of the white noise terms has a stationary covariance matrix and is completely independent from previous and future white noise term. Often the term 'random walk' is used instead. See Buscher (2002), p. 143.

with ε_t being a white noise process with $E(\varepsilon_t)=0$ and $var(\varepsilon_t)=\sigma^2$.[545] MA(q) models are always stationary, as the data generation process is based exclusively on white noise observations.

In AR(p) models, the current value of Y_t is a linear combination of its p lagged values of the following type:

$$Y_t = \beta_0 + \beta_1 Y_{t-1} + \beta_2 Y_{t-2} + \ldots + \beta_p Y_{t-p} + \varepsilon_t \quad (2)$$

with $E(\varepsilon_t|Y_{t-1}, Y_{t-2}, \ldots)=0$.[546] In contrast to an MA(q) process, AR(p) processes may be non-stationary.[547]

ARMA (p,q) models are a combination of MA(q) and AR(p) models, whereby target variable Y_t is determined accordingly by a linear combination of its own p previous values (AR(p)-component) as well as q white noise innovations (MA(q)-component):[548]

$$Y_t = \beta_0 + \beta_1 Y_{t-1} + \beta_2 Y_{t-2} + \ldots + \beta_p Y_{t-p} + \ldots + \alpha_1 \varepsilon_{t-1} + \alpha_2 \varepsilon_{t-2} + \ldots + \alpha_q \varepsilon_{t-q} + \varepsilon_t \quad (3)$$

Time series models that use as input real historical data frequently face the issue of non-stationary (see also section 4.2.3, B on stationarity). In order to model a stationary ARMA-type model, therefore, it is essential to eliminate the source of non-stationarity. Should the series be non-stationary in its mean, it is possible to difference or integrate it to obtain a stationary data sequence. This model is denominated an Integrated ARMA (or ARIMA) model. Its model specifications are:[549]

$$W_t = \Delta^d Y_t = \beta_0 + \beta_1 W_{t-1} + \beta_2 W_{t-2} + \ldots + \beta_p W_{t-p} + \varepsilon_t + \alpha_1 \varepsilon_{t-1} + \alpha_2 \varepsilon_{t-2} + \ldots + \alpha_q \varepsilon_{t-q} \quad (4)$$

So far, all ARIMA models have been univariate models, in which just one dependent variable was fitted. However, it is also possible to generalise ARIMA models to compute multivariate vector time series. Such models, denominated Vector ARIMA Models or simply VARIMA, could be potentially more suitable for

545 See Buscher (2002), p. 172 et seq.
546 See Stock, Watson (2012), p. 572.
547 See Buscher (2002), pp. 205-208, for a detailed discussion on the requirements for a AR(p) process to be stationary.
548 See Brooks (2008), pp. 223-225.
549 See Chatfield (2004), p. 48.

the purposes of our analysis, as we are analysing various variables simultaneously. Additionally, VARIMA models allow for the inclusion of exogeneity and contemporaneous relationships.[550] Nonetheless, as discussed in Tsay (2002), VARIMA models can have serious identification problems that require special attention and therefore seem less appropriate for our analysis. Moreover, VAR models are sufficient for most of financial time-series modelling purposes.[551] Nonetheless, for variables that do not exhibit cointegration dynamics (VEC model) with other variables or are not dynamically related via a VAR-approach, the ARIMA(p,q) model is the adequate modelling concept and will be used in our regression analysis.

C. VAR (Vector Auto Regressive) Models

Vector autoregressions (VAR) are a special case of a VARMA model. "In essence, a VAR model is a fairly unrestricted (flexible) approximation to the reduced form of a wide variety of dynamic econometric models".[552] VAR processes are multivariate systems allowing the researcher for the inclusion of dynamic, inter-temporal features that could exist amongst the explanatory variables used in the model.[553] The structure of the VAR system includes feedback loops as the variables are enabled to impact each other, a flexibility not available in traditional structural models or ARIMA models.[554] Applying simple VARs for the modelling of returns of financial assets is a suitable technique and frequently applied in economic research.[555]

The simplest VAR specification is the bivariate case with two equations and an identical lag structure with p lags in each equation. It can be described by the following VAR (p) model:

$$Y_{1,t} = \beta_{10} + \beta_{11} Y_{1,t-1} + \ldots + \beta_{1p} Y_{1,t-p} + \phi_{11} Y_{2,t-1} + \ldots + \phi_{1p} Y_{2,t-p} + \varepsilon_{1,t}$$

$$Y_{2,t} = \beta_{20} + \beta_{21} Y_{1,t-1} + \ldots + \beta_{2p} Y_{1,t-p} + \phi_{21} Y_{2,t-1} + \ldots + \phi_{2p} Y_{2,t-p} + \varepsilon_{2,t} \quad (5)$$

---

[550] See De Gooijer, Hyndman (2006), p. 449.
[551] See Tsay (2002), pp. 322-324. To avoid the identification issue, Tsay proposes a structural specification following the suggestions of Tiao, Tsay (1989).
[552] De Gooijer, Hyndman (2006), p. 449.
[553] See Luetkepohl (2004, b), p. 86.
[554] See Enders (2010), p. 298.
[555] See Tsay (2002), p. 309.

with $\beta_{i,j}$, $\Phi_{k,l}$, i=1,2 and j=1,…,p, k=1,2 and l=1,…p as the respective coefficients of the VAR, whereas $\varepsilon_{1,t}$, $\varepsilon_{2,t}$ are the error terms of the equation system. The general, multivariate VAR can be described as a set of k different regression equations for which the regressors are the respective lagged values of all k time series.[556] As the formula for $Y_{1,t}$ states, the current value of the dependent variable will be estimated based on lagged values of the same variable, lagged values of explanatory variable $Y_{2,t}$ and a stochastic error term $\varepsilon_{1,t}$. The same logic applies to the second variable $Y_{2,t}$. Now the explanatory variable has become the dependent variable. The error terms can have a direct effect on their corresponding dependent variable (for example ε_{1t} on $Y_{1,t}$), but also an indirect impact on the second equation. As the right-hand-side of the equations in the VAR system includes exclusively predetermined variables and we have assumed that the error terms are serially uncorrelated and have a constant variance,[557] all the parameters of the VAR model can be estimated using OLS (Ordinary-Least-Squares) regression.[558]

It is debatable whether the variables of the VAR need to be stationary. While the majority of econometricians argue that the variables estimated in the VAR should indeed be stationary, there are a number of academics that disagree on this point. Sims (1980) as well as Sims et al. (1990), for example, are in favour of using non-stationary data series and not adjust for potential stochastic or deterministic trends, as in their view VAR analysis aims to determine the interrelationships among the target variables, not to calculate the parameter estimates.[559] "The common practice of attempting to transform models to stationary form by difference or cointegration operators whenever it appears likely that the data are integrated is in many cases unnecessary. … It will be often the case that the statistics of interest have distributions unaffected by the non-stationarity, in which case the hypotheses can be tested without first transforming to stationary regressors."[560] The predominant consensus view amongst ac-

556 See Stock, Watson (2012), p. 674.
557 There can be, nonetheless, correlation between the error terms of the respective equations for the same time period t (therefore between ε_{1t} and ε_{2t}).
558 See Tsay (2002), p. 314. For a more detailed discussion on the so-called 'multivariate least squares estimation' for multi-equation VAR models, see Luetkepohl (2006), pp. 70-77.
559 See Enders (2010), p. 303, quoted after Sims (1980) and Sims et al. (1990).
560 Sims et al. (1990), p. 136.

ademics remains though to use exclusively stationary time series for VAR modelling purposes.[561]

D. VEC (Vector Error Correction) Models

D.1 Definition

Should some of the explanatory variables of a VAR model be cointegrated, VEC modelling methodologies are the appropriate technique to capture the statistical properties of the data generating process. Cointegration can occur when several variables are driven by a common stochastic trend in the long run. This means, that the time series used in the model move together (for more details on cointegration, see following section D.2).[562]

The formal definition of the VEC Model with two dependent variables and p lags for each equation is:

$$\Delta Y_{1,t} = \beta_{10} + \beta_{11}\Delta Y_{1,t-1} + \ldots + \beta_{1p}\Delta Y_{1,t-p} + \phi_{11}\Delta Y_{2,t-1} + \ldots + \phi_{1p}\Delta Y_{2,t-p}$$
$$+\alpha_1(Y_{1,t-1} - \delta_1 Y_{2,t-1}) + \varepsilon_{1,t}$$

$$\Delta Y_{2,t} = \beta_{20} + \beta_{21}\Delta Y_{1,t-1} + \ldots + \beta_{2p}\Delta Y_{1,t-p} + \phi_{21}\Delta Y_{2,t-1} + \ldots + \phi_{2p}\Delta Y_{2,t-p}$$
$$+\alpha_2(Y_{1,t-1} - \delta_1 Y_{2,t-1}) + \varepsilon_{2,t} \quad (6)$$

The light-grey highlighted terms in formulas (6) are called the error correction terms.[563] These error correction terms play a crucial role when cointegration is present amongst the dependent variables. As formulas (6) describe, the current value of the target variable (for example $Y_{1,t}$) is not simply dependent on lagged values of the same variable as well as past values of the explanatory variables (here $\Delta Y_{2,t}$) in the equation system, but also on the response of $Y_{1,t}$ to the deviation from the long-run equilibrium that we assume exists between $Y_{1,t}$ and $Y_{2,t}$. This adjustment is regulated via the error correction terms. Parameters α_1 and α_2 are thereby responsible for the speed of adjustment to the long-run-equilibrium. The larger their respective values are, the faster the corresponding

---

[561] See Enders (2010), p. 303 et seq.
[562] See Luetkepohl (2004, b), p. 86 et seq.
[563] See Hill et al. (2008), p. 348.

dependent variables will react in this period to a deviation to the long-run equilibrium in the previous period.[564]

For many VEC model applications, an n-equation system will be required, as a bivariate system may be insufficient to include all the dependent (endogenous) variables of a research study. For n-equations and an equal number of p-lags, it is practical to use the matrix notation to represent the entire equation system, as will be done in our empirical analysis in section 5.3.2:[565]

$$\begin{bmatrix} \Delta Y_{1,t} \\ \Delta Y_{2,t} \\ \vdots \\ \Delta Y_{n,t} \end{bmatrix} = \begin{bmatrix} \alpha_{11} & \alpha_{12} & \alpha_{13} & \dots & \alpha_{1r} \\ \alpha_{21} & \alpha_{22} & \alpha_{23} & \cdots & \alpha_{2r} \\ \vdots & \vdots & \vdots & \cdots & \vdots \\ \alpha_{n1} & \alpha_{n2} & \alpha_{n3} & \cdots & \alpha_{nr} \end{bmatrix} * \begin{bmatrix} ecm_{1,t-1} \\ ecm_{2,t-1} \\ \vdots \\ ecm_{r,t-1} \end{bmatrix}$$

$$+ \begin{bmatrix} \phi_{11} & \phi_{12} & \phi_{13} & \dots & \phi_{1n} \\ \phi_{21} & \phi_{22} & \phi_{23} & \cdots & \phi_{2n} \\ \vdots & \vdots & \vdots & \cdots & \vdots \\ \phi_{q1} & \phi_{q2} & \phi_{q3} & \cdots & \phi_{qn} \end{bmatrix} * \begin{bmatrix} \Delta Y_{1,t-1} \\ \Delta Y_{2,t-1} \\ \vdots \\ \Delta Y_{n,t-1} \end{bmatrix} + \dots$$

$$+ \begin{bmatrix} \gamma_{11} & \gamma_{12} & \gamma_{13} & \dots & \gamma_{1n} \\ \gamma_{21} & \gamma_{22} & \gamma_{23} & \cdots & \gamma_{2n} \\ \vdots & \vdots & \vdots & \cdots & \vdots \\ \gamma_{s1} & \gamma_{s2} & \gamma_{s3} & \cdots & \gamma_{sn} \end{bmatrix} * \begin{bmatrix} \Delta Y_{1,t-p} \\ \Delta Y_{2,t-p} \\ \vdots \\ \Delta Y_{n,t-p} \end{bmatrix}$$

$$+ \begin{bmatrix} \pi_1 \\ \pi_2 \\ \vdots \\ \pi_x \end{bmatrix} + \begin{bmatrix} \psi_1 \\ \psi_2 \\ \vdots \\ \psi_y \end{bmatrix} * \begin{bmatrix} d_1 \\ d_2 \\ \vdots \\ d_y \end{bmatrix} + \begin{bmatrix} \varepsilon_{1,t} \\ \varepsilon_{2,t} \\ \vdots \\ \varepsilon_{n,t} \end{bmatrix} \quad (7)$$

and

$$ecm_{j,t-1} = Y_{j,t-1} - \sum_{\substack{k=1 \\ k \neq j}}^{n} \beta_{j,k} Y_{k,t-1} + \mu_j \quad (8)$$

where r=0,…n (max) represents the cointegration rank, $ecm_{j,t-1}$ is the j-th error correction mechanism with j=1,…r, π_x (with x=0,…,n (max)) are the constants in the short-term part of the VEC model, Ψ_y*d_y (with y=0,…,n (max)) po-

564 See Enders (2010), p. 366 et seq.
565 See Hendry, Juselius (2001), p. 79.

tential dummy data and μ_j (with j=0,...n (max)) corresponds to the constants in the cointegration equations . The error term $\varepsilon_{n,t}$ is supposed to be distributed NI $[0,\Omega_\varepsilon]$, with Ω as the positive-definite, symmetric covariance matrix of the error process.[566] The VECM in formula (7) is displayed in reduced form, as all dependent variables are regressed on lagged values. The system can also be represented in just a single equation:[567]

$$\Delta \boldsymbol{Y}_t = \boldsymbol{\Gamma}_1 \Delta \boldsymbol{Y}_{t-1} + \ldots + \boldsymbol{\Gamma}_{p-1} \Delta \boldsymbol{Y}_{t-p+1} + \boldsymbol{\Pi} \boldsymbol{Y}_{t-1} + \boldsymbol{\varepsilon}_t \quad (9)$$

with p as the number of lags, $Y_t=[Y_1, Y_2,\ldots,Y_n]'$, $\boldsymbol{\Gamma}_i=-(\mathbf{I}-\mathbf{A}_1-\ldots-\mathbf{A}_i)$, (i=1,..., p-1), $\boldsymbol{\Pi}=-(\mathbf{I}-\mathbf{A}_1-\ldots-\mathbf{A}_p)$ and A_i an nxn matrix of parameters. The $\boldsymbol{\Pi}=\boldsymbol{\alpha}\boldsymbol{\beta}'$ matrix contains the speed of adjustment $\boldsymbol{\alpha}$ as well as the long-run coefficients $\boldsymbol{\beta}$.[568] Assuming interventions have no impact on the long-run equilibrium, the VEC equation could be expanded with an additional summand $\boldsymbol{\Psi}\mathbf{D}_t$. Matrix D would include all intervention dummies the researcher deems necessary for an adequate estimation of the regression model. Furthermore, while for the VAR model we assumed that variables $Y_{1,t}$ and $Y_{2,t}$ are stationary I(0), the VEC model assumes that $Y_{1,t}$ and $Y_{2,t}$ are non-stationary I(1)[569] and cointegrated.[570]

D.2 Cointegration

Cointegration is the key concept in the VEC model. In financial and economic time series analysis, two or more data series frequently appear to have the same stochastic trend in common. This means that both series seem to share the same long-run movement. When subtracting one time series from the other results in the loss of this common trend in each series, we conclude that they both share the same trend.[571] Such series are defined to be cointegrated.[572] The concept of cointegration was initially applied in academic studies in the context of economic equilibrium theories that involved non-stationary varia-

---

566 The error terms $\varepsilon_{n,t}$ are independent, identically distributed (iid) Gaussian vectors with mean 0 and positive-definite, symmetric covariance matrix Ω. See Saikkonen, Luetkepohl (2000), p. 452.

567 Letters in bold indicate a matrix representation.

568 See Harris (1995), p. 63 and p. 81.

569 I(1): Integrated of order 1.

570 See Hill et al. (2008), p. 347 et seq. Some financial data can also be I(2), in which case it is necessary to differentiate twice to obtain a stationarity series. See Hendry, Juselius (2001), p. 76.

571 By subtracting we refer to differencing both variables and analyzing the difference for stationarity.

572 See Stock, Watson (2012), p. 691.

bles.[573] Under an economic equilibrium system, any potential deviation from the equilibrium requires that a combination of the variables be stationary, so that the departure from the long-term relationship is temporary.[574] As many statistical models and tests in empirical finance cannot be applied to data with stochastic trends, the range of financial theories that can be tested is restricted. Consequently, the formulation of the error correction model represents an important achievement in modern econometrics.[575]

Engle and Granger define the concept of cointegration in their seminal research papers published in 1987.[576] In summary, when time series vectors $Y_{t,1}$ and $Y_{2,t}$ are both I(d), then their resulting linear combination $Z_t=Y_{1,t}-\beta Y_{2,t}$ will generally also be I(d). Nevertheless, should for a particular linear combination $Z_t \sim I(d-b)$, with b>0 (i.e. with a level of integration lower than the initial order d), a constraint on the long-run elements of the joint time series Z_t occurs. The special case for which d=b=1, makes both $Y_{t,1}$ and $Y_{2,t}$ I(1) and in some circumstances the combined Z_t can be I(0) and therefore stationary. In this case, the long-run factors of both vectors $Y_{t,1}$ and $Y_{2,t}$ cancel each other out and are considered to be cointegrated of order CI (d,b). Here, the vector (1,ß) is called the co-integrating vector.[577]

Cointegration for financial variables has been analysed in numerous empirical research studies over the last 25 years and many of these analysis have been able to detect cointegrated relationships. Some of these relationships are contractually caused (for example the relationship between spot and futures prices), supported by economic theory (relation between the purchasing power

---

573 Enders (2010), p. 358 mentions three examples of such micro- and macroeconomic equilibrium theories: the consumption function theory, the unbiased forward rate hypothesis and the purchasing power parity.

574 See Enders (2010), p. 358 et seq. In the context of univariate modeling, in case of non-stationarity, the usual procedure for modeling purposes is to use first differences (if I(1)). While for such model types this is the correct approach, if the objective of the modeling exercise is to capture long term trends amongst the variables observed, such a method is not appropriate. Models using first differences have no long-run solution and will not be able to analyse the equilibrium relationship that potentially may exist. See also Brooks (2008), p. 338.

575 See Brenner, Kroner (1995), p. 23 et seq.

576 As a side note, Granger was awarded the Prize in Economic Sciences in Memory of Alfred Nobel (equivalent to the Nobel Prize in Economics) in 2003 for his achievements in the area of cointegration. See The Royal Swedish Academy of Sciences (2003).

577 See Engle, Granger (1987), p. 252 et seq. It depends on the constant β if Z_t can be I(0). Only for cointegrated vectors β will result in a combined stationary series. For some time series, no β will be computable that will make $Z_t \sim I(0)$. Another important point to consider is that two variables with different orders cannot be cointegrated. See Enders (2010), p. 360.

parity and the forward rate hypothesis) or simply driven by the dynamics of financial markets (international interest rates or share prices within an industry sector).[578]

Understanding which asset classes are cointegrated and quantifying this relationship is a powerful portfolio management tool, in particular for long-term investors like pension funds or insurance companies. From a purely portfolio risk management perspective, cointegration is an excellent indicator as to which degree assets or international markets are connected to each other in the long-run. Consequently, it should be in the interest of a portfolio manager to allocate asset classes into his portfolio that have a 'weak' cointegration relationship, as this will increase risk diversification of his basket of assets.[579] In addition, the portfolio manager can estimate with a VEC model the common stochastic trend and should the price gap of two cointegrated variables widen in the short-term, cointegration will ensure that this gap will narrow again, so that a frequent and costly rebalancing of the portfolio can be avoided.

The presence of cointegration dynamics can play an essential role in our empirical analysis. First, should cointegration be present and statistically significant using appropriate testing procedures, ignoring such relationships will lead to poor forecasting power and therefore distort the significance of our results. Second, cointegration can be an important factor for the strategic investment management of long-term investors, as it allows fund managers to better risk-manage their overall portfolio allocation.

[578] The most relevant academic studies for cointegration analysis on financial assets are: (1) Baillie, Bollerslev (1989) establish that sets or pairs of exchange rates are cointegrated, (2) Barnhardt, Szakmary (1991) find cointegrated relationships for foreign currency spot and forward rates, (3) in a similar analysis, Kroner, Sultan (1993) detect cointegration for foreign currency spot and futures rates, (4) interest rates of different maturities (Engle, Granger (1987)) and (5) interest rates in different countries (Akella, Patel (1996)) have been verified to follow a common long-term trend, (6) international equity markets (Taylor, Tonks (1989)), (7) share prices within a given industry (Cerchi, Havenner (1988)) as well as (8) dividend payments and stock prices (Campbell, Shiller (1987)) also follow a (statistically significant) cointegration behaviour. For commodities markets, on the other hand, cointegration has not been verified (see Brenner, Kroner (1995)).

[579] See Brooks (2008), p. 357.

4.2.2 Rationale for VEC Models

A. Advantages

A.1 Forecasting Precision and Economic Foundation

Despite ARMA models generating adequate forecasting results that generally outperform structural models, they lack any theoretical (economic) foundation. As a consequence, they are for example not suitable for the validation of economic theories. VEC models, on the other hand, enable researcher to benefit from the precision of ARMA forecasting results while enabling for some economic foundation, without the requirement however to have the same in-depth theoretical knowledge as may be required for structural models. For VECMs, it is sufficient to know which variables may have an impact on the dependent variable. Statistical tests will help to determine the exact relationships amongst them.[580] In addition, VEC models do not restrict the variables to be exogenous, as it is the case for ARMA models. Furthermore, VECMs are considered to be more suitable for forecasting purposes in comparison to structural models, in particular with regards to out-of-sample forecasting accuracy.[581]

A.2 Inclusion of Long-term Trends

VEC systems offer a self-correction mechanism that ensures that for cointegrated variables any deviation from the long-run equilibrium in the data generation process reverts back. Moreover, impulse-response functions can be applied to see how each variable of the equation system reacts to external shocks and recalibrates over time. For portfolio management purposes, in particular, such dynamic features make VECMs appealing.[582]

Cointegration can be used in portfolio management in particular for allocations in long-only positions and for long-term investing horizons, therefore being a suitable tool for the investment process for Pension Insurance Funds.[583] Due to the long investment horizon of occupational pension schemes, it is appropriate to base investment decisions on common long-term trends in asset prices. As such, costly portfolio rebalancing can be decreased considerably. Moreover,

---

[580] See Winker (2002), pp. 214-217.
[581] See Brooks (2008), p. 292.
[582] See Alexander (2008), p. 251.
[583] See Clare et al. (1995), p. 315 et seq.

should the pension fund track or follow a benchmark index, as it is frequently the case in pension fund management, then the investment portfolio should be cointegrated with the respective benchmark, so that in the long-run both are tied together via their cointegration relationship.[584]

A.3 Mutually Consistent Forecasts

Using a single model that is able to forecast various target variables at the same time will allow the researcher to obtain mutually consistent forecasts. The alternative approach would be to forecast each variable separately, what is cumbersome and inefficient.[585] In case of existing cointegration relationships amongst the variables, such a method would be unable to capture the dynamics implicit in the set of variables. Given that we want to analyse the existence of cointegration relationships amongst our target variables and produce consistent return forecasts, the single model methodology appears more suitable for the objectives of our research study.

A.4 Reduction in Multicollinearity

Multicollinearity, i.e. the undesirable effect that the explanatory variables in the VEC model are correlated with one another, which is frequently present in financial time series data, is considerably reduced in the error-correction form. Low multicollinearity will lead thereby to more reliable estimation results of the regression exercise.[586]

B. Concerns

B.1 Selecting Optimal Lag Structure

Due to the rather a-theoretical structure of VECMs in the context of financial (non-economic) data, theoretical concepts will frequently not provide sufficient guidance to determine the optimal lag structure of the model. The application of information criteria, in particular, will help to establish the appropriate lag length for the VEC model.[587]

[584] See Alexander (2008), p. 252.
[585] See Stock, Watson (2012), p. 674.
[586] See Juselius (2006), p. 60.
[587] See Brooks (2008), p. 293.

B.2 Inadequacy for Estimating Structural Models

VEC models have been criticised for not obtaining robust results, in particular in connection with macroeconomic variables. Early studies by Sims (1980), for example, attempted to proof macroeconomic theories with structural VEC analysis techniques. Economist back then disapproved Sims' methodology and results as his conclusions contradicted economic theory. Subsequently published research studies by King (1986) and Spencer (1989) challenged Sim's work and exposed some of the flaws in his calculations. As Todd (1990) concludes, VEC models remain an adequate technique for forecasting purposes, but have limitations when used for approving theoretical models.[588] Nonetheless, cointegration analysis remains a popular econometric technique for empirical analysis in areas in which long-run relationships have an impact on current values of target variables. Many acclaimed cointegration studies relying on economic theory have been published since Sim's criticisms.[589]

4.2.3 Identification

A. Overview

Following the Box-Jenkins method of time series analysis, the identification phase is the pre-step analysis before the estimation of a time series model can be computed. The identification phase for the VEC estimation will include unit root testing, cointegration analysis, lag length determination as well as considerations on intervention dummies. Unit root testing focuses on analysing the data we will analyse as input for the VEC model and determine whether the time series are stationary or non-stationary and may therefore require differencing or not. The cointegration test following the Johansen approach[590] will allow establishing the existence of cointegration relationships amongst the assets included in the portfolio. For the estimation of the VEC model, we have to determine an adequate lag length. We will therefore present information criteria methodologies that will facilitate an appropriate lag length selection. Additionally, we will assess the inclusion of intervention dummies.

---

588 See Todd (1990), pp. 19-21.

589 See The Royal Swedish Academy of Sciences (2003), p. 9 et seq. Acclaimed research studies using cointegration analysis and that are based on economic theory include: Cochrane (1994) and Lettau, Ludvigson (2001) on the predictability of stock returns, Johansen, Juselius (1990) on money demand analysis, Hall et al. (1992) and Culver, Papell (1999) on tests on the interest rate term structure.

590 See Johansen (1988).

B. Stationarity and Unit Root Tests

B.1 Definition

A time series is weakly stationary if it has a constant mean, constant variance and auto-covariance matrix. The stationarity condition therefore implies that the probability distribution of a time series Y_t remains unchanged over time if the joint distribution of (Y_{s+1}, Y_{s+2}, Y_{s+T}) are independent of both s and T.[591] Shocks to stationary time series data are by definition temporary, so that over time any shock will vanish and the underlying series will revert back to its long-run average. Non-stationary data (also denominated unit roots), on the other hand, will include permanent shock components so that mean and/or variance will become time-dependent. Non-stationarity will ultimately lead to time series with no long-run mean to which the data will revert back and variance levels that will increase in time.[592] Ignoring unit roots can cause several problems in our analysis. First, including non-stationary data in an econometric model may lead to spurious regression, i.e. regression results that suggest the existence of a statistically significant relationship amongst the variables, even though these links may be just contemporaneous correlation effects rather than proper economic causal relationships.[593] Second, usual OLS t-statistics may have non-normal distributions under the null hypothesis, with the result that standard hypothesis testing is not valid anymore.[594]

The common approach in time series analysis to eliminate non-stationarity in the underlying time series data is differencing (for stochastic trends) and detrending (for trend-stationary processes). It is critical to determine precisely which method to apply to which data series. While the Box-Jenkins method recommends differencing for non-stationary data, for long-term time horizons the existence of a trend and its precise form becomes relevant. The definition of stationarity implies the absence of a trend and long-run mean reversion, while the presence of a deterministic trend will lead to steady increases or decreases

591 See Stock, Watson (2012), p. 578.
592 See Asteriou, Hall (2007), p. 288.
593 See Harris, Sollis (2003), p. 26.
594 See Stock, Watson (2012), p. 591 et seq.

in the future. Forecasts with a stochastic trend, on the other hand, move towards a steady level.[595]

Fortunately for the purpose of our empirical analysis, the majority of financial time series that have unit roots are of the type I(1), so that differencing once results in an I(0) stationary series.[596] Nonetheless, the possibility of unit roots in financial data requires an adequate set of reliable testing techniques to detect non-stationarity.

B.2 Augmented Dickey-Fuller Test (ADF-Test)

The econometricians Dickey and Fuller were the first to define a formal procedure that allows determining the existence of stationarity in a time series, the so-called augmented Dickey-Fuller (ADF) unit root test.[597] The ADF test assumes as null hypothesis H_0 that the underlying time series is non-stationary (i.e. has a unit root). Dickey and Fuller provide the critical values for this test, as the usual t-statistics for OLS regressions do not apply in this case.[598] In essence, the ADF test is based on a simple autoregression with/without a constant and with/without a trend. The corresponding regression equations would be:

$$
\begin{aligned}
Y_t &= \rho Y_{t-1} + \varepsilon_t \\
Y_t &= \mu + \rho Y_{t-1} + \varepsilon_t \\
Y_t &= \mu + \beta t + \rho Y_{t-1} + \varepsilon_t \quad (10)
\end{aligned}
$$

with H_0: $\rho=1$.[599] In case the null hypothesis is rejected, you assume that the underlying time series has no unit root.[600]

B.3 Philipps-Perron Test (PP-Test)

The main limitation of the ADF is its assumption that the error terms ε_t in the regression equations are independent and have constant variance. Phillips and Perron developed a testing methodology that is based on a less strict supposi-

---

[595] See Enders (2010), p. 257.
[596] See Brooks (2008), p. 323.
[597] See Dickey, Fuller (1979).
[598] See Kugler (2002), p. 267. The majority of software packages use actually the critical values calculated by MacKinnon (1991).
[599] See Dickey, Fuller (1979), p. 427 et seq.
[600] Strictly speaking the test result of 'no unit root' does not imply that the data is stationary, merely that there is not sufficient statistical evidence for accepting a unit root.

tion on the error terms (in particular by allowing autocorrelation), as for many financial data series, the ADF assumptions impose strong limitations that distort test results. The PP-test, nonetheless, remains a modification of the ADF test, so that H_0 assumes again non-stationarity.[601] More importantly, the PP-test appears to have better power properties than asymptotically equivalent unit root tests for many different time series specifications.[602]

B.4 Kwiatkowski-Philipps-Schmidt-Shin Test (KPSS-Test)

The publication of numerous empirical studies suggesting standard unit root tests fail frequently to reject the null hypothesis of a unit root led to the development of the KPSS-test. This test is intended to complement the ADF and PP unit root tests. The KPSS-test is considered a stationarity test that assumes under the null hypothesis stationarity of the underlying time series, therefore reverting the testing hypothesis of the standard unit root tests.[603] The rationale behind the KPSS-test is that in the standard unit root tests (ADF, PP), the null is accepted unless there is sufficient statistical evidence against it. However, should the data not be very informative about the existence of a unit root or the power of the test low, standard unit root test will wrongly assume non-stationarity.[604]

For our modelling purposes, we will apply all three tests procedures in our empirical analysis to ensure that our conclusions with respect to (non-) stationarity of our financial time series data are correct and robust from a statistical standpoint.

C. Johansen's Cointegration Test

C.1 Definition

In academic literature, there are primarily three approaches to determine the existence of cointegration dynamics amongst time series: (1) Economic theory and expert knowledge, (2) visualising time series to detect common trends and

---

601 See Asteriou, Hall (2007), p. 298 et seq.

602 See Phillips, Perron (1988), p. 345.

603 See Kwiatkowski et al. (1992), p. 160 and p. 176 for a detailed explanation on the testing methodology of the KPSS-test.

604 See DeJong et al. (1992), p. 423 et seq. This research paper suggests traditional Dickey-Fuller tests have low power in detecting stationary AR processes that have roots close to 1.

(3) using statistical tests.[605] Within the statistical tests available to detect cointegration, the Engle-Granger approach for single equations and the Johansen methodology for multivariate systems are amongst the most popular techniques in financial econometrics.[606] Due to the multivariate character of our research study, we will focus primarily on the Johansen approach, although we will compute the Engle-Granger test statistics to counter-check the results obtained via the Johansen method.

In comparison to the Engle-Granger method, which relies on ordinary-least-squares regression, the Johansen approach assumes Gaussian error terms. This will allow us to use maximum likelihood estimates (MLE). While presenting all the technical details of Johansen's procedure is beyond the scope of this research study, it is important to understand the main concept of the technique.[607] In essence, returning to our previous VEC representation,

$$\Delta \boldsymbol{Y}_t = \boldsymbol{\Gamma}_1 \Delta \boldsymbol{Y}_{t-1} + \ldots + \boldsymbol{\Gamma}_{p-1} \Delta \boldsymbol{Y}_{t-p+1} + \boldsymbol{\Pi} \boldsymbol{Y}_{t-1} + \boldsymbol{\varepsilon}_t \quad (11)$$

with $\boldsymbol{\Pi}=\boldsymbol{\alpha\beta}'$. If we assume that vector $\mathbf{Y}_t$ is I(1) (non-stationary) and all terms in the equation that involve $\Delta\mathbf{Y}_{t-i}$ are I(0), for $\boldsymbol{\varepsilon}_t$ to be I(0), $\boldsymbol{\Pi}\mathbf{Y}_{t-1}$ must also be stationary. There are three scenarios that can occur for the condition $\boldsymbol{\Pi}\mathbf{Y}_{t-p}$~I(0) to be met. The relevant one for us is when there are (n-1) cointegration relationships so that $\boldsymbol{\beta}'\mathbf{Y}_{t-1}$ is also stationary. There could be r<=(n-1) cointegration vectors and (n-r) non-stationary vectors in $\boldsymbol{\beta}$**.** Only the cointegration vectors will be included in $\boldsymbol{\beta}$ to ensure that $\boldsymbol{\Pi}\mathbf{Y}_{t-1}$ is stationary, what suggests that the last (n-r) columns of vector $\boldsymbol{\alpha}$ in $\boldsymbol{\Pi}=\boldsymbol{\alpha\beta}'$ are effectively zero. Testing for cointegration relationships therefore comes down to finding the number of linearly independent columns in matrix $\boldsymbol{\Pi}$ or, what is equivalent, determine the rank of $\boldsymbol{\Pi}$. For a reduced rank of $\boldsymbol{\Pi}$, there will be r<=(n-1) cointegration vectors. The Johansen method enables to obtain estimates for $\boldsymbol{\alpha}$ as well as $\boldsymbol{\beta}$ using a technique called reduced rank regression.[608] The cointegration procedure leads to two test statis-

---

[605] See Stock, Watson (2012), pp. 693-695.

[606] A third estimator is the dynamic OLS (DOLS) estimator developed by Stock, Watson (1993), which is popular particularly in US research studies.

[607] See Johansen (1988) for the original research paper on the Johansen procedure.

[608] See Harris (1995) pp. 77-79. For similar explanations on the Johansen procedure, see also Luetkepohl (2004, b), pp. 112-116.

tics, the trace test and the maximum eigenvalue test.[609] Which test is superior is an open debate in academia. Independently we will compute both statistics and in case of contradicting outcomes apply our own judgement.

C.2 Limitations

The Johansen procedure has become a very popular method and has been applied in many empirical studies to test the presence of cointegration in economic theories. Nonetheless, we acknowledge that the method relies on strong assumptions that can cause issues when estimating the correct cointegration rank of a VEC system. First, the procedure depends on the assumption of independent and Gaussian (iid) distributed residuals.[610] For regressions where this condition for the error terms is not given, the power of the Johansen procedure is distorted so that more often it will reject the null hypothesis of no cointegration (therefore wrongly concluding that cointegration relationships exist).[611] Second, for time series that under the standard unit root tests are considered I(1) but in reality depart from this assumption without the testing procedure being able to capture it, the corresponding cointegration test using Johansen's method will result in spurious regressions.[612]

Research findings, nonetheless, have provided empirical evidence that for forecasting purposes using VEC models, even incorrectly assuming cointegration relationships will produce good forecasting results, in particular for long time periods. Forecasting errors of VECMs are lower by up to 20% in comparison to a VAR or BVAR (Bayesian VAR) models.[613] Even erroneously imposing unit roots on a VECM yields better forecasting results than regression models that do not enforce unit roots.[614]

D. Lag Structure

An important element of any VEC estimation is to determine the adequate lag-length for the regression analysis. The general problem with the estimation

---

[609] See Maddala, Kim (1998), p. 211.
[610] We acknowledge that this is an assumption that in practice may not hold.
[611] See Huang, Yang (1996), p. 970 et seq. Nonetheless, the empirical analysis also shows that the erroneous rejection probability decreases with the number of lags used in the regression. For lag length >5, more satisfactory and robust results are obtained.
[612] See Gonzalo, Lee (1998), p. 149.
[613] See LeSage (1990), p. 671.
[614] See Maddala, Kim (1998), p. 187, quoted after Ohanian (1990).

of the lag structure is that too few lags will diminish forecast accuracy as the VEC model may not capture relevant information adequately, whereas adding too many lags will increase the estimation uncertainty and reduce the degrees of freedom ('overfitting'). As a consequence, the benefits of including additional lags must be counterbalanced against the costs of running more estimations and increasing both regression uncertainty and estimation imprecisions.[615] For VECMs, it is standard to use initially the same lag length for all equations, as this preserves the symmetry of the system and allows applying OLS estimation techniques efficiently. Once we complete the optimization of the overall VEC lag structure, however, we will obtain unequal lag lengths amongst the different equations so that the SUR (Seemingly Unrelated Regressions) methodology for parameter estimation will be applied (see also section 4.2.4,C).

The initial lag length will be fixed using the recommendation by Saikkonen, Luetkepohl (1996) or Mills (1998) for initiating the estimation process with $T^{1/3}$ as maximum lag length for the unrestricted VAR on price levels, with T as the maximum number of periods of the underlying time series data. Subsequently we will apply an information criterion to refine the length that is adequate for the regression process.[616]

For the purpose of determining the VEC structure of our analysis, we will use the AIC information criterion defined by Akaike (1976)[617], as it asymptotically overestimates the order of the model, whereas the alternative methods, HQ (Hannan-Quinn) and SC (Schwartz), tend to underestimate the true order.[618] We generally have a preference for a longer lag length structure as it allows us to better capture the dynamics of the underlying data. Besides, as Luetkepohl (2006) suggests, for moderate samples sizes, the AIC may provide superior results in terms of forecasting precision.[619]

---

615 See Stock, Watson (2012), p. 587.

616 See Saikkonen, Luetkepohl (1996), p. 819 or Mills (1998), p. 5. Philips applies in his simulation studies the BIC and PIC (posterior information criterion) information criteria. See Philips (1998), p. 30.

617 See Akaike (1976) for the original findings on this information criterion.

618 See Luetkepohl (2004, b), p. 111 et seq. and Winker (2000), p. 90 et seq., on a more detailed comparison amongst the three information criteria. For the original papers on these information criteria, see Hannan, Quinn (1979) and Schwarz (1978).

619 See Luetkepohl (2006), p. 156 et seq.

E. Intervention Dummies and Structural Breaks

E.1 Structural Breaks

Applied time series analysis is based on the concept of stationary, i.e. that parameters like the mean, variance and autocovariance of a time series remain constant over time.[620] In reality, however, this assumption may not always hold, as structural breaks or extreme one-off events to the data-generating process can be frequently observed.[621] Examples of such occurrences in recent times are for example the impact on financial markets by the oil price shock in 1973, events such as the 9/11 attacks in the US, the Lehman bank collapse in 2008 or the effects of the sovereign debt crisis in Europe since 2009. Regression models that do not consider such events (breaks) may produce misleading inferences and forecasts. Breaks can occur unexpectedly and suddenly (also called 'distinct changes') or evolve over time ('slow evolution').[622]

It is essential for our analysis that we are able to detect any potential structural break in the data series and adjust our estimation models accordingly. We will apply primarily the recursive CUSUM test developed by Brown et al. (1975). In their research study, the researchers present a testing procedure that analyses the constancy of regression relationships. Only under the validity of constant parameters an econometrical model should be used for forecasting purposes.[623]

E.2 Intervention Dummies

As the ordinary-least-squared (OLS) regression technique is based on squared deviations, any extreme event will have a significant impact on the estimators, in particular if the sampling universe is not large. Academics have elaborated a range of methodologies that will facilitate better regression results when outliers are present.[624] The inclusion of intervention dummies is hereby a commonly used methodology to handle extreme events.[625] In general, any ex-

---

620 See Hansen (2001), p. 117.
621 See Enders (2010), p. 103 et seq.
622 See Stock, Watson (2012), p. 598 et seq.
623 See Brown et al. (1975).
624 See Greene (2012), pp. 139-142. Doornik et al. (1998), p. 550, state that intervention dummies could either be ignored, entered unrestrictedly in the VEC model, restricted to the cointegration space only or included as a mixture of both.
625 For the purpose of our research study, intervention dummies are 0 everywhere except for the date of the extreme event, for which they will take the value 1.

treme one-off event should be eliminated from the regression as its inclusion prevents from estimating a stable and robust model.[626]

Apart from obvious extreme political or economic extreme events, many researchers advise to include dummies for those data points, for which the corresponding standardized residuals of the regression are larger than a pre-specified tolerance level.[627] The aim of such an intervention is to enforce normal residuals in the regression model.[628] We will apply the same logic to our models in case of extreme events or large outliers. An important consideration in this context is that intervention dummies do not impact the properties of the likelihood ratio tests for cointegration and therefore will not distortion our conclusions with respect to the number of cointegration relationships.[629]

4.2.4 Estimation

A. Model Reduction Techniques: Sequential Elimination Method (SER)

Once the cointegration relationships have been determined using the Johansen methodology and the adequate number of lags for the regression model chosen, the parameters of the VEC equations will be efficiently estimated using the ordinary least squares (OLS) method.[630] Following this procedure will lead to equations that have the same number of lagged values. It is however unavoidable to have insignificant regressors in the estimated model, so that some form of optimization or model reduction technique should be considered to obtain a more parsimonious and efficient regression and no degrees of freedom are wasted.

[626] See the VEC model example in Greene (2012), p. 1004. Greene uses several intervention dummies to single out the currency crisis in September 1992. Beyer (1998), p. 59, uses intervention dummies to eliminate exceptional movements in interest rates due to inflationary expectations after the reunification of the Federal Republic of Germany with the German Democratic Republic in 1989. Luetkepohl (2004, b), p. 117 also uses a 0/1-type intervention dummy to remove the impact on economic and financial data by the events linked to the German reunification.

[627] See Luetkepohl (2004, b), p. 76. Luetkepohl recommends to eliminate outliers for which the standardized residual is larger than |3|. Hendry, Juselius (2001), p. 85, apply the same approach. In Juselius, MacDonald, (2004), p. 23, the authors suggest as threshold level of |3.3| the standardized residual if the outlier corresponds to a known event.

[628] See Harris, Sollis (2003), p. 167.

[629] See Luetkepohl (2006), p. 335, Nielsen (2004), p. 249 or Juselius (2006), p. 139.

[630] See Rao (2007), p. 73 et seq., Harris, Sollis (2003), p. 173 et seq. or Harris (1995), p. 134.

Econometricians have developed different approaches for how to effectively realise such a model reduction. Brueggemann (2006) and Brueggemann et al. (2002) propose a Sequential Elimination of Regressors (SER) process whereby variables that have a t-value smaller than a predefined threshold value will be sequentially deleted. They determine the threshold value based on the sample size of the VECM, the reduction step realised as well as the information criterion used.[631] Bonham et al.'s (2009) model applies a simpler method by just deleting those parameters from the VEC that have a t-value of less than 2, starting from the smallest number.[632] We will follow the SER methodology presented in Luetkepohl (2006) as it is the more sophisticated approach and provides a well-defined set of process steps.

In a first step, an appropriate information criterion needs to be selected. Luetkepohl proposes a calculation method that includes either AIC, HQ or SC information criteria.[633] The elimination strategy presented is based on a sequential elimination of regressors that have t-values lower than a given threshold value λ. Once a regressor is excluded from an equation, new t-ratios are calculated for the reduced model.[634] This process is repeated until all respective t-statistics are significant. The value for λ is defined as:

$$\lambda = \left\{ \left[\exp\left(\frac{c_T}{T} \right) - 1 \right] \left[T - N + j - 1 \right] \right\}^{\frac{1}{2}}$$
$$c_T(AIC) = 2$$
$$c_T(HQ) = 2 \ln \ln T$$
$$c_T(SC) = \ln T \quad (12)$$

with j as the j-th step in the elimination process, T as the sample size and N as the total number of regressors.[635]

C. SUR (Seemingly Unrelated Regression)

The sequential elimination procedure will lead to individual equations with an unequal lag length structure, so that the VEC system cannot be estimated any-

---

[631] See Brueggemann (2006), p. 421 or Brueggemann et al. (2002), p. 3.
[632] See Bonham et al. (2009), p. 541.
[633] For cointegration purposes, we will apply the AIC information criterion in our analysis.
[634] This procedure is realised on individual equations of the initially estimated VEC. The estimation of these single equations occurs via OLS.
[635] See Luetkepohl (2006), p. 211 et seq. and p. 344.

more using OLS estimation. In such instances, the Seemingly Unrelated Regression (SUR) technique provides efficient estimates of the coefficients.[636] While each equation is a classical regression and could therefore be estimated by OLS, the SUR methodology applies the Generalized Least Squares (GLS) estimator, which is a more efficient estimator than OLS. In the GLS, the equations of the VEC are linked purely by their disturbances only.[637]

As stated by Zellner, who published the SUR methodology in 1962, the efficiency will be larger (1) if the variables in the different equations are not highly correlated and (2) if the respective disturbance terms in the different equations are highly correlated.[638] These conclusions also hold for finite moderate sample sizes.[639] In this context, Binkley (1982) demonstrates that the efficiency gain by using SUR versus OLS depends not only on the correlation of variables across equations, but also on the multicollinearity within equations. The higher the multicollinearity amongst the variables of the same equation, the higher will be the efficiency gain by applying SUR estimators. "It is reasonable to expect that, given a level of interequation correlation, the likelihood that it will reflect existing multicollinearity among the variables within an equation will be greater the greater is the already existing multicollinearity."[640] The efficiency gain of GLS estimator versus OLS will be considerably reduced or even entirely eliminated if the variance-covariance matrix of the residuals is diagonal.[641] Moreover, if the individual equations have identical explanatory variables or the regressors in one set of equations are a subset of those in another, then GLS is equal to OLS.[642]

4.2.5 Diagnostic Checking

A. Rationale

To ensure that an estimated regression fulfils the underlying theoretical model assumptions, a range of diagnostic tests for the residuals is commonly con-

[636] See Enders (2010), p. 315 and p. 375.
[637] See Greene (2012), pp. 333-335.
[638] See Zellner (1962), p. 348. In Zellner's empirical example, the gain in efficiency versus equation-by-equation application of least-squares is up to 20% in smaller coefficient estimator variance. See Zellner (1962), p. 363.
[639] See Zellner (1963), p. 988.
[640] Binkley (1982), p. 894.
[641] See Kennedy (2003), p. 198.
[642] See Greene (2012), p. 334.

sidered: tests for residual autocorrelation, multivariate tests for non-normality as well as conditional heteroskedasticity checks.[643] In addition, we will also assess the suitability of the model in terms of forecasting accuracy, as this is a good indication of how appropriate the final model will be for simulation purposes.

B. Normality Tests

Normality tests for the regression residuals are an important element of any diagnostic checking. In case non-normality should be detected, this could be caused by an initial model misspecification. Nonetheless, as stated in Enders (2010), "much of the asymptotic theory in which inference in dynamic models is based, strictly speaking, works also for certain non-normal residual distributions".[644]

The most common normality test is the Jarque-Bera (JB) test, developed by Jarque, Bera (1987), which is based on preliminary findings by Lomnicki (1961). In essence, the JB test focuses on the departure from normality due to skewness and excess kurtosis, the third and fourth moment of a distribution.[645] This test statistic is simple to compute, as it requires only the first four moments of the regression residuals. The measurement is asymptotically distributed as a Chi-squared distribution, with 2 degrees of freedom.[646]

C. Autocorrelation

The Ljung-Box Q-statistics (1978) examines the overall significance of the residual autocorrelation up to a certain lag length m. It can be applied to single equations as well as to multivariate models (also called Portmanteau test). For our purposes, we will compute both the Portmanteau as well as the Adjusted Portmanteau statistics for the multivariate case, whereas for the single equations, we will apply the univariate Q-statistics and additionally the Breusch-Godfrey Serial Correlation LM test.

C.1 Ljung-Box Q-Statistic

The Q-statistic is based on the first m autocorrelations of the residuals from a fitted VEC model. The residual autocorrelation is defined as

---

[643] See Luetkepohl (2004, b), p. 125 and p. 144.
[644] Enders (2010), p. 46.
[645] See Lomnicki (1961), p. 37.
[646] See Jarque, Bera (1987), p. 167. The detailed test statistic is represented on p. 167.

$$r_k = \frac{\sum_{t=k+1}^{T} \hat{\varepsilon}_t \hat{\varepsilon}_{t-1}}{\sum_{t=1}^{T} \hat{\varepsilon}_t^2} \quad (13)$$

with k=(1,2,...,T-1), and is subsequently used in the test statistic

$$Q_m = T(T+2)\sum_{k=1}^{m} \frac{r_k^2}{(T-k)} \quad (14)$$

with T as the number of observations. For large T, the test statistic would be distributed as a Chi-squared distribution with m degrees of freedom.[647] While initially the authors suggest values for m in the range of 20-30, in a later study they demonstrate that Q_m could actually be improved by using lower values for m, so that we feel confident that m=12 for our analysis is an adequate figure.[648]

C.2 Breusch-Godfrey Serial Correlation LM Test

The Breusch-Godfrey LM test is appropriate for testing low order residual autocorrelation, whereas the Q-statistic is in comparison more suitable for longer lag lengths. Applying both tests for the same VEC model allows therefore a more accurate detection of potential autocorrelation effects and consequently reduces any misspecification of the underlying regression model. We will apply the LM test for our research study using 1, 2 and 4 lags for single equations.

The LM method as defined by Breusch and Godfrey is obtained by fitting an AR(h) model to the residuals of the original regression. The test assesses whether the h-th order residual autocorrelations of a regression equation follow the model:

$$r_t = B_1 r_{t-1} + \ldots + B_h r_{t-h} + error_t \quad (15)$$

[647] See Ljung, Box (1978), p. 297 et seq.
[648] See Ljung (1986), pp. 727-729. For details on the multivariate version of this test statistic, see Ahn (1988), p. 592.

and are tested against the null hypothesis $H_0=B_1=\ldots=B_h=0$. The respective LM test statistic follows a Chi-squared (h) distribution if no autocorrelation is present.[649]

D. Heteroskedasticity

Engle developed a powerful testing procedure to examine whether the resid uals of a linear regression follow an ARCH process or are Gaussian distributed. ARCH-type processes are thereby defined as zero mean, serially uncorrelated processes with non-constant variances conditional on the past. As Engel proofs, for regression models with varying residual variances, ARCH models can improve the performance of least square estimators and obtain more realistic forecast variances.[650]

The ARCH test statistic is Chi-squared distributed with q degrees of freedom (with q as the number of lags) and has as null hypothesis that there is no conditional heteroskedasticity present.[651] An important aspect for the objectives of our research study is that ARCH effects in the residuals do usually not produce biased inference, even though they may affect our estimation efficiency. The potential presence of ARCH effects in some of our equations of the fitted VECMs will be analysed thoroughly and appropriate adjustments may be necessary. For only weak ARCH effects, nonetheless, no particular adjustments will be required.[652]

E. Forecasting Precision

E.1 Overview

A regression model that has been fitted adequately and therefore is able to capture the underlying data generating process should also generate satisfactory forecasts.

Numerous research studies have compared different time-series models with respect to their forecasting accuracy. The main conclusion is that VECMs con-

---

[649] See Luetkepohl (2004, a), p. 44 et seq. quoted after Breusch (1978) and Godfrey (1978), (1988). In Luetkepohl (2004, a), p.47, a similar lag structure to ours has been applied for a VEC model example.

[650] See Engle (1982), p. 987 and p. 1004.

[651] See Brooks (2008), pp. 389-392 for more details on the test for ARCH-effects.

[652] See Juselius, MacDonald (2004), p. 25, Luetkepohl (2004, b), p.131 or Juselius (2006), p. 47.

sistently outperform other time series methods. In general, however, all models included in the studies achieve satisfactory results. Brooks et al. (2001), for example, compares VECMs to ARMA and VAR models. The forecasting exercise is realised by applying out-of-sample forecasting techniques. The forecasting results are compared using Root-Mean Squared Errors (RMSE), Mean Absolute Errors (MAE) as well as Percentage of Correct Direction Predictions. The results indicate that VECMs perform better than VARs and ARMA models in terms of forecasting precision.[653] A similar structured, recent study conducted by Rajagura, Pattnayak (2007) draws the same conclusions.[654]

Moreover, recent research studies have verified that overly parsimonious time-series models obtain in general considerably better forecasting results than complex, large models, which may be more consistent with the actual data-generating process (issue of 'overfitting'). Research studies by Clark, West (2007), in particular, as well as Dimitrios, Guerard (2004) and Liu, Enders (2003) show that out-of-sample forecasts of simple time-series models very often outperform forecast results of more complex methods.[655]

E.2. Static Forecasts (One-step Ahead Predictions)

Static forecasts are computed to obtain one-step ahead forecasts ('in-of-sample') over the historical data with the objective to assess the historical fit of the model. A static approach can therefore not be applied to forecast more than one observation into the future. To realize static predictions, "values of the endogenous variables up to the previous period are used each time the model is solved. Lagged endogenous variables and ARMA terms in the model are based on actual values of the endogenous variables".[656] The graphical depiction of static forecasts is an indicator of the strength of the model in predicting one-step ahead predictions.[657]

E.3 Correct Sign Predictions

We will also assess the accuracy of forecasting power of our fitted VEC models by computing the correct sign prediction of the change of the dependent

---

[653] See Brooks et al. (2001), p. 40.
[654] See Rajaguru, Pattnayak (2007), p. 81.
[655] See Enders (2010), p. 85, quoted after Clark, West (2007), Dimitrios, Guerard (2004) and Lui, Enders (2003).
[656] Quantitative Micro Software (2007), p. 441.
[657] See Quantitative Micro Software (2007), p. 441.

variable. This test is particularly suitable when the underlying probability distribution refers to large, non-linear dynamic econometric models.[658] The corresponding formula for the forecasting indicator is:

$$Correct\ \ Sign\ \ Predictions\ \ (\%) = \frac{1}{T - T_1} \sum_{t=T_1}^{T} z_{t+n} \quad (16)$$

with $z_{n+1}>1$ if $(x_{t+n}*f_{t,n})>0$ and $z_{n+1}=0$ otherwise. X_{t+n} is hereby the actual return in period t+n, $f_{t,n}$ is the forecast in period t for period n, T is the number of observations and T_1 represent the observations not included in the overall calculation. As the formula indicates, the prediction is irrespective of the magnitude of the change.[659] As input data, we will use the continuously compounded returns estimated in our VEC model.

4.2.6 Conclusions

Stochastic time series models offer a powerful tool to capture the underlying data generation process of either a single equation or a multivariate system. For cointegrated variables, we will apply the VEC methodology, as it is a particularly suitable method to capture both short- and long-term dynamics. For pension fund managers, especially, cointegration relationships can be a useful portfolio management tool.

The Johansen procedure will allow us to detect cointegration relationships, whereas the VEC regression, combined with the optimization procedure to obtain more efficient parameter estimators and the application of the SUR regression technique, will ensure that we get a well-fitted, parsimonious regression model. The analysis of the regression residuals as well as forecasting precision will be essential tools to test the quality and suitability of the estimated stochastic model.

Once we have captured the data generating process of our underlying time series data, we will run in section 4.3 bootstrap simulations that will generate stochastic return distributions for our 3-year observation period.

---

658 See Pesaran, Timmermann (1992), p. 461. The details for a simple example on this test can be found on p. 461 et seq.

659 See Brooks (1997), p. 127 and p. 134.

4.3 Bootstrap Simulation

4.3.1 Definition

When a suitable VEC model is estimated that describes the data generating process of the underlying data, we will use bootstrap simulations to generate future return paths of the target assets included in our portfolios.

The bootstrap technique has been in use for many years in econometric research studies. The method was first introduced by Efron in 1979 and is nowadays a common procedure for simulation exercises. In its basic form, the objective of the bootstrap technique is to estimate the sampling distribution of a specified random variable R (X, F), which depends on X as well as the unknown distribution for F, on the basis of the available data points of x.[660] The principal concept is to resample the original observations "to construct "pseudo-data" on which the estimator of interest is exercised. More specifically, the theoretical distribution of an unobservable disturbance term is approximated by the empirical distribution of an observable set of residuals."[661] The bootstrap system consequently permits to replace the unknown distribution of a target variable by the empirical distribution we obtain through the resampling process.[662] Initially, the bootstrap methodology as introduced by Efron was applied to econometric models that assumed iid (independent and identically distributed) random variables, even though later on its applicability was extended to include regressions, AR(p) and multiequation models.[663]

The step-by-step process of a bootstrap simulation can be summarised as follows:[664]

(1) Fit the data generating process with an adequate econometric model (in our case the VEC model) and estimate its parameters. Maintain these parameters fixed at their estimated values.

(2) The fundamental idea is that the residuals of the regression (VEC) are subsequently used for resampling purposes. An important condition is

660 See Efron (1979), p. 2.
661 Freedman, Peters (1981), p. 150.
662 See Holbert, Son (1986), p. 3670.
663 See Thombs, Schucany (1990), p. 486.
664 See Freedman, Peters (1981), p. 151.

that their stochastic structure will be preserved. This also implies that the econometric model chosen will be tested against its own initial assumptions.

(3) When running the simulation, new errors will be added randomly to the econometric model with fixed parameters. These errors are thereby drawn from the residuals obtained in the first place when the regression was estimated.

(4) This resampling process will generate new data that enables us to obtain the estimator of interest (in our case future return distributions of the target variables in the VEC).

An important aspect of this form of simulation is the high frequency of resampling that is required to get an adequate distribution of potential values. Apart from computational capacity needed to run multiple repetitions, a researcher will also be interested in how many data points are necessary to sufficiently replicate the target variable. While the answer will obviously depend on the objective of the respective study, there are some indications in academic literature that may help us in choosing a satisfactory number for our analysis. For estimating standard errors, for example, up to 100 replications seem sufficient, whereas for setting bootstrap confidence intervals, at least 1,000 repetitions should be computed.[665] In Schroeder (2010), in which future return paths for financial data are simulated, 10,000 data points per quarter and asset class are simulated.[666]

4.3.2 Rationale

The rationale for using the bootstrap simulation for our research study is manifold. First, bootstrap simulation permits concluding inferences without making strong assumptions about the distribution of the target variable, as the distribution employed in the simulation is that of the actual underlying data. In effect, bootstrapping assumes that the sample data is treated as the actual population from which the samples are drawn.[667] Also, bootstrap techniques are the appropriate methodology when finite sample theory is problematic to derive, or,

---

665 See Efron, Tibshirani (1986), p. 72, Hatemi-j, Shukur (1999), p. 642 or Greene (2012), p. 654.

666 See Schroeder (2010), p. 87.

667 See Brooks (2008), p. 553 et seq.

as it is the case for time series analysis, only asymptotic theory is obtainable.[668] In time series models, the error terms may exhibit some conditional heteroskedasticity. For monthly financial data, in particular, this is a frequent issue. In such instances, simply resampling residuals would be inappropriate, as that would eliminate the dependency structure. Bootstrap simulations, nonetheless, enable to maintain the dependency by resampling the entire vector with all residuals estimated in time t.[669] This will become relevant for our study in the context of multiequation models, as we will attempt to maintain the correlation structure unchanged amongst the different equations of the VEC model. Furthermore, the distribution of the errors can easily be computed or programmed using the Monte-Carlo simulation method by simply repeating the procedure a large number of times.[670]

4.3.3 Implementation

Taking into consideration the objectives of our simulation study, we will run our bootstrap process with 10,000 repetitions per month and asset class, following the resampling with replacement method.[671] As we are running a multi-equation VEC model, we have to ensure that the correlation structure amongst the error terms of the respective endogenous variables remains complete. To achieve that, we will ensure that the resampling with replacement process maintains the error vector $\boldsymbol{\varepsilon}_t$ for a given time period t intact.[672] Moreover, as the results for the estimated VEC will demonstrate in section 5.3.3,B the autocorrelation of each error term with its previous realizations will be negligible, so that resampling repeatedly will not lead to any forecasting errors due to dependency.[673] Figure 38 summarises the details of our bootstrapping procedure.

668 See Souza, Neto (1996), p. 344.
669 See Freedman (1981), p. 1220.
670 See Freedman, Peters (1981), p. 152.
671 We follow here the recommendations from Schroeder (2010), p. 86 et seq. in which a similar bootstrap simulation process is described for a VEC model in connection with financial data. Also Elton et al. (2011), pp. 268-270, follow an analogous methodology for an ARMA-style time series model.
672 This procedure is also called 'block bootstrap sampling'. See Greene (2012), p. 654.
673 See Eling, Parnitzke (2007), p. 43.

Figure 38: Bootstrap Simulation Process

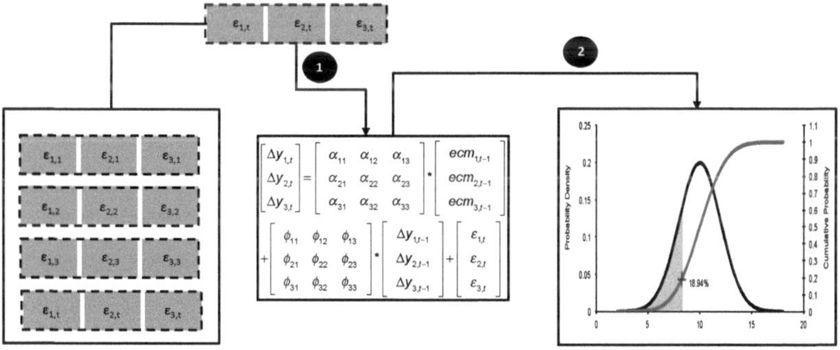

Source: Own figure, for illustrative purposes only. Neither the VEC model nor the distribution chart is related to the actual data of our empirical study.

As the figure illustrates, once we have estimated the VEC model based on historical data, we will use the residuals of the regression as our resampling universe. For each of the 10,000 repetitions we will run in our simulation study, we will randomly choose a vector with residuals from the VEC model and add it to the forecasted values of the endogenous variables to obtain the new asset return (see step 1 in figure 38). This vector will be available for subsequent drawings to ensure that we adhere to the principle of repeated sampling with replacement. For each of the endogenous variables of the model, only the corresponding residuals will be added. Besides, our approach also allows us to keep the correlation structure of the residuals drawn in time t unchanged. Repeating this process for each endogenous variable and each time step of our forecasting period will ultimately lead to the return distributions we will afterwards use as input for our investment strategies (see step 2 in figure 38).

4.3.4 Conclusions

The bootstrap simulation facilitates the generation of a return path based on the estimated VEC model and the residuals of the same regression. An essential feature of bootstrapping is that the correlation structure of the residuals in time t remains intact. Additionally, the technique does not make any assumptions about the distribution of the underlying variables, so that a realistic picture of potential return distributions is obtained. The high frequency of the generated data will also create a dense return distribution that allows us drawing important conclusions on the dispersion of returns and the downside risk of the investment strategies considered in our empirical study.

The specific investment strategies that we will focus on will be discussed in subsequent section 4.4.

4.4 Strategic Asset Allocation Strategies

4.4.1 Overview

Using the return distributions created by the bootstrap simulation as input parameters, we can replicate asset allocation strategies that are appropriate for German Pension Insurance Funds, both from an economic and regulatory standpoint. Despite the rather conservative portfolio profile German Pension Insurance Funds have followed in the last years (see also our analysis in section 2.5.2) and the tight regulation imposed by the BaFin that limits considerably the investment flexibility of fund managers, different permitted portfolio management strategies can lead to diverse investment return distributions.

In this chapter, we will describe the strategic investment strategies we perceive as suitable for Pension Insurance Funds but that also have been used in research papers and empirical studies. We are aware of the limitation our selection may impose in comparison to all the possible strategies that could be implemented. However, we believe our selection represents a broad spectrum of methods that encompasses the majority of strategic investment approaches a portfolio manager at a pension fund institution could pursue.

An important aspect of our study is the fact that our allocation strategies via the simulation procedure do not represent explicitly an optimization process in the classical way, as investment choices are not ranked based on a utility criterion.[674] One major limitation of these mathematical optimization models is their inflexibility in terms of changing the portfolio policy or active investing decisions over time. Moreover, it is problematic to include in the decision process the en-

---

[674] See Elton et al. (2011), p. 270 et seq. For pension fund models that focus on the maximizetion of intertemporal expected utility, see Rudolf, Ziemba (2004), in which assets and liabilities of pension funds and life insurers are modeled as stochastic processes. The modeling exercise of the study is thereby based on a four-fund theorem for intertemporal surplus optimizers (i.e. pension funds). See also Carino, Ziemba (1998) for a multistage stochastic linear program for an insurance company that has to consider a long-term asset liability management as part of its business strategy. Merton (1993) models the portfolio allocation for a university endowment with the main objective of maximizing the lifetime utility of the university.

tire spectrum of possible investment choices available.[675] Computing an investment simulation, on the other side, "is a critical tool for investment planning and provides potentially detailed and accurate answers to questions about future return distributions and future investment policies".[676] However, we have to assume that the prevailing asset allocation of German Pension Insurance Funds implicitly assumes some form of portfolio optimization in the classical way, realised by the respective asset manager. Nevertheless, we will not make any assumption at this stage on the form this maximization process may take.

While the mean-variance approach introduced by Markowitz in 1952 is the predominant model in classical finance literature,[677] alternative models may also apply, for example a geometric mean return approach, in which the investor would select the portfolio that is expected to generate the highest maximum growth.[678] For a rationally acting investor, the decision which approach is more suitable to him will depend on his personal risk preference. For those investors characterised by a logarithmic utility function, the geometric mean return method is more appropriate, whereas investors with a quadratic utility function should pursue a mean-variance optimizing method.[679] Under the assumption that portfolio managers of Pension Insurance Funds adhere to their fiduciary duty with respect to their pension contribution payers and considering the regulatory investment environment in which pension funds operate in Germany, it seems plausible to assume a risk-averse investor, who, for an adequate risk profile, attempts to maximise the return of the portfolio and consequently his utility.

---

675 See Elton et al. (2011), p. 266.

676 Elton et al. (2011), p. 270.

677 Markowitz's research findings are considered a groundbreaking achievement for mean-variance based portfolio models. See Markowitz (1952). For continuous-time approaches, see Merton (1969), who introduced the first optimal portfolio selection and consumption rules for an investor in an intertemporal investment horizon. For the latest dynamic allocation methodologies in this context, see Amenc et at. (2011), pp. 179-196, in which dynamic allocation decisions to performance-seeking and liability-hedging portfolios are presented.

678 See Latane, Young (1969), p. 610 et seq.. Roll (1973), p. 565, argues that the investor should prefer the "growth-optimum portfolio; that is, the portfolio with the highest expected rate of increase in value". Maier et al. (1977) published a research study on the optimal geometric mean portfolios that do not rely on (log-) normally distributed returns of the individual assets. The researchers determined optimal portfolios by means of a Monte-Carlo study.

679 See Breuer et al. (2006), p. 69 et seq.

4.4.2 Main Assumptions

A. Regulatory Constraints on Investing

Any investment strategy that will be used in our simulation study needs to comply with the regulatory rules of the VAG, the AnlV and the circular letter R4/2011 we referred to in section 2.5.1, in particular with respect to the maximum allowed allocations into single asset classes. These maximum caps will have a meaningful impact on our simulation, as we have to ensure that, independently of the underlying investment strategy, these allocation limits are not breached. In case the weight of a particular asset class exceeds one of these limits, we will adjust the portfolio allocation accordingly. The frequency of these adjustments will depend on the investing strategy. The predominant factor, however, are the reporting requirements by the BaFin that German Pension Insurance Funds have to fulfil. Our simulation model assumes that in case of potential imbalances an adjustment has to occur (at least on reporting dates). The most relevant reporting events are hereby: every quarter, the fund has to report to the BaFin the composition of the investment portfolio[680] and at the end of each fiscal year the annual report has to be produced.[681] Moreover, as defined in Sec. 16 Par. 1 BetrAVG, the employer has to review every three years his contribution and benefit commitments and adjust if appropriate to new economic conditions.[682]

B. Length of Forecasting Period

For the VEC regression to yield satisfactory estimates and consequently acceptable forecasting data, we need to use a long time period of historical data. Our model is based on 10-year monthly data. This time frame is conditioned on the availability of historical data from the index providers and the various financial data platforms we have used. The 10-year historical data will also determine the length of the forecasting period for the simulation study. While there is no rule that determines the relationship between the time period of historic data available and the length of the forecasting period, academic research studies

680 Based on circular letter 'Anordnung betreffend die Anzeige- und Berichtspflichten der Versicherungsunternehmen ueber ihre Kapitalanlagen'. See BaFin (2011, c).
681 See BaFin (2011, b), R4/2011, section B.2.5.
682 As stated in Sec. 16 Par. 3 No. 3 BetrAVG, offering Defined Contribution with Capital Guarantee benefits already fulfills this three-year review requirement by the legislator.

tend to have a 3 to 5-year forecasting window.[683] A 3-year window would match also the reporting requirements of the BaFin (see above) and be appropriate in relation to the 10-year time series data we have available to estimate our regression models.

C. ESG Screening Methodology for SRIs

For those indices that will be replicated in our empirical study following an ESG-screening methodology,[684] we will apply a best-in-class (BiC) approach with negative screening, excluding companies that generate revenues from alcohol, gambling, tobacco, armaments, firearms and adult entertainment (AGTAFA) businesses. The corresponding indices that pursue screening methods are provided by STOXX in case of the equity index and ECPI for the corporate bond indices.[685] The government bond index includes sovereign bonds that are eligible under the screening methodology of ECPI, which emphasizes primarily the compliance to international conventions, treaties and standards.[686]

The rationale for using a combined BiC with negative screening methodology for equities as well as corporate bonds is based on the fact that it is the most applied SRI screening approach in practise by institutional investors in Europe.[687] Moreover, it allows investors to choose the best performers within a region or industry sector based on a quantifiable, predetermined set of KPIs (BiC approach), while excluding sectors or business activities commonly rejected by society (negative screening criterion), which might ultimately prevent criticism from stakeholders or external pressure groups.[688]

---

683 See Schroeder (2010), p. 87, in which 126 data points per endogenous variable in the VEC model were available (corresponding to 25 years of historical data) and a 5-year foreasting period was computed (20 data points).

684 This will be the case for the SRI- and the Alternative Portfolios in our empirical analysis in section 5.4.

685 See STOXX (2012, a) and ECPI (2012) for brief company descriptions. For details on the respective indices, see appendix B.

686 The most relevant ones are: death penalty, civil liberties and political rights and the ratification of the main conventions on labor rights, human rights and environmental protection. See ECPI (2010), p. 2. This index follows therefore a positive screening approach. Due to the nature of EMU government bonds, a positive screening selection process appears as the most suitable technique.

687 See figure 29 in section 3.2.3.

688 See also section 3.2.2, D and 3.2.7, B on the rationale and benefits of including negative screening criteria as part of a strategic asset management policy.

4.4.3 Outright Strategies

Both outright strategies considered in our research study (Buy-and-Hold, Constant-Mix) represent the benchmark strategies for our empirical analysis. We will use them as a reference to compare results obtained from more sophisticated investment approaches.

B. Buy-and-Hold

In a Buy-and-Hold strategy, the Pension Insurance Fund invests into an initial mix of assets that satisfies the legal and regulatory investment requirements of the BaFin. Once the investment portfolio is acquired, it is held over time. No further adjustments will be conducted.[689] Such portfolio strategies are also called 'do-nothing' investment methods, as independently of the movement of the relative values of the assets in a portfolio, no rebalancing will be realised. Buy-and-Hold methods act frequently in academic studies as anchor points for more complex models. Some general features of these strategies are that (1) the payoff function of the strategy is linear, (2) the portfolio value moves as a function of the value of a single asset at a rate that is equal to the proportion of the asset in the initial portfolio mix and (3) the upside potential is unlimited.[690] Buy-and-Hold strategies are well-suited investing methods for long-term investors, as many research studies provide evidence that they outperform short-term focused outright investment strategies.[691] Index benchmarking, a strategy followed by many pension funds, is very often classified as a Buy-and-Hold strategy, as the weights of the index components rarely changes.[692] For German occupational pension funds, in particular, Buy-and-Hold policies represent the basic, passive portfolio strategy for investing schemes targeting capital preservation.[693]

Given our research focus, the Buy-and-Hold approach we are pursuing is not a pure Buy-and-Hold strategy, as we will have to readjust the allocation weights

---

[689] See Fabozzi et al. (2011), p. 245.

[690] See Perold, Sharpe (1995), p. 149 et seq.

[691] See Malkiel (2003), p. 62 et seq. The study provides evidence that momentum-driven trading strategies that attempt to profit from short-term momentum in financial markets do consistently underperform Buy-and-Hold methods. With outright strategies we refer to long-only approaches in which neither derivative overlays nor short-selling activities are implemented.

[692] See Cesari, Cremonini (2003), p. 989.

[693] See John (2009), p. 125 or Haferstock, Hilka (2009), pp. 211-213.

depending on the possibility that one of the regulatory allocation limits are breached. As a consequence, every three months, in accordance with the reporting requirements for Pension Insurance Funds, a screening of the proportions of each individual asset class will be conducted and adjustments be made in case of any breach.

C. Constant-Mix (Proportional Portfolio Strategy)

Constant-Mix asset allocation strategies, also referred to as Proportional Portfolio methods, play a central role in modern portfolio theory. They are part of the dynamic asset allocation strategies, as an investor that follows a Constant-Mix technique continuously rebalances his portfolio with the objective of maintaining a fixed constant percentage of the portfolio value invested in the underlying assets at each point in time.[694] This constant rebalancing involves buying securities when their prices drop relative to the other assets in the portfolio, and vice versa, selling assets when the prices have increased. Constant-mix policies are often used in the portfolio management practice and have a range of optimal characteristics for the ordinary asset allocation problem.[695]

The implementation of a Constant-Mix method usually requires from the portfolio manager to define a rule regarding the exact price levels at which a trading activity may be triggered. Common trading rules could for example imply a change of the respective asset or portfolio by a certain percentage.[696] For the purposes of our analysis, nevertheless, we will neither pursue a continuous rebalancing[697] nor will we include a certain percentage level that automatically triggers buying or selling activity. Instead, we will readjust the portfolio back to its initial constant proportions every month of our forecasting period. We implement a monthly rebalancing frequency as in our discrete time frame the underlying time series data has one month as the smallest time unit.

D. Comparison Buy-and-Hold vs. Constant-Mix Strategies

Buy-and-Hold strategies will behave differently to Constant-Mix methods depending on the price movements of the portfolio components. As mentioned

---

694 See Browne (1998), p. 216.
695 See Browne (1999), p. 278.
696 See Perold, Sharpe (1995), p. 151.
697 Our simulation analysis is based on monthly data and therefore has discrete time intervals that for the purpose of our analysis are sufficiently small.

earlier, in the Buy-and-Hold scenario, initial quantities and allocations are kept constant over time, so that the payoff of the portfolio is linear.[698] For Constant-Mix methods, on the other hand, the portfolio manager maintains the initial portfolio proportions fixed. As the asset prices randomly change over time, the portfolio manager is obliged to buy or sell continuously to sustain the fixed weight proportions of the underlying assets. This portfolio composition will lead to a concave payoff structure. In addition, it implies that the link between quantity held of an asset and its price is countervarying, so that when the asset price rises, the quantity demanded decreases and vice versa ('buy low and sell high' rule).[699]

The relative outperformance of one investment strategy versus the other will depend on the price movements of the underlying assets during the observation period. For scenarios in which the price levels end up near the initial value, Constant-Mix will generally outperform, whereas for price movements far from the initial level, Buy-and-Hold approaches may yield better returns.[700]

4.4.4 Derivative Overlays

A. Regulatory Framework

For derivative overlay strategies suitable for German insurance companies and Pension Insurance Funds, BaFin circular letter R3/2000 describes the characteristics these derivative contracts can have in terms of maximum size, option type and strikes.[701] The relevant features of R3/2000 are summarised in table 14.

Table 14: Feasible Derivative Structures for Pension Insurance Funds based on Circular Letter R3/2000

Derivative Strategy	Reference in R3/2000	Size Constraints	Strikes	Maturity
Put Option	A.II.3.a	100% AuM	No reference	No reference
Collar	A.II.4	100% AuM	No reference	No reference
Long Call	A.II.3.b	7.5% AuM	Max. 15% OTM	No reference
Short Call	A.II.3.c	7.5% AuM	No reference	No reference

Source: Own representation.

[698] See Cesari, Cremonini (2003), p. 989. We assume for this comparison that no adjustments occur caused by a potential breach of one of the regulatory asset caps.
[699] See Dhaene et al. (2005), p. 254.
[700] See Perold, Sharpe (1995), p. 154.
[701] See BaFin (2000), R3/2000.

For all derivatives structures, the pension fund can at maturity either physically deliver the underlying or cash-settle the contract.[702] We will assume cash-settlement for all our transactions as well as a 1-year maturity.

All our derivative pricings have been calculated using the Black-Scholes option pricing formula, modified for European options.[703] As volatility input, we have used the annualised standard deviation based on monthly returns over the last 10 years. While the limitations of the Black-Scholes formula are widely known to both academics and practitioners,[704] the methodology remains still the most-used option pricing approach in finance as it allows computing an indicative option price in nearly real-time. Hence, its application seems appropriate and justifiable for the purpose of our analysis.

B. Hedging – Put Options (Option Based Portfolio Insurance, OBPI)

The Option Based Portfolio Insurance (OBPI) is a popular portfolio hedging strategy that should be considered as part of an adequate investment strategy for German Pension Insurance Funds.[705] OBPI methods were introduced first by Leland and Rubinstein in 1976.[706] They basically consist of acquiring a risky asset and simultaneously writing a put on it (also called 'protective put'). The strike of the put represents thereby the insured amount of the portfolio.[707] Pension funds, in particular, are considered the ideal investor type for OBPI structures, as they "at all costs must exceed a minimum value, but thereafter can accept reasonable risks. 'Safety-first' investors would find portfolio insurance attractive on this basis".[708] While the OBPI approach can be applied to a number of different asset classes (e.g. fixed-income portfolios, foreign exchange funds), the most common asset type insured by this technique are usually equity investments. Besides, the most frequent strike level tends to be at-the-money (ATM), so that the portfolio value is hedged at nominal terms.[709]

---

[702] See BaFin (2000), R3/2000, section A.II.2.
[703] See Black, Scholes (1973). Given that we are pricing exclusively options on equity indices, no further adjustments are required to the original Black-Scholes formulas.
[704] Primarily the assumptions about risk-neutrality, continuous securities trading, constant risk-free rate and constant volatility. See Hull (2006), pp. 289-291.
[705] See John (2009), p. 125.
[706] See Leland, Rubinstein (1976).
[707] See Bertrand, Prigent (2003), p. 462.
[708] See Leland (1980), p. 582.
[709] See Bird et al. (1990), p. 1.

In the first section of our empirical analysis, the option-based strategy will be applied only to the equity portion of the portfolio. At inception of the investment horizon, the equity portfolio is protected with ATM put options that have a one-year maturity. After each annual period, the equity portfolio will be protected recursively for another year at the then prevailing market value. A credit risk-hedging scenario is simulated later in section 5.5.4 of our study.

The rationale for limiting the application of option derivative overlay structures to the equity part of the portfolio in section 5.4 is manifold:

1. In practise, large derivative transactions are restricted by the ability of the counterparty to hedge its position. Hedging large proportions of a portfolio with a financial institution is generally not feasible or only at an excessive cost that would question the whole purpose the transaction.
2. As figure 41 as well as table 23 illustrate, equity assets chosen for our simulation have historically represented the riskiest asset class from a mean-variance perspective. For our 10-year observation period, the high equity volatility was thereby not compensated by higher realised returns. Downside risk of our target portfolios is therefore higher due to the equity allocation. This rationale becomes more obvious in the alternative models we consider in section 5.5 that have higher equity allocations, in particular the UK and Dutch scenarios (see 5.5.2).

C. Hedging – Collar

As detailed in circular R3/2000, collar strategies are a permitted derivative overlay structure for German Pension Insurance Funds. They are considered 'combined strategies' as they include the purchase of a put option combined with the sale of an upper strike call. The German regulator expects pension funds and insurers to use collars as a hedging instrument, analogous to the put option approach. From a regulatory standpoint, therefore, collar derivative overlays are simply more cost efficient put-option hedging instruments, in which the premium received from the call option subsidises the cost of the put premium the investor needs to pay at inception.[710]

[710] See BaFin (2000), R3/2000, A.II.4.

The collar we will implement in our empirical analysis will have an ATM put strike and a call strike of 115% of spot price. While the legislator does not impose restrictions on the respective strikes of the collar, we will use the ATM strike for the put as we are interested in capital guarantee at nominal terms, while the 115 strike on the call replicates the maximum strike the long call position can have as defined in A.II.3.b of R3/2000.

D. Bond-Call Option Strategy (Portfolio Insurance with Call Options)

Bond-Call Option strategies (also called Portfolio Insurance with Call Option methods) enable a portfolio manager to preserve principal capital value while maintaining exposure to favourable price movements of a risky asset class (in our analysis, equity investments). The structure consists of a long position in a call option on a risky (equity) index, while the remaining assets of the portfolio are invested in low-risk fixed-income instruments.[711] The central element of this structure is that the entire exposure to the risky asset class is obtained via the call option position, no outright investment will be undertaken. The freed-up proceeds from the sell-down of the risky asset will be reinvested into the other assets of the portfolio. At maturity of the call option, should the underlying trade below the strike, the portfolio suffers only the loss of the option premium, whereas for any price movement above the strike, the fund participates in all upside at a levered rate to the initial call option investment. Due to its conservative risk-return profile, Bond-Call Option strategies are suitable for German Pension Insurance Funds.[712]

Current German regulation allows the implementation of the Bond-Call Option technique for the investment management of Pension Insurance Fund, based on the wording of circular letter R3/2000.[713] The regulator, however, has imposed some restrictions on the allowed call strikes and the maximum nominal amount. The former is not allowed to exceed 115% of current spot value, whereas the nominal amount of the option shall not surpass 7.5% of the total AuM of the fund.[714] For our analysis, we will use an ATM call option with a 1-year maturity. At the end of each year during our forecasting period, we will

---

[711] See Carletti, Weigel (1992), p. 76.
[712] See John (2009), p. 125 et seq.
[713] Based on the working of circular letter R3/2000. See BaFin (2000), R3/2000, A.II.3.b.
[714] See BaFin (2000), R3/2000, A.II.3.b.

cash-settle the derivative contract and recursively acquire a new 1-year ATM call. The equity funds will be completely sold at inception and the proceeds proportionally distributed amongst the remaining (less risky) asset classes of the investment portfolio.

E. Yield Enhancement (Covered Call Writing)

Yield Enhancement strategies by means of selling call options on existing securities (also denominated 'covered call writing') are the most popular options strategies in modern portfolio management and a topic frequently covered in academic research studies.[715] In theory, writing calls on an existing portfolio should lead to a reduction of the portfolio variance, as in bearish markets the call will remain unexercised,[716] while for rising share prices, the variance should be smaller.

There appears to be evidence that Yield Enhancement strategies are already frequently used in portfolio management of occupational pension funds in countries like the UK, the Netherlands and Germany.[717] For our research study, we will follow the structural possibilities circular R3/2000 offers in relation to short call strategies, in particular with respect to sizing restrictions (maximum of 7.5% of total AuM).[718] To maintain consistency with the collar overlay considered in our empirical analysis, we will fix the strike of the short call at 115% of initial spot of the underlying equity index.

4.4.5 Conclusions

The German regulator allows Pension Insurance Funds a wide range of different investment strategies that enable portfolio managers to pursue their individual investment preferences. The objective of our empirical analysis is to generate for each of these portfolio strategies possible future return paths and portfolio value distributions. The benchmarks of our simulation study are outright strategies. The simplest one is the Buy-and-Hold approach, a passive in-

---

715 See Board et al. (2000), p. 1 and p. 5. On page 5, a summary of the most relevant research studies on the topic since 1960 are presented. As the overview shows, the vast majority of academic papers are US-market focused.

716 In this scenario, the variance of the portfolio with call option overlay and the outright portfolio without derivative will be identical.

717 See Simeonova (2008), p. 3, quoted after Dreyer, Vischer (2004), pp. 10-14.

718 See BaFin (2000), R3/2000, A.3.c.

vesting strategy, whereas the Constant-Mix requires continuous adjustments. Both strategies are anchor-methods for our more sophisticated derivative overlays, in particular as all derivative strategies use as base strategy one of these two outright methods.

The investment strategies of our analysis will allow portfolio managers to implement simple long-only outright strategies, hedging methods, yield enhancement techniques as well as bond-call investment styles. Figure 39 summarises our strategies for the empirical simulation.

Figure 39: Summary of Investment Strategies for the Simulation Study

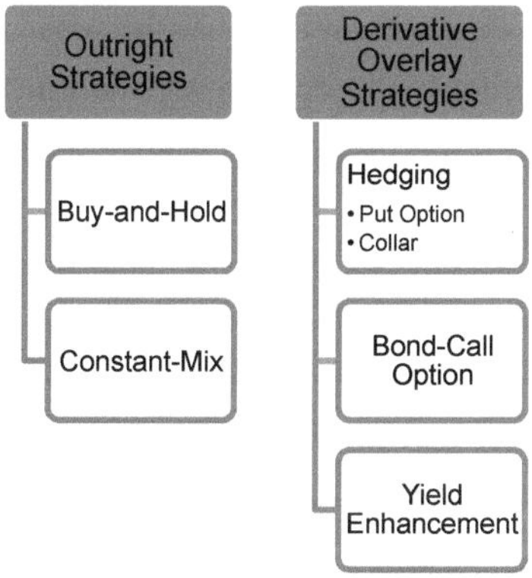

Source: Own representation.

There are numerous academic papers available that either analyse these strategies from a theoretical aspect or include them in empirical studies. Moreover, we have ensured that our methods are fully compliant with prevailing German regulation. Considering a broad range of different investment strategies will also support our research objectives of (1) obtaining representative results that are valid under varying investment approaches, (2) allowing us to give recommendations that are suitable for investors with different risk-preferences and (3) enabling us to order investment styles by appropriateness for the general investment objectives of German Pension Insurance Funds.

The performance measures that will enable us to rank the performance of a particular investment strategy in terms of downside risk are presented in section 4.5.

4.5 Performance Measurement

4.5.1 Asymmetric Risk-Return Measures

To assess the dominance or suitability of a specific investment strategy over other approaches considered in our analysis, we need to define adequate performance measurements. Under the assumption of normally distributed portfolio returns, the classical mean-variance selection rule is the optimal methodology to rank investment strategies for risk-averse investors with increasing and concave utility functions.[719] However, for asymmetric return distributions, variance is not the appropriate risk measurement metric.[720] Moreover, as numerous research studies have verified, in particular in the area of behavioural finance, variance as a risk measure is not coherent with the individual perception investors have of investment risk.[721] Investment alternatives that have a high probability of causing either large losses or below-target returns, for example, cannot always be counterbalanced by possible gains, regardless of how large they may be.[722] Such anomalies are defined in behavioural finance as 'loss aversion', a phenomenon that occurs when "the disutility of giving up an object is greater than the utility associated with acquiring it."[723] These research findings suggest new investment selection techniques are required that are based on a more accurate assumption about investors' risk preferences and perceptions.

Roy (1952) presented the first of the so-called 'risk-reward' measures in what he denominated the 'safety-first principle'. In his model, Roy describes the concern investors may have for not achieving a minimum return or suffering catastrophic losses (shortfall risk) and the efforts they may be willed to undertake to avoid such occurrences. Roy's risk-reward scaling criterion can be consequently applied to rank investment preferences.[724] Fishburn (1977) argued that mean-risk dominance models, in which both the mean as well as the expected loss below a target return t determine the dominance of one distribution versus the other, were "motivated by the observation that decision makers in invest-

---

[719] See Bawa (1976), p. 1169.
[720] See Estrada (2007), p. 170.
[721] See Harlow (1991), p. 29.
[722] See Libby, Fishburn (1977), p. 273 and p. 289.
[723] Kahneman et al. (1991), p. 194, making reference to a previous definition by Kahneman, Tversky (1984).
[724] Roy (1952), p. 432 et seq.

ment contexts frequently associate risk with failure to attain a target return".[725] Fishburn also introduced the concept of 'Lower Partial Moments' (LPM).[726]

$$F_{\alpha}(t) = \int_{-\infty}^{t} (t - r)^{\alpha} dF(r) \quad (17)$$

with α>0 and in which t represents the target return, α the degree of moment and r a random variable.[727] For empirical analysis in a discrete time frame, following formula for the LPM is commonly used:[728]

$$F_{\alpha}(t) = LPM_{\alpha}(t) = \frac{1}{N} * \sum_{t=1}^{N} (t - r)^{\alpha}$$

with r<=t and N as the total number of observations, or alternatively as

$$F_{\alpha}(t) = LPM_{\alpha}(t) = \frac{1}{N} * \sum_{t=1}^{N} \max\left[t - r_t, 0\right]^{\alpha} \quad (18)$$

For different values of α, the risk aversion of the investor will change. While α=0 just determines the probability of not achieving target return t, α=1 calculates the expected value below t[729] and α=2 returns the semi-variance of the underlying distribution. For increasing α, the weight of the deviation of x from t increases, suggesting a higher-order risk-aversion of the investor. In practise, only values α=0, 1, 2 are usually computed, even though we will also compute α=3 for the Kappa 3 risk measure.[730]

The corresponding economic justification for LPM-based performance measures in the context of portfolio management becomes obvious in the following comparison: while the traditional mean-variance framework, as described by Markowitz (1952), requires a restrictive set of assumptions to enable the use of the variance as a risk measurement,[731] the LPM framework entails

725 Fishburn (1977), p. 123.
726 Fishburn called his formulation the α-t model.
727 See Fishburn (1977), p. 116.
728 See Schroeder (1999), p. 385.
729 In more detail, α=1 calculates for the investor the expected value of the shortfall-loss, e.g. the sum of the weighted deviations of the returns below the target return t. See Zimmermann, Portmann (2000), p. 511.
730 See Schroeder (1999), p. 385.
731 The assumptions being that either asset returns are normally distributed or investors have a quadratic utility function.

only general assumptions about the underlying utility function of the investor[732] and the respective distribution of the asset, which itself can take any shape defined by the mean and the corresponding standard deviation.[733] Moreover, pursuing a portfolio allocation in the downside-risk framework allows the formation of "an investment opportunity set for downside-averse investors that is at least as efficient as that derived using conventional techniques. More generally, the downside-risk approach offers the potential for portfolios that are more attractive than mean-variance portfolios."[734] In conclusion, the downside-risk perspective can lead to a portfolio risk reduction while simultaneously maintaining or even improving the level of expected returns offered by the traditional mean-variance methods.[735]

4.5.2 Downside Risk Performance Indicators

The LPM findings in the context of the downside-risk approach have subsequently led to a number of useful risk-reward measures that are popular in modern portfolio management for performance assessment. They are particularly suitable for the risk assessment of German Pension Insurance Funds given their focus on downside-risk. Our empirical analysis will therefore consider the most appropriate of these measurements for the evaluation of our investment strategies. In particular, we have focused on Downside Deviation, Omega measure, Sortino Ratio, Kappa 3 as well as the Upside Potential Ratio.

A. Downside Deviation

The Downside Deviation (DD), also denoted downside standard deviation or semi-deviation, is defined as:[736]

$$DD = \sqrt{\frac{1}{N} * \sum_{t=1}^{N} \max\left[MAR - r_t, 0\right]^2} \quad (19)$$

MAR is thereby the Minimum Acceptable Return, which represents the minimum return a portfolio manager is required to achieve, N the number of total

---

732 Primarily risk aversion and preference for skewness.
733 See Harlow (1991), p. 31.
734 Harlow (1991), p. 39.
735 See Harlow (1991), p. 39.
736 See Estrada (2008), p. 69, or Estrada (2007), p. 172.

observations and r_t is the random return the portfolio or the asset yields in time period t.[737] The Downside Deviation measures the downside volatility of the return distribution, or more strictly speaking, the return volatility below the MAR.[738] Depending on the skewness of a given return distribution, some portfolios or investment strategies will be riskier below the MAR-level than others. In terms of our empirical analysis, some investment strategies will have a higher accumulated return distribution below the MAR than others, e.g. they will be riskier in terms of downside risk as the probability of obtaining a return below the minimum acceptable level is higher.

B. Omega

The Omega measure calculates the probability-weighted ratio of gains to losses relative to the MAR. The corresponding formula is:

$$\Omega_r(MAR) = \frac{\int_{MAR}^{+\infty} (1 - F(r))d_r}{\int_{-\infty}^{MAR} F(r)d_r} \quad (20)$$

in which F(r) is the cumulative distribution function of asset return r.[739] The calculation of Omega involves therefore dividing the cumulative return distribution of the portfolio returns into losses and gains above and below the MAR level and then computing the (probability weighted) ratio of returns above and below this division. For each level of targeted return, the Omega enables a fund manager to determine the probability-adjusted ratio of gains to losses relative to the target return.[740] An equivalent representation for Omega, which is easier to compute in a discrete time frame, is:

$$Omega = \frac{r^d - MAR}{LPM_1(MAR)} + 1 \quad (21)$$

with

[737] The level of the MAR will obviously depend on the circumstances. For Pension Insurance Funds, a guarantee at nominal terms implies MAR=0%.
[738] See Estrada (2008), p. 69.
[739] See Bertrand, Prigent (2011), p. 1814.
[740] See Keating, Shadwick (2002), p. 2 and p. 4.

$$LPM_1(MAR) = \frac{1}{N} * \sum_{t=1}^{N} \max\left[MAR - r_t, 0\right]^1 \quad (22)$$

with r^d as the average (monthly) return of the underlying asset or portfolio and LMP_1 as the respective Lower Partial Moment of order 1.[741]

C. Sortino Ratio

The calculation of the Sortino Ratio (SR) is similar to that of Omega. The Sortino Ratio, however, considers the semi-deviation below the MAR, instead of the LPM of order 1. The formula is thereby:[742]

$$SR = \frac{r^d - MAR}{\sqrt[2]{LPM_2(MAR)}} \quad (23)$$

In essence, for a given distribution of portfolio returns, the Sortino Ratio computes the average excess return relative to the downside deviation of the distribution below the MAR.[743]

D. Kappa 3

The Kappa 3 measure considers the LPM of order 3 and is hence a suitable risk coefficient for very risk-averse investor types[744]. The calculation is given by the following formula:[745]

$$Kappa\ 3 = \frac{r^d - MAR}{\sqrt[3]{LPM_3(MAR)}} \quad (24)$$

E. Upside Potential Ratio

The Upside Potential ratio (UPR) calculates the ratio of the Higher Partial Moment (HPM) of order 1 over the LPM of order 2:[746]

$$UPR = \frac{HPM_1(MAR)}{\sqrt[2]{LPM_2(MAR)}} \quad (25)$$

741 See Eling, Schuhmacher (2007), p. 2635. We make reference to the average of monthly returns as this is the time interval of the time series data used in our empirical analysis.
742 See Kaplan, Knowles (2004), p. 44.
743 See Chaudhury, Johnson (2008), p. 489.
744 As we mentionned earlier, the more risk-averse an investor is, the higher the respective LPM order should be. See Eling, Schuhmacher (2007), p. 2635.
745 See Kaplan, Knowles (2004), p. 44.
746 See Farinelli, Tibiletti (2008), p. 1545, quoted after Sortino et al. (1999).

with

$$HPM_1(MAR) = \frac{1}{N} * \sum_{t=1}^{N} \max\left[r_t - MAR, 0\right]^1 \quad (26)$$

The Higher Partial Moment computes the excess return of the distribution over the MAR, so that the Upside Potential Ratio measures the reward the investor is receiving (above MAR) for being exposed to the downside risk, which is defined as the semi-deviation of returns below MAR.[747]

4.5.3 Conclusions

Classical risk-return performance measures are based on some (strong) assumptions with respect to the distribution of the underlying returns and the risk behaviour of investors. As we will realise in our simulation study, return distributions for investment strategies that include derivative overlays tend to be skewed, so that traditional risk-return measures do not appear appropriate.[748] Moreover, as different studies in the field of behavioural finance suggest, investors tend to have an asymmetrical risk (variance) perception between losses and potential gains, in particular for risk-averse investor types ('loss aversion').

As a consequence, risk-reward methods based on Lower Partial Moments are more suitable risk measures for the assessment of investment strategies for Pension Insurance Funds. These methods focus on the inherent risk or probability of a (potentially asymmetrical) return distribution to underperform a minimum acceptable return (MAR). In this chapter we have introduced those risk measurements we think are the most appropriate for the purpose of our research study: Downside Deviation, Omega, Sortino Ratio, Kappa 3 and the Upside Potential Ratio. These measures will enable us to rank investment strategies and to judge which portfolios are more in accordance with the investment objectives of Pension Insurance Funds.

---

[747] See Leggio, Lien (2003), p. 83, and Lien (2001), p. 486, quoted after Sortino et al. (1999).

[748] This will be particularly the case for the Alternative Investment Scenarios in section 5.5, in which large proportions of the investment portfolios have derivative overlays.

4.6 Summary

In chapter 4, we have presented a coherent theoretical methodology that sets the framework for our empirical analysis. The principal elements of our theoretical foundation are the stochastic time series regression model and the bootstrap simulation technique, as both will enable us to generate future return paths for the underlying investment portfolios we will examine in more detail in the following chapter. Rigid testing procedures both in the identification and the diagnostic checking phase of the regression model, combined with 'optimised regressions' for the VEC model itself, will ensure that our fitted model adequately captures the data generating process of the underlying time series data.

Moreover, we have defined a number of investment allocation strategies that will allow portfolio managers not only to replicate prevailing outright strategies followed by Pension Insurance Funds, but also to explore the structural flexibilities the German regulator BaFin allows these investors in terms of derivative overlay structures. The aim of defining these investing approaches has been to outline allocation strategies that represent a wide range of possible investment opportunities for pension fund managers, depending on their respective risk appetite. The return distributions obtained from the bootstrap simulation will act as input for these allocation strategies. Chapter 5 will present the results of simulating all investment strategies defined in this section.

Traditional mean-variance performance measures will not suffice to assess the suitability of the investment strategies under consideration. Due to the risk-averse portfolio allocation and investment style German Pension Insurance Funds have showed in the past and the capital preservation character of pension plans with defined-contributions with capital-guarantee, a new set of performance measures is required. We define in this chapter risk measurements based on lower partial moments (LPMs), as they allow for return distributions that are non-normally distributed. Furthermore, these measures offer an adequate downside risk assessment so that we can determine which investment strategies combined with which portfolio allocations yield more appropriate risk-return combinations.

The same concept will also be applied in chapter 5.5 when we consider additional investment approaches and portfolio structures that do not comply with current German regulations, but that attempt to explore potential alternative investment methods for Pension Insurance Funds.

5. Empirical Analysis

5.1 Objectives[749]

Chapter 5 summarises the main results of our empirical analysis and is based on the methodologies and techniques we discussed in chapter 4. This section therefore represents the core part of our research study that will enable us to provide answers by means of empirical evidence to the research questions we defined in our research proposal in part 1.3.1.

First, we will describe the three main portfolios we will be using as benchmarks to simulate future asset returns.

1. Portfolio 1, the Standard Portfolio, simply reflects the average portfolio allocation German Pension Insurance Funds have invested in in the last five years. As we have already seen in section 2.5.2, this allocation has been relatively stable over this time period.
2. The SRI Portfolio (Portfolio 2) replicates both the equity proportion as well as all fixed-income assets in SRI filtered manner, following the characteristics and methods we have described in chapter 3.2.
3. The Alternative Portfolio, the third fund contemplated, will be similar to the SRI Portfolio with the main difference that 10% of the assets under management are allocated to alternative investments.[750] We discussed in chapter 3.3.3 the relevance alternative assets do already play for pension funds outside Germany and the benefits they can provide when added to an investment portfolio.

The advanced econometric model we have chosen as our principal regression model is the VEC model, due to its ability to capture long-term cointegration relationships as well as short-term dynamics amongst the asset classes included in a portfolio. Moreover, as we mentioned in 4.2.5, E, VEC models provide satisfactory forecasting results that are superior to many other commonly used time-series models. After estimating the coefficients of the VEC model us-

[749] While we have included in section 5 the most relevant parts of the empirical analysis, some output analyses have been left out due to the sizing constraints of our thesis. The author can deliver these outputs upon request.

[750] In connection with this allocation into alternative investments, bond investments, both corporate and government bonds, will decrease accordingly by 10 points.

ing the SUR method and optimizing the overall structure with a model reduction technique, we will present the final structure of the respective VEC model for all three portfolios. For all our econometric calculations, we have used the software application EViews 6 (Enterprise Edition) except for the cointegration relation graphs, for which we have employed the software package R.[751]

The estimated VEC model will subsequently be used in connection with the bootstrap simulation technique to generate future return paths for every asset class used in the portfolios. We will insert these returns as inputs for the portfolio management strategies we have selected. The portfolio values of the derivative-based strategies will be contrasted with the results obtained from outright (benchmark) investing methods. For the large part of our empirical analysis, we will focus primarily on mitigating downside risk so as to avoid future investment shortfalls that could threaten the viability of a pension fund to fulfil its fiduciary obligations. To measure this downside risk, we will apply different risk indicators based on lower partial moments, as discussed in part 4.5.2, which provide valuable information on the likelihood of a particular investment strategy to underperform a minimum acceptable return.

As the investment framework imposed by the German regulator is relative restrictive in terms of asset allocation and strategies, we will explore in 5.5 alternative asset allocation models that could potentially be suitable for the strategic asset management of Pension Insurance Fund under a modified regulation. Moreover, we will dedicate a section to get a better understanding of how inflationary pressure can distort our portfolio performance results. This analysis is optional as we restrict our research study to pension plans with defined-contributions with capital guarantee, a contribution form that offers capital preservation at nominal terms only.

Chapter 5 starts with the description of the various investment portfolios included in our empirical study (5.2), subsequently presents the results of our VEC regression analysis (5.3) before running the bootstrap simulation in section

---

[751] In comparison to EViews, R allows plotting existing correlation relations that are corrected for short-term effects. We have also recalculated all our VEC analysis with R to double check the validity of the results obtained with EViews 6.

5.4 for our three standard models contemplated. Section 5.5 completes our empirical analysis with the computation of alternative investment models.

5.2 Description of the Investment Portfolios

5.2.1 Matching Principle

Each of the three portfolios used in our empirical analysis will be composed of a certain number of indices, each of which will represent a particular asset class. For both the Standard Portfolio as well as the SRI Portfolio, there will be five asset classes included in total, following the most relevant asset classes that German Pension Insurance Funds have been invested in in the last 5 years: (1) equities, (2) government bonds, (3) corporate bonds, (4) real estate investments and (5) money market. The Alternative Portfolio will include in addition (6) hedge fund investments as well as (7) commodities as part of the alternative investments. Table 15 summarises the investment opportunity set each of the asset classes will have in the respective investment portfolios.

Table 15: Investment Approach per Asset Class

Asset Class	Regional Focus	Proposed Investment Approach for German Pension Insurance Funds
(1) Equities	Europe	• European focus, including UK and Switzerland • Total return approach to benefit from dividend payments of the underlying shares
(2) Government Bonds	Europe	• Government bonds from the Euro area • Euro denominated to have a better currency-risk control, as Pension Insurance Funds are not allowed to invest more than 30% of the investment portfolio in non-euro denominated assets[752] • Total return approach, so that coupons are reinvested into the index
(3) Corporate Bonds	Europe	• Exclusively investment grade corporate bonds will be considered to fulfil the regulatory requirements • Euro-denominated, total return method
(4) Real Estate	Europe	• European real estate companies or real-estate funds as well as tax-efficient REITS, as allowed by AnlV[753] • Represents investments into the equity of the company or the fund

[752] See R4/2011, section B.7.
[753] See AnlV, Sec. 2, Par. 1, No. 14.

Asset Class	Regional Focus	Proposed Investment Approach for German Pension Insurance Funds
(5) Money Market	Europe	• We assume that the portfolio manager allocates excess cash proceeds into a money market fund • For modelling purposes, this money market fund will be replicated via the 1-year Euribor rate
(6) Hedge Funds	Global	• Investment into a wide range of different hedge fund strategies • No single strategy will be chosen to avoid any biasedness and subjectivity • Investment via a fund-of-funds principle
(7) Commodities	Global	• Investment into a basket of commodities, as allowed by AnlV[754] and section B.6.1-c R4/2011[755]

Source: Own representation.

To enable an adequate and representative comparison amongst the different portfolios, it has been an essential requirement in the index selection process that the indices chosen follow a matching principle. This method implies that for each asset class in the respective portfolio, a comparable index is selected that shows a similar composition. In general, any of the underlying SRI indices will have their respective counterpart in the Standard Portfolio as benchmark. This principle is applied in particular to the asset classes 'equities' as well as 'government bonds' and 'corporate bonds', for which sustainable investment and screening methods are used. A similar matching principle has been applied in various academic papers, in which SRI fund performance has been compared to non-SRI funds as well as SRI indices versus classical benchmark indices.[756] Schroeder (2004) highlights in his study the advantages of using SRI indices for such comparative analysis instead of SRI funds: (1) methodological problems are avoided and (2) the performance of the underlying SRI assets are tested directly and "these tests are not distorted by (transaction) costs or the ability of the fund management".[757]

754 See AnlV, Sec. 3 Par. 2 No. 3.

755 See R4/2011, section B.6.1-c.

756 For comparison amongst investment funds, see Mallin et al. (1995), Gregory et al. (1997) for UK investment funds, Statman (2000) for US funds, Kreander et al. (2005) for European funds and Bauer et al. (2005) for an international mix. For pure SRI-index performance studies, see Sauer (1997), Kurtz, diBartolomeo (1996) and Statman (2006).

757 Schroeder (2004), p. 125.

The applied matching principle in our analysis as well as the main characteristics on the indices chosen are reflected in table 16. A detailed description of each of these indices can be found in appendix B.

Table 16: Indices used in the Empirical Analysis

Asset Class	Index	Region	Price/Total Return	Currency
(1) Equities	Stoxx Europe 600	Europe	Net return	EUR
	Stoxx Europe Sustainability	Europe	Net return	EUR
(2) Government Bonds	Iboxx Eurozone	Eurozone	Total return	EUR
	ECPI Euro Government Bonds	Eurozone	Total return	EUR
(3) Corporate Bonds	Iboxx Corporates	EUR denominated	Total return	EUR
	ECPI Corporate Bonds	EUR denominated	Total return	EUR
(4) Real Estate	FTSE Developed Europe[758]	Europe	Total return	EUR
(5) Money Market	1-year Euribor	Eurozone	N/A	EUR
(6) Hedge Funds	DJ Credit Suisse Hedge Fund	Global	Price return[759]	EUR
(7) Commodities	DJ UBS Commodity	Global	Total return	EUR

Source: Own representation.

The above-mentioned matching principle is thereby reflected in the comparison between standard and SRI indices. This approach guarantees that the respective asset classes in the three portfolios have a similar industry- and country allocation and hence any form of allocation tilt is avoided.

Figure 40: Matching Principle for SRI Indices

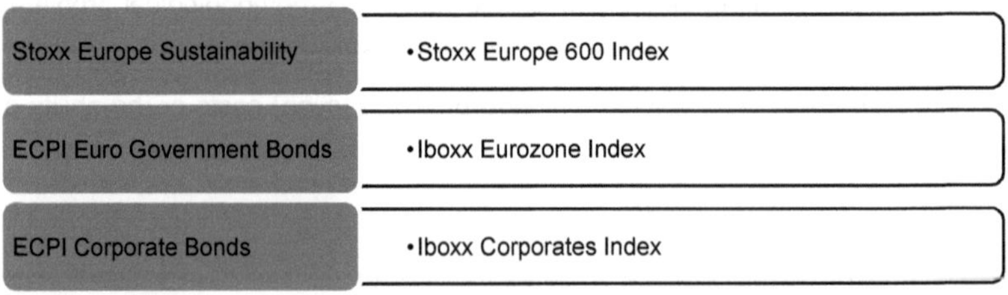

Source: Own figure.

[758] The real estate index we will use in our empirical analysis replicates the equity price evolution of real estate companies and REITs. The investor is therefore subject to equity risk. For investments in physical real estate objects, indices provided by IPD can be used instead. Due to data license restrictions, however, we did not have access to IPD calculated index numbers. See IPD (2012) for more details on the available product range.

[759] To our knowledge, no total return hedge fund index with at least a 10-year time series history is currently available.

Moreover, the matching principle also ensures that the SRI screening and selection methodology that underlie both the Stoxx Europe Sustainability index and the ECPI Corporate Bonds index are the same, so that the final asset pool for corporate bonds is selected following a similar procedure than the one applied to the equity portfolio.[760] With the selected indices, we have also envisaged to use benchmark indices that are broad in terms of the number of underlying assets and have a wide regional coverage and balanced industry weights. This methodology guarantees that the empirical results are as representative as possible and recommendations for the strategic asset allocation of German Pension Insurance Funds are universally valid.

5.2.2 Descriptive Statistics

A. Portfolio 1: Standard Portfolio

The Standard Portfolio represents the basic benchmark portfolio of our analysis, as it replicates the average investment portfolio of all German Pension Insurance Funds. Its initial allocation (base case scenario) follows the allocation data of all 150 Pension Insurance Funds supervised by the BaFin and is an average value for the investment portfolios over the last 5 years. The initial asset split will be 5% of assets under management into equities, 45% into government bonds, 40% in corporate bonds, 5% in real estate assets and 5% in money market instruments. As for all price data used in our models, we will transform price levels into the logs of the prices levels.[761]

In table 17, we summarise the main characteristics of the log prices of the indices included in Portfolio 1.

Table 17: Descriptive Statistics Standard Portfolio: Log Prices (Monthly)[762]

	Equities	Corporate Bonds	Government Bonds	Real Estate	Money Market
Mean	5.98	4.94	4.96	7.58	-3.65
Median	5.99	4.96	4.96	7.57	-3.74

[760] Both indices follow a best-in-class approach with a negative screening ex-AGTAFA. More details on the index methodologies can be found in STOXX (2012, b) for the Stoxx Europe Sustainability index and ECPI (2011, b) for the ECPI Corporate Bonds index.

[761] Log transformation will be convenient for the empirical analysis, as it allows for continuous compounding and has the advantage of being time-additive. See Brooks (2008), p. 8 et seq.

[762] All historical data we have used in our empirical analysis has been downloaded from the respective platform of data providers Bloomberg, DataStream and VWD, unless stated otherwise.

	Equities	Corporate Bonds	Government Bonds	Real Estate	Money Market
Maximum	6.39	5.14	5.17	8.28	-2.92
Minimum	5.47	4.69	4.70	6.99	-4.41
Std. Dev.	0.23	0.11	0.13	0.35	0.42
Skewness	-0.17	-0.22	-0.23	0.15	-0.07
Kurtosis	2.25	2.55	2.19	2.09	2.09
Jarque-Bera	3.41	2.04	4.37	4.65	4.21
Probability	0.18	0.36	0.11	0.10	0.12
Observations	120	120	120	120	120

Source: Own representation. Asset classes are represented by the following indices: 'Equities'=Stoxx Europe 600 index, 'Corporate Bonds'=Iboxx Corporates index, 'Government Bonds'=Iboxx Eurozone index, 'Real Estate'=FTSE Developed Europe index, 'Money Market'=1-year Euribor rate. Data history: monthly prices, 10-year time horizon from Dec-2001 to Nov-11.

As can be seen from the descriptive statistics, log price distributions tend to be normally distributed,[763] though slightly skewed (not symmetric around its mean) and platykurtic (distribution is flat relative to the normal). Continuously compounded (cc) returns for the Standard Portfolio, on the other hand, are predominantly non-normally distributed, with skewed distributions and leptokurtosis.

Table 18: Descriptive Statistics Standard Portfolio: Returns (Monthly)

	Equities	Corporate Bonds	Government Bonds	Real Estate	Money Market
Mean	0.06%	0.35%	0.34%	0.43%	-0.40%
Median	0.92%	0.40%	0.52%	1.40%	0.83%
Maximum	13.34%	3.59%	3.67%	18.33%	11.56%
Minimum	-15.15%	-4.91%	-2.61%	-24.23%	-27.52%
Std. Dev.	4.95%	1.15%	1.09%	5.66%	6.15%
Skewness	-0.70	-0.79	-0.06	-0.76	-1.60
Kurtosis	4.05	6.48	3.25	6.02	7.45
Jarque-Bera	15.05	72.68	0.37	56.71	149.10
Probability	0.01	0.00	0.83	0.00	0.00
Observations	119	119	119	119	119

Source: Own representation. Note: The return for the money market asset represents the change in the 1-year Euribor interest rate. This is equivalent to a mark-to-market on the proceeds invested.

In terms of riskiness, money market,[764] real estate assets and equities are the most volatile asset categories during our observation period, with annual-

[763] The Jarque-Bera statistics (the null H_0 assumes normality of the underlying data) shows evidence for normality at the 10% confidence level for all five indices. For details on this test statistic, see Jarque, Bera (1987).

[764] The return on the money market investments represent the change of the returns an investor receives on his investments. The actual return for this asset category is represented by the actual price level, i.e. the 1-year Euribor rate.

ised volatilities of 21.3%, 19.6% and 17.2%, respectively. The least-risky asset class, government bonds, only records 3.8% of annualised volatility.[765]

B. Portfolio 2: SRI Portfolio

The equivalent descriptive statistics for the SRI Portfolio indicate similar patterns than we found for the Standard Portfolio: log price distributions tend to follow a normal distribution, despite having less pronounced skewness and platykurtosis, while returns exhibit non-normality, excess kurtosis and skewness.

Table 19: Descriptive Statistics SRI Portfolio: Log Prices (Monthly)

	SRI Equities	SRI Corporate Bonds	SRI Government Bonds	Real Estate	Money Market
Mean	4.66	9.52	9.51	7.58	-3.65
Median	4.68	9.53	9.51	7.57	-3.74
Maximum	5.06	9.71	9.72	8.28	-2.92
Minimum	4.19	9.28	9.25	6.99	-4.41
Std. Dev.	0.21	0.12	0.12	0.35	0.42
Skewness	-0.11	-0.22	-0.23	0.15	-0.07
Kurtosis	2.32	2.56	2.19	2.09	2.09
Jarque-Bera	2.58	1.96	4.39	4.65	4.21
Probability	0.28	0.38	0.11	0.10	0.12
Observations	120	120	120	120	120

Source: Own representation. Asset classes are represented by the following indices: 'Equities'=Stoxx Europe Sustainability index, 'Corporate Bonds'=ECPI Corporates index, 'Government Bonds'=ECPI Euro Government index, 'Real Estate'=FTSE Developed Europe index, 'Money Market'=1-year Euribor rate. Data history: monthly prices, 10-year time horizon from Dec-2001 to Nov-11.

Table 20: Descriptive Statistics SRI Portfolio: Returns (Monthly)

	SRI Equities	SRI Corporate Bonds	SRI Government Bonds	Real Estate	Money Market
Mean	-0.05%	0.33%	0.33%	0.43%	-0.40%
Median	0.71%	0.39%	0.53%	1.40%	0.83%
Maximum	15.07%	3.85%	3.65%	18.33%	11.56%
Minimum	-15.94%	-4.68%	-3.55%	-24.23%	-27.52%
Std. Dev.	5.09%	1.18%	1.12%	5.66%	6.15%
Skewness	-0.59	-0.622	-0.25	-0.76	-1.60
Kurtosis	4.25	6.12	3.76	6.02	7.45
Jarque-Bera	14.78	56.00	4.16	56.71	149.10
Probability	0.00	0.00	0.12	0.00	0.00
Observations	119	119	119	119	119

Source: Own representation. Note: The return for the money market asset represents the change in the 1-year Euribor interest rate.

[765] See Hull (2006), p. 286. These numbers are calculated as follows: annual volatility=standard deviation (monthly returns) * $\sqrt[2]{12}$.

SRI indices have similar volatility figures than their benchmark references, with the equity index having 17.6% (vs. 17.2% in the Standard Portfolio) while the most conservative asset category, government bonds, reach 3.9% of annualised volatility (versus 3.8% in the Standard Portfolio).

C. Portfolio 3: Alternative Portfolio

The Alternative Portfolio only differs from the SRI Portfolio with respect to the inclusion of hedge fund and commodity indices. The descriptive statistics for the remaining assets of this portfolio are the same than for the SRI Portfolio. Focusing therefore exclusively on the statistics of the hedge fund and commodities log prices as well as related returns, we conclude that both asset classes do not show evidence of normality neither in their log prices nor in their log returns.

Table 21: Descriptive Statistics Alternative Portfolio: Log Prices (Monthly)

	SRI Equities	SRI Corp. Bonds	SRI Gov. Bonds	Real Estate	Mon. Markets	Hedge Funds	Comm.
Mean	4.66	9.52	9.51	7.58	-3.65	5.77	5.68
Median	4.68	9.53	9.51	7.57	-3.74	5.80	5.67
Max	5.06	9.71	9.72	8.28	-2.92	6.05	6.01
Min	4.19	9.28	9.25	6.99	-4.41	5.421	5.43
Std. Dev.	0.21	0.12	0.12	0.35	0.42	0.19	0.15
Skewness	-0.11	-0.22	-0.23	0.15	-0.07	-0.46	0.02
Kurtosis	2.32	2.56	2.19	2.09	2.09	2.06	1.75
JB	2.58	1.96	4.39	4.65	4.21	8.58	7.81
Prob.	0.28	0.38	0.11	0.10	0.12	0.01	0.02
Obs.	120	120	120	120	120	120	120

Source: Own representation. Asset classes are represented by the following indices: 'Equities'=Stoxx Europe Sustainability index, 'Corporate Bonds'=ECPI Corporates index, 'Government Bonds'=ECPI Euro Government index, 'Real Estate'=FTSE Developed Europe index, 'Money Market'=1-year Euribor rate, 'Hedge Funds'=DJ Credit Suisse Hedge Fund index, 'Commodities'=DJ UBS Commodity index. Data history: monthly prices, 10-year time horizon from Dec-2001 to Nov-11.

Table 22: Descriptive Statistics Alternative Portfolio: Returns (Monthly)

	SRI Equities	SRI Corp. Bonds	SRI Gov. Bonds	Real Estate	Mon. Markets	Hedge Funds	Comm.
Mean	-0.05%	0.33%	0.33%	0.43%	-0.40%	0.49%	0.22%
Median	0.71%	0.39%	0.53%	1.40%	0.83%	0.75%	0.71%
Max	15.07%	3.85%	3.65%	18.33%	11.56%	3.74%	9.53%
Min	-15.94%	-4.68%	-3.55%	-24.23%	-27.52%	-7.1%	-13.71%
Std. Dev.	5.09%	1.18%	1.12%	5.66%	6.15%	1.71%	4.57%
Skewness	-0.59	-0.62	-0.25	-0.76	-1.60	-1.70	-0.72
Kurtosis	4.25	6.12	3.76	6.02	7.45	8.08	3.56

	SRI Equities	SRI Corp. Bonds	SRI Gov. Bonds	Real Estate	Mon. Markets	Hedge Funds	Comm.
JB	14.78	56.00	4.16	56.71	149.10	185.3	11.95
Prob.	0.00	0.00	0.12	0.00	0.00	0.00	0.00
Obs.	119	119	119	119	119	119	119

Source: Own representation. Note: The return for the money market asset represents the change in the 1-year Euribor interest rate.

From a risk perspective, the inclusion of hedge fund and commodities investments seems to be beneficial (assuming less than perfect positive correlation), with annualised volatilities of 5.9% and 15.8%, respectively, and hence lower than the SRI equity assets and real estate investments. For allocation purposes, the Alternative Portfolio will have 5% invested in European equities, 35% in corporate bonds (-5 percentage points in comparison to both the Standard and SRI Portfolio), 40% government bonds (-5 percentage points), 5% real estate, 10% alternative investments (50% hedge fund assets, 50% commodities) and 5% money market instruments.

D. Risk-Adjusted Benchmarking of Input Assets

Figure 41 plots the risk-return combinations of each asset class we are using as input for our empirical analysis. The riskiness of each asset is hereby calculated as the annualised average standard deviation over the 10-year time period of our historical data, whereas the asset returns are determined as the average annual historical returns. Plotting the respective assets in a risk-return matrix results in interesting findings: equity assets, which are together with real estate investments the riskiest asset categories in terms of annual volatility, underperform considerably with respect to average return generated for investors.

Figure 41: Risk-Return Distributions of Input Assets (Average Values Last 10 Years)

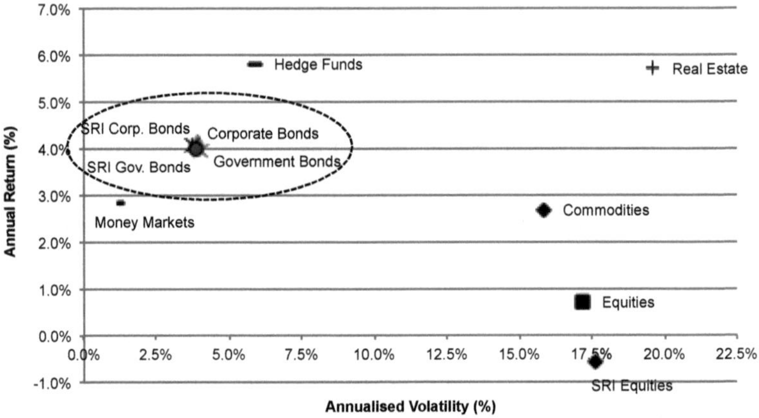

Source: Own figure. Note: Time period used for the calculation of the average return and the standard deviation is the 10-year time horizon from Dec-2001 to Nov-11. The money market risk-return figures reflect the average 1-year Euribor rate over the observation period and the corresponding standard deviation.

For the risk-adjusted comparison, we calculate for each asset class the respective Sharpe and Sortino ratios, using as risk-free rate the average 1-year Euribor rate over our observation period. Table 23 ranks the individual asset classes in descending order by the value of the Sortino ratio. On a risk-adjusted basis, equity assets underperform all other asset categories contemplated in the analysis, while hedge fund investments as well as all bond indices offer attractive risk-return constellations. The weak performance of equity assets will have a meaningful impact on our simulation study, as we will discuss in more detail in section 5.4.

Table 23: Risk-Adjusted Benchmarking: Sharpe Ratio and Sortino Ratio[766]

Rank	Asset Class	Portfolio Represented	Sharpe Ratio	Sortino Ratio
1	Hedge Funds	3	0.51	0.19
2	Government Bonds	1	0.33	0.14
3	Corporate Bonds	1	0.33	0.13
4	SRI Gov. Bonds	2	0.30	0.12
5	SRI Corp. Bonds	2	0.28	0.11
6	Real Estate	1,2,3	0.15	0.04
7	Money Markets	1,2,3	0.00	0.00
8	Commodities	3	(0.01)	0.00
9	Equities	1	(0.12)	(0.05)
10	SRI Equities	2	(0.19)	(0.07)

Source: Own representation. Abbreviations used: '1'=Standard Portfolio, '2'=SRI Portfolio, '3'=Alternative Portfolio.

5.2.3 Conclusions

The matching principle we have rigorously applied in the composition of our three reference portfolios ensures that SRI indices (equities, corporate and government bonds) have as benchmark the respective indices in the Standard Portfolio and consequently guarantee a high degree of comparability. Moreover, the SRI screening methodology is the same for both the equity and corporate bond indices (i.e. best-in-class with negative screening), in order to avoid a distortion of the results obtained due to different selection approaches.

The descriptive statistics reveal that log asset prices within the chosen portfolios and time horizon are normally distributed, whereas there is no statistical evidence that asset returns follow a normal distribution. The only exceptions to these findings are hedge fund and commodities, for which normality is rejected for both the log of asset prices as well as returns. Calculating risk-adjusted performance measures that do allow for the inclusion of non-normally distributed returns, we have benchmarked each individual asset class of our empirical study versus the risk-free rate. The Sortino ratio thereby ranks hedge funds as well as all four bond indices applied as preferable asset categories. Equity indi-

766 See Schroeder (1999), p. 386 et seq. As stated by Schroeder, the Sharpe ratio is only applicable if the asset returns follow approximately a normal distribution. The statistical evidence we have obtained in tables 18, 20 and 22, however, contradicts this assumption. We present the results for the Sharpe ratio therefore just for illustrative purposes. To obtain more reliable results for our benchmarking analysis, we have calculated the Sortino ratio proposed by Schroeder, which uses in the denominator instead of the realized standard deviation the square root of the lower partial moment of order 2. For the minimum acceptable return, we have included the risk-free rate based on the average 1-year Euribor of our observation period.

ces, nevertheless, both conventional and SRI-screened, underperform in comparison to all other assets considered.

Next chapter 5.3 will provide the results of our VEC regression analysis as well as outcomes of the respective diagnostic checks for the three main portfolios considered in our empirical analysis (Standard, SRI, Alternative Portfolio).

5.3 Vector Error Correction Modelling

5.3.1 Identification

Within the identification process, unit root tests, stationarity tests, considerations on dummy data as well as tests for cointegration relations are the most relevant techniques, as we have discussed in section 4.2.3.

A. Unit Root Tests

Applying the previously described unit root tests, the ADF-approach[767] and the PP-procedure[768] as well as the KPSS method[769] for stationarity testing, we obtain the following results for the indices of the three portfolios:

Table 24: Results for the Unit Root and Stationarity Tests

	ADF-Test[770] ------------- PP-Test			KPSS-Test		
	No Intercept, no trend	**Intercept, no trend**	**Intercept, trend**	**Intercept, no trend**	**Intercept, trend**	**Result[771]**
(1) Standard Portfolio						
Equities	I(1) / I(0)*** ---------- I(1) / I(0)***	I(1) / I(0)*** ---------- I(1) / I(0)***	I(1) / I(0)*** ---------- I(1) / I(0)***	I(1)* / I(0)	I(1)** / I(0)	Yes
Corporate Bonds	I(1) / I(0)*** ---------- I(1) /	I(1) / I(0)*** ---------- I(1) /	I(1) / I(0)*** ---------- I(1) /	I(1)*** / I(0)	I(1)* / I(0)	Yes

[767] Augmented Dickey-Fuller Test. See Cheung, Lai (1998), p. 58 et seq. and Dickey, Fuller (1979).

[768] Phillips-Perron Test. See Phillips, Perron (1988).

[769] Kwiatkowski-Philips-Schmidt-Shin Test. See Kwiatkowski et al. (1992).

[770] The upper data refers to the ADF-Test, whereas the number below the dashed line refers to the test results from the PP-Test.

[771] A 'Yes' indicates there is sufficient statistical support to assume that I(0), and therefore that returns have no unit roots (ADF, PP) or are stationary (KPSS test).

	ADF-Test[770] ------------- PP-Test			KPSS-Test		
	I(0)***	I(0)***	I(0)***			
Govern-ment Bonds	I(1) / I(0)*** ---------- I(1) / I(0)***	I(1) / I(0)*** ---------- I(1) / I(0)***	I(1) / I(0)*** ---------- I(1) / I(0)***	I(1)*** / I(0)	I(1)** / I(0)	Yes
Real Estate	I(1) / I(0)*** ---------- I(1) / I(0)***	I(1) / I(0)*** ---------- I(1) / I(0)***	I(1) / I(0)*** ---------- I(1) / I(0)***	I(1)* / I(0)	I(1)*** / I(0)	Yes
Money-Market	I(1) / I(0)*** ---------- I(1) / I(0)***	I(1) / I(0)*** ---------- I(1) / I(0)***	I(1) / I(0)*** ---------- I(1) / I(0)***	I(1)* [772] / I(0)	I(1)** / I(0)	Yes
(2) SRI Portfolio						
SRI Equities	I(1) / I(0)*** ---------- I(1) / I(0)***	I(1) / I(0)*** ---------- I(1) / I(0)***	I(1) / I(0)*** ---------- I(1) / I(0)***	I(1)* [773] / I(0)	I(1)** / I(0)	Yes
SRI Corporate Bonds	I(1) / I(0)*** ---------- I(1) / I(0)***	I(1) / I(0)*** ---------- I(1) / I(0)***	I(1) / I(0)*** ---------- I(1) / I(0)***	I(1)*** / I(0)	I(1)* / I(0)	Yes
SRI Govern-ment Bonds	I(1) / I(0)*** ---------- I(1) / I(0)***	I(1) / I(0)*** ---------- I(1) / I(0)***	I(1) / I(0)*** ---------- I(1) / I(0)***	I(1)*** / I(0)	I(1)* [774] / I(0)	Yes
(3) Alternative Portfolio						
Hedge Funds	I(1) / I(0)*** ---------- I(1) / I(0)***	I(1) / I(0)*** ---------- I(1) / I(0)***	I(1) / I(0)*** ---------- I(1) / I(0)***	I(1)*** / I(0)	I(1)** / I(0)	Yes
Commodi-ties	I(1) / I(0)*** ---------- I(1) / I(0)***	I(1) / I(0)*** ---------- I(1) / I(0)***	I(1) / I(0)*** ---------- I(1) / I(0)***	I(1)* [775] / I(0)	I(1)** / I(0)	Yes

Source: Own representation. For the ADF- and PP-test, the legend has the following meaning: */**/*** - H_0, which tests for the presence of unit roots, will be rejected at the 1%/5%/10% significance level for I(0), whereas there is no statistical evidence for rejecting H_0 for I(1) at any of the three significance levels. For the KPSS test, on the other hand, */**/*** represents the significance level at which H_0 and therefore the stationarity assumption will be rejected for I(1).

[772] Using a user-specified bandwidth of 6.
[773] Using a user-specified bandwidth of 7.
[774] Using a user-specified bandwidth of 7.
[775] Using a user-specified bandwidth of 7.

The results for the ADF- as well as the PP-test offer a clear picture: all financial time series data we are using as input variables in the simulation analysis show statistical evidence for unit roots in the price levels. Differencing once[776] to I(0) results in the rejection of the presence of unit roots. While both tests use as null hypothesis the assumption of unit roots for the data, the KPSS test assumes stationarity under the null. Therefore applying both testing procedures simultaneously increases considerably the reliability of the results. The outcome of the KPSS-test supports the evidence obtained with the ADF- and PP-tests. For all of these tests, we have calculated different assumptions on the selection of the deterministic term.[777]

B. Cointegration Relationships

First, we choose the number of lags for the unrestricted VAR employing an information criterion at price levels.[778] The initial lag length is fixed at $T^{1/3}$, with T representing the total number of observations[779], while the final lag length was estimated with the AIC[780] information criterion.[781] For all three portfolios, the AIC information criterion suggests an optimal lag length of 6. Trace statistics as well as maximum eigenvalues for the respective cointegration rank tests using the Johansen method described in 4.2.3, C for the three portfolios are summarised in tables 25 to 27.

---

776 Given that we are using log prices, differencing once to I(0) implies obtaining continuously compounded returns.

777 (1) No intercept, no trend in the data, (2) intercept, no trend, (3) intercept, trend.

778 See Enders (2010), p. 401 for this approach.

779 See Saikkonen, Luetkepohl (1996), p. 819 and Mills (1998), p. 5. Initial lag length in our empirical analysis is therefore $120^{1/3}$=4.93, rounded up to 5. To be able to capture semi-annual effects or dynamics our data may have, we use 6 lags (i.e. 6 months) as starting point. Winker (1999), p. 273, for example uses 6 months as it proofs to be a sufficiently large lag length structure to eliminate autocorrelation in the residuals.

780 See Akaike (1974).

781 As shown in Luetkepohl (2006), p. 156 et seq., in small samples, the information criterion AIC gives superior results in terms of forecast precision than HQ (see Hannan and Quinn, 1979) or SC (see Schwartz, 1978).

B.1 Standard Portfolio

Table 25: Test for the Cointegration Rank of the Standard Portfolio[782]

Hypothesized No. of CE(s)	Trace Statistic	P-Value[783]	Max. Eigenvalue Statistic	P-Value
None	99.26	0.00%	49.72	0.00%
At most 1	49.54	3.44%	30.09	2.33%
At most 2	19.45	46.08%	17.10	16.72%
At most 3	2.35	98.87%	1.81	99.44%
At most 4	0.54	46.35%	0.54	46.35%

Own representation. Abbreviations used: 'CE' = Cointegration equation, 'P-Value'=probability value. Note: these test values refer to a 5% critical value.

Both cointegration test statistics using the Johansen methodology conclude there are 2 cointegration equations at the 5% level within the assets of the Standard Portfolio. Also the corresponding graphs (figures 42) of the two cointegration relations support this result, as the processes appear stationary. We have hereby corrected the standard cointegration relations for short-run dynamics, as proposed by Johansen, Juselius (1992), as we are primarily focused on the long-run relations for this section of the analysis. This approach has the advantage that (short-run) large shocks to the system that may push the model away from the equilibrium path are avoided.[784]

782 These figures refer to the number of potential cointegration equations indicated by the Trace statistic (second column) and the Maximum Eigenvalue statistic (fourth column). For the deterministic trend assumption of the test, we allowed for a linear deterministic trend in the data, with an intercept (no trend) in the cointegration equation and a trend in the short-term dynamics of the VAR. This conclusion is based on the fact that our time series show a deterministic trend in their levels, whereas for the cointegration relations there are only constants present. See Neusser (2011), p. 241. See also Johansen (1995), pp. 80–84, on a more technical discussion on how to choose the adequate deterministic trend.

783 EViews applies hereby the MacKinnon-Haug-Michelis p-values. See MacKinnon, Haug (1999).

784 See Johansen, Juselius (1992), pp. 220-222.

Figure 42: Cointegration Relations in the Standard Portfolio

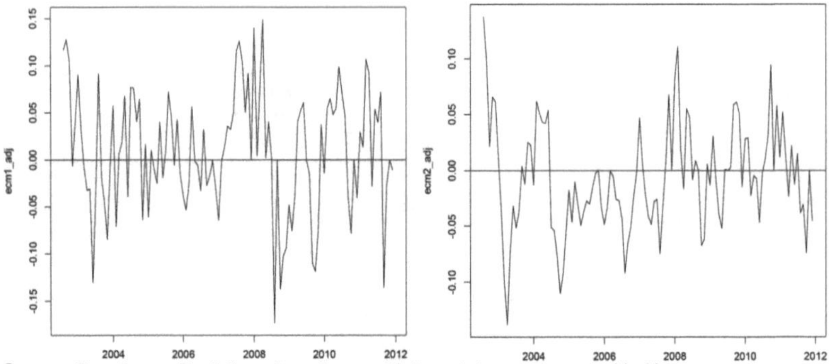

Source: Own figure. Deviations from the equilibrium state are measured in %.

The equilibrium cointegration relations we have established for the Standard Portfolio applying the Johansen technique are depicted in figure 42. Both cointegration relations are mean reverting as well as return back to the equilibrium state frequently. For both charts, no trend is observable.[785]

For the two cointegration equations, we impose three restrictions in total on the cointegrating vector β,[786] so that the final equations for the ecms become:[787]

$$CE\ 1_{t-1} = 18.77 * Equities_{t-1} - 13.26 * Real\ Estate_{t-1} + 1.86 * Money\ Market_{t-1} - 4.70 \quad (27)$$

$$CE\ 2_{t-1} = -30.28 * Corporate\ Bonds_{t-1} + 32.81 * Government\ Bonds_{t-1} - 2.86 * Real\ Estate_{t-1} + 2.08 * Money\ Market_{t-1} + 16.15 \quad (28)$$

785 Weakly mean-reverting error correction mechanisms, nonetheless, are often found in academic research studies. See for example Juselius, MacDonald (2002), p. 23, Juselius, MacDonald (2004), pp. 27-29 or Johansen, Juselius (1990), p. 187 and p. 191.

786 These three restrictions on the cointegration vector β were approved with a probability of 64.2% using the Likelihood Ratio statistic.

787 EViews 6 presents the cointegration coefficients in normalized form, so that the coefficient value of the first variable in the cointegration is set by the application equal to 1. This results in a normalized cointegration vector. However, as soon as restrictions are imposed on the cointegration vectors, as we have done in our analysis, the normalization is reversed. See Brooks (2008), p. 373.

B.2 SRI Portfolio

Table 26: Test for the Cointegration Rank of the SRI Portfolio

Hypothesized No. of CE(s)	Trace Statistic	P-Value	Max. Eigenvalue Statistic	P-Value
None	130.42	0.00%	59.67	0.00%
At most 1	70.75	0.00%	45.27	0.00%
At most 2	25.49	14.45%	19.92	7.32%
At most 3	5.57	74.54%	3.47	91.03%
At most 4	2.10	14.75%	2.10	14.75%

Source: Own representation. Abbreviations used: 'CE' = Cointegration equation, 'P-Value'=probability value. Note: these test values refer to a 5% critical value.

Also for the SRI Portfolio, the cointegration rank tests indicate there are two cointegration relations present at the 5% critical value threshold. The two error correction mechanisms estimated for the SRI Portfolio are represented in figure 43. The graphical depiction of the cointegration relations supports the conclusion from the rank tests, as both charts are stationary and return to the equilibrium frequently and in short time intervals.

Figure 43: Cointegration Relations in the SRI Portfolio

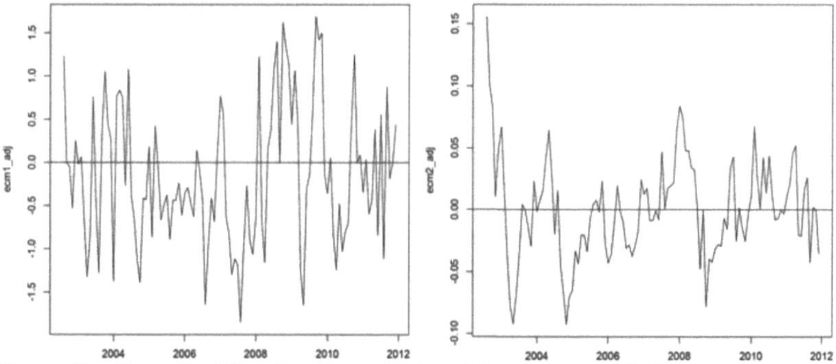

Source: Own figure. Deviations from the equilibrium state are measured in %.

The two restrictions we have imposed on the cointegration vector β have been approved with a probability of 34.5% using the Likelihood Ratio statistic.

$$CE\ 1_{t-1} = 19.15 * SRI\ Equities_{t-1} + 9.92 * SRI\ Corporate\ Bonds_{t-1} - 15.39 * Real\ Estate_{t-1} + 4.34 * Money\ Market_{t-1} - 50.85 \quad (29)$$

$$CE\ 2_{t-1} = -7.34 * SRI\ Equities_{t-1} - 55.67 * SRI\ Corporate\ Bonds_{t-1} + 55.73 * SRI\ Government\ Bonds_{t-1} + 2.86 * Money\ Market_{t-1} + 44.58 \quad (30)$$

B.3 Alternative Portfolio

Table 27: Test for the Cointegration Rank of the Alternative Portfolio

Hypothesized No. of CE(s)	Trace Statistic	P-Value	Max. Eigenvalue Statistic	P-Value
None	248.99	0.00%	89.24	0.00%
At most 1	159.74	0.00%	62.81	0.00%
At most 2	96.93	0.00%	41.01	0.01%
At most 3	55.92	0.07%	25.66	8.63%
At most 4	30.26	4.42%	20.39	6.33%
At most 5	9.87	29.06%	7.58	42.28%
At most 6	2.29	13.01%	2.29	13.01%

Source: Own representation. Abbreviations used: 'CE' = Cointegration equation, 'P-Value'=probability value. Note: these test values refer to a 5% critical value.

For the Alternative Portfolio, the trace statistic and the maximum eigenvalue statistic yield different results. This ambiguous outcome occurs often in empirical cointegration analysis, as the test procedures have in general low power for cases when the cointegration relation is relatively close to the nonstationary test limits.[788] Based on academic literature, there is no clear view on which of the two tests (maximum eigenvalue test or trace test) should be *a priori* preferred. While Luetkepohl et al. (2001) conclude that neither of the tests is to be prioritized in practice, there may be nonetheless differences in small samples. The maximum eigenvalue test "seem to have smaller size distortions than the trace test."[789] Enders (2010) states that the "λ_{max} test has the sharper alternative hypothesis. It is usually preferred for trying to pin down the number of cointegrating vectors".[790] Johansen, Juselius (1990) prefer the maximum eigenvalue test to the trace test, even though they recommend in general examining the estimated cointegration equation in case both tests yield conflicting results and base the final choice on the interpretability of the cointegration relationship.[791] Cheung, Lai (1993) conclude that the trace test is more robust to nonnormality than the maximum eigenvalue tests and therefore generates more robust results.[792] Based on these research recommendations and the analysis of the graphical representations of the respective cointegration relations we obtain for

[788] See Johansen, Juselius (1992), p. 221, quoted after Johansen (1991).
[789] Luetkepohl et al. (2001), p. 304.
[790] Enders (2010), p. 392.
[791] See Johansen, Juselius (1990), p. 181.
[792] See Maddala, Kim (1998), p. 217, quoted after Cheung, Lai (1993).

the Alternative Portfolio, we conclude there are three cointegration equations present.

Figure 44: Cointegration Relations in the Alternative Portfolio

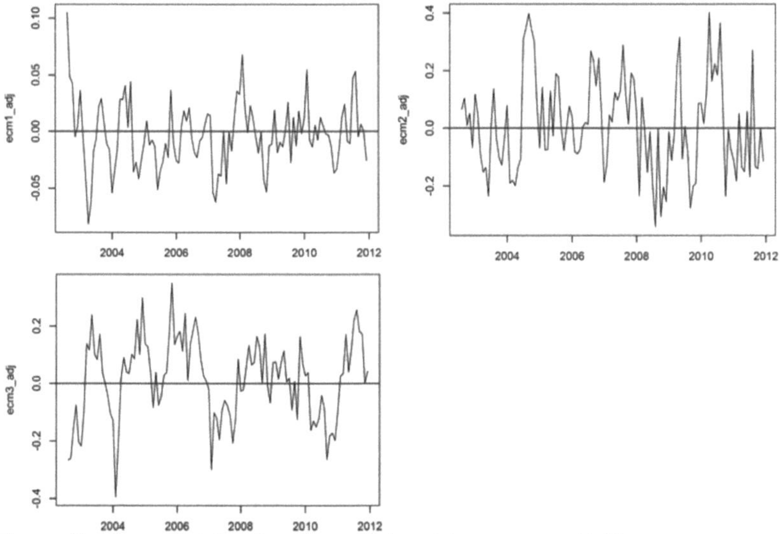

Source: Own figure. Deviations from the equilibrium state are measured in %.

As figure 44 illustrates, all 3 error correction mechanisms are stationary and cross the x-axis repeatedly, so that deviations from the long-term equilibrium amongst the cointegrated assets do not last for long.[793]. The corresponding charts for higher order ranks (>3) we have plotted separately, on the other hand, show non-stationary behaviour. Therefore our assumption of 3 cointegration equations seems plausible and justifiable.

$$CE\ 1_{t-1} = -7.69 * SRI\ Corporate\ Bonds_{t-1} - 2.51 * Money\ Market_{t-1} + 1.80 * Hedge\ Funds_{t-1} + 7.24 * Commodities_{t-1} + 12.53 \quad (31)$$

$$CE\ 2_{t-1} = 97.29 * SRI\ Corporate\ Bonds_{t-1} - 96.22 * SRI\ Government\ Bonds_{t-1} + 9.89 * Real\ Estate_{t-1} - 25.03 * Commodities_{t-1} + 56.22 \quad (32)$$

$$CE\ 3_{t-1} = -28.30 * SRI\ Equities_{t-1} + 24.36 * Real\ Estate_{t-1} - 2.73 * Hedge\ Funds_{t-1} - 22.74 * Commodities_{t-1} + 91.86 \quad (33)$$

[793] The 10 restrictions on the cointegration vector β have been approved with a probability of 57.8% using the Likelihood Ratio statistic.

5.3.2 Estimation

Using the VEC modelling approach described in section 4.2.4 of chapter 4, in particular the optimization algorithm to achieve efficient coefficient estimates as well as the SUR methodology, we obtain for each of the three portfolios contemplated an estimated VEC model for the time period Dec-2001 until Nov-2011 (incl.).[794]

A. Standard Portfolio

The estimated VEC model for the Standard Portfolio is presented in matrix form in formula 34.

$$
\begin{aligned}
\begin{pmatrix} \Delta EQ_t \\ \Delta CB_t \\ \Delta GB_t \\ \Delta RE_t \\ \Delta MM_t \end{pmatrix} = &
\begin{pmatrix} -0.008 & 0.000 \\ 0.000 & 0.000 \\ -0.002 & 0.002 \\ 0.000 & 0.010 \\ 0.011 & -0.030 \end{pmatrix} \cdot \begin{pmatrix} CE1_{t-1} \\ CE2_{t-1} \end{pmatrix} +
\begin{pmatrix} 0.00 & 0.00 & 1.28 & 0.00 & 0.23 \\ 0.00 & 0.00 & 0.00 & 0.00 & 0.00 \\ -0.07 & 0.00 & 0.00 & -0.03 & 0.00 \\ 0.76 & 2.24 & 0.00 & 0.00 & 0.34 \\ 0.00 & -0.97 & 0.00 & 0.16 & 0.39 \end{pmatrix} \cdot \begin{pmatrix} \Delta EQ_{t-1} \\ \Delta CB_{t-1} \\ \Delta GB_{t-1} \\ \Delta RE_{t-1} \\ \Delta MM_{t-1} \end{pmatrix} \\
& + \begin{pmatrix} 0.00 & 0.00 & -0.90 & 0.12 & -0.30 \\ 0.00 & -0.33 & 0.21 & 0.00 & 0.00 \\ 0.00 & 0.00 & -0.18 & 0.00 & 0.00 \\ 0.00 & 0.00 & 0.00 & 0.00 & -0.20 \\ -0.25 & 0.00 & 0.00 & 0.25 & -0.20 \end{pmatrix} \cdot \begin{pmatrix} \Delta EQ_{t-2} \\ \Delta CB_{t-2} \\ \Delta GB_{t-2} \\ \Delta RE_{t-2} \\ \Delta MM_{t-2} \end{pmatrix} +
\begin{pmatrix} 0.00 & 0.00 & 0.00 & 0.00 & -0.04 \\ 0.00 & 0.00 & 0.00 & 0.00 & 0.00 \\ 0.00 & 0.00 & 0.00 & -0.04 & 0.02 \\ 0.00 & 1.04 & -1.06 & 0.00 & 0.00 \\ -0.30 & -0.49 & 0.00 & 0.15 & 0.00 \end{pmatrix} \cdot \begin{pmatrix} \Delta EQ_{t-3} \\ \Delta CB_{t-3} \\ \Delta GB_{t-3} \\ \Delta RE_{t-3} \\ \Delta MM_{t-3} \end{pmatrix} \\
& + \begin{pmatrix} 0.00 & 0.00 & 0.00 & 0.00 & 0.00 \\ 0.00 & 0.00 & -0.17 & 0.00 & 0.00 \\ 0.04 & 0.38 & -0.25 & 0.00 & 0.00 \\ 0.18 & 0.00 & 0.66 & 0.00 & 0.41 \\ -0.16 & 0.00 & 0.00 & 0.00 & 0.00 \end{pmatrix} \cdot \begin{pmatrix} \Delta EQ_{t-4} \\ \Delta CB_{t-4} \\ \Delta GB_{t-4} \\ \Delta RE_{t-4} \\ \Delta MM_{t-4} \end{pmatrix} +
\begin{pmatrix} 0.00 & -1.71 & 1.93 & 0.00 & -0.29 \\ 0.00 & 0.24 & 0.00 & 0.00 & 0.00 \\ 0.00 & 0.00 & 0.00 & 0.00 & 0.00 \\ 0.12 & -1.11 & 1.60 & 0.20 & -0.33 \\ 0.00 & -0.74 & 0.00 & -0.12 & -0.39 \end{pmatrix} \cdot \begin{pmatrix} \Delta EQ_{t-5} \\ \Delta CB_{t-5} \\ \Delta GB_{t-5} \\ \Delta RE_{t-5} \\ \Delta MM_{t-5} \end{pmatrix} \\
& + \begin{pmatrix} 0.23 & 0.00 & -1.03 & 0.19 & 0.00 \\ 0.00 & 0.00 & 0.00 & 0.00 & -0.05 \\ 0.00 & 0.00 & 0.00 & 0.00 & 0.00 \\ 0.00 & 0.00 & 0.00 & 0.00 & 0.22 \\ 0.00 & 0.00 & 0.00 & 0.00 & 0.00 \end{pmatrix} \cdot \begin{pmatrix} \Delta EQ_{t-6} \\ \Delta CB_{t-6} \\ \Delta GB_{t-6} \\ \Delta RE_{t-6} \\ \Delta MM_{t-6} \end{pmatrix} +
\begin{pmatrix} 0.00 & -0.12 & 0.00 & 0.08 & -0.09 \\ 0.03 & -0.05 & 0.00 & -0.04 & 0.00 \\ 0.02 & 0.00 & -0.03 & -0.04 & 0.00 \\ -0.06 & 0.00 & -0.05 & 0.00 & 0.00 \\ -0.14 & 0.08 & 0.00 & 0.00 & 0.00 \end{pmatrix} \cdot \begin{pmatrix} DUM1_{t-4} \\ DUM2_{t-4} \\ DUM3_{t-4} \\ DUM4_{t-4} \\ DUM5_{t-4} \end{pmatrix} \\
& + \begin{pmatrix} 0.00 \\ 0.00 \\ 0.00 \\ -0.01 \\ 0.00 \end{pmatrix} + \begin{pmatrix} \hat{\varepsilon}_{t-1} \\ \hat{\varepsilon}_{t-2} \\ \hat{\varepsilon}_{t-3} \\ \hat{\varepsilon}_{t-4} \\ \hat{\varepsilon}_{t-5} \end{pmatrix} \qquad (34)
\end{aligned}
$$

with EQ=equities, CB=corporate bonds, GB=government bonds, RE=real estate, MM=money market. DUM1 refers to an intervention dummy that is 1 for Jul-2009 and 0 anywhere else. The same logic applies to DUM2=Sep-2008,

---

[794] For the estimation process, we have used intervention dummies for assets that have standardized residuals larger than $\pm 3\hat{\sigma}$. This approach is necessary for the residuals to approximately satisfy the normality requirement. For a similar intervention on outliers, see Juselius, MacDonald (2004), p. 25, Hendry, Juselius (2001), p. 85 or Luetkepohl (2004, a), p. 76. For studies using intervention dummies in general, see Beyer (1998), p. 62, Brooks (2008), p. 166 or Harris, Sollis (2003), p. 167.

DUM3=Nov-2010, DUM4=Nov-2011 and DUM5=Dec-2007. We also allow for an intercept in the cointegration relation. Both cointegration equations are as defined in formulas (27) and (28).

B. SRI Portfolio

$$
\begin{pmatrix} \Delta EQSRI_t \\ \Delta CBSRI_t \\ \Delta GBSRI_t \\ \Delta RE_t \\ \Delta MM_t \end{pmatrix} = \begin{pmatrix} -0.013 & 0.000 \\ 0.000 & 0.002 \\ 0.000 & 0.002 \\ -0.001 & 0.000 \\ 0.000 & -0.018 \end{pmatrix} * \begin{pmatrix} CE1_{t-1} \\ CE2_{t-1} \end{pmatrix} \begin{pmatrix} 0.00 & 0.00 & 0.00 & 0.00 & 0.00 \\ 0.00 & 0.29 & 0.00 & 0.00 & 0.07 \\ 0.00 & 0.22 & 0.00 & -0.02 & 0.06 \\ 0.00 & 1.13 & 0.00 & 0.00 & 0.00 \\ -0.13 & -1.47 & 0.00 & 0.00 & 0.27 \end{pmatrix} * \begin{pmatrix} \Delta EQSRI_{t-1} \\ \Delta CBSRI_{t-1} \\ \Delta GBSRI_{t-1} \\ \Delta RE_{t-1} \\ \Delta MM_{t-1} \end{pmatrix}
$$

$$
+ \begin{pmatrix} 0.00 & 0.00 & 0.00 & -0.11 & 0.00 \\ 0.00 & 0.00 & 0.00 & 0.00 & 0.00 \\ 0.00 & 0.00 & -0.22 & 0.00 & 0.00 \\ 0.00 & 0.00 & 0.00 & 0.00 & 0.00 \\ -0.25 & 0.64 & 0.00 & 0.25 & 0.00 \end{pmatrix} * \begin{pmatrix} \Delta EQSRI_{t-2} \\ \Delta CBSRI_{t-2} \\ \Delta GBSRI_{t-2} \\ \Delta RE_{t-2} \\ \Delta MM_{t-2} \end{pmatrix} + \begin{pmatrix} 0.00 & 0.00 & 0.00 & 0.00 & 0.00 \\ 0.00 & 0.12 & 0.00 & 0.00 & 0.00 \\ 0.06 & 0.00 & 0.18 & -0.05 & 0.00 \\ 0.00 & 0.71 & -1.11 & 0.00 & 0.00 \\ -0.12 & -0.92 & 0.00 & 0.00 & -0.23 \end{pmatrix} * \begin{pmatrix} \Delta EQSRI_{t-3} \\ \Delta CBSRI_{t-3} \\ \Delta GBSRI_{t-3} \\ \Delta RE_{t-3} \\ \Delta MM_{t-3} \end{pmatrix}
$$

$$
+ \begin{pmatrix} 0.00 & 0.00 & 0.00 & 0.00 & 0.00 \\ 0.00 & 0.00 & 0.00 & 0.00 & 0.00 \\ 0.00 & 0.25 & 0.00 & 0.00 & 0.06 \\ 0.00 & 0.00 & 0.00 & 0.00 & 0.00 \\ 0.00 & 1.24 & -1.40 & 0.00 & 0.00 \end{pmatrix} * \begin{pmatrix} \Delta EQSRI_{t-4} \\ \Delta CBSRI_{t-4} \\ \Delta GBSRI_{t-4} \\ \Delta RE_{t-4} \\ \Delta MM_{t-4} \end{pmatrix} + \begin{pmatrix} 0.00 & 0.00 & 0.00 & 0.00 & -0.22 \\ 0.00 & 0.00 & 0.00 & 0.00 & -0.04 \\ -0.03 & 0.00 & 0.00 & 0.00 & 0.00 \\ 0.00 & 0.00 & 0.00 & 0.00 & -0.18 \\ 0.00 & -0.72 & 0.00 & -0.10 & -0.36 \end{pmatrix} * \begin{pmatrix} \Delta EQSRI_{t-5} \\ \Delta CBSRI_{t-5} \\ \Delta GBSRI_{t-5} \\ \Delta RE_{t-5} \\ \Delta MM_{t-5} \end{pmatrix}
$$

$$
+ \begin{pmatrix} 0.00 & 0.00 & 0.00 & 0.00 & 0.00 \\ 0.00 & 0.00 & 0.00 & 0.00 & 0.00 \\ 0.00 & 0.00 & 0.00 & 0.00 & 0.00 \\ 0.00 & 0.00 & 0.00 & 0.00 & 0.00 \\ 0.00 & 0.00 & 0.00 & 0.00 & 0.00 \end{pmatrix} * \begin{pmatrix} \Delta EQSRI_{t-6} \\ \Delta CBSRI_{t-6} \\ \Delta GBSRI_{t-6} \\ \Delta RE_{t-6} \\ \Delta MM_{t-6} \end{pmatrix} + \begin{pmatrix} 0.00 & 0.00 & 0.00 \\ -0.02 & -0.04 & -0.05 \\ -0.04 & -0.05 & 0.00 \\ 0.00 & 0.00 & 0.00 \\ 0.00 & -0.07 & 0.07 \end{pmatrix} * \begin{pmatrix} DUM1_{1,t} \\ DUM2_{2,t} \\ DUM3_{3,t} \end{pmatrix}
$$

$$
+ \begin{pmatrix} 0.00 \\ 0.00 \\ 0.00 \\ 0.00 \\ 0.00 \end{pmatrix} + \begin{pmatrix} \hat{\varepsilon}_{1,t} \\ \hat{\varepsilon}_{2,t} \\ \hat{\varepsilon}_{3,t} \\ \hat{\varepsilon}_{4,t} \\ \hat{\varepsilon}_{5,t} \end{pmatrix} \quad (35)
$$

with EQSRI=SRI equities, CBSRI=SRI corporate bonds, GBSRI=SRI government bonds, RE=real estate, MM=money market and the following intervention dummies: DUM1=Nov-2010, DUM2=Nov-2011 and DUM3=Sep-2008. The details on the error correction mechanisms CE1 and CE2 for this portfolio are presented in formulas (29) and (30).

C. Alternative Portfolio

The Alternative Portfolio has just two intervention dummies: DUM1=Sep-2008 and DUM2=Nov-2011. The estimated VEC model becomes then:

$$\begin{pmatrix} \Delta EQSRI_t \\ \Delta CBSRI_t \\ \Delta GBSRI_t \\ \Delta RE_t \\ \Delta MM_t \\ \Delta HF_t \\ \Delta CO_t \end{pmatrix} = \begin{pmatrix} 0.015 & -0.003 & 0.013 \\ -0.004 & 0.000 & 0.000 \\ -0.004 & 0.000 & 0.000 \\ 0.000 & -0.004 & 0.001 \\ 0.058 & 0.013 & -0.001 \\ 0.000 & 0.000 & 0.002 \\ 0.000 & 0.005 & 0.000 \end{pmatrix} * \begin{pmatrix} CE1_{t-1} \\ CE2_{t-1} \\ CE3_{t-1} \end{pmatrix} + \begin{pmatrix} 0.00 & 0.00 & 0.00 & 0.00 & 0.00 & 0.00 & 0.00 \\ 0.00 & 0.00 & 0.00 & 0.00 & 0.00 & 0.00 & 0.00 \\ 0.00 & 0.00 & 0.00 & -0.03 & 0.00 & 0.00 & 0.00 \\ 0.00 & 1.88 & 0.00 & 0.00 & 0.19 & 0.00 & 0.00 \\ -0.15 & -1.29 & 0.00 & 0.00 & 0.00 & 0.00 & -0.29 \\ 0.00 & 0.59 & -0.49 & 0.00 & 0.00 & 0.00 & 0.00 \\ -0.25 & 1.61 & -1.35 & 0.00 & 0.00 & 0.00 & 0.00 \end{pmatrix} * \begin{pmatrix} \Delta EQSRI_{t-1} \\ \Delta CBSRI_{t-1} \\ \Delta GBSRI_{t-1} \\ \Delta RE_{t-1} \\ \Delta MM_{t-1} \\ \Delta HH_{t-1} \\ \Delta CO_{t-1} \end{pmatrix}$$

$$+ \begin{pmatrix} 0.00 & 0.00 & 0.00 & -0.22 & 0.16 & 0.64 & 0.19 \\ 0.00 & 0.00 & 0.00 & 0.00 & 0.00 & -0.15 & 0.00 \\ 0.00 & 0.38 & -0.48 & 0.00 & 0.00 & -0.33 & 0.00 \\ 0.00 & 0.00 & 0.00 & 0.00 & 0.00 & 0.00 & 0.00 \\ -0.27 & 0.00 & 0.83 & 0.28 & 0.00 & 0.00 & 0.00 \\ 0.00 & 0.00 & 0.00 & 0.00 & 0.00 & 0.00 & 0.00 \\ 0.00 & -0.76 & 0.74 & 0.00 & 0.00 & 0.00 & 0.12 \end{pmatrix} * \begin{pmatrix} \Delta EQSRI_{t-2} \\ \Delta CBSRI_{t-2} \\ \Delta GBSRI_{t-2} \\ \Delta RE_{t-2} \\ \Delta MM_{t-2} \\ \Delta HH_{t-2} \\ \Delta CO_{t-2} \end{pmatrix}$$

$$+ \begin{pmatrix} 0.00 & 0.00 & -0.52 & 0.00 & 0.00 & 0.00 & 0.36 \\ 0.00 & 0.00 & 0.00 & 0.00 & -0.03 & 0.00 & 0.03 \\ 0.00 & 0.00 & 0.00 & 0.00 & 0.00 & 0.00 & 0.00 \\ 0.00 & 1.49 & -2.11 & 0.00 & 0.00 & 0.00 & 0.35 \\ -0.26 & -0.49 & 0.00 & 0.21 & 0.00 & 0.00 & 0.00 \\ 0.00 & 0.00 & 0.00 & 0.00 & 0.00 & 0.00 & 0.00 \\ 0.18 & 0.00 & 0.00 & 0.00 & -0.21 & 0.49 & -0.18 \end{pmatrix} * \begin{pmatrix} \Delta EQSRI_{t-3} \\ \Delta CBSRI_{t-3} \\ \Delta GBSRI_{t-3} \\ \Delta RE_{t-3} \\ \Delta MM_{t-3} \\ \Delta HH_{t-3} \\ \Delta CO_{t-3} \end{pmatrix}$$

$$+ \begin{pmatrix} 0.00 & 0.00 & 0.00 & 0.00 & 0.00 & 0.00 & 0.00 \\ 0.00 & 0.00 & 0.00 & 0.00 & 0.00 & 0.15 & 0.00 \\ 0.00 & 0.33 & -0.23 & 0.00 & 0.00 & 0.00 & 0.00 \\ 0.00 & 0.00 & 0.00 & 0.00 & 0.28 & 0.00 & 0.00 \\ -0.14 & 0.74 & -1.21 & 0.00 & -0.21 & 0.00 & 0.00 \\ 0.00 & 0.00 & 0.00 & 0.00 & 0.00 & 0.00 & 0.06 \\ 0.00 & -0.90 & 0.00 & 0.00 & 0.00 & 0.00 & 0.21 \end{pmatrix} * \begin{pmatrix} \Delta EQSRI_{t-4} \\ \Delta CBSRI_{t-4} \\ \Delta GBSRI_{t-4} \\ \Delta RE_{t-4} \\ \Delta MM_{t-4} \\ \Delta HH_{t-4} \\ \Delta CO_{t-4} \end{pmatrix}$$

$$+ \begin{pmatrix} 0.00 & 0.82 & -0.86 & -0.18 & 0.00 & 0.00 & 0.00 \\ 0.00 & 0.00 & 0.00 & 0.00 & 0.00 & 0.00 & 0.00 \\ 0.00 & -0.22 & 0.00 & 0.00 & 0.00 & 0.00 & 0.00 \\ 0.13 & 0.00 & 0.67 & 0.00 & -0.28 & -0.59 & 0.00 \\ 0.00 & 0.00 & -0.47 & -0.15 & -0.22 & 0.00 & -0.15 \\ 0.00 & 0.20 & 0.00 & -0.04 & 0.00 & 0.00 & 0.00 \\ 0.00 & 0.84 & 0.00 & 0.00 & 0.00 & -0.70 & 0.00 \end{pmatrix} * \begin{pmatrix} \Delta EQSRI_{t-5} \\ \Delta CBSRI_{t-5} \\ \Delta GBSRI_{t-5} \\ \Delta RE_{t-5} \\ \Delta MM_{t-5} \\ \Delta HH_{t-5} \\ \Delta CO_{t-5} \end{pmatrix}$$

$$+ \begin{pmatrix} 0.00 & 0.00 & 0.00 & 0.00 & 0.00 & 0.00 & 0.00 \\ 0.00 & 0.00 & 0.00 & 0.00 & -0.06 & 0.00 & 0.00 \\ 0.00 & 0.00 & 0.00 & 0.00 & 0.00 & 0.00 & 0.00 \\ 0.00 & 0.00 & 0.00 & 0.00 & 0.19 & 0.00 & 0.00 \\ 0.00 & 0.00 & 0.00 & 0.00 & -0.13 & -0.63 & 0.00 \\ 0.00 & 0.00 & 0.00 & 0.00 & 0.00 & 0.00 & 0.00 \\ 0.29 & 0.00 & 0.74 & -0.26 & 0.00 & 0.00 & 0.00 \end{pmatrix} * \begin{pmatrix} \Delta EQSRI_{t-6} \\ \Delta CBSRI_{t-6} \\ \Delta GBSRI_{t-6} \\ \Delta RE_{t-6} \\ \Delta MM_{t-6} \\ \Delta HH_{t-6} \\ \Delta CO_{t-6} \end{pmatrix}$$

$$+ \begin{pmatrix} 0.00 & 0.00 \\ -0.05 & -0.05 \\ 0.00 & -0.05 \\ -0.05 & 0.00 \\ 0.00 & 0.00 \\ -0.06 & -0.04 \\ 0.00 & 0.00 \end{pmatrix} * \begin{pmatrix} DUM1_{1,t} \\ DUM2_{2,t} \end{pmatrix} + \begin{pmatrix} 0.00 \\ 0.00 \\ 0.01 \\ 0.00 \\ 0.00 \\ 0.00 \\ 0.00 \end{pmatrix} + \begin{pmatrix} \hat{\varepsilon}_{1,t} \\ \hat{\varepsilon}_{2,t} \\ \hat{\varepsilon}_{3,t} \\ \hat{\varepsilon}_{4,t} \\ \hat{\varepsilon}_{5,t} \\ \hat{\varepsilon}_{6,t} \\ \hat{\varepsilon}_{7,t} \end{pmatrix} \quad (36)$$

5.3.3 Diagnostic Checking

Once a VEC model has been estimated, it is necessary to assess if the model is an "adequate representation of the Data Generation Process underlying the time series set of interest".[795] Should the model have non-normally distributed residuals or residuals that are autocorrelated, then it can be concluded that the estimated VEC is a weak representation of the DGP.[796]

A. Goodness-of-Fit

The Adjusted-R^2 figure is a good and commonly used goodness-of-fit statistic that indicates how much variation of the dependent variable is explained by the estimated model.[797] Moreover, we will also plot the F-statistic, which tests the hypothesis that all of the slope coefficients of the regression are zero. The p-value represents thereby the marginal significance level of the F-test.[798]

Table 28: Considerations on Adjusted-R^2 and F-Statistic

	Adjusted.-R^2 [799]	**p-Value F-Statistic**
(1) Standard Portfolio		
Equities (equation 1 in VECM)	37.4%	0.00%
Corporate Bonds (equation 2)	49.9%	0.00%
Government Bonds (equation 3)	33.0%	0.00%
Real Estate (equation 4)	72.0%	0.00%
Money Market (equation 5)	77.0%	0.00%
(2) SRI Portfolio		
SRI Equities (equation 1)	32.1%	0.00%
SRI Corporate Bonds (equation 2)	48.1%	0.00%
SRI Government Bonds (equation 3)	33.3%	0.00%
Real Estate (equation 4)	35.6%	0.00%
Money Market (equation 5)	74.7%	0.00%
(3) Alternative Portfolio		
SRI Equities (equation 1)	46.9%	0.00%
SRI Corporate Bonds (equation 2)	47.6%	0.00%
SRI Government Bonds (equation 3)	30.8%	0.00%

795 Luetkepohl (2004, b), p. 125.
796 See Luetkepohl (2004, b), p. 125.
797 See Brooks (2008), p. 110 et seq.
798 See Quantitative Micro Software (2007), p. 15.
799 To compare these results with similar academic studies that use VEC model regressions, see for example Juselius (1998), p. 406, Bonham et al. (2009), p. 542, Hendry, Juselius (2001), p. 105 or Juselius (2006), p. 73. On the basis of a relative comparison to these studies in terms of the Adjusted-R^2 number, our results are satisfactory.

	Adjusted.-R^2 [799]	p-Value F-Statistic
Real Estate (equation 4)	46.7%	0.00%
Money Market (equation 5)	82.0%	0.00%
Hedge Funds (equation 6)	40.9%	0.00%
Commodities (equation 7)	37.1%	0.00%

Source: Own representation.

B. Normality, Autocorrelation and Heteroskedasticity of Residuals

For each individual estimated equation, the underlying asset should have residuals that are asymptotically normally distributed and show no autocorrelation. For our analysis, we have used the Jarque-Bera test (see also section 4.2.5, B on a detailed explanation) to assess normality, while for autocorrelation we have applied the Ljung-Box Q-statistics[800] and the Breusch-Godfrey Serial Correlation LM test[801] (see section 4.2.5, C) for individual asset classes whereby for the entire portfolio the Portmanteau-test[802] was used. Heteroskedasticity effects were assessed with the ARCH test explained in 4.2.5, D. The respective results are summarised in table 29.

Table 29: Normality, Autocorrelation and Heteroskedasticity Tests (p-values)

	Normality	Autocorrelation[803]	Heteroskedasticity
(1) Standard Portfolio		98.9%	
Equities	22.2%	60.0%/89.8%/57.3%80.2%	46.4%
Corporate Bonds	25.6%	70.1%/40.7%/61.5%/91.1%	26.2%
Government Bonds	76.2%	21.5%/83.1%/31.3%/36.3%	12.9%
Real Estate	29.5%	44.0%/92.6%/65.0%/83.3%	90.5
Money Market	13.8%	99.5%/94.4%/94.8%/90.3%	8.6%
(2) SRI Portfolio		89.9%	
SRI Equities	89.1%	96.7%/98.4%/76.0%/94.1%	3.7%*[804]
SRI Corporate Bonds	52.1%	88.4%/18.6%/18.1%/19.7%	34.4%
SRI Government Bonds	16.8%	72.4%/72.4%/93.6%/96.2%	75.5%
Real Estate	91.4%	98.4%/94.0%/24.2%/34.5%	85.5%
Money Market	86.0%	81.0%/69.1%/89.2%/51.9%	98.4%

[800] See Ljung, Box (1979).
[801] See Luetkepohl (2006), pp. 171-174.
[802] See Luetkepohl (2006), pp. 169-171.
[803] For the entire portfolio, the corresponding value refers to the Portmanteau-test, whereas for each individual asset class, the first value corresponds to the Ljung-Box Q-statistics with 12 lags whereas values 2-4 belong to the results of the Breusch-Godfrey Serial Correlation LM test for one lag, two lags and four lags, respectively.
[804] Heteroskedasticity in the residuals of VEC regressions may affect estimation efficiency but should not produce biased inference, so that they do not represent a serious issue for our purposes. See Juselius, MacDonald (2004), p. 25, Luetkepohl (2004, b), p. 131 or Juselius (2006), p. 47.

	Normality	Autocorrelation[803]	Heteroskedasticity
(3) Alternative Portfolio		99.9%	
SRI Equities	96.1%	83.9%/42.0%/59.1%/50.2%	0.9%*
SRI Corporate Bonds	38.8%	52.4%/52.0%/74.6%/94.7%	6.8%
SRI Government Bonds	66.3%	98.4%/89.6%/82.8%/78.0%	58.5%
Real Estate	75.0%	91.9%/64.7%/69.3%/85.3%	65.9%
Money Market	84.4%	50.7%/48.0%53.7%/81.7%	98.7%
Hedge Funds	59.5%	98.5%/93.9%/98.3%/99.8%	73.1%
Commodities	95.4%	7.7%/19.5%/15.2%/22.3%	0.1%*

Source: Own representation. Values highlighted with a * indicate figures that are rejected at the 5% confidence level.

Using a significance level of 5%, we conclude that the residuals of the individual asset classes used in the estimation of the VEC models are normally distributed and do not exhibit evidence of autocorrelation. The respective residuals for the entire portfolio do also not show autocorrelation effects, as indicated by the Portmanteau test statistic. Moreover, the vast majority of single assets are homoscedastic, even though the three cases of heteroskedasticity do not cause an issue for our modelling purposes. In summary, the individual variables we have used for the optimised VEC models do fulfil the statistical requisites for being used in the regressions.

C. Forecasting Quality

The forecasting methods described in section 4.2.5, E yield the following results:

C.1 Static Forecasts (1-Month Ahead Predictions)

As we explained earlier, static forecasts allow us to obtain one-step ahead forecasts over the historical data used in the analysis, with the objective to assess the historical fit of the VEC model. For our three portfolios, 1-month ahead forecasts for each individual asset classes are depicted in figures 70-72 in appendix C. In all portfolios, the simulated forecasts achieve a high degree of precision, so that we conclude that the underlying estimated regression model is suitable to capture the data generating process of the time series data and provide satisfying forecasts.

C.2 Correct Sign Predictions

Table 30 summarises our forecasting indicator test presented in section 4.2.5, E3 that enables us to assess the forecasting ability of the underlying

VECM. The predictions are hereby calculated on a 1-month forward basis, similar therefore to the graphs we have exhibited in appendix C.

Table 30: Correct Sign Prediction Across Portfolios

Portfolio	Asset Category	Proportion of Correct Sign Predictions
(1) Standard Portfolio		61.3%[805]
	Equities	*58.9%*
	Corporate Bonds	*47.7%*
	Government Bonds	*52.3%*
	Real Estate	*77.6%*
	Money Market	*70.1%*
(2) SRI Portfolio		60.0%
	SRI Equities	*56.1%*
	SRI Corporate Bonds	*54.2%*
	SRI Government Bonds	*57.0%*
	Real Estate	*64.5%*
	Money Market	*68.2%*
(3) Alternative Portfolio		60.9%
	SRI Equities	59.8%
	SRI Corporate Bonds	55.1%
	SRI Government Bonds	56.1%
	Real Estate	63.6%
	Money Market	73.8%
	Hedge Funds	59.8%
	Commodities	57.9%

Source: Own representation.

The overall results are satisfactory, as on average all three models manage to predict the signs of next month returns in 60% or more of the cases. These numbers compare favourably to similar research studies.[806]

5.3.4 Conclusions

We have been able to establish cointegration relationships amongst the assets used in all three portfolios applying the Johansen cointegration test methodology. Consequently, the VEC model is an appropriate time-series model to capture the data generating process of the underlying assets as it also allows for the inclusion of error correction mechanisms. Our optimized and final VEC models have all efficient and robust coefficient estimates thanks to the model

805 Equally-weighted average value.

806 See Brooks (1997), pp. 137-139. Brooks compares the predictive power of different time series models on foreign exchange data and obtains for the majority of these models a predicttive power in terms of correct sign prediction in the range of 41%-54%. He also applies in his study 1-step ahead forecasts.

reduction technique applied and the SUR estimation method. Goodness-of-fit statistics as well as the analysis of the model residuals confirm the satisfactory outcome of our regression exercise. Moreover, our forecasting assessments support the appropriateness of our models for forecasting and ultimately simulation purposes.

In subsequent chapter 5.4, we will present the results of the various simulations of the different investment strategies contemplated for the three standard investment models. For each portfolio, we will provide the data output in a table as well as in chart format. While sections 5.4.2-5.4.5 include the performance results by investment strategy for all three portfolios, section 5.4.6 groups the data by portfolio across investment strategies. In 5.4.7, we run a benchmarking analysis across portfolios and investment strategies to determine best- and worst-performing strategies amongst the standard investment models contemplated in our analysis.

5.4 Simulation of Investment Management Strategies

5.4.1 Modelling Assumptions

Our estimated VEC models, combined with the randomly selected error terms via the bootstrap simulation method, enable us to generate 10,000 returns per month per asset class, for a total forecasting period of 3 years. These returns represent the input for our various portfolio management strategies. The final implementation of these strategies relies on some modelling assumptions that are summarised in this section.

A. Average Asset Allocation for Portfolios

The initial asset allocation we will assume for our Standard and SRI Portfolios replicate the average asset allocation of German Pension Insurance Funds. The respective asset class proportion is thereby the average value for the last 5 years (see section 2.5.2 on the allocation statistics). For the Alternative Portfolio, we will include in addition 5% of hedge fund and commodity assets, respectively. The overall allocation structures for all three portfolios are summarised in table 31.

Table 31: Asset Allocation Assumptions

Standard Portfolio		SRI Portfolio		Alternative Portfolio	
Asset Class	**Weight (%)**	**Asset Class**	**Weight (%)**	**Asset Class**	**Weight (%)**
Equities	5%	SRI Equities	5%	SRI Equities	5%
Corp. Bonds	40%	SRI Corp. Bonds	40%	SRI Corp. Bonds	35%
Govern. Bonds	45%	SRI Govern. Bonds	45%	SRI Govern. Bonds	40%
Real Estate	5%	Real Estate	5%	Real Estate	5%
Money Market	5%	Money Market	5%	Money Market	5%
				Hedge Funds	5%
				Commodities	5%
Total	**100%**		**100%**		**100%**

Source: Own representation.

B. Maximum Guaranteed Return

Since 01-Jan-2012, German Life Insurers and Pension Insurance Funds can only offer to their clients a maximum guaranteed return of 1.75% per annum on their pension contributions, down from the 2.0% guarantee in place until the end of 2011.[807] While for pension plans with defined contributions with capital guarantee (DCCG)[808] the pensioner is only entitled to receive the sum of all contributions accumulated until the moment an insured event occurs plus any excess returns the invested capital has achieved until that point (minimum legal requirement), we will assume that the pension fund and ultimately the sponsoring company offers its employees the maximum guaranteed return of 1.75% p.a.. Consequently, 1.75% is deducted from the nominal value of the portfolio on an annual basis.

C. Cost of Insuring Biometric Risks

No assumptions have been made with respect to the costs a Pension Insurance Fund may incur to hedge biometric risk. This cost would have to be deducted from the net value of the portfolio on a periodic basis.

D. Inflation

All our prices and returns are in nominal terms, so that no adjustment for inflation will be considered. The rationale for using nominal terms is related to the capital guarantee pension plans with defined contributions with capital guaran-

[807] See Gesamtverband der Deutschen Versicherungswirtschaft (2012).
[808] As worded in Sec. 1 Par. 2 No. 2 BetrAVG.

tee offer their members, which is expressed in nominal terms. We will nonetheless make reference to the potential impact inflation could have on our results within the respective investment strategies, as from an investor's perspective a professional investment management does have to take into account for increasing price levels. As a reference value for inflation, we have calculated an average annual inflation of 2.06% over the last 10 years using the data published by the ECB.[809] Continuously compounding this inflation number over 3 years and using an initial investment value of 100, we obtain a minimum value for the portfolio of 106.36 that would need to be achieved at the end of our investment period to obtain capital guarantee in real terms. Furthermore, we have dedicated an entire section on inflation considerations given the importance price change aspects should play in modern pension fund management (see section 5.5.3)

E. Total Return Considerations

As we are using total return indices for our simulations, any return in the form of dividend and/ or coupon payments will be reinvested into the index. Apart from the 1.75% annual pay-out, no further capital reduction will occur during the investment period.

F. Minimum Acceptable Return for Lower Partial Moments

For the calculation of the Lower Partial Moments, which will enable us to assess the downside risk of our investment strategies, we have used as Minimum Acceptable Return (MAR) 0% per annum. We therefore expect the strategy to achieve at least 0%, post the 1.75% p.a. for the Maximum Guaranteed Return that have already been deducted from the gross portfolio values at the end of each year.

As such, a pension beneficiary can be certain to receive his 1.75% return plus benefit from capital protection on the funds invested. Any strategy that on average does not achieve the minimum overall return is not suitable (i.e. 1.75% Maximum Guaranteed Return plus 0% MAR).

---

[809] The number published by the ECB is the annual inflation rate published on a monthly basis. The time period considered is identical to the one used for our empirical analysis, i.e. Dec-2001 until Nov-2011. See ECB (2012, a).

G. Transaction Costs

For all investment strategies, we have assumed zero transaction costs.[810] While this is not realistic in capital markets, ignoring such costs facilitates considerably the extensive simulation studies.

H. Tax Aspects

Our empirical analysis does not consider any taxation aspects that may come up as part of the daily business within the investment management of a Pension Insurance Fund. Nonetheless, the overall tax treatment of pension contributions for occupational pension schemes in Germany is beneficial for the pension plan, as based on Sec. 4c Par. 1 EStG, any contribution by the sponsoring company into the Pension Insurance Fund will be tax deductible. Moreover, for the beneficiary, pension benefits are fully taxable as defined in Sec. 22 Par. 5 No. 1 EStG if the contributions paid into the pension plan benefited initially from the tax-exemption of Sec. 3 Par. 63 EStG that refers to the social security cost exemption for pension contributions.[811] Due to the deferred taxation of pension benefits, our assumption of ignoring tax aspects seems therefore plausible.

I. Size Considerations Derivative Overlays

Derivative transactions, like the collar contemplated in our analysis, are usually OTC contracts, in which the counterparty is normally a financial institution. The counterparty usually hedges some risks associated with being either long or short a collar. Such hedging techniques are dependent, amongst other factors, on the liquidity of the underlying, so that possibly not all sizing considerations we have used in our analysis could be executed in a real life deal situation. We will focus exclusively on derivative strategies for the equities portion of the overall fund, which at inception represents 5% of the total AuM. Derivatives on other asset classes are not considered in section 5.4 (for alternative models, nonetheless, see chapter 5.5).

---

[810] Main transaction costs that could be incurred with our investment strategies are bid-ask spreads, brokerage fees as well as potential price impacts when large portfolio reallocations occur.

[811] See Wolf (2011), p. 216.

5.4.2 Outright Strategies

In the Buy-and-Hold outright strategy, the investor maintains the initial portfolio weights unchanged during the entire investment period of one year. At the end of this period, the initial weights are reinstated. During the year a rebalancing could only occur should one of the regulatory maximum caps for the asset classes be reached. In such an instance, the portfolio would be returned again to its initial weights. In all subsequent analyses of investment strategies, we will focus primarily on those approaches that pose the largest threat to capital preservation. We therefore maintain our conservative investor perspective when comparing results, as ultimately our research interest is concentrated primarily on the suitability of strategies for pension funds that are bound by regulatory obligations to offer capital guarantee to their beneficiaries. In chapter 5.5, nonetheless, we will contemplate alternative investment scenarios that do not have to comply with the regulatory investment limitations imposed by the German regulator BaFin.

In the Constant-Mix scenario, the portfolio is rebalanced at the end of every month to its initial portfolio weights. This method leads thus to a lower probability of breaching the regulatory caps. Constant-Mix methods lead to an asset allocation in year 3 that is similar in its asset weights to the one at inception. It is therefore characterised as a very rigid investment methodology.

A. Buy-and-Hold: Outright

A.1 Value Distribution after 3 Years

Figure 45: Buy-and-Hold Outright Strategies Across Portfolios (Value after 3yrs)

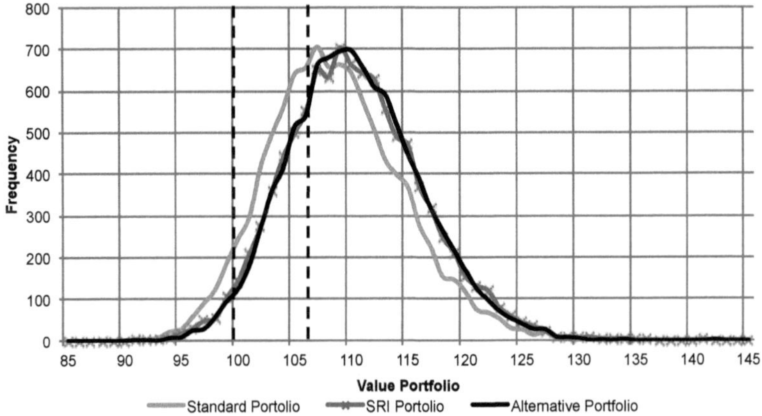

Source: Own figure. The first dotted black line indicates par value, while the second line reflects par value after three years taking into account for inflation. This line is positioned at 106.36, what corresponds to an average annual inflation rate of 2.06%, continuously compounded over three years and an initial investment value of 100.

A.2 Risk, Return and Distribution Characteristics over Investment Period

Table 32: Risk, Return and Distribution Measures: Buy-and-Hold Outright Strategy

	Standard Portfolio			SRI Portfolio			Alternative Portfolio		
	YR 1	YR2	YR3	YR 1	YR2	YR3	YR 1	YR2	YR3
Performance									
Average Value	100.16	103.84	108.07	101.09	105.81	109.75	101.77	106.78	***109.79***
CAGR (%)	0.16	1.88	2.59	1.09	2.83	3.10	1.75	3.28	***3.11***
Maximum	111.46	125.96	135.42	114.98	129.10	140.59	114.79	126.50	***141.14***
Minimum	89.89	90.61	87.89	89.32	91.77	***90.20***	91.09	90.78	89.77
Median	100.08	103.66	107.69	100.95	105.49	109.43	101.68	106.56	***109.46***
Distribution Analysis									
Std. Dev. Returns (%)[812]	2.60	4.28	5.47	3.20	4.63	5.46	2.86	4.53	***5.28***
Skewness	-0.02	-0.01	-0.01	-0.02	-0.01	0.00	-0.03	-0.05	-0.04
Skewness T-Ratio	0.86	0.48	0.58	0.97	0.45	0.00	1.14	2.11	1.63
Kurtosis	-0.05	-0.03	0.01	0.02	-0.02	0.05	0.06	-0.02	-0.02
Kurtosis T-Ratio	0.94	0.61	0.30	0.43	0.43	1.01	1.25	0.45	0.35

[812] Calculated as standard deviation of cumulated returns at the end of year 3.

	Standard Portfolio			SRI Portfolio			Alternative Portfolio		
Downside Risk Measures (LPMs)									
Omega	1.13	9.50	44.84	2.29	25.97	110.37	4.60	49.38	***131.26***
Downside Dev. (%)	1.74	1.26	0.82	1.65	0.87	0.55	1.17	0.65	***0.51***
Sortino Ratio	0.07	2.91	9.22	0.63	6.38	16.54	1.46	9.94	***17.99***
Kappa 3	0.05	1.87	4.97	0.45	3.71	8.05	0.98	5.33	***8.32***
Upside Pot. Ratio	0.63	3.26	9.43	1.12	6.63	16.69	1.87	10.14	***18.13***

Source: Own representation. Bold and in italic highlighted numbers indicate the best-performing investment strategy (taking into consideration the conservative investment objectives of German Pension Insurance Funds) within the respective category after an investment period of 3 years, whereas underlined numbers denote the worse performing approach in the corresponding group. For skewness and kurtosis, no highlighting will be applied. Abbreviations used: 'CAGR'=compounded annual growth rate, 'Std. Dev.'=standard deviation.

A.3 Observations

Comparing the performance of the three portfolios with respect to the Buy-and-Hold outright strategy at the end of year 3 reveals the overall outperformance both the SRI as well as the Alternative Portfolio achieve vs. the Standard Portfolio. This conclusion can be generalised to almost all strategies analysed in our study. For the Buy-and-Hold outright scenario, the Alternative Portfolio reaches at the end of year 3 both the highest absolute value with 141.14%[813] of the initial par value of 100 (11.49% annual continuous return) as well as the highest average with 109.79% (3.11%). The price distributions for all three portfolios show statistical evidence for normality (see both skewness and kurtosis ratios).

On downside risk aspects we have contemplated, the Standard Portfolio has across all three periods the lowest values. Consequently, it poses the highest risk of not achieving the envisaged capital guarantee after our investment period of 3 years. The value for the Sortino Ratio of 9.22 for year 3 implies that an investor would receive on average 9.22% of excess return over MAR for every 1.00% of downside risk he incurs below the MAR, while the equivalent ratio for the Alternative Portfolio is 17.99%. Considering the impact of an estimated annual inflation of 2.06%, all three portfolios reach capital guarantee in nominal terms.

[813] When we show the portfolio value in % (e.g. 105%), we mean the value as percentage of the initial par value of 100 units. For absolute portfolio values (e.g. 105), on the other hand, we refer to the portfolio value in monetary units.

B. Constant-Mix: Outright

B.1 Value Distribution after 3 Years

Figure 46: Constant-Mix Outright Strategies Across Portfolios (Value after 3yrs)

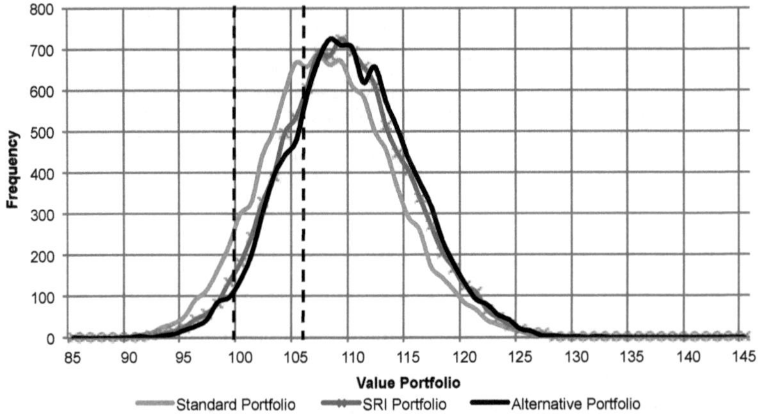

Source: Own figure. The first dotted black line indicates par value, while the second line reflects par value after three years taking into account for inflation. This line is positioned at 106.36, what corresponds to an average annual inflation rate of 2.06%, continuously compounded over three years and an initial investment value of 100.

B.2 Risk, Return and Distribution Characteristics over Investment Period

Table 33: Risk, Return and Distribution Measures: Constant Mix Outright Strategy

	Standard Portfolio			SRI Portfolio			Alternative Portfolio		
	YR 1	YR2	YR3	YR 1	YR2	YR3	YR 1	YR2	YR3
Performance									
Average Value	100.01	103.40	107.34	101.00	105.33	108.82	101.72	106.49	***109.28***
CAGR (%)	0.01	1.67	2.36	1.00	2.60	2.82	1.70	3.15	**2.96**
Maximum	111.03	123.25	129.85	114.23	124.14	***133.48***	114.73	125.48	131.17
Minimum	88.82	89.09	85.82	88.45	90.64	89.18	90.11	89.47	***89.84***
Median	99.95	103.30	107.16	100.92	105.17	108.67	101.68	106.45	***109.12***
Distribution Analysis									
Std. Dev. Returns (%)	2.83	4.43	5.42	3.26	4.56	5.24	2.98	4.45	**5.13**
Skewness	-0.03	-0.01	-0.02	-0.03	-0.01	-0.01	-0.03	-0.05	-0.04
Skewness T-Ratio	1.17	0.39	0.71	1.26	0.48	0.26	1.21	2.15	1.68
Kurtosis	-0.07	-0.10	-0.05	-0.04	-0.09	-0.05	0.06	-0.09	-0.11
Kurtosis T-Ratio	1.52	1.96	0.94	0.82	1.84	0.94	1.18	1.93	2.18
Downside Risk Measures (LPMs)									
Omega	0.97	6.44	27.70	2.07	18.36	66.69	4.06	37.63	***92.84***
Downside	2.02	1.61	1.08	1.78	1.06	0.71	1.31	0.77	***0.61***

	Standard Portfolio			SRI Portfolio			Alternative Portfolio		
Dev. (%)									
Sortino Ratio	-0.02	2.02	6.44	0.53	4.80	11.65	1.26	8.03	***14.31***
Kappa 3	-0.01	1.33	3.64	0.38	2.86	5.95	0.86	4.39	***6.94***
Upside Pot. Ratio	0.55	2.39	6.68	1.02	5.07	11.83	1.68	8.25	***14.47***

Source: Own representation. Bold and in italic highlighted numbers indicate the best-performing investment strategy (taking into consideration the conservative investment objectives of German Pension Insurance Funds) within the respective category after an investment period of 3 years, whereas underlined numbers denote the worse performing approach in the corresponding group. For skewness and kurtosis, no highlighting will be applied. Abbreviations used: 'CAGR'=compounded annual growth rate, 'Std. Dev.'=standard deviation.

B.3 Observations

Constant-Mix outright strategies obtain lower average values for all three portfolios analysed in comparison to corresponding strategies for Buy-and-Hold approaches. Moreover, the Constant-Mix method reaches the lowest value of 85.82 for the Standard Portfolio in year 3. Within the downside risk measures we are considering, all Constant-Mix strategies do have worse values than their Buy-and-Hold counterparts, indicating therefore that the former investment strategies pose a higher risk of not achieving capital guarantee at the end of the investment period. As a comparison, while in the Buy-and-Hold scenario the Alternative Portfolio achieves an Omega value of 131.26, in the Constant Mix the corresponding value is 92.84 (-29.27%). Overall, using our annual inflation assumption, all three portfolios achieve on average capital guarantee.

5.4.3 Hedging

In our simulation analysis, we will assess the impact the hedging of equity assets with put and collar derivative overlays would have on the risk-return constellation of the entire portfolio values at the end of the 3-year investment period.

A put-option based investment strategy involves acquiring an ATM strike, 1-year maturity put on the total value of the equity portfolio. At the end of each year, the options are cash-settled and new options with the same structural characteristics are bought on the new nominal value of the equity portion of the fund. For the collar strategies, the investment manager purchases an ATM put option on the underlying equity assets and sells a call option with a 15% premium. Both options will have a 1-year maturity. All collars are cash-settled at maturity and new collars, with the same terms, are bought recurrently for another 1 year.

A. Buy-and-Hold: Put Option

A.1 Value Distribution after 3 Years

Figure 47: Buy-and-Hold ATM Put Option Strategies Across Portfolios (Value after 3yrs)

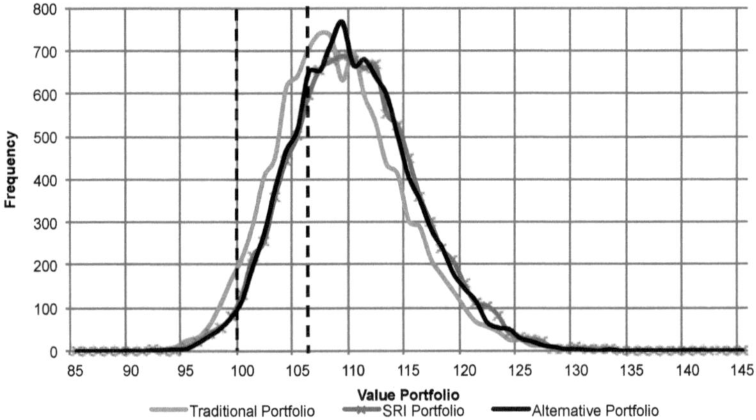

Source: Own figure.

A.2 Risk, Return and Distribution Characteristics over Investment Period

Table 34: Risk, Return and Distribution Measures: Put Option ATM, Buy-and-Hold

	Standard Portfolio			SRI Portfolio			Alternative Portfolio		
	YR 1	YR2	YR3	YR 1	YR2	YR3	YR 1	YR2	YR3
Performance									
Average Value	100.60	104.16	108.15	101.25	105.84	***109.68***	101.83	106.59	109.45
CAGR (%)	0.60	2.04	2.61	1.24	2.84	***3.08***	1.82	3.19	3.01
Maximum	111.09	125.12	136.88	114.60	128.23	140.06	114.41	125.65	***140.61***
Minimum	91.48	91.85	89.83	90.79	91.86	***91.47***	91.84	91.79	89.83
Median	100.53	103.93	107.72	101.11	105.51	***109.37***	101.74	106.36	109.11
Distribution Analysis									
Std. Dev. Returns (%)	2.31	4.00	5.19	2.95	4.43	5.25	2.62	4.34	***5.06***
Skewness	-0.01	-0.01	-0.01	-0.02	-0.01	-0.00	-0.03	-0.05	-0.05
Skewness T-Ratio	0.50	0.53	0.47	0.75	0.51	0.06	1.24	2.02	1.98
Kurtosis	-0.00	-0.01	0.04	0.07	-0.00	0.07	0.10	-0.00	0.01
Kurtosis T-Ratio	0.08	0.22	0.88	1.42	0.10	1.35	2.08	0.03	0.17
Downside Risk Measures (LPMs)									
Omega	1.88	14.56	64.84	2.84	32.54	141.26	5.78	57.02	***147.66***

	Standard Portfolio			SRI Portfolio			Alternative Portfolio		
Downside Dev. (%)	1.30	0.96	0.64	1.39	0.74	0.46	0.96	0.57	***0.46***
Sortino Ratio	0.44	4.14	11.95	0.86	7.57	19.64	1.85	11.10	***19.43***
Kappa 3	0.32	2.55	6.18	0.61	4.31	***9.32***	1.22	5.88	8.85
Upside Pot. Ratio	0.95	4.45	12.14	1.32	7.81	***19.78***	2.23	11.30	19.56

Source: Own representation.

A.3 Observations

Using ATM-strike put options to hedge the downside (equity) risk leads to an improvement of the overall risk profile of all three portfolios. The minimum values for the Standard and the SRI portfolios, for example, increase (from 87.89 for the Standard Portfolio to 89.83, from 90.20 to 91.47 for the SRI fund), whereas the minimum for the Alternative Portfolio remains almost unchanged.

On a relative basis, the numbers indicate that the SRI portfolio would benefit the most from the put option hedging approach. The reduced riskiness of this strategy is reflected for example in a lower standard deviation (5.25% vs. 5.46% outright) and a considerable increase in Omega from 110.37 in the outright strategy to 141.26 (+27.99%). The superior downside risk profile of the put option method, however, comes at the cost of a lower average final value in all three portfolios. While the Standard and SRI average values decrease by a mere 8bps and 7bps respectively, the average for the Alternative fund declines by 34bps. As it is the case for both outright strategies, the Alternative Portfolio offers the portfolio manager the most conservative downside risk profile.

B. Constant Mix: Put Option

B.1 Value Distribution after 3 Years

Figure 48: Constant-Mix ATM Put Option Strategies Across Portfolios (Value after 3yrs)

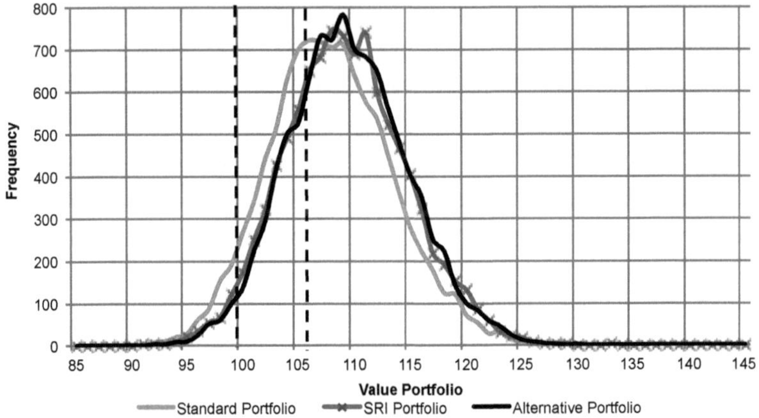

Source: Own figure.

B.2 Risk, Return and Distribution Characteristics over Investment Period

Table 35: Risk, Return and Distribution Measures: Put Option ATM, Constant-Mix

	Standard Portfolio			**SRI Portfolio**			**Alternative Portfolio**		
	YR 1	**YR2**	**YR3**	**YR 1**	**YR2**	**YR3**	**YR 1**	**YR2**	**YR3**
Performance									
Average Value	100.45	103.68	107.38	101.16	105.33	108.71	101.78	106.28	***108.91***
CAGR (%)	0.45	1.81	2.37	1.15	2.60	2.78	1.77	3.04	***2.84***
Maximum	110.66	122.57	128.91	113.85	123.58	***132.88***	114.34	124.64	129.78
Minimum	90.41	90.71	87.96	89.92	92.08	***90.62***	91.33	90.54	89.89
Median	100.39	103.55	107.16	101.07	105.14	108.52	101.72	106.18	***108.74***
Distribution Analysis									
Std. Dev. Returns (%)	2.50	4.06	5.07	2.99	4.31	4.99	2.72	4.23	***4.89***
Skewness	-0.02	-0.01	-0.02	-0.03	-0.01	-0.01	-0.03	-0.05	-0.05
Skewness T-Ratio	0.84	0.41	0.64	1.05	0.50	0.26	1.31	2.03	1.94
Kurtosis	-0.04	-0.09	-0.04	-0.01	-0.09	-0.05	-0.09	-0.09	-0.10
Kurtosis T-Ratio	0.74	1.85	0.87	0.20	1.74	0.95	1.79	1.82	2.05
Downside Risk Measures (LPMs)									
Omega	1.52	9.44	39.33	2.55	23.00	85.70	5.06	42.93	***104.83***
Downside Dev. (%)	1.53	1.23	0.84	1.50	0.88	0.59	1.08	0.67	***0.54***
Sortino Ratio	0.27	2.87	8.37	0.74	5.76	13.96	1.60	8.94	***15.48***
Kappa 3	0.20	1.84	4.58	0.52	3.39	6.97	1.06	4.85	***7.38***

	Standard Portfolio			SRI Portfolio			Alternative Portfolio		
Upside Pot. Ratio	0.79	3.21	8.59	1.21	6.03	14.13	2.00	9.16	***15.63***

Source: Own representation.

B.3 Observations

With a CAGR of 2.37%, the Standard Portfolio achieves the lowest return of all three portfolios. It also exhibits the highest investment risk, in particular with respect to the minimum value (87.96 of par) and downside risk measures. Nevertheless, the implementation of the put option strategy leads to a better downside risk profile in comparison to the outright method. All risk measures based on Lower Partial Moments improve. Using the Standard Portfolio as reference again, the Upside Potential Ratio, for example, increases from 6.68 to 8.59 (+28.59%), whereas the downside volatility below MAR declines from 1.08% to 0.84% (-22.22%).

As figure 47 indicates, the Alternative Portfolio yields the lowest downside risk exposure. The downside deviation is with 0.54% 30bps below the figure for the Standard Portfolio. The overall risk mitigation by the put option strategy becomes obvious when comparing the change in Omega value (increase by 41.99% for the Standard Portfolio and 12.91% for the Alternative Portfolio) between these two portfolios as well as the improvement of the Sortino Ratio (+29.97% vs. 8.18% respectively) versus the respective outright strategies. For upside focused investors, the Alternative Portfolio benefits from the highest Upside Potential Ratio. In comparison to the outright portfolio, the put option hedging has lead to a rise of 8.02% from 14.47 to 15.63.

C. Buy-and-Hold: Collar

C.1 Value Distribution after 3 Years

Figure 49: Buy-and-Hold Collar Strategies Across Portfolios (Value after 3yrs)

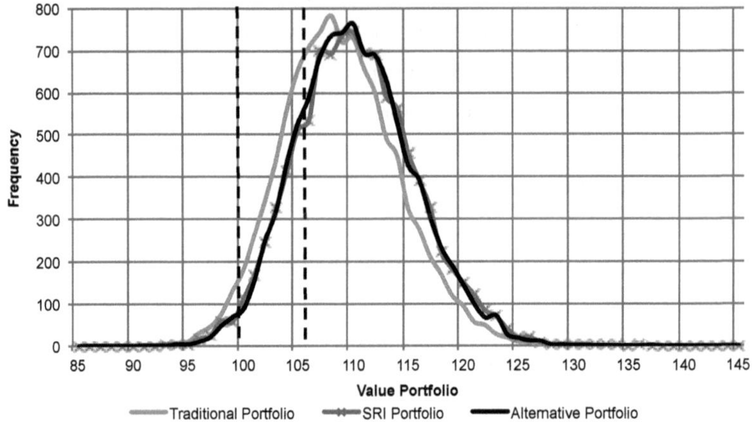

Source: Own figure.

C.2 Risk, Return and Distribution Characteristics over Investment Period

Table 36: Risk, Return and Distribution Measures: Collar (100/115), Buy-and-Hold

	Standard Portfolio			SRI Portfolio			Alternative Portfolio		
	YR 1	YR2	YR3	YR 1	YR2	YR3	YR 1	YR2	YR3
Performance									
Average Value	100.81	104.38	108.30	101.45	105.98	***109.78***	102.04	106.73	109.67
CAGR (%)	0.81	2.14	2.66	1.44	2.90	***3.11***	2.02	3.26	3.08
Maximum	110.69	122.43	131.97	114.79	125.49	135.80	114.62	124.99	***136.45***
Minimum	91.69	92.21	90.35	91.00	92.27	***92.03***	92.05	92.17	90.40
Median	100.74	104.22	108.04	101.33	105.75	***109.55***	101.95	106.58	109.42
Distribution Analysis									
Std. Dev. Returns (%)	2.30	3.81	4.83	2.93	4.21	4.95	2.61	4.12	***4.82***
Skewness	-0.01	-0.01	-0.01	-0.02	-0.01	-0.00	-0.03	-0.05	-0.04
Skewness T-Ratio	0.51	0.39	0.44	0.77	0.52	0.09	1.19	2.08	1.75
Kurtosis	-0.01	-0.08	-0.01	0.05	-0.03	0.02	0.08	-0.04	-0.03
Kurtosis T-Ratio	0.24	1.68	0.18	0.99	0.70	0.45	1.64	0.74	0.68
Downside Risk Measures (LPMs)									
Omega	2.37	18.61	87.86	3.43	40.90	184.59	7.20	73.72	***200.29***
Downside Dev. (%)	1.19	0.85	0.55	1.29	0.65	0.40	0.88	0.49	***0.39***
Sortino Ratio	0.66	4.95	14.40	1.08	8.82	23.20	2.25	13.06	***23.45***
Kappa 3	0.47	2.96	7.14	0.76	4.88	***10.59***	1.46	6.68	10.20

	Standard Portfolio			SRI Portfolio			Alternative Portfolio		
Upside Pot. Ratio	1.14	5.23	14.57	1.53	9.04	23.33	2.62	13.24	***23.56***

Source: Own representation.

C.3 Observations

Hedging the equities downside risk with a 100/115 collar has a measurable impact on downside risk measures. For the Alternative Portfolio, which has the lowest risk profile after hedging with the collar, Omega jumps to 200.29 (+52.59% versus 131.26 in the outright scenario), whereas the Sortino Ratio rises from 17.99 previously to 23.45 (+30.35%). Moreover, the minimum values increase in all three portfolios, trading above the 90 price level. For the Standard Portfolio, this means an improvement of 261 basis points, for the SRI Portfolio of 183 basis points and for the Alternative Portfolio of 63 basis points in comparison to the outright scenarios. Nevertheless, the negative impact of the collar structure is the slight decrease in the maximum values in comparison to the outright strategies: for the Standard Portfolio, the maximum declines from 135.42 to 131.97 (-2.55%), for the SRI Portfolio from 140.59 to 135.80 (-3.41%) and for the Alternative Portfolio from 141.14 to 136.45 (-3.32%).

D. Constant-Mix: Collar

D.1 Value Distribution after 3 Years

Figure 50: Constant-Mix Collar Strategies Across Portfolios (Value after 3yrs)

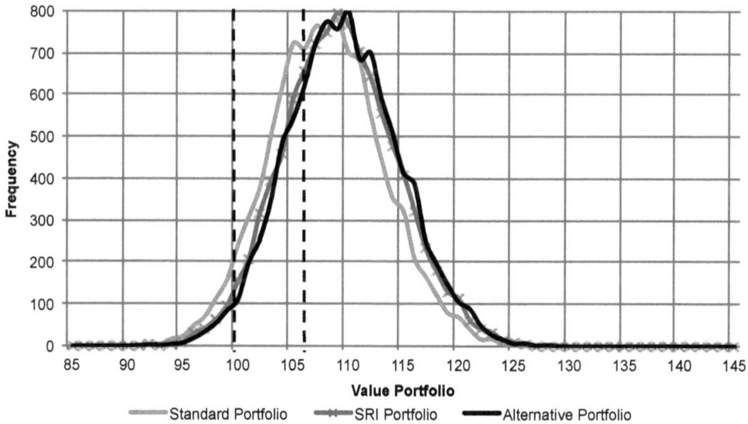

Source: Own figure.

D.2 Risk, Return and Distribution Characteristics over Investment Period

Table 37: Risk, Return and Distribution Measures: Collar (100/115), Constant-Mix

	Standard Portfolio			SRI Portfolio			Alternative Portfolio		
	YR 1	YR2	YR3	YR 1	YR2	YR3	YR 1	YR2	YR3
Performance									
Average Value	100.66	103.89	107.51	101.36	105.44	108.75	101.99	106.39	***109.09***
CAGR (%)	0.66	1.91	2.41	1.35	2.65	2.80	1.97	3.10	***2.90***
Maximum	110.87	120.22	126.74	114.04	123.63	***128.85***	114.56	124.02	128.64
Minimum	90.62	91.11	88.54	90.13	92.50	***91.23***	91.55	90.96	90.50
Median	100.60	103.85	107.42	101.28	105.28	108.60	101.93	106.36	***108.98***
Distribution Analysis									
Std. Dev. Returns (%)	2.49	3.86	4.73	2.97	4.09	4.74	2.71	4.02	***4.68***
Skewness	-0.02	-0.01	-0.02	-0.03	-0.02	-0.00	-0.03	-0.05	-0.04
Skewness T-Ratio	0.84	0.27	0.65	1.07	0.61	0.19	1.26	2.07	1.67
Kurtosis	-0.04	-0.12	-0.06	-0.02	-0.08	-0.05	0.07	-0.10	-0.11
Kurtosis T-Ratio	0.85	2.54	1.24	0.44	1.69	1.05	1.47	2.00	2.30
Downside Risk Measures (LPMs)									
Omega	1.88	11.90	52.05	3.07	28.16	106.86	6.21	54.37	***137.45***
Downside Dev. (%)	1.42	1.09	0.71	1.40	0.79	0.52	0.99	0.59	***0.47***
Sortino Ratio	0.44	3.43	10.03	0.94	6.63	15.99	1.95	10.40	***18.36***
Kappa 3	0.32	2.14	5.28	0.66	3.80	7.75	1.27	5.46	***8.46***
Upside Pot. Ratio	0.94	3.75	10.22	1.39	6.87	16.14	2.32	10.60	***18.50***

Source: Own representation.

D.3 Observations

Similar to the impact the 100/115 collar has on the Buy-and-Hold strategies, the risk measures for the Constant-Mix methods also improve versus the outright strategy. The minimum values, in particular, experience considerable upward shifts, reducing therefore the risk of a shortfall during the investment period: from 85.82 for the Standard Portfolio to 88.54 (+272bps), 89.18 to 91.23 (+205bps) for the SRI Portfolio and from 89.84 to 90.50 (+66bps) for the Alternative Portfolio. With regards to the downside risk profile, the Standard Portfolio improves the most in relative terms amongst all three funds. As a reference, Omega jumps from 27.70 to 52.05 (+87.91%) whereas the Sortino Ratio surges from 6.44 to 10.03 (+55.75%). The Upside Potential Ratio expands by 52.99% from 6.68 to 10.22. In summary, all three portfolios benefit from the implementation of the collar structure in terms of downside risk management, so that the costs incurred to acquire the derivative overlay and the capped upside above the upper call strike are more than offset by the benefits of the downside protection through the ATM put option.

5.4.4 Bond-Call Option Strategy

The Bond-Call Option strategy implies the acquisition of an ATM call option on the entire nominal amount of the equity allocation (in our case 5% at inception). The equity portion of the fund will subsequently be sold down to 0%. Therefore, the entire equity exposure of the fund is replicated via the ATM call option. This option has a 1-year maturity and will be cash-settled at the end of the investment period. At the beginning of the following year, a new ATM call option on 5% of the underlying equity is acquired.

A. Buy-Hold: Bond-Call Option

A.1 Value Distribution after 3 Years

Figure 51: Buy-and-Hold Bond-Call Option Strategies Across Portfolios (Value after 3yrs)

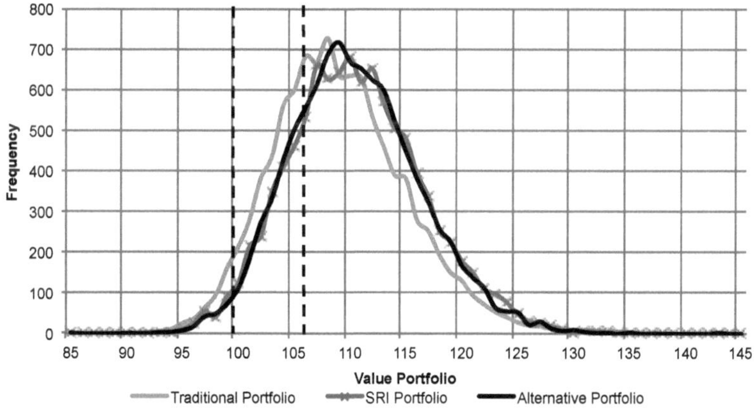

Source: Own figure.

A.2 Risk, Return and Distribution Characteristics over Investment Period

Table 38: Risk, Return and Distribution Measures: Bond-Call Option (Call ATM), Buy-and-Hold

	Standard Portfolio			SRI Portfolio			Alternative Portfolio		
	YR 1	YR2	YR3	YR 1	YR2	YR3	YR 1	YR2	YR3
Performance									
Average Value	100.63	104.32	108.52	101.31	106.09	***110.09***	101.94	106.91	109.93
CAGR (%)	0.63	2.11	2.73	1.30	2.95	***3.20***	1.92	3.34	3.16

	Standard Portfolio			SRI Portfolio			Alternative Portfolio		
Maximum	111.60	126.20	137.81	115.33	129.55	142.10	115.14	126.95	***142.91***
Minimum	91.00	91.50	89.34	90.22	91.46	***91.21***	91.42	91.43	89.37
Median	100.55	104.07	108.06	101.18	105.75	***109.74***	101.84	106.67	109.57
Distribution Analysis									
Std. Dev. Returns (%)	2.44	4.17	5.43	3.10	4.63	5.50	2.75	4.54	***5.30***
Skewness	-0.01	-0.01	-0.01	-0.02	-0.01	-0.00	-0.03	-0.05	-0.05
Skewness T-Ratio	0.57	0.49	0.46	0.79	0.54	0.06	1.23	2.03	1.90
Kurtosis	-0.00	-0.02	0.04	0.06	-0.01	0.07	0.10	-0.00	0.01
Kurtosis T-Ratio	0.07	0.32	0.73	1.25	0.15	1.36	1.99	0.10	0.18
Downside Risk Measures (LPMs)									
Omega	1.86	14.32	64.32	2.83	31.40	133.18	5.83	57.05	***147.81***
Downside Dev. (%)	1.38	1.01	0.68	1.47	0.79	0.50	1.01	0.59	***0.48***
Sortino Ratio	0.43	4.09	11.90	0.85	7.37	18.85	1.86	11.10	***19.47***
Kappa 3	0.32	2.53	6.16	0.60	4.21	***9.01***	1.23	5.88	8.86
Upside Pot. Ratio	0.94	4.40	12.08	1.32	7.61	19.00	2.24	11.30	***19.60***

Source: Own representation.

A.3 Observations

The Bond-Call Option strategy has a beneficial overall effect for Buy-and-Hold strategies. Apart from (minor) increases in the average value after 3 years (45bps for Standard Portfolio, 34bps for the SRI Portfolio and 14bps for the Alternative Portfolio) and rises in the maxima (by 239bps, 151bps and 177bps, respectively), also the minima improve for the Standard and SRI portfolios: for the former one, the minimum value grows from 87.89 to 89.34 (+1.65%) and for the latter one from 90.20 to 91.21 (+1.12%). The minimum for the Alternative Portfolio, on the other hand, decreases slightly by 40bps to 89.37. The resulting downside risk measures improve for all three portfolios, but in particular for the Standard Portfolio, for which the Sortino Ratio increases by 29.07% from 9.22 to 11.90 and Omega rises by 43.44% from 44.84 to 64.32.

Overall, the Bond-Call Option strategy seems to be an attractive alternative for Pension Insurance Funds, as risky equity assets are replicated via option strategies and therefore do not suffer downside risk. In our simulation analysis, the cost of the call option premium appears to be compensated by the levered upside participation above the call strike for those periods in which share prices rise.

B. Constant-Mix: Bond-Call Option

B.1 Value Distribution after 3 Years

Figure 52: Constant-Mix Bond-Call Option Strategies Across Portfolios (Value after 3yrs)

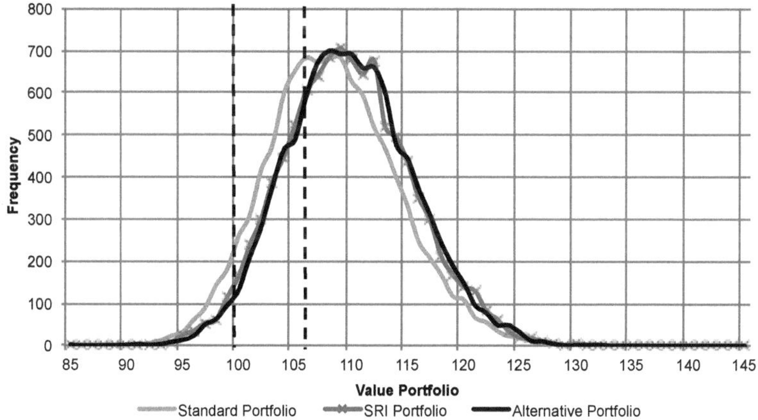

Source: Own figure.

B.2 Risk, Return and Distribution Characteristics over Investment Period

Table 39: Risk, Return and Distribution Measures – Bond-Call Option (Call ATM), Constant-Mix

	Standard Portfolio			SRI Portfolio			Alternative Portfolio		
	YR 1	YR2	YR3	YR 1	YR2	YR3	YR 1	YR2	YR3
Performance									
Average Value	100.51	103.91	107.82	101.23	105.63	109.20	101.87	106.60	***109.38***
CAGR (%)	0.51	1.92	2.51	1.23	2.74	2.93	1.85	3.20	***2.99***
Maximum	111.18	123.92	131.33	114.48	124.72	***134.96***	115.04	125.73	131.61
Minimum	90.15	90.25	87.61	89.59	91.61	***90.20***	90.88	90.09	89.31
Median	100.44	103.77	107.57	101.12	105.40	108.99	101.80	106.48	***109.19***
Distribution Analysis									
Std. Dev. Returns (%)	2.59	4.25	5.32	3.12	4.52	5.23	2.83	4.44	***5.12***
Skewness	-0.02	-0.01	-0.02	-0.02	-0.01	-0.01	-0.03	-0.05	-0.05
Skewness T-Ratio	0.81	0.44	0.64	1.02	0.44	0.26	1.33	2.00	1.99
Kurtosis	-0.03	-0.08	-0.03	-0.01	-0.08	-0.04	0.09	-0.08	-0.10
Kurtosis T-Ratio	0.60	1.65	0.69	0.19	1.69	0.84	1.74	1.71	1.96
Downside Risk Measures (LPMs)									
Omega	1.59	9.83	41.15	2.61	23.40	87.77	5.09	43.24	***106.28***
Downside Dev. (%)	1.56	1.26	0.85	1.55	0.92	0.61	1.12	0.70	***0.57***
Sortino Ratio	0.31	2.98	8.66	0.76	5.85	14.21	1.61	8.99	***15.60***
Kappa 3	0.23	1.90	4.71	0.54	3.43	7.08	1.07	4.87	***7.43***

	Standard Portfolio			SRI Portfolio			Alternative Portfolio		
Upside Pot. Ratio	0.83	3.32	8.88	1.23	6.11	14.38	2.01	9.20	***15.75***

Source: Own representation.

B.3 Observations

Similar to the Buy-and-Hold strategy, the Portfolio Insurance investment method does provide improvement for the Constant-Mix method with respect to downside risk characteristics in comparison to the outright strategy: (1) small increases in average values during and at the end of the investment period, (2) lower standard deviations of portfolio returns, (3) lower downside risk as indicated by our selected risk measures. Omega, for example, grows for all three portfolios from 27.70, 66.69 and 92.84 for the Standard, SRI and Alternative Portfolio, respectively, to 41.15 (+48.56%), 87.77 (+31.61%) and 106.28 (+14.48%).

In direct comparison to the outright investment strategies, the computed simulation results provide evidence that the Bond-Call Option method is a suitable investing approach and superior to the outright Constant-Mix method.

5.4.5 Yield Enhancement

Selling OTM call options on an existing equity portfolio is a common strategy to increase the overall yield of the fund. In our analysis, a 115-strike, 1-year maturity call option is sold at the beginning of each period on the nominal amount of the equities portfolio. For share price movements above the strike at maturity, the portfolio will forego upside, whereas for any value below the strike, the returns of the fund will be enhanced by the option premium received at inception. This premium can also be interpreted as a risk buffer against downside moves, as the share price needs to drop by more than the initial option premium for the equity assets to suffer any loss.

A. Buy-and-Hold: Yield Enhancement

A.1 Value Distribution after 3 Years

Figure 53: Buy-and-Hold Yield Enhancement Strategies Across Portfolios (Value after 3yrs)

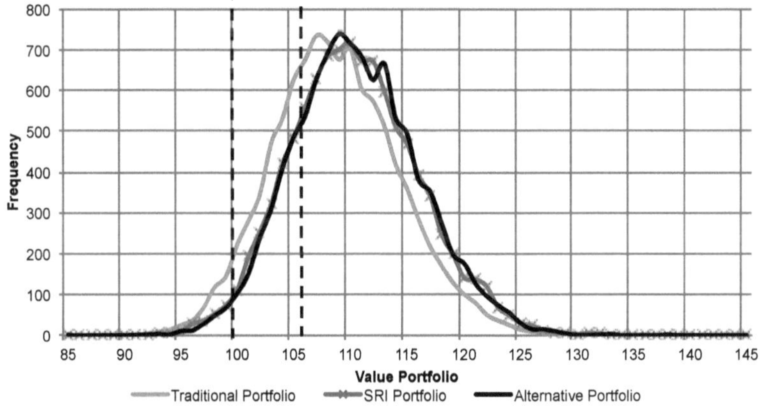

Source: Own representation.

A.2 Risk, Return and Distribution Characteristics over Investment Period

Table 40: Risk, Return and Distribution Measures: Yield Enhancement (Short Call 115), Buy-and-Hold

	Standard Portfolio			SRI Portfolio			Alternative Portfolio		
	YR 1	YR2	YR3	YR 1	YR2	YR3	YR 1	YR2	YR3
Performance									
Average Value	100.37	104.06	108.21	101.30	105.95	109.84	101.98	106.91	***110.01***
CAGR (%)	0.37	1.99	2.63	1.29	2.89	3.13	1.96	3.34	***3.18***
Maximum	111.07	123.06	130.60	115.18	126.36	136.43	115.01	125.86	***137.51***
Minimum	90.10	90.99	88.41	89.53	92.18	***90.75***	91.30	91.16	90.34
Median	100.29	103.94	107.98	101.16	105.71	109.61	101.89	106.78	***109.75***
Distribution Analysis									
Std. Dev. Returns (%)	2.59	4.10	5.13	3.17	4.41	5.17	2.85	4.32	***5.05***
Skewness	-0.02	-0.01	-0.01	-0.02	-0.01	-0.00	-0.03	-0.05	-0.03
Skewness T-Ratio	0.85	0.34	0.52	1.00	0.47	0.01	1.10	2.17	1.41
Kurtosis	-0.05	-0.09	-0.03	0.00	-0.05	0.02	0.04	-0.05	-0.05
Kurtosis T-Ratio	1.09	1.85	0.56	0.07	0.93	0.32	0.89	1.01	1.08
Downside Risk Measures (LPMs)									
Omega	1.38	11.74	57.92	2.71	31.91	139.84	5.58	62.28	***172.62***
Downside Dev. (%)	1.62	1.14	0.71	1.54	0.77	0.48	1.08	0.57	***0.44***
Sortino Ratio	0.21	3.43	10.87	0.80	7.33	19.09	1.77	11.52	***21.35***

	Standard Portfolio			SRI Portfolio			Alternative Portfolio		
Kappa 3	0.15	2.15	5.65	0.57	4.16	9.02	1.17	5.98	***9.50***
Upside Pot. Ratio	0.74	3.75	11.06	1.27	7.57	19.23	2.15	11.71	***21.47***

Source: Own representation.

A.3 Observations

Yield enhancement strategies by way of selling OTM call options are a suitable strategy as long as the underlying asset does not trade above the strike at maturity. For Buy-and-Hold investment strategies, our results suggest a considerable reduction of the downside risk can be achieved by simply benefiting from the option premium received, which functions as a cushion against price declines.

In this scenario, Omega values increase from 44.84 / 110.37 / 131.26 at the end of year 3 for the Standard, SRI and the Alternative Portfolio outright strategies, correspondingly, to 57.92 (+29.17%) / 139.84 (26.70%) / 172.62 (+31.51%) for the Yield Enhancement investing approach. The average portfolio values, at the same time, remain almost unchanged. The yield enhancement comes at an opportunity cost, as the upside of the equity allocation is capped above the 115-strike, which leads to a noticeable drop for the maximum values across all three portfolios from 135.42 / 140.59 / 141.14 for outright strategies, respectively, to 130.60 (-3.56%) / 136.43 (-2.96%) / 137.5 (-2.57%) for the derivative overlay structures.

Overall, the Alternative Portfolio achieves the best downside risk measures of all three portfolios contemplated.

B. Constant-Mix: Yield Enhancement

B.1 Value Distribution after 3 Years

Figure 54: Constant-Mix Yield Enhancement Strategies Across Portfolios (Value after 3yrs)

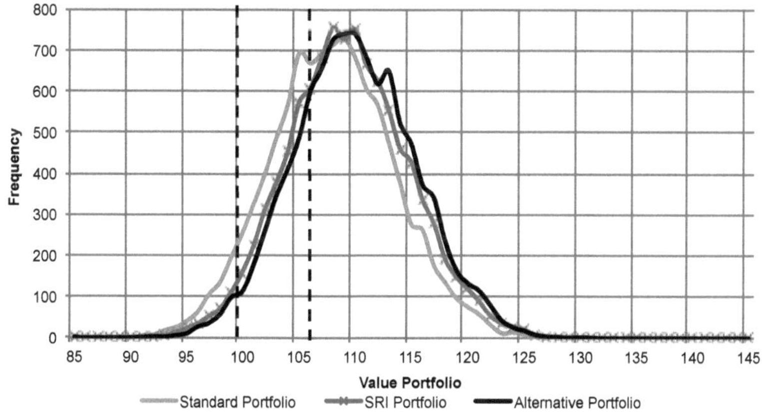

Source: Own figure.

B.2 Risk, Return and Distribution Characteristics over Investment Period

Table 41: Risk, Return and Distribution Measures: Yield Enhancement (Short Call 115), Constant-Mix

	Standard Portfolio			SRI Portfolio			Alternative Portfolio		
	YR 1	YR2	YR3	YR 1	YR2	YR3	YR 1	YR2	YR3
Performance									
Average Value	100.22	103.62	107.47	101.21	105.44	108.87	101.93	106.61	***109.47***
Cum. Returns (%)	0.22	1.78	2.40	1.20	2.65	2.83	1.91	3.20	***3.02***
Maximum	111.25	120.90	127.76	114.42	124.16	129.45	114.94	124.86	***130.03***
Minimum	89.03	89.47	86.39	88.67	91.06	89.79	90.33	89.89	***90.44***
Median	100.16	103.59	107.42	101.14	105.32	108.73	101.89	106.62	***109.34***
Distribution Analysis									
Std. Dev. Returns (%)	2.83	4.23	5.10	3.24	4.35	5.01	2.97	4.25	***4.94***
Skewness	-0.03	-0.01	-0.02	-0.03	-0.02	-0.00	-0.03	-0.05	-0.04
Skewness T-Ratio	1.16	0.27	0.69	1.29	0.63	0.20	1.16	2.18	1.43
Kurtosis	-0.08	-0.12	-0.06	-0.05	-0.09	-0.04	0.05	-0.10	-0.12
Kurtosis T-Ratio	1.60	2.43	1.15	1.01	1.77	0.89	0.92	2.03	2.37
Downside Risk Measures (LPMs)									
Omega	1.17	7.82	34.91	2.45	22.00	80.68	4.88	46.28	***117.53***
Downside Dev. (%)	1.90	1.45	0.94	1.67	0.96	0.64	1.22	0.69	***0.54***
Sortino Ratio	0.09	2.38	7.51	0.69	5.43	13.04	1.53	9.20	***16.66***

	Standard Portfolio			SRI Portfolio			Alternative Portfolio		
Kappa 3	0.07	1.54	4.12	0.49	3.17	6.49	1.02	4.89	***7.84***
Upside Pot. Ratio	0.64	2.73	7.73	1.16	5.69	13.20	1.92	9.40	***16.80***

Source: Own representation.

B.3 Observations

The results of the Yield Enhancement strategy for the Constant-Mix method are analogous to those of the Buy-and-Hold portfolios: downside risk profiles improve, maximum portfolio values decline due to the capped upside of the equity allocation and portfolio standard deviations decrease. In addition, we experience a minor increase in the average portfolio values. These conclusions are applicable to all three portfolios.

5.4.6 Performance Comparison by Portfolio

In this section, we will contrast the results of the various investment strategies contemplated for each of the three portfolios separately. This comparison will enable us to determine the optimal strategy for each individual portfolio.

A. Standard Portfolio

A.1 Value Distribution after 3 Years

Figure 55: Buy-and-Hold Strategies Standard Portfolio (Value after 3yrs)

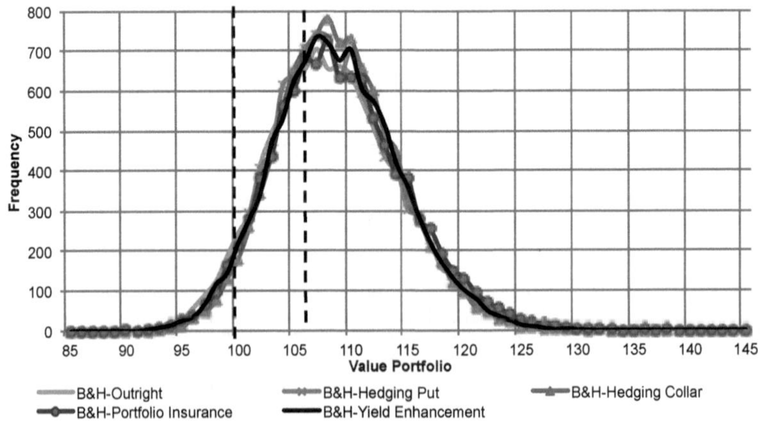

Source: Own figure. Abbreviations used: 'B&H'=Buy-and-Hold.

Figure 56: Constant Mix Strategies Standard Portfolio (Value after 3yrs)

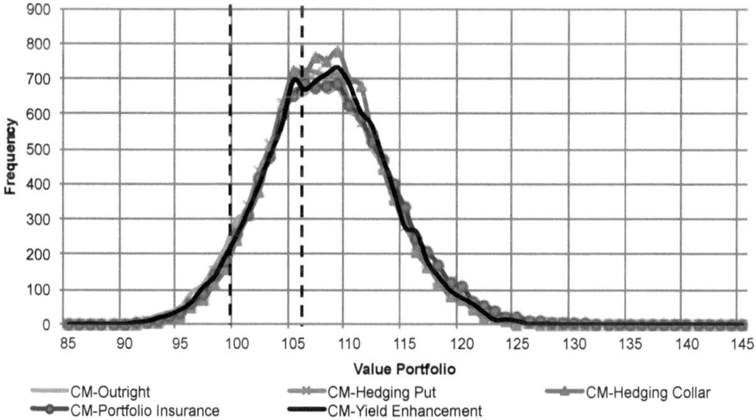

Source: Own figure. Abbreviations used: 'CM'=Constant-Mix.

A.2 Risk, Return and Distribution Characteristics over Investment Period

Table 42: Comparison across Investment Strategies – Standard Portfolio (After Year 3)

	Aver. Value	Max	Min	Std. Dev. Returns (%)	Omega	Downs. Dev. (%)	Sortino Ratio	Ups. Pot. Ratio
Buy & Hold								
Outright	108.07	135.42	87.89	5.47	44.84	0.82	9.22	9.43
Hedging Put	108.15	136.88	89.83	5.19	64.84	0.64	11.95	12.14
Hedging Collar	108.30	131.97	***90.35***	4.83	***87.86***	***0.55***	***14.40***	***14.57***
Bond-Call Option	***108.52***	***137.81***	89.34	5.43	64.32	0.68	11.90	12.08
Yield En-hanc.	108.21	130.60	88.41	5.13	57.92	0.71	10.87	11.06
Constant Mix								
Outright	107.34	129.85	85.82	5.42	27.70	1.08	6.44	6.68
Hedging Put	107.38	128.91	87.96	5.07	39.33	0.84	8.37	8.59
Hedging Collar	107.51	126.74	88.54	***4.73***	52.05	0.71	10.03	10.22
Bond-Call Option	107.82	131.33	87.61	5.32	41.15	0.85	8.66	8.88
Yield En-hanc.	107.47	127.76	86.39	5.10	34.91	0.94	7.51	7.73

Source: Own representation.

A.3 Observations

The best performing strategy for the Standard Portfolio based on our results is the hedging approach via the collar. This investment strategy yields the highest minimum values (90.35 for Buy-and-Hold and 88.54 for Constant-Mix) during the investment period as well as the most risk-averse downside measures (Omega value of 87.86 for the collar versus 27.70 measured for the lowest value across all strategies that corresponds to the Constant-Mix outright approach). On an absolute basis, the Buy-and-Hold collar hedging strategy outperforms all other simulated strategies.

As already eluded to in the previous sections of our simulation results, collar structures do not tend to generate the highest average values, as the net cost of the derivative impacts the maximum level achievable and the upside is capped above the upper call strike. Instead, the highest average portfolio values are obtained via the Bond-Call Option investment methods, as the downside risk on the equity portfolio is reduced due to the lower direct exposure to the underlying but simultaneously higher potential (levered) upside participation in case of a stock price increase. In both the Buy-and-Hold as well as the Constant-Mix scenarios, Bond-Call Option strategies also generate the highest maximum portfolio end values.

The investment strategies with the weakest price performance and highest downside risk profiles correspond to both outright strategies. They return the lowest average portfolio values after 3 years, suffer the largest downside risks in absolute terms (minimum values of 87.89 for the Buy-and-Hold strategy and 85.82 for the Constant-Mix approach) and the highest portfolio return volatilities (5.47% and 5.42% respectively). In absolute terms, the worse performing strategy is the outright method following a Constant-Mix approach.

B. SRI Portfolio

B.1 Value Distribution after 3 Years

Figure 57: Buy-and-Hold Strategies SRI Portfolio (Value after 3yrs)

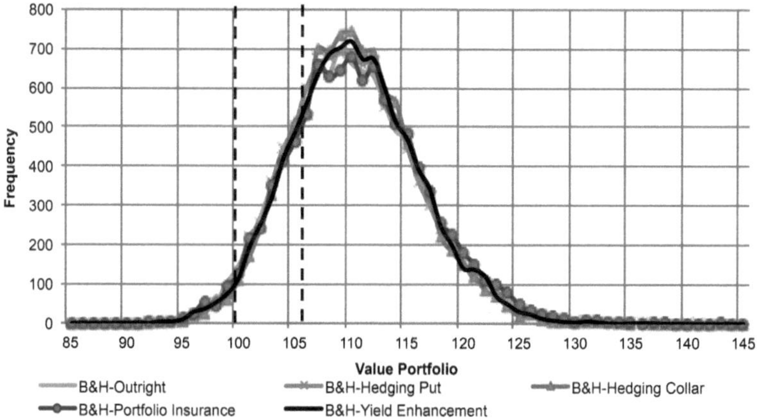

Source: Own figure. Abbreviations used: 'B&H'=Buy-and-Hold.

Figure 58: Constant-Mix Strategies SRI Portfolio (Value after 3yrs)

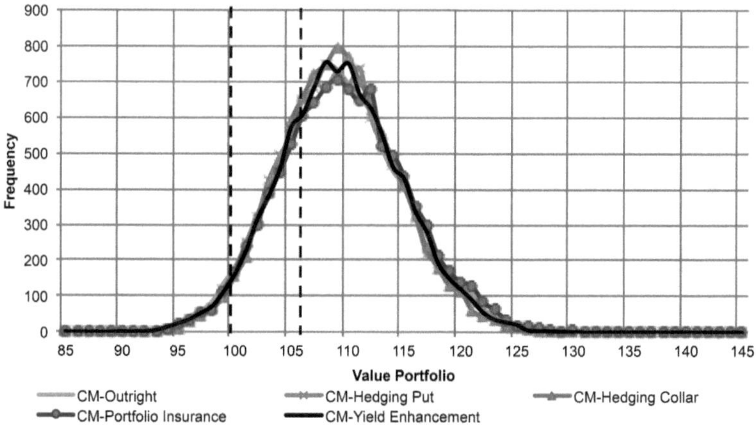

Source: Own figure. Abbreviations used: 'CM'=Constant-Mix.

B.2 Risk, Return and Distribution Characteristics over Investment Period

Table 43: Comparison across Investment Strategies – SRI Portfolio (After Year 3)

	Aver. Value	Max	Min	Std. Dev. Returns (%)	Omega	Downs. Dev. (%)	Sortino Ratio	Ups. Pot. Ratio
Buy & Hold								
Outright	109.75	140.59	90.20	5.46	110.37	0.55	16.54	16.69
Hedging Put	109.68	140.06	91.47	5.25	141.26	0.46	19.64	19.78
Hedging Collar	109.78	135.80	***92.03***	4.95	***184.59***	***0.40***	***23.20***	***23.33***
Bond-Call Option	***110.09***	***142.10***	91.21	5.50	133.18	0.50	18.85	19.00
Yield Enhanc.	109.84	136.43	90.75	5.17	139.84	0.48	19.09	19.23
Constant Mix								
Outright	108.82	133.48	89.18	5.24	66.69	0.71	11.65	11.83
Hedging Put	108.71	132.88	90.62	4.99	85.70	0.59	13.96	14.13
Hedging Collar	108.75	128.85	91.23	***4.74***	106.86	0.52	15.99	16.14
Bond-Call Opt.	109.20	134.96	90.20	5.23	87.77	0.61	14.21	14.38
Yield Enhanc.	108.87	129.45	89.79	5.01	80.68	0.64	13.04	13.20

Source: Own representation.

B.3 Observations

The empirical results for the SRI Portfolio look comparable to those of the Standard Portfolio. The hedging strategy with collar overlays leads to the best downside risk characteristics for the fund (Omega values of 184.59 for Buy-and-Hold and 106.86 for Constant-Mix, downside deviations of 0.40% and 0.52% and standard deviations of 4.95% and 4.74% respectively). The highest average portfolio values, on the other hand, are obtained again with Bond-Call Option methods (110.09 for Buy-and-Hold, 109.20 for Constant-Mix), whereas simple outright strategies pose the largest downside threats of all methods considered. The main difference to the Standard Portfolio is that both outright strategies yield slightly better or similar average portfolio values than hedging strategies (both collar and put option approaches), with values at the end of year 3 of 109.75 (Buy-and-Hold) and 108.82 (Constant-Mix). Comparing results across strategies, we conclude that Constant-Mix outright strategies are the least suitable approaches within the SRI portfolio universe for the investment objectives of German Pension Insurance Funds.

C. Alternative Portfolio

C.1 Value Distribution after 3 Years

Figure 59: Buy-and-Hold Strategies Alternative Portfolio (Value after 3yrs)

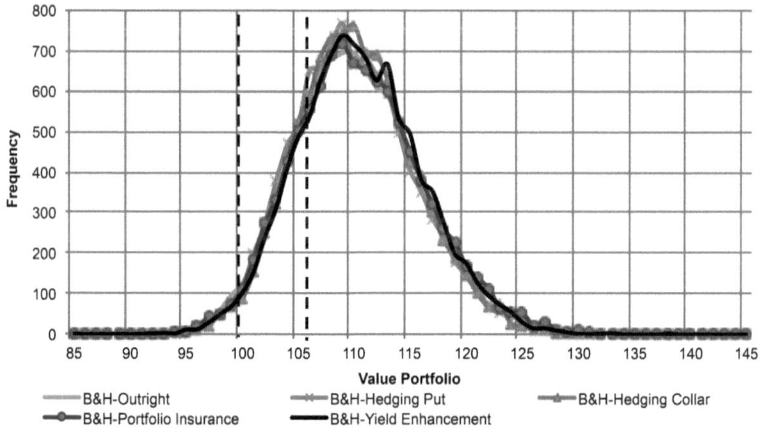

Source: Own representation. Abbreviations used: 'B&H'=Buy-and-Hold.

Figure 60: Constant Mix Strategies Alternative Portfolio (Value after 3yrs)

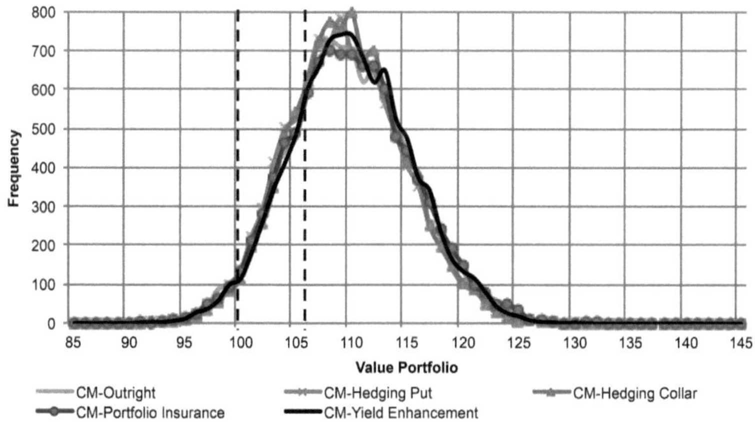

Source: Own representation. Abbreviations used: 'CM'=Constant Mix.

C.2 Risk, Return and Distribution Characteristics over Investment Period

Table 44: Comparison across Investment Strategies – Alternative Portfolio (After Year 3)

	Aver. Value	Max	Min	Std.Dev. Returns (%)	Omega	Downs. Dev. (%)	Sortino Ratio	Ups. Pot. Ratio
Buy & Hold								
Outright	109.79	141.14	89.77	5.28	131.26	0.51	17.99	18.13
Hedging Put	109.45	140.61	89.83	5.06	147.66	0.46	19.43	19.56
Hedging Collar	109.67	136.45	90.40	4.82	***200.29***	***0.39***	***23.45***	***23.56***
Bond-Call Opt.	109.93	***142.91***	89.37	5.30	147.81	0.48	19.47	19.60
Yield Enhanc.	***110.01***	137.51	90.34	5.05	172.62	0.44	21.35	21.47
Constant Mix								
Outright	109.28	131.17	89.84	5.13	92.84	0.61	14.31	14.47
Hedging Put	108.91	129.78	89.89	4.89	104.83	0.54	15.48	15.63
Hedging Collar	109.09	128.64	***90.50***	***4.68***	137.45	0.47	18.36	18.50
Bond-Call Opt.	109.38	131.61	89.31	5.12	106.28	0.57	15.60	15.75
Yield Enhanc.	109.47	130.03	90.44	4.94	117.53	0.54	16.66	16.80

Source: Own representation.

C.3 Observations

From a downside risk management perspective, hedging strategies, in particular the collar overlay, are the most suitable investment strategies for Pension Insurance Funds within the Alternative Portfolio scenario. A 100/115 collar overlay allows the portfolio manager to reduce the minimum value (worse case scenario) to 90.40 (Buy-and-Hold) and 90.50 (Constant-Mix) at the end of year 3. This is an improvement in comparison to the respective outright strategies, with minimum values of 89.77 and 89.84, respectively. In addition, the collar strategies achieve the highest downside risk measures of all portfolios, with Omega figures of 200.29 and 137.45 for the Buy-and-Hold and Constant-Mix methods, correspondingly, and Sortino Ratios of 23.45 and 18.36. The highest portfolio values, nevertheless, are obtained with Bond-Call Option approaches (142.91 and 131.61), as the premium generated by the short call position subsidizes downward price movements of the remaining assets of the portfolio.

5.4.7 Benchmarking Across Investment Strategies

Comparing the results from our simulation studies across all portfolios and investment strategies will allows us to rank each strategy by its suitability within a certain performance or risk indicator. The focus of our comparison will thereby be to select strategies that reduce the downside risk exposure of the fund. Simultaneously, the strategy needs to generate at least the Maximum Guaranteed Return of 1.75% per annum.

Table 45 summarises the best and worse performing strategies simulated in chapter 5.4. In terms of portfolio approach, our results provide empirical evidence that the SRI-structured portfolios (both the SRI Portfolio as well as the Alternative Portfolio) consistently outperform the Standard Portfolio, both for the outright scenarios as well as the various derivative overlay structures contemplated. While the performance difference is on average not excessive, it is nonetheless consistent. More importantly for the purpose of our research study, SRI portfolios yield overall better downside risk figures than conventional portfolios do, indicating a more conservative risk exposure in bearish market environments, consequently minimizing tail-risk.

The overall conclusion in terms of downside risk is apparent: outright strategies using Constant-Mix methods emerge as the least appropriate investment strategies for Pension Insurance Funds. In more detail, within the downside risk measures we have determined, the worse performers are strategies from the Standard Portfolio using Constant-Mix methods as underlying strategy. In addition, outright strategies rank hereby as the worst performers overall. With regards to minimum values obtained after our 3-year investment horizon, the outright strategy as well as the Yield Enhancement techniques within the Standard Portfolio yield the lowest values. When using average portfolio values as indicator of suitability of a respective investment strategy, again the Standard Portfolio produces the lowermost figures. We therefore conclude that based on the outcome of our simulation study, a combination of Standard Portfolio, Constant-Mix and outright methods represent the worse downside risk profiles for German Pension Insurance Funds.

The most appropriate investment strategies for a risk-averse manager of a Pension Insurance Fund, on the contrary, are predominantly collar hedging derivative overlays, as they allow the portfolio manager to optimise the risk management on the risky equity portion of his investment portfolio. The premium generated by the upper strike call subsidises thereby the cost of implementing the structure and leads to a better downside risk profile than simply acquiring put options. Collar derivatives, combined with Buy-and-Hold methods in particular, enable a portfolio manager to get the best downside risk profile of all strategies simulated. Collars also generate the highest minimum values, reducing consequently the risk of a major one-off shortfall event in the equities markets, and yield the lowest portfolio volatility. For those managers focused on generating high yielding investment portfolios, the Bond-Call Option methodology, combined with the Buy-and-Hold technique, will return the best results.

Table 45 replicates our best and worse performing portfolio strategies from different investment perspectives.

Table 45: Relative Comparison across Portfolios and Investment Strategies

Average Portfolio Value				**Maximum**			
Best Value		**Worst Value**		**Best Value**		**Worst Value**	
1. SRI: Bond Call Option-B&H	***110.09***	1. SP: Outright-CM	107.34	1. AP: Bond Call Option-B&H	***142.91***	1. SP: Collar-CM	126.74
2. AP: Yield Enhanc.-B&H	***110.01***	2. SP: Put-CM	107.38	2. SRI: Bond Call Option-B&H	***142.10***	2. SP: Yield Enhanc.-CM	127.76
3. AP: Bond Call Option-B&H	***109.93***	3. SP: Yield Enhanc.-CM	107.47	3. AP: Outright-B&H	***141.14***	3. AP: Collar-CM	128.64

Minimum				**Standard Deviation Returns (in %)**			
Best Value		**Worst Value**		**Best Value**		**Worst Value**	
1. SRI: Collar-B&H	***92.03***	1. SP: Outright-CM	85.82	1. AP: Collar-CM	***4.68***	1. SRI: Bond Call Option-B&H	5.50
2. SRI: Put-B&H	***91.47***	2. SP: Yield Enhanc.-CM	86.39	2. SP: Collar-CM	4.73	2. SP: Outright-B&H	5.47
3. SRI: Collar-CM	***91.23***	3. SP: Bond Call Option-B&H	87.61	3. SRI: Collar-CM	***4.74***	3. SRI: Outright-B&H	5.46

Omega				**Downside Deviation (in %)**			
Best Value		**Worst Value**		**Best Value**		**Worst Value**	
1. AP: Collar-B&H	***200.29***	1. SP: Out-right-CM	27.70	1. AP: Collar-B&H	***0.39***	1. SP: Out-right-CM	1.08
2. SRI: Collar-B&H	***184.59***	2. SP: Yield Enhanc.-CM	34.91	2. SRI: Collar-B&H	***0.40***	2. SP: Yield Enhanc.-CM	0.94
3. AP: Yield Enhanc.-B&H	***172.62***	3. SP: Put-CM	39.33	3. AP: Yield Enhanc.-B&H	***0.44***	3. SP: Bond Call Option-CM	0.85

Sortino Ratio				**Upside Potential Ratio**			
Best Value		**Worst Value**		**Best Value**		**Worst Value**	
1. AP: Collar-B&H	***23.45***	1. SP: Out-right-CM	6.44	1. AP: Collar-B&H	***23.56***	1. SP: Out-right-CM	6.68
2. SRI: Collar-B&H	***23.20***	2. SP: Yield Enhanc.-CM	7.51	2. SRI: Collar-B&H	***23.33***	2. SP: Yield Enhanc.-CM	7.73
3. AP-Yield Enhanc.-B&H	***21.35***	3. SP: Put-CM	8.37	3. AP: Yield Enhanc.-B&H	***21.47***	3. SP: Put-CM	8.59

Source: Own representation. Abbreviations used: 'B&H'=Buy-and-Hold, 'CM'=Constant Mix, 'Yield Enhanc.'=Yield Enhancement, 'SP'=Standard Portfolio, 'SRI'=SRI Portfolio, 'AP'=Alternative Portfolio. Bold and in italic highlighted numbers indicate an SRI-based investment strategy (both for the SRI Portfolio and the Alternative Portfolio) that obtains results that correspond to the top three best-performing investment strategies in the respective category. Underlined numbers, on the contrary, designate investment strategies belonging to the Standard Portfolio that generate a performance that belongs to the worse three portfolio returns in that category.

5.4.8 Conclusions

Chapter 5.4 is of crucial importance for our research study, as it summarises the results of our empirical analysis for the standard models. All three simulated portfolios are presented with corresponding investment strategies. Investment results have been analysed primarily from the perspective of a risk-averse portfolio manager of a German Pension Insurance Fund, focused primarily on fulfilling his investment objectives of capital preservation under the prevailing regulatory framework.

From the viewpoint of capital guarantee of invested funds, all three portfolios achieve their objectives (on average) in all strategies used. However, as the downside risk measures indicate, some investing approaches imply a larger risk of missing capital preservation at the end of the investment period, while other strategies enable the portfolio manager to better risk control the composition of his asset allocation.[814] While our analysis has been focused predominantly on returns and portfolio values in nominal terms, we have made reference to the impact inflation could have on the results. Based on an average European infla-

[814] As a reminder: all strategies at the end of year 3 have already suffered a deduction of 1.75% per annum to take into account for the Maximum Guaranteed Return.

tion rate for the last 10 years, our performance results across portfolios are on average sufficient to offer capital guarantee in nominal and real money terms.

The side-by-side comparison of portfolios invested exclusively in conventional asset classes versus SRI-structured portfolios offers unambiguous results: SRI portfolios outperform in all contemplated investment scenarios, independently of the underlying investing strategy. Furthermore, Alternative Portfolios that invest up to 10% of the total asset allocation in alternative investments (hedge fund assets and commodities) perform on average better than the corresponding SRI Portfolio. This conclusion applies to average achieved returns as well as downside risk measures calculated for our analysis. Our results suggest therefore that Pension Insurance Funds should consider SRI assets as part of their strategic asset allocation consideration. Furthermore, our preliminary conclusions are aligned with those of similarly structured research studies that focus on a direct comparison of conventional assets versus SRI assets.[815]

Overall, analysing the return distributions of the contemplated investment strategies reveals that outright strategies underperform more complex portfolio methods from a return perspective, volatility aspect as well as from a downside risk angle. Between the two outright strategies, Buy-and-Hold is the dominant methodology for all three portfolios simulated. Within the three portfolios simulated, the Alternative Portfolio generates overall the best investment results for a portfolio manager, in particular with regards to downside risk mitigation and absolute maxima.

Collar hedging strategies with 100/115 strikes, in particular, combined with an underlying Buy-and-Hold technique achieve the best downside risk protection in all three portfolios, while also minimising the volatility of portfolio returns. These derivative overlays seem therefore suitable for the asset management of German Pension Insurance Funds. However, should the objective of the portfolio strategy be to obtain the highest absolute portfolio values, Bond-Call Option methods yield maximum returns as well as the highest average portfolio values, independently of the portfolio chosen.

[815] See section 3.2.5 that refers to empirical research studies that compare conventional to SRI asset performances.

It is important to acknowledge that our modelling results rely on certain assumptions that may not hold in a real life situation, but which are nonetheless necessary to make the simulations viable from a computational standpoint. Moreover, we have restricted our modelling exercise to a time frame of 3 years. This time horizon seems appropriate to us given that the VEC model as well as the bootstrap simulation rely on 10 years of historical monthly data. Longer forecasting time periods would lead to more forecasting errors and increase therefore the uncertainty of our conclusions. Furthermore, the presented derivative strategies are subject to the limitations imposed by the regulatory framework of BaFin's circular letter R3/2000[816]. Our conclusions do ultimately also depend on the estimated VEC models that attempt to capture the dynamic features and interdependencies of the underlying assets, but cannot by definition be all-encompassing methods.

An area of interest not covered in our simulation study is the application of SRI structured derivatives. While this is to date an almost untouched research topic, it may gain relevance in future academic studies as well as for SRI-focused practitioners that use derivatives as part of their tactical asset allocation.

Section 5.5 presents the simulation results of our alternative models. 5.5.2 includes the data for the equity-dominated UK and Dutch portfolio models, whereas 5.5.3 attempts to create an asset allocation appropriate to pension funds suffering from rising inflation pressure. Section 5.5.4 is dedicated to the Credit Risk Hedging model, a scenario that includes derivative overlays for both the equity and corporate bond segments of our portfolios. In 5.5.5, we will benchmark all strategies simulated in our research study, including results obtained in 5.4 as well as in section 5.5.

[816] See BaFin (2000).

5.5 Alternative Investment Scenarios

5.5.1 Objectives

The main objective of this chapter is to run alternative investment scenarios to those models analysed in section 5.4. The focus now will be to ignore the restrictive regulatory environment under which Pension Insurance Funds operate in Germany and simulate strategies that have asset allocations geared towards a higher equity exposure, include more alternative investments as well as overlay derivative structures on various asset classes simultaneously. The motivation for this exercise is to get a better understanding of how alternative pension portfolios may perform with the aim to draft a recommendation for policy makers on whether the prevailing regulatory framework for Pension Insurance Funds in Germany may be appropriate or require amendments.

In section 5.5.2, we replicate the average portfolio allocation for pension funds in the UK and the Netherlands, the two largest pension fund systems in Europe. Based on a total AuM base of European pension funds of €4,170bln for 2009, Dutch and UK pension funds obtained a total market share of 62.8%. The German pension fund market, on the other hand, only represented 4.2% of the overall market.[817] In terms of relevance of the pension fund system in relation to the GDP of the respective country, the Netherlands is the undisputed leader within all OECD countries, with a figure of 129.8% of GDP. The UK, with 73.0% of GDP, is also above the weighted average of 67.1% of GDP. In Germany the asset base of domestic pension funds reaches a mere 5.2% of GDP.[818]

As can be seen from figure 61 and figure 63, the pension systems in the UK and the Netherlands have on average considerably higher allocation into equity investments than German Pension Insurance Funds do. UK pension funds, with an average equity allocation of 54.0%, have historically relied heavily on equities and regularly invested a significant portion of their funds into this asset

[817] See Eurosif (2011), p. 14.
[818] See OECD (2010), p. 8.

class, while in the Netherlands pension funds have in the past invested approximately 28.8% of their portfolios into equity securities.[819]

In section 5.5.3, we will present the Inflation Hedge model, an alternative fund that pursues to generate a suitable inflation hedge. The particular asset mix of this portfolio has been hereby determined based on academic evidence with respect to inflation-hedging suitability of certain underlying asset classes, in particular real estate and commodities. The Inflation Hedge model could become relevant should the on-going loose monetary policy of the ECB be maintained, to avoid the collapse of the monetary union despite rising prices. Such a scenario would lead to a yield-trap for Pension Insurance Funds given their high exposure to fixed-income securities.

Subsection 5.5.4 includes the empirical results we obtain for the Credit Risk Hedging model, a fund specification that pursues a better risk-management of credit risk by overlaying fixed-income derivatives to the corporate bond allocations. The underlying benchmark strategy for this simulation is the Alternative Portfolio we have used in section 5.4, as it consistently outperformed the other portfolio models calculated.

For all alternative models of section 5.5, the portfolios will invest into equities and bonds in a SRI-screened manner, following the same screening methods we applied in chapter 5.4.[820] Due to the outperformance of Buy-and-Hold outright strategies in comparison to Constant-Mix methods in all simulations we have run previously, we will apply exclusively the Buy-and-Hold approach in this section. To ensure that our previous conclusions with respect to the outperformance of SRI-filtered assets as well as Buy-and-Hold outright strategies do also hold for the alternative portfolio allocations of section 5.5, we have performed additionally a test for both traditional assets as well as Constant-Mix strategies and concluded that our prior recommendations are also valid for the new asset allocation scenarios. Moreover, we will include again the derivative overlay structures we used in our previous simulation studies, ignoring now though the

---

[819] All allocation data used for the UK and the Dutch pension markets in this section are based on the annual Mercer 'Asset Allocation Survey' for European pension plans. The survey for 2011, for example, covered over 1,100 plans from 13 different European countries with a total investment base of more than €550bln AuM. See Mercer (2007) – Mercer (2011).

[820] In practical terms, we have used the same underlying sustainability indices than in section 5.4, just with varying portfolio weights.

sizing restrictions imposed by BaFin circular R3/2000.[821] For the Credit Risk hedging model, we will have in addition to the equity derivative models of section 5.4 similarly structured fixed-income derivatives that will allow to risk-manage the corporate bond segment of the portfolio.

5.5.2 Equity-focused Approach: UK- and Dutch-Model

A. UK Pension Fund Model

A.1 Assumptions on Asset Allocation

Based on the historical asset allocation of UK pension funds as depicted in figure 61 and the corresponding average values over the last 5 years, we have run our simulations on an asset allocation of 55% equities, 40% bonds (with a split of 60% European government bonds and 40% European corporate bonds), 1% real estate investments and 4% alternative assets (50% commodities, 50% hedge fund assets).

An interesting observation derived from the UK allocation is the steadily decreasing equity proportion within the overall portfolios. Triggered potentially by the turmoil of the global credit crisis from 2007 onwards and the spillover effects from the subsequent European sovereign debt crisis in since autumn 2009,[822] UK pension fund managers have shifted away from risky equity investments into more conservative assets like government and corporates bonds.

[821] See BaFin (2000).
[822] See Featherstone (2011), p. 194.

Figure 61: Historic Asset Allocation for UK Pension Funds (2007-2011)

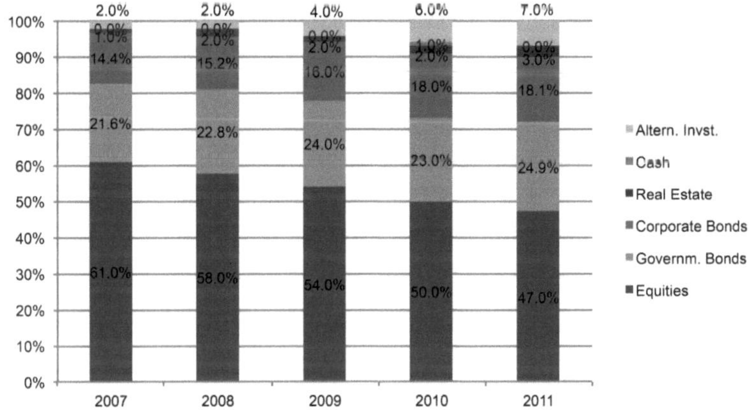

Source: Own representation, on the basis of Mercer (2077) - Mercer (2011). The asset split between corporate and government bonds for 2011 and 2010 is based on actual data, whereas for 2007-2009 we have assumed the arithmetic averages of 2011 and 2010.

A.2 Value Distribution after 3 Years

Figure 62: Buy-and-Hold Strategies UK-Style Portfolio (Value after 3yrs)

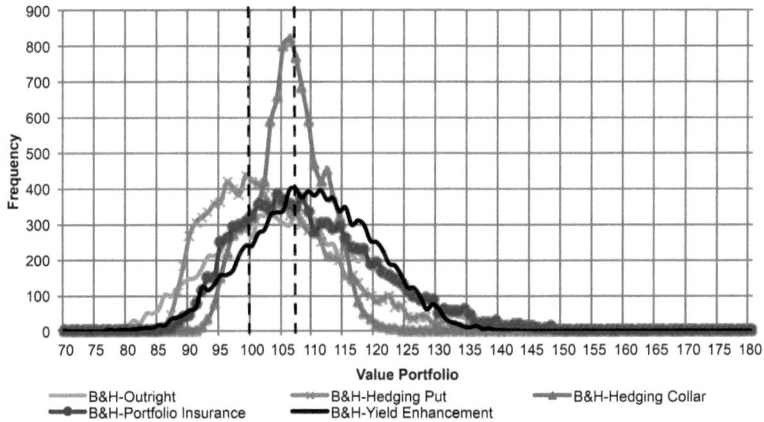

Source: Own representation. Abbreviations used: 'B&H'=Buy-and-Hold.

A.3 Risk, Return and Distribution Characteristics over Investment Period

Table 46: Comparison Across Investment Strategies – UK Pension Fund Model (After Year 3)

	Aver. Value	Max	Min	Std. Dev. Returns (%)	Omega	Downs. Dev. (%)	Sortino Ratio	Ups. Pot. Ratio
Outright	106.55	***181.88***	70.81	11.95	3.29	5.47	1.03	1.48
Hedging Put	103.05	161.58	83.12	9.44	1.99	4.65	0.55	1.10
Hedging Collar	105.55	126.01	***89.28***	***5.21***	***11.43***	***1.50***	***3.52***	***3.86***
Bond-Call Opt.	108.91	177.13	80.47	10.28	8.43	2.76	2.90	3.29
Yield Enhanc.	***109.09***	141.78	76.19	9.20	9.01	3.12	2.66	2.99

Source: Own representation.

A.4 Observations

Allowing the initial equity allocation for the simulation to start in t=0 at 55% yields remarkable results with regard to portfolio performance as well as downside risk measures. The outright strategy, for example, leads to the highest maximum portfolio value of all strategies considered in our research study so far (181.88 in year 3), in comparison to our previous absolute maximum of 142.91 (+27.27%) for the Alternative Portfolio applying the Bond-Call Option strategies in the Buy-and-Hold approach. At the same time, however, the outright strategy of the UK model also leads to the lowest portfolio value recorded, with 70.81, and therefore more than 17.49% below our previous minimum of 85.82 recorded for the outright strategy (Constant-Mix) of the Standard Portfolio.

From a downside risk perspective, the collar derivative structure yields again the most risk-averse profile: (1) a minimum value of 89.28 and hence 18.47 percentage points above the minimum for the outright strategy, (2) a standard deviation for the portfolio returns of 5.21%, which is 6.74 points lower than the volatility of the outright portfolio with 11.95% and (3) the best downside risk indicators of all five major LPM-based risk measures contemplated in this scenario. The cost of the collar structure is the considerably capped maximum achievable value of 126.01 (-30.72% below the Outright strategy). The particular return distribution for the collar structure can be seen in figure 62. The shape of the graph is thereby leptokurtic, with a kurtosis t-ratio of 5.13. This result represents a stark contrast to the price distributions we had beforehand, which were largely (log)-normally distributed.

In the UK model scenario, for a portfolio manager focused on achieving high portfolio values while benefiting from a better downside protection than in the outright case, the Bond-Call option method, in which the entire equity portfolio exposure is replicated with call options, seems suitable.

B. Dutch Pension Fund Model

B.1 Assumptions on Asset Allocation

The assumed asset allocation for the Dutch pension fund model is as follows: equities 30%, bonds 60% (85% European government bonds, 15% European corporate bonds), 5% real estate and 5% alternative investments (50% commodities, 50% hedge fund assets). These numbers are based on the average allocation for the time period 2007-2011. As figure 63 depicts, Dutch pension funds have also decreased their equity exposure since 2007 (from 35.0% down to 26.0%), while simultaneously increasing their investments into government bonds (from 47.6% up to 54.8%).

Figure 63: Historic Asset Allocation for Dutch Pension Funds (2007-2011)

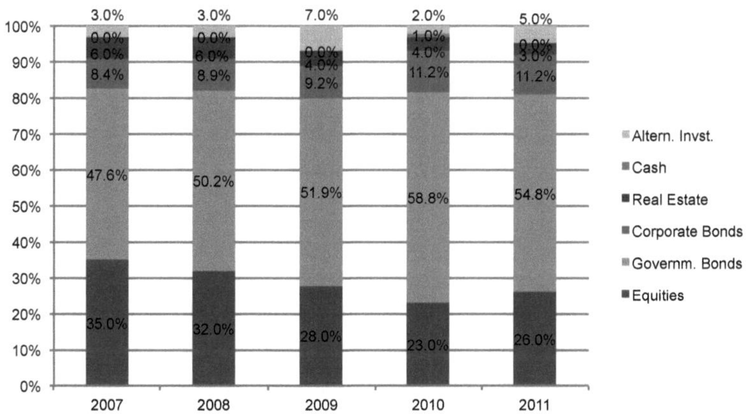

Source: Own representation, on the basis of Mercer (2077) - Mercer (2011). The asset split between corporate and government bonds for 2011 and 2010 is based on actual data, whereas for 2007-2009 we have assumed the arithmetic averages of 2011 and 2010.

B.2 Value Distribution after 3 Years

Figure 64: Buy-and-Hold Strategies Dutch-Style Portfolio (Value after 3yrs)

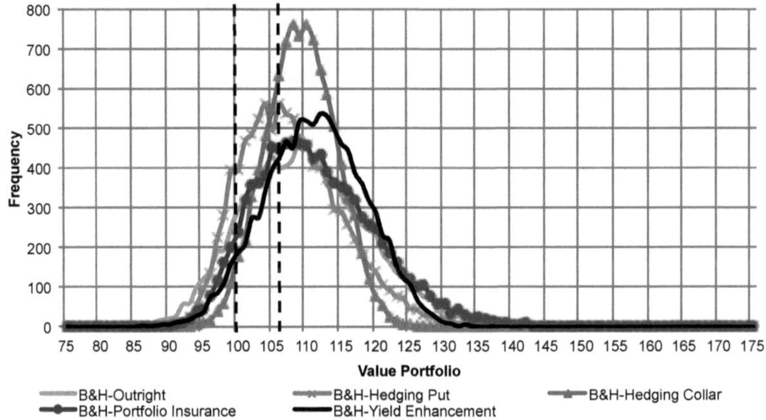

Source: Own representation. Abbreviations used: 'B&H'=Buy-and-Hold.

B.3 Risk, Return and Distribution Characteristics over Investment Period

Table 47: Comparison Across Investment Strategies – Dutch Pension Fund Model (After Year 3)

	Aver. Value	Max	Min	Std. Dev. Returns (%)	Omega	Downs. Dev. (%)	Sortino Ratio	Ups. Pot. Ratio
Outright	109.30	157.36	82.41	8.22	15.54	1.99	4.29	4.59
Hedging Put	107.32	148.37	87.91	6.83	16.95	1.36	5.03	5.35
Hedging Collar	108.67	127.50	***91.21***	***4.67***	***108.99***	***0.50***	***16.27***	***16.42***
Bond-Call Opt.	***110.74***	***159.78***	85.43	7.84	39.29	1.13	8.76	8.99
Yield Enhanc.	110.66	136.48	85.54	6.61	44.32	1.14	8.72	8.92

Source: Own representation.

B.4 Observations

Lowering the equity exposure to 30% of the overall allocation in the Dutch model, in comparison to the UK approach with a 55% equity proportion, has a significant impact on the risk profile of the portfolio values at the end of year 3. For the Outright strategies, the maximum achievable value decreases by -13.48% from 181.88 to 157.36, the minimum value shifts by 11.60 points to 82.41 and the downside risk measures improve considerably as does the Upside Potential Ratio (by factor 3.1x from 1.48 to 4.59).

Both hedging strategies (put and collar), despite generating the lowest average portfolio values, yield nevertheless also the highest minima. The collar structure, in particular, offers the most conservative risk profile in terms of downside risk measures. Its Omega value, for example, is with 108.99 more than 7.0x higher than the corresponding number for the outright strategy. Furthermore, the collar offers the highest upside potential with an Upside Potential Ratio of 16.42, 3.6x the respective outright number. The Bond-Call Option strategy, with an average portfolio value of 110.74 (versus 109.30 for the outright method), has an attractive downside profile (Sortino Ratio of 8.76 in comparison to 4.29 for the outright approach) and an appealing upside participation (Upside Potential Ratio of 8.99 vs. 4.59 outright).

5.5.3 Inflation Hedge Model

A. Rationale

The current capital markets environment of historically low interest rates and record-high spreads for government bonds, particularly from peripheral European sovereigns (see also figure 65) make investments into fixed-income bonds in general a riskier proposition than in the past. This becomes even more relevant in the current environment of financial turmoil caused by the European sovereign debt crisis. German Pension Insurance Funds that invest approximately 85% of their total asset base in low-risk fixed-income instruments may have to reconsider their investment policy if they want to maintain a viable portfolio management.

Figure 65: Interest Rate and Credit Environment (Dec-2001 to Nov-2011)

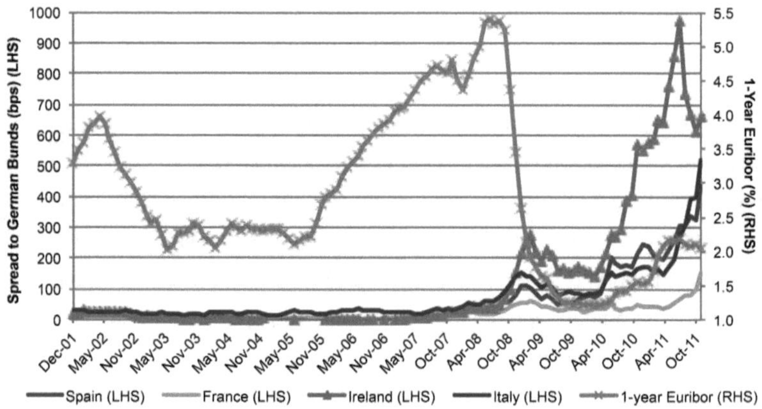

Source: Own representation. Based on data provided by the ECB. See ECB (2012, d) and ECB (2012, f). Note: Spread to German Bunds is calculated as the difference in secondary market yields between the local government debt and German government bonds of the same duration (approximately 10 years).

Furthermore, should the response of the ECB to the financial crisis in form of further loose monetary policy continue in the upcoming years,[823] the increased money supply might lead in some countries of the European Union to inflationary pressure.[824] We acknowledge at this point that our simulation study has not considered in-depth the potential impact of inflation on portfolio performance. Inflation impact merits nonetheless some consideration as ignoring it could lead to misleading portfolio performances in real money terms. A historic analysis of inflation in the European Monetary Union (EMU) provides important conclusions (see figure 66): inflation numbers followed a steady path within a tight band width of 1.0-3.0% before the outbreak of the credit crisis in 2007/2008, at which point large swings were measured, caused predominantly by the massive monetary interventions at that time operated by the European Central Bank to stabilise the markets. As a consequence of this volatile pattern of the inflation number, we will focus in this section on the analysis of extreme inflation environments similar to those registered historically for the EMU and contrast them with the performance the Inflation Hedge Model generates. This side-by-side analysis will enable us to test the robustness of the Inflation Hedge Model to withstand high-inflationary time periods.

[823] See ECB (2011, a), p. 114.
[824] See ECB (2011, b), p. 36 et seq.

Figure 66: Inflation Environment in Europe (Dec-2001 to Nov-2011)

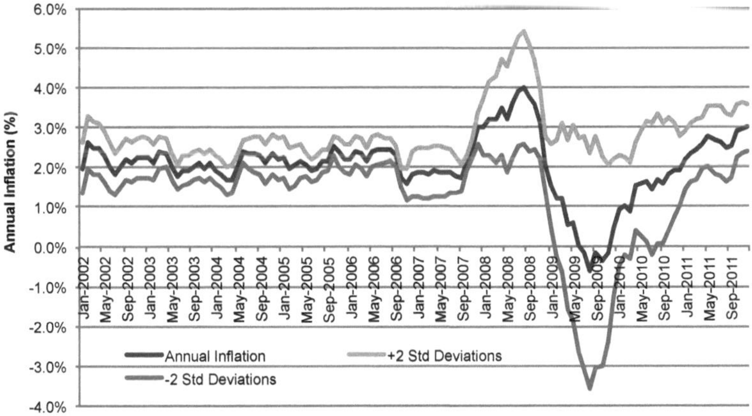

Source: Own representation. Based on data provided by the ECB. See ECB (2012, a).

In summary, this section will attempt to engineer an asset portfolio mix, the Inflation Hedge Model, that based on previously obtained academic evidence should provide an adequate inflation hedge for Pension Insurance Funds. As we did in the section for the UK- and Dutch-model, we will ignore in this section for our allocation prevailing regulatory constraints imposed by the BaFin in Germany.

B. Assumptions on Asset Allocation

In our understanding, an asset provides inflation hedge “if it offers “protection” against inflation, which in turn means the elimination or at least the reduction of the possibility that the real rate of return on the security will fall below some specified “floor” value such as zero”, so that the nominal rate of return of an investments is at least the rate of inflation.[825] This understanding is based on an earlier definition of inflation hedge by Reilly et al. (1970).[826] Therefore we will conclude that our Inflation Hedge Model provides an adequate inflation hedge if it generates a return that is at least as high as the increase in price levels.

We already discussed in detail in section 3.3.4 the inflation hedge benefits commodity investments can offer to an asset portfolio. Moreover, we highlighted the positive diversification impact both hedge fund and commodity assets can provide to a portfolio manager. These two asset classes will therefore play a

[825] See Bodie (1976), p. 460.
[826] See Reilly et al. (1970), p. 105.

more relevant role in this section than in previous portfolio models considered so far.

In addition, academic research findings underline the inflation proxy hedging features of real estate assets. Numerous academic papers support this assumption. Fama, Schwert (1977), for example, proved that "private residential real estate is a complete hedge against both expected and unexpected inflation [.]"[827] The inflation hedge properties of unsecuritized real estate have been already proved in various early academic articles, in particular Hoag (1980) and Brueggeman et al. (1984).[828] More recently, Zhou et al. (2005) conclude that real estate asset groups (industrial real estate, residential real estate, commercial real estate) offer in general a good inflation hedge proxy, whereby industrial real estate assets achieve the best results in this context.[829] For REIT structures that have as underlying real assets, on the other hand, the inflation hedge results are rather mixed.[830]

The suitability of equity assets as inflation hedge yields a mixed picture in terms of academic findings: while Reilly et al. (1970) found partial inflation hedge properties,[831] Bodie (1976) showed that real returns on equity assets were negatively correlated to inflation, therefore rejecting the assumption of common stock as a suitable inflation hedge.[832] Jaffe, Mandelker (1976) and Fama, Schwert (1977) confirm these findings in their respective empirical studies.[833] Gultekin (1983) expands the analysis to a total of 26 countries and find no evidence of hedging properties.[834] These research findings therefore contradict the 'Fisher effect', i.e. that nominal interest rates or returns should reflect future inflation rates.[835] Firth (1979), on the contrary, obtains robust results that

827 Fama, Schwert (1977), p. 144. This research analysis used time series data for the time period 1953-1977 for the US real estate market.
828 See Hoag (1980), p. 577 and Brueggeman et al. (1984), p. 351.
829 See Zhou et al. (2005), p. 44 et seq. Empirical study based on time series data from 1979-2003 for the New Zealand real estate market.
830 See Glascock et al. (2002), p. 316.
831 See Reilly et al. (1970), p. 110.
832 See Bodie (1976), p. 469. Bodie's results actually suggest that shorting equities would provide a suitable inflation hedge.
833 See Jaffe, Mandelker (1976), p. 457 and Fama, Schwert (1977), p. 145.
834 See Gultekin (1983), p. 64.
835 See Fisher (1930).

confirm a proxy inflation hedge by common stock.[836] Moreover, a research paper by Boudoukh, Richardson (1993), which focuses on very long-term time series data, confirms the Fisher-type effect for both the US and the UK equity markets.[837]

In conclusion, while inflation hedge properties have been consistently achieved for commodity assets and are also robust for real estate investments, the suitability of equities remains ambiguous. We therefore propose an asset allocation with an overweight allocation into commodity assets, real estate (both for their inflation hedge characteristics) and hedge fund strategies (diversification effect, alpha generation). We will assign a 25% weight to each of these asset classes, 10% to equities given their rather mixed results in terms of inflation hedge properties and 5% respectively for corporate bonds, government bonds and money market. As underlying investment strategy, we rely on the Buy-and-Hold approach as so far it has consistently achieved better results than the Constant-Mix technique. Furthermore, we have used as asset base the indices we had for the Alternative Portfolio in section 5.4, as it was the alternative that yielded the best performance results for our research objectives. This implies that the asset categories equities, corporate bond as well as government bonds will be replicated following SRI-screening techniques that follow a combined BiC and negative screening approach.

While the asset weights for the Inflation Hedge Model have been chosen randomly, they nonetheless reflect our objective of simulating a portfolio that should provide a good inflation hedge (therefore the 50% overall allocation in real estate and commodities), benefit from the advantages hedge fund investments can offer, while minimising the exposure to fixed-income securities.

C. Different Inflation Scenarios as Benchmark

Before analysing the results of the simulation study for the Inflation Hedge Model, we have to determine the various minimum inflation threshold levels we will use to benchmark our results against. Apart from using historical annual inflation figures for the EMU as inflation input (see also figure 66), we have also

---

[836] See Firth (1979), p. 747 et seq. Firth uses UK stock market data for the time period 1950-1976.

[837] See Boudoukh, Richardson (1993), p. 1354. The empirical study uses as time period historical stock market data from 1802-1990 for the US and 1820-1988 for the US.

added a 95% confidence band around the average (represented by ±2 standard deviations around the mean)[838] that we will use as risk parameter for our calculations and that will also represent our 'extreme inflation' scenarios. The precise threshold levels are summarised in table 48.

Table 48: European Annual Inflation – Sensitivity Analysis

	European Inflation	2 Std. Deviations Band
Main Numbers		
Average	2.06%	2.06%
Abs. Maximum	4.01%	5.42%
Abs. Minimum	-0.62%	-3.59%
3-year Number[839]		
Average	6.36%	6.36%
Maximum	12.77%	17.65%
Threshold Portfolio Value[840]		
Average	106.36	106.36
Maximum	112.77	117.65

Source: Own representation. Time period for data used: Dec-2001 until Nov-2011. Based on data provided by the ECB. See ECB (2012, a).

Using the average annual inflation number of 2.06% for the last 10 years, the portfolio value of the Pension Insurance Fund needs to reach a final value of 106.36 at the end of year 3 to compensate investors for inflation. Applying the maximum inflation point measured during this time period of 4.01% as constant inflation input, a three-year investment would need to achieve a value of 112.77. Within our risk parameters of 2*trailing 12-month standard deviation, the final number (for the absolute maximum recorded) accrues to 117.65 of par. We will apply these figures as minimum thresholds in our downside risk measures to see how the respective risk profile of our investment strategies may change. We acknowledge that the assumption of such high inflation numbers over a longer

[838] Both confidence intervals are calculated as the trailing 12-month standard deviation of the inflation number multiplied by 1.96. Under the assumption of a normally distributed function, 95% of all values would lie within ±1.96 standard deviations. We have hereby allowed for negative weights. See Brooks (2008), p. 55.
Based on a Jarque-Bera test of normality, however, European inflation numbers do not show statistical evidence of normality (test statistic of 33.59). We use the 2-standard deviation band nonetheless as it is a commonly used risk parameter in finance, in particular in modern risk management.

[839] This number is the continuously compounded figure over three years assuming that the value itself from above remains constant.

[840] This number indicates the minimum value the portfolio needs to achieve at the end of year 3 to be able to offer capital guarantee in real money terms, i.e. including the effect of inflation.

period of time is not very likely[841] given the ECB's prime objective of price stability within the Euro area.[842] Nevertheless we believe that this type of analysis should still be run from a risk management perspective,[843] especially as the expansionary monetary policies of the ECB might fuel inflation in the next few years.

D. Value Distribution after 3 Years

Figure 67: Buy-and-Hold Strategies Inflation Hedge Model (Value after 3yrs)

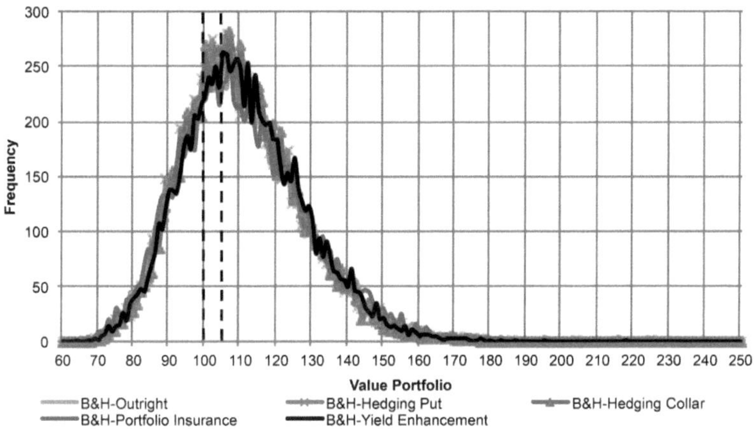

Source: Own representation. Abbreviations used: 'B&H'=Buy-and-Hold.

E. Risk, Return and Distribution Characteristics over Investment Period

Table 49: Comparison Across Investment Strategies – Inflation Hedge Model (After Year 3)

	Aver. Value	Max	Min	Std. Dev. Returns (%)	Omega	Downs. Dev. (%)	Sortino Ratio	Ups. Pot. Ratio
Outright	109.90	226.82	62.68	15.50	3.87	6.70	1.23	1.66
Hedging Put	109.25	224.46	65.92	14.88	3.78	6.40	1.21	1.64
Hedging Collar	109.71	215.55	***66.89***	***14.38***	4.31	***5.92***	1.39	1.81

841 As a reference point: In May 2012, the ECB inflation forecast for 2016 was 2.0%, with a standard deviation of 0.2%. Nonetheless, 18.3% of the replies of the survey expected inflation to exceed the 2.5% number over this time period. See ECB (2012, b).

842 Price stability is defined by the ECB as the first element of the central bank's strategy. See ECB (2012, c).

843 Using ECB inflation numbers going back until 1990, annual inflation in Europe reached 4.92% in Jul-1991. See ECB (2012, a).

	Aver. Value	Max	Min	Std. Dev. Returns (%)	Omega	Downs. Dev. (%)	Sortino Ratio	Ups. Pot. Ratio
Bond-Call Opt.	110.24	***239.68***	62.43	16.33	3.72	7.10	1.18	1.62
Yield Enhanc.	***110.36***	217.91	63.62	15.02	**4.38**	6.24	***1.40***	***1.81***

Source: Own representation.

F. Inflation Stress Testing

Table 50: Portfolio Return Comparison in Different Inflation Environments (at End of Year 3)

	Average Portfolio Value[844]	Scenario 1: 2.06% Inflation-106.36[845]	Scenario 2: 4.01% Inflation-112.77	Scenario 3: 5.42% Inflation-117.65
Outright	109.90	3.54%[846]	-2.87%	-7.75%
Hedging Long Put	109.25	2.89%	-3.52%	-8.40%
Hedging Long Collar	109.71	3.35%	-3.06%	-7.94%
Bond-Call Option	110.24	3.88%	-2.53%	-7.41%
Yield Enhanc.	110.36	4.00%	-2.41%	-7.29%

Source: Own representation.

Table 51: Inflation Impact on Inflation Hedge Model, Buy-and-Hold (at End of Year 3)

	Omega	Downs. Dev. (%)	Sortino Ratio	Kappa 3	Ups. Pot. Ratio
(1) Inflation Assumption: Constant Annual Inflation of 2.06%[847]					
Outright	1.35 (3.87)	9.79 (6.70)	0.19 (1.23)	0.14 (0.85)	0.73 (1.66)
Hedging Long Put	1.26 (3.78)	9.55 (6.40)	0.14 (1.21)	0.11 (0.84)	0.69 (1.64)
Hedging Long Collar	1.38 (4.31)	8.98 (5.92)	0.21 (1.39)	0.16 (0.96)	0.75 (1.81)
Bond-Call Option	1.37 (3.72)	10.22 (7.10)	0.20 (1.18)	0.15 (0.83)	0.74 (1.62)
Yield Enhanc.	1.48 (4.38)	9.24 (6.24)	0.25 (1.40)	0.19 (0.96)	0.78 1.81)
(2) Inflation Assumption: Constant Annual Inflation of 4.01% (Maximum for European Inflation)					
Outright	0.48	13.59	-0.33	-0.27	0.31
Hedging Long	0.43	13.44	-0.38	-0.31	0.28

[844] Refers to the average value we obtain for the Inflation Hedge Model simulation.

[845] Under the assumption of a constant annual inflation rate of 2.06%, the final value of the Alternative Portfolio needs to exceed 106.36 to compensate pension beneficiaries for the potential devaluation of their investments due to inflation. The values in this column indicate the spread or risk cushion of the average portfolio value versus the minimum value of 106.36. Analogous approaches are run for Scenario 2 and Scenario 3. The numbers are shown as percentage points.

[846] This number indicates by what percentage points the average portfolio value is above/below the minimum threshold value of 106.36.

[847] In brackets the previous numbers obtained in the simulation for the Inflation Hedge Model from table 49.

	Omega	Downs. Dev. (%)	Sortino Ratio	Kappa 3	Ups. Pot. Ratio
Put					
Hedging Long Collar	0.45	12.81	-0.36	-0.29	0.30
Bond-Call Option	0.51	14.02	-0.31	-0.25	0.33
Yield Enhanc.	0.51	12.98	-0.31	-0.25	0.32
(3) Inflation Assumption: Constant Annual Inflation of 5.42% (Maximum for 2 Std. Deviation Band)					
Outright	0.22	16.91	-0.56	-0.47	0.16
Hedging Long Put	0.19	16.83	-0.59	-0.50	0.14
Hedging Long Collar	0.20	16.16	-0.58	-0.49	0.14
Bond-Call Option	0.24	17.31	-0.53	-0.45	0.17
Yield Enhanc.	0.23	16.26	-0.55	-0.46	0.16

Source: Own representation.

G. Observations

G.1 Performance Inflation Hedge Model

The Inflation Hedge model yields widespread price distributions at the end of year 3 of our simulation period. With maxima well above 200 and minima in the low 60s, the range of prices we obtain is considerably more widespread than in any other investment strategy contemplated in section 5.4. Also within our alternative models so far, no approach generates a similarly wide price range. The maximum of 236.68 belonging to the Bond-Call Option approach is significantly above the previous absolute value of 177.13 measured for the same strategy in the UK model. The lowest absolute value beforehand corresponded to the Outright method in the UK model (70.81), whereas the minimum of the Bond-Call Option for the Inflation Hedge is at 62.43 and therefore -8.38 percentage points lower. The increased riskiness of the new portfolio price distributions we have obtained is also reflected in the volatility of portfolio returns. The 16.33% for the Bond-Call Option method are +4.38 points above the 11.95% for the UK outright scenario.

In terms of average portfolio figures, the results seem more appealing. The highest average value of 110.36 for the Yield Enhancement portfolio is the third highest average measured in our simulation study. Even the Put strategy at 109.25 yields a better result than any of the UK models, but moreover also outperforms many strategies contemplated within the standard investment methods of section 5.4.

From a downside risk perspective, the Inflation Hedge portfolios offer rather disappointing results: high downside deviations below the 0% MAR threshold, Omega values in the range of 3.72-4.38 and Upside Potential Ratios of 1.62-1.81 are considerably weaker than the downside profile of the Dutch model and even the majority of the strategies considered in the UK model. The standard portfolios in section 5.4 also obtain consistently better downside risk numbers (see also table 45 with all the results from section 5.4). As we saw with the UK and the Dutch models, a shift into riskier asset classes (bearing in mind that the real estate exposure was obtained via investments in the equity capital of real estate companies) will not automatically be compensated by higher average returns. Based on our empirical analysis, also a high exposure into alternative investments (50% of the total allocation) does not yield the expected results. However, the Inflation Hedge model is undoubtedly suitable for (highly) risk-seeking portfolio managers that pursuit high returns at the cost of potentially suffering significant losses and managing a portfolio with a large downside risk exposure. On average, nonetheless, our empirical evidence does not suggest that the Inflation Hedge Model is a suitable method for Pension Insurance Funds.

G.2 Inflation Hedging Adequacy

More importantly for our research purposes at this point is the adequacy of the Inflation Hedge model to offer portfolio managers an appropriate inflation hedge. Tables 50 and 51 present the numbers obtained. The results in table 50 indicate for inflation scenario 1 that the performance achieved by the various investment strategies of the Inflation Hedge model is sufficient to compensate portfolio managers for both the inflation impact and also generate the 1.75% annual maximum guaranteed return that pension beneficiaries obtain. For higher inflationary environments (scenario 2, 3), however, the portfolios underperform. For the worse case scenario (scenario 3), the underperformance is in the range of -8.40 to -7.29 percentage points over the 3-year simulation period.

Table 51 centres on the impact on downside risk measures if the MAR is set at different average annual inflation figures rather than at 0% as we have assumed in all previous simulation scenarios.[848] The impact on overall portfolio performance in real money terms is considerable. For inflation scenarios 2 and 3, in particular, the results are disencouraging. A high increase in downside deviation to values of 12.81-14.02% for scenario 2 and 16.16-17.31% for scenario 3, alongside negative values for the Sortino Ratio as well as Kappa 3, should be interpreted as a warning to portfolio managers to not underestimate the effect inflation can have on portfolio performance during high-inflationary periods.

5.5.4 Credit Risk Hedging

A. Rationale

Derivative overlay structures used in our portfolio scenarios so far have been used exclusively in connection with the equity segment of the respective portfolio. While in our view such a limitation is justified for various reasons (see section 4.4.4 with our rationale), we will nonetheless analysis the impact the hedging of credit risk can have on overall performance. In conclusion, we will have two derivative overlay structures in parallel, one for the equity allocation and one for the corporate bond portfolio. At this stage, we assume the government bond portfolio is of sufficiently low default risk that such a hedging effort is not necessary. We are aware, as mentioned already in previous sections, that in the context of the European sovereign debt crisis such 'risk-free' assumption may not hold anymore.

B. Assumptions for the Credit Risk Hedging Model

The most common valuation approach for options on bonds would be to apply a multi-factor interest rate model (see Fong, Vasicek (1991), Longstaff, Schwartz (1992), Chen (1996), Balduzzi et al. (1996)) in which the dynamics of interest rates are exogenously specified as well as interest rate volatility and mean values modelled.[849] Once the theoretical interest rate curve has been specified, the model would be calibrated using market prices of reference bonds to obtain values for the various model parameters. Finally, using the estimated parameters, option prices could be calculated. Alternatively, arbitrage models

---

[848] For scenario 1, MAR will be 2.06% per annum instead of 0% we have used in all previous calculations. In scenario 2, MAR=4.01% and in scenario 3 MAR=5.42%. Any portfolio strategy contemplated in our analysis already has included the 1.75% annual maximum guaranteed return.

[849] See Martellini et al. (2003), p. 392 et seq.

can also be suitable methods, as they overcome one of the major limitations of multi factor models that interest rates are derived endogenously. Arbitrage models, on the other hand, are consistent with the actual observed interest rate curve and prices of bonds. These prices are subsequently used to price derivatives.[850] Most common models are the Ho, Lee (1986) approach, the Hull, White (1990) model, the Heath, Jarrow, Morton technique (1990, 1992) or the Moraleda, Vorst (1997) method.

While both multi-factor models as well as arbitrage methods are useful to price single bond options, in practise, any investment professional managing a corporate bond portfolio would most probably hedge default risk via CDS contracts, an OTC credit derivative that offers the buyer protection against default of the underlying entity. This protection is obtained by paying the protection seller a fixed premium over the life of the CDS contracts. The premium paid is commonly known as CDS spread.[851] For an entire corporate bond portfolio, a basket of CDS could be applied, with individual CDS for each bond.[852]

The selection of the most adequate credit hedging model for our simulation study is a challenging task, as many of the key assumptions of the multi-factor models, bond option or CDS valuation approaches discussed beforehand do not apply in our case. With respect to bond option pricing, our corporate bond index (1) applies to a large number of corporate bonds (around 1,000 at a given valuation date), (2) the index does not have a contractual maturity like single bonds usually do (with the exception of subordinated, perpetual bonds frequently in use for bank capital purposes) so that the before-mentioned 'duration' effect is not given, (3) is a total return index that reinvests any coupons paid on the underlying bonds. As described in the index methodology of our corporate bond index, the bond rebalances the index components on a monthly basis to maintain a constant duration and an average investment grade profile of the portfolio.[853] CDS contracts, while appealing from a practical standpoint, require as essential input the risk-neutral probability that the underlying entity will de-

---

[850] See Martellini et al. (2003), p. 396.
[851] See Bouzoubaa, Osseiran (2010), p. 293.
[852] See Hull (2006), p. 516.
[853] See ECPI (2011, b), p. 2 et seq.. We assume at this point that we will model exclusively the Alternative Portfolio given its superior risk-return characteristics discussed in chapter 5.4.

fault at different time periods in the future as well as a recovery rate.[854] While for single corporate bonds this input is relatively straightforward to obtain, for a corporate bond index such an exercise is excessively cumbersome. Moreover, simply applying the Black-Scholes option pricing model is also suboptimal, as the constant volatility and interest rate assumptions do not hold, as any change to the interest rate will affect the underlying instrument and impact the entire yield curve structure.[855] Furthermore, the majority of these more complex interest rate option techniques are not implementable in a bootstrap simulation framework due to the various thousands of different pricings that would need to be calculated almost simultaneously by the model.

For our modelling purposes with respect to the corporate bond portfolio, consequently, there does not exist an obvious superior valuation approach. Practitioners, nonetheless, apply frequently the so-called 'Black-76' model when pricing bond options.[856] This derivative model, an extension of the Black-Scholes formula, was initially developed by Black (1976) and is a popular method for valuing European-style interest rate options.[857] Originally, the Black model was presented as a commodity option pricing method and subsequently adjusted to price bond options. The Black model assumes that bond prices are log-normally distributed at the maturity of the option and uses yield volatility as key input rather than price volatility.[858] One of the main advantages of the Black-76 model for practitioners is that it is very fast in calculating option prices. For fixed-income derivative desks that manage trading books with thousands of bond options, computational speed is an essential factor.[859] Due to the model complexity of our simulation study and the computational constraints we are working under, the Black-76 will enable us to calculate for each of the 10,000 data points we have and for each of the input variables, the respective bond option price.

---

[854] See Hull (2006), p. 510.
[855] See Martellini et al. (2003), p. 488.
[856] See Hull, White (1990), p. 585.
[857] See Black (1976).
[858] See Hull (2006), pp. 615-617.
[859] See Bouzoubaa, Osseiran (2010), p. 268.

D. Main Input Parameters

For the respective strikes of the fixed-income derivative overlay structures, we will fix the ATM level at par value plus the average coupon we will receive during the 1-year maturity of the option. In comparison to any uncertain dividend payments we may receive on an equity portfolio, we assume that the average coupon will be received with certainty during the next period and therefore act as a cushion against price drops of the credit portfolio. With an average coupon rate of 5.15% p.a.,[860] we fix the ATM strikes at 105.15% of spot for the put, the collar and the ATM long call strategies. For the upper strikes on the collar and the Yield Enhancement strategy, we maintain the previously used levels of 115% of spot. These assumptions seem reasonable to us in the context of an investment grade portfolio of corporate bonds with a large number of underlying bonds. We hereby perceive the average cash coupon as a certain value accretion our credit portfolio will benefit from during the year, so that the actual portfolio value drop would be less the coupon amount received. All bond option pricings for the credit portfolio will be calculated with the Black-76 pricing method. The strikes and features of the derivatives for the equity portfolio remain identical to the ones used in previous chapters and are determined with the Black-Scholes method.

Even though we are primarily interested in hedging the credit portfolio against price declines and / or potential defaults, we will for the sake of completeness also calculate the returns obtained for the remaining investment strategies we simulated in section 5.4. This will enable us to draw direct comparisons among all the various strategies and different scenarios we have been contemplated in our research study. Our reference portfolio will be the Alternative Portfolio of section 5.4, given that our previous simulation results have proven that including SRI assets for the equity, corporate and government bond segments of the portfolio and having an allocation into alternative investments achieved overall the best portfolio results in terms of downside risk mitigation without impacting average portfolio returns. We therefore continue to focus on exploring the advantages SRI-structured portfolios have under different deriva-

[860] See ECPI (2011, c), p. 2.

tive overlay structures to obtain potentially an investment strategy that may yield superior risk-return results for German Pension Insurance Funds.

E. Value Distribution after 3 Years[861]

Figure 68: Buy-and-Hold Strategies Credit Risk Hedging Portfolio (Value after 3yrs)

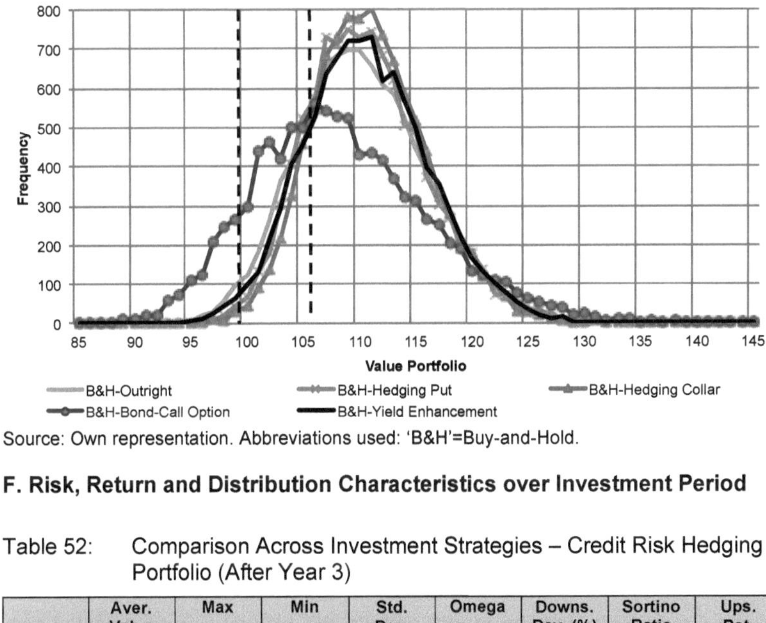

Source: Own representation. Abbreviations used: 'B&H'=Buy-and-Hold.

F. Risk, Return and Distribution Characteristics over Investment Period

Table 52: Comparison Across Investment Strategies – Credit Risk Hedging Portfolio (After Year 3)

	Aver. Value	Max	Min	Std. Dev. Returns (%)	Omega	Downs. Dev. (%)	Sortino Ratio	Ups. Pot. Ratio
Outright	109.79	141.14	89.77	5.28	131.42	0.51	18.00	18.14
Hedg-ing Put	110.13	147.30	94.69	4.85	448.52	0.23	41.13	41.22
Hedg-ing Col-lar	***110.52***	143.85	***95.41***	***4.57***	***796.23***	***0.17***	***58.17***	***58.24***
Bond-Call	107.95	***166.39***	84.92	7.20	16.50	1.61	4.59	4.89

[861] Main pricing input assumptions used for the credit derivatives in the Black-76 pricing formula: bond price volatility based on the ECPI Corporate Bond index for the last 10 years of 11.54% p.a., yield curve spreads -47bps for 1 months, -30bps for 3 months, -13bps for 6 months, +39bps for 3 years and +72bps for 5 years based on the average spreads of the respective Euribor rates to the 1-year rate for the last 10 years. For each repricing date, a new yield curve is calculated based on the stochastic 1-year Euribor rate on the end of the year. Yield spreads, however, remain constant over our simulation period of 3 years. Aver-age duration of the portfolio is 4.07 years and average coupon 5.15%, with one annual cou- pon payment. See ECPI (2011,c) p. 2. Input data used as provided by VWD data provider.

	Aver. Value	Max	Min	Std. Dev. Returns (%)	Omega	Downs. Dev. (%)	Sortino Ratio	Ups. Pot. Ratio
Opt.[862]								
Yield En-hanc.	110.17	143.00	90.50	5.04	191.34	0.42	22.77	22.89

Source: Own representation.

G. Observations

The inclusion of credit derivatives concurrently to the equity derivative overlays discussed in previous chapters yields very favourable results in terms of downside risk mitigation. In comparison to the investment strategies simulated in chapter 5.4, the Credit Risk Hedging portfolio using collar structures for both the equity and corporate bond portfolios achieves the most risk-conservative value distribution of all portfolios contemplated in our research study.

The absolute minimum value recorded, for example, is with 95.41 the lowest of all portfolios simulated. The previously lowest value belonged to the collar in the SRI portfolio (92.03). In terms of return volatility after three years, the collar obtains a standard deviation of 4.57%, the lowest figure recorded in our research study across all investment strategies. The previous minimum of 4.67% corresponded to the Constant–Mix collar in the Dutch Pension Fund model. With regards to Omega, which reflects the probability-weighted ratio of gains to losses relatively to a minimum return of 0% (see also section 4.5.2), the collar for the Credit Risk Hedging model records the highest upside potential with 796.23, +298% the previously highest number obtained of 200.29 for the collar in the Alternative Portfolio in the Buy-and-Hold scenario. Downside deviation below a MAR of 0% is with 0.17% significantly more risk-averse in relative terms than the 0.39% observed for the collar in the Alternative Portfolio. The Sortino Ratio, a figure that expresses the average excess return of the strategy relative to the downside deviation below 0%, is at 58.17 more than double the previous value of 23.56 for the collar-method in the Alternative Portfolio. With respect to the Upside Potential Ratio that reflects the excess return of the portfolio distribution over the minimum return of 0%, the Credit Risk Hedging portfo-

862 In the Bond-Call Option method, both the equity as well as corporate bond segments are closed out and replaced with long call option positions.

lio yields 58.24 (for the collar) again the best results based on the data obtained by our simulation study.

The improved downside risk profile of the collar structure in the Credit Risk Hedging Portfolio does not impact the expected average return a portfolio manager can obtain. With an average portfolio value of 110.52 after year 3, this investment strategy generates the third largest average return of all strategies, just below the 110.74 the Bond-Call Option strategy and the Yield Enhancement method with 110.66, both for the Dutch model. The opportunity cost of the structure, nonetheless, is reflected in the lower absolute maximum value we achieve during the observation period. With 143.85% of the initial portfolio value, the maximum is considerably below the 239.68% and 226.82% figures observed in the Inflation Hedge model for the Bond-Call Option strategy and the Outright approach, respectively.

An important observation is also the performance of the put option strategy. Hedging both the equity and the corporate bond portfolios with ATM options seems to generate satisfactory performance numbers. For the majority of observed downside risk measures, this strategy actually offers the second best results of all strategies contemplated in terms of minimum value (94.69), Omega (448.52), Sortino Ratio (41.13) and Upside Potential (41.22).

An unusual result is the weak performance of the Bond-Call Option scenario, in which we replicate the entire exposure into equities as well as corporate bonds via ATM call options. This strategy can only convince with the largest absolute value observed amongst the five portfolios within the Credit Risk Hedging section. In relative comparison to the other four models, however, the overall performance achieved appears less suitable for Pension Insurance Funds.

The overall superiority of the Credit Risk Hedging scenario (see also subsequent section 5.5.5 in which we will compare all strategies across all investment models analysed in our research study) is also a manifest of the superior performance observed for SRI-structured portfolios across all our different portfolios in this thesis. With the Credit Risk Hedging approach, we have been able to provide empirical evidence that independently of the derivative overlays applied or the underlying allocation weights, SRI portfolios consistently outperform similarly structured conventional asset classes. In this section, we have been able to improve the downside risk characteristics of the previously best-performing Alternative Portfolio that invests its equity, corporate and government bond allocations in SRI-filtered manner.

5.5.5 Benchmarking Across All Strategies and Portfolios

After completion of the various model specifications and portfolio alternatives in our empirical analysis, we have summarised all results obtained in one single table. This overview will enable us to draw conclusions with respect to the suitability of a particular investment strategy for the strategic asset allocation of German Pension Insurance Funds. While previous table 45 summarised exclusively the results obtained for the standard management strategies simulated in section 5.4, table 53 below encompasses all results from both section 5.4 as well as the alternative investment models from 5.5.

Table 53: Relative Comparison across all Portfolios and Investment Strategies (After Year 3)

Average Portfolio Value				**Maximum**			
Best Value		**Worst Value**		**Best Value**		**Worst Value**	
1. DM: Bond-Call Option	***110.74***	1. UK: Put	103.05	1. IH: Bond-Call Option	***239.68***	1. UK: Collar	126.01
2. DM: Yield Enhanc.	***110.66***	2. UK: Collar	105.55	2. IH: Outright	***226.82***	2. SP: Collar-CM	126.74
3. CH: Collar	***110.52***	3. UK: Outright	106.55	3. IH: Put	***224.46***	3. DM: Collar	127.50

Minimum				**Standard Deviation Returns (in %)**			
Best Value		**Worst Value**		**Best Value**		**Worst Value**	
1. CH: Collar	***95.41***	1. IH: Bond-Call Option	62.43	1. CH: Collar	***4.57***	1. IH: Bond-Call Option	16.33
2. CH: Put	***94.69***	2. IH: Outright	62.68	2. DM: Collar-B&H	***4.67***	2. IH: Outright	15.50
3. SRI: Collar-B&H	92.03	3. IH: Yield Enhanc.	63.62	3. AP: Collar-CM	4.68	3. IH: Yield Enhanc.	15.02

Omega				**Downside Deviation (in %)**			
Best Value		**Worst Value**		**Best Value**		**Worst Value**	
1. CH: Collar	***796.23***	1. UK: Put	1.99	1. CH: Collar	***0.17***	1. IH: Bond-Call Option	7.10
2. CH: Put	***448.52***	2. UK: Outright	3.29	2. CH: Put	***0.23***	2. IH: Outright	6.70
3. AP: Collar-B&H	200.29	3. IH: Bond-Call Option	3.72	3. AP: Collar-B&H	0.39	3. IH: Put	6.40

Sortino Ratio				Upside Potential Ratio			
Best Value		Worst Value		Best Value		Worst Value	
1. CH: Collar	***58.17***	1. UK: Put	<u>0.55</u>	1. CH: Collar	***58.24***	1. UK: Put	<u>1.10</u>
2. CH: Put	***41.13***	2. UK: Outright	<u>1.03</u>	2. CH: Put	***41.22***	2. UK: Outright	<u>1.48</u>
3. AP: Collar-B&H	23.45	3. IH: Bond-Call Option	<u>1.18</u>	3. AP: Collar-B&H	23.56	3. IH: Bond-Call Option	<u>1.62</u>

Source: Own representation. Abbreviations used: 'B&H'=Buy-and-Hold, 'CM'=Constant Mix, 'Yield Enhanc.'=Yield Enhancement, 'SP'=Standard Portfolio, 'SRI'-SRI Portfolio, 'AP'=Alternative Portfolio, 'UK'=UK Model, 'DM'=Dutch Model, 'IH'=Inflation Hedge Model, 'CH': Credit Risk Hedging Model. All alternative models (UK, DM, IH, CH) are based on SRI-screening methods for equities, corporate bonds as well as government bonds. The underlying investment strategies for all alternative models of section 5.5 follow a Buy-and-Hold approach. Bold and in italic highlighted numbers denote alternative strategies that have outperformed those investment methods from section 5.4 for the standard models. Underlined numbers highlighting strategies belonging to alternative models from section 5.5 that have yielded worse results than those from section 5.4.

As the colour coding in table 53 already indicates, including the performance results from the alternative models of section 5.5 changes considerably the overall picture of best/worst performing investment strategies. Our main conclusions across all strategies are hereby:

1. SRI strategies[863] consistently perform better than portfolios with conventional assets. This applies to both outright as well as all derivative overlays contemplated in section 5.4. Moreover, the Buy-and-Hold approach generates better results than the Constant-Mix methodology.
2. Adding alternative investments (hedge funds, commodities) to the asset mix enhances the risk-return profile of the overall portfolio. The Alternative Portfolio in section 5.4, which implemented SRI screening methods as well as allocated 10% of the total funds into alternative investments, outperformed both the Standard Portfolio as well as the SRI fund.
3. For the alternative models in chapter 5.5, we used as benchmark portfolio SRI-screened assets for the equities, corporate and government bond segments of the portfolio given their superior returns established previously. As underlying investment technique, we used across all alternative models in 5.5 the Buy-and-Hold methodology.
4. Due to the weak total return of equity investments during the 10-years of time series data we have used as input, portfolios with a high allocation into equities underperform versus funds that have an overweight in fixed-

[863] For all strategies simulated, SRI followed for equities and corporate bonds a BiC approach combined with negative screening, whereas for government bonds a positive screening method was implemented.

income securities. This explains also why the UK and the Dutch models rather disappoint in our empirical study and why the Inflation Hedge model does not generate the results we hoped. Nonetheless, returns from the Inflation Hedge model at least partially offer inflation hedge. In addition, its performance is also an indication that portfolios invested excessively in alternative investments tend not to outperform.

5. The results from the alternative models in 5.5 provide sufficient empirical evidence for Pension Insurance Funds to consider derivative overlay structures also on the corporate bond segment. Such overlays enable the portfolio manager to better risk-manage his credit risk exposure. Our results indicate that from a downside risk perspective, the Credit Risk Hedging model achieves the best results of all investment strategies considered.
6. Within the Credit Risk Hedging model, the hedging overlays (put, collar) offer superior downside risk profiles. In terms of absolute minima, downside risk measures, volatility of portfolio returns as well as upside potential, both the put and the collar overlay yield satisfactory results. Also average portfolio values after our 3-year observation period are respectable. The opportunity cost of these strategies is reflected in the lower absolute maximum values these strategies achieve.

5.5.6 Conclusions

The results obtained in chapter 5.5 have offered us valuable information in terms of potential alternative strategic asset allocation models for Pension insurance Funds. Ignoring prevailing regulatory constraints imposed by the BaFin for the portfolio management has enabled us to expand considerably our investment horizon:

1. The more equity-focused portfolios of section 5.5.2 allowed us to replicate portfolio allocations followed by pension funds in the UK and the Netherlands, two of the largest and most significant markets in Europe for capital-funded pension investing. These two models are essential, as German Pension Insurance Funds that at current maintain on average a 85% of their asset base in fixed-income securities may consider replicat-

ing asset allocations that leading pension funds in other countries are pursuing.

2. The Inflation Hedge model is an attempt to create a portfolio mix suitable for providing an inflation (proxy) hedge for portfolio managers. Based on academic findings, we focused our asset mix on real estate assets and commodity investments. The motivation of presenting the Inflation Hedge model is to allow Pension Insurance Funds to react to inflationary pressures should the on-going loose monetary policy of the ECB persist, which could potentially lead to price level increases in the future.
3. The simulation of the Credit Risk Hedging model provides crucial observations, as it enables pension fund managers to calibrate the risk-management of the overall portfolio to also consider the negative effects credit or default on corporate bonds might cause to portfolio performance. In particular since the outbreak of the credit crisis, the overall pool of highly rated corporate bonds has shrunk considerably, therefore reducing the investable universe for pension funds.

Our results show that both the Dutch and the UK pension fund model change significantly the risk-return profile of portfolio value distributions (versus the standard models in section 5.4), especially in terms of downside risk management. While this is justifiable and appropriate for pension fund systems that do not offer their beneficiaries capital guarantee on their contributions, such asset allocations pose a challenge for defined-contributions with capital guarantee pension models.

The Inflation Hedge model, on the other hand, provides at least a partial inflation hedge, even though it would underperform in times of high inflation. This is a fundamental conclusion for pension funds in general and divisive in the prevailing fragile and (almost) unique macroeconomic situation: while under traditional monetary theory an inflationary environment should lead to an increase of interest rates, the current interest rate policy of the ECB amid the European sovereign debt crisis is primarily focused on rescuing the structural framework of the monetary union rather than pursuing classical monetary policy. This is a highly controversial situation for long-term investors like Pension Insurance Funds, as the ECB's efforts to rescue the monetary union may be financed at the cost of investors that suffer a high inflation environment and simultaneously low interest rates. In our view, therefore, Pension Insurance Funds should seriously revise their excessive allocations into fixed-income securities, as they could find themselves in the near future in a difficult position of facing low-yielding bond assets, while inflation is corroding their returns in real money terms. Given the strict investment framework Pension Insurance Funds are subject to, it appears essential to us that a reconsideration of this topic needs to occur by the German regulator. A more flexible investment opportunity set should be implemented to allow pension fund managers to re-allocate their assets in case the interest rate environment should turn hostile.

The Credit Risk Hedging model has provided valuable answers to Pension Insurance Fund managers that are exposed to corporate bonds. Our empirical results suggest that a tailor-made risk-management approach, which allows using derivative overlay structures for both the equity and corporate bond segments of the portfolio, can lead to performance results that in the current regulatory investment framework generate superior portfolio risk-return distributions. Moreover, this model has relied on asset allocations that are feasible under current regulation for Pension Insurance Funds and could therefore be implemented immediately by practitioners. Nonetheless, we acknowledge that the credit risk tools used in our simulation study do not cover all instruments commonly applied by practitioners. Credit-default swaps, in particular, have become very popular risk management tools that could be used instead of the instruments we have considered in our analysis.

5.6 Summary

Chapter 5 summarises the empirical results we require to provide appropriate answers to our research proposals. The results from the VEC model estimation, combined with the bootstrap simulation and the various investment strategies we have run, give a robust methodological framework to compare portfolio performances and assess the suitability of certain asset classes and fund strategies for long-term pension investors.

The starting point of our study is the benchmark portfolio (Standard Portfolio) that represents adequately the current (average) asset allocation of German

Pension Insurance Funds. The individual asset classes within this fund have been replicated with large and representative benchmark indices. As alternative portfolios, we have created the SRI as well as the Alternative Portfolio. The former reproduces the same asset allocation than the Standard Portfolio, with the main difference that equities as well as all bond investments are generated in SRI-structured manner following the SRI methods described in chapter 3.2.3, in particular BiC with negative screening for equities and corporate bonds. The Alternative fund, on the other hand, invests 10% of its allocation into alternative investments.[864] An important aspect of both the SRI and Alternative portfolios is that the selected SRI indices use as benchmark indices the conventional indices from the Standard Portfolio, so that a high degree of similarity in terms of the number of underlying individual assets, sector and country allocation is guaranteed (following a 'matching principle').

We recognise at this point the limitation imposed on our analysis by the underlying screening methodology of the SRI indices, as they apply the BiC with negative screening filter.[865] As we discussed in section 3.2.5, existing research studies have analysed the performance of different SRI indices against traditional asset classes. While the overall conclusion is that SRI-screened assets perform at least as well as conventional assets do, there exist performance differences amongst the numerous SRI methods we have considered in section 3.2.3. One of the main reasons for using BiC with negative screening on corporate securities is also the fact that it represents the most popular strategy implemented by practitioners (see also figure 29 in section 3.2.3). Furthermore, the strategy allows pension fund managers to select the best performing companies within an industry (BiC), while the negative screening overlay simultaneously pre-empts activism by shareholders or external pressure groups. Also, the exclusion criteria considered in the negative screening method (ex-AGTAFA) represent business practises and industry sectors that are commonly rejected or disapproved by society.

Using the bootstrap simulation technique to generate thousands of potential future return paths enables us to get empirical evidence on the relative ad-

[864] This allocation leads to an overall reduction in the bond investments by 10 points.
[865] For equities and corporate bonds. Government bonds follow a positive screening approach.

vantage and suitability of certain investment strategies over others. Downside risk measures, in particular, are excellent indicators and assessors of downside risk. The respective investment strategies chosen allow portfolio managers to pursue different investing objectives: outright investing, hedging, yield enhancement or bond-call option approaches. Stress-testing our portfolios under different investment strategies permits us to recommend the most appropriate strategies for Pension Insurance Funds.

The results of our analysis provide the empirical verification that modifying the asset allocation in general and the screening methodology for the underlying assets in particular can offer substantial benefits to achievable portfolio returns. Moreover, allowing equities as well as all bond investments to be invested via SRI-screening methods yields consistently better average returns as well as a lower downside risk profile than investments in conventional assets, as represented in our analysis by the Standard Portfolio. Moreover, adding alternative investments (in our case for the Alternative Portfolio) also shifts the computed risk-return characteristics of the portfolio to the benefit of the Pension Insurance Fund. In general, we have observed that Buy-and-Hold investment methods are superior to Constant-Mix approaches across portfolios and strategies.

Additionally, the derivative overlay structures allowed under BaFin's circular R3/2000[866] enable portfolio managers to fine-tune the portfolio to their investment preferences. Assuming a risk-averse investor that is concerned primarily in conserving his capital over time while maintaining some upside potential, hedging the equity allocation within his fund with a collar structure generates the best downside-risk protected portfolio values. The collar structure actually obtains consistently the best downside-risk results of all strategies in all our portfolios. Consequently, our empirical evidence suggests the inclusion of these derivative overlays in the traditional portfolio management of German Pension Insurance Funds. Another important conclusion from our study is that outright strategies tend to underperform the vast majority of methods that consider also derivative overlays, particularly with respect to downside-risk. Our data therefore indicates that fund managers of Pension Insurance Funds may use the

[866] See Bafin (2000).

possibilities the BaFin permits in terms of derivatives. For high-yield seeking investment strategies, the Bond-Call Option methodology seems appropriate. While this technique may add return volatility to the overall fund performance, the data from our simulation shows that it generates the highest average portfolio values as well as yields the highest maxima.

Our assessment of the relative advantage of portfolios applying current asset allocation of German Pension Insurance Funds versus the so-called Dutch- and UK-models provide robust empirical evidence that under current regulation, the strategic asset allocation followed so far in practise is adequate. Based on our time series data, it appears challenging that portfolios under the Dutch or UK-model can achieve a capital guarantee for the invested pension contributions.[867] We understand that the allocation practise by Dutch and UK pension funds is not intended to offer such guarantees but rather to enable future pension beneficiaries to benefit from capital appreciation in the long-term for generally higher-yielding (and riskier) assets than those currently in use by German Pension Insurance Funds.

Any modern portfolio management should consider inflation implications, in particular for fund managers of pension schemes, given their long-term investment horizon. Inflation contemplations for the risk-management of Pension Insurance Fund are even more crucial due to the high exposure into fixed-income securities. As we discussed beforehand, at current, pension funds face a challenging investment environment as the ECB may be inclined to deviate from a traditional monetary policy to rescue the framework of the monetary union to the extend that a low interest rate environment may be artificially maintained even in a high inflation period. Our Inflation Hedge model is an attempt to engineer an asset structure that, based on academic evidence, should provide an adequate inflation hedge. Real estate investments and commodity assets, in particular, are regularly advocated by academics as suitable inflation hedges. While our results support at least partially the inflation hedging assumption, the Inflation Hedge model would underperform in very high inflation circumstances. Beyond the inflation hedging suitability, we have provided empirical evidence that

[867] We assume again defined-contributions with capital guarantee as a reference.

despite the beneficial characteristics of alternative investments, an excessive allocation into this asset class will not lead automatically to an outperformance.

We have also considered the impact on performance a proper credit risk management would have for Pension Insurance Funds. With an average allocation of 40% (see also section 2.5.2 for a detailed historical breakdown) into corporate bonds, it is fundamental for a portfolio manager to manage the inherent credit or default risk these securities have. For this model scenario, we have used as benchmark portfolio the Alternative Portfolio of section 5.4, as it yielded consistently higher results than those obtained by the Standard and SRI portfolios. Using the Black-Scholes pricing method for the equity derivatives instruments and the Black-76 for the various bond option structures considered, we obtain overall superior performance results in terms of downside risk measures and portfolio return volatility. For a risk-averse fund manager of a Pension Insurance Fund, the Credit Risk Hedging, in particular the put and the collar structures, offer the best downside risk of all alternatives simulated in our empirical study.

A key takeaway from our simulation study across all strategies and portfolios is that alternative models that go beyond the current regulatory framework German Pension Insurance Funds are currently operating in have not yielded better results than portfolio strategies that have considered the status quo in their asset allocation. Both high equity funds (UK and Dutch model) as well as the Inflation Hedge model, which has an overall 75% of the assets invested in real estate and alternative investments, could not outperform the Credit Risk Hedging portfolio that was based on the specifications of the Alternative Portfolio from section 5.4. This conclusion is highly relevant for any occupational pension scheme in Germany that is based on the capital-funded principle and offers defined contributions with capital guarantee benefit structures.

Overall, the disappointing performance of equity assets during our 10-year observation period from Dec-2001 to Nov-2011 has undoubtedly influenced our conclusions and recommendations, as portfolios with high equity allocations have generally underperformed fixed-income focused funds. A reversal of this performance relationship amongst the asset classes considered due to external major shocks or regulatory intervention could undoubtedly lead to different empirical results and therefore conclusions. Furthermore, replicating real estate investments via equity investments in real estate companies may most probably not yield the same risk-return profile than investing directly into real estate objects. We admit that this aspect is a limitation to the validity of our conclusions with respect to real estate investments by pension funds. This is an area where we see considerable potential for future research studies, in particular in combination with sustainability considerations.

6. Conclusion, Criticism and Outlook

6.1 Conclusion

6.1.1 General Observations

Our research study has provided substantiated arguments and empirical evidence that SRIs are suitable for the strategic asset management of German Pension Insurance Funds. SRI assets fit into the prevailing regulatory framework in Germany and also obtain superior performance results than conventional investments portfolios do. An important contribution in this context has been the development of SRI screening methods for fixed-income securities and their inclusion in an empirical analysis, given their overall relevance in the average portfolio allocation. SRI structured portfolios not only yield better average portfolio results than the respective Standard Portfolio, but achieve also superior downside risk measures. Our research results support hereby similar outcomes of recent research studies that compared the performance of conventional assets to SRI-screened investment strategies.[868]

Furthermore, the inclusion of alternative assets (hedge funds, commodities) has led to a positive effect to the overall performance of the respective funds. The Alternative Portfolio, which consists of SRI-screened assets as well as alternative investments, generates the highest performance of all standard portfolios analysed in our study. The product range available for alternative investments enable portfolio managers to include them via fund-of-fund structures or ETFs, therefore minimising an extensive investment process that would be required if a pension fund would decide to invest directly into this asset class. The empirical results of our dissertation suggest the use of derivative overlay structures as part of the strategic portfolio management of a Pension Insurance Fund. The different strategies allowed by the German regulator offer pension fund managers a better risk management for their investment portfolios, independently of the investment strategy pursued. For investors with a focus on downside risk mitigation, collar structures, in particular, obtain the best results.

[868] See also our summary of relevant research studies on this topic in section 3.2.5.

The simulation of alternative portfolio models with a high allocation into equity investments, on the other hand, has yielded mixed results. The returns obtained by the UK and Dutch models, respectively, appear rather surprising given the higher risk equity assets imply in comparison to highly rated fixed-income securities. In the Markowitz mean-variance context, higher incurred risks would have to be compensated by higher average performance returns. This is not the case in our research study. The fact that our simulation actually leads to weaker average values for equity-dominated portfolios has a simple yet plausible explanation: as we highlighted in section 5.2.2, D, equities have underperformed both corporate bonds as well as government securities in the time period Dec-2001 to Nov-2011 in terms of total return[869] of the underlying assets, despite recording higher realised volatilities.[870] This *prima facie* contradictory and irrational result may be explained by the safety-focused investment behaviour large institutional investors show in uncertain times. In search of safe havens, they shift their allocation to a large extend into highly-rated bond securities at the expense of equities. The effects of the 2007/2008 credit crisis, combined with the extraordinary events in connection with the European sovereign debt crisis since autumn 2009[871] may explain the relative performance of equities versus fixed-income securities.

The disillusioning performance of the Inflation Hedge model, on the other hand, is partially a result of the high exposure of the fund (25% of AuM) to the particular real estate index we have chosen. The underlying investments are essentially equity stakes in the respective real estate companies and therefore not proper investments in real estate objects. While many investors may replicate physical real estate investments via acquiring the respective shares in the open market, more risk-averse investors may rather target commercial or residential buildings directly. The impact of a transition into physical real estate investments remains unanswered in our research study due to the unavailability of long-term time series data on our side.[872] Nonetheless, the Inflation Hedge

[869] Price performance plus dividend payments.

[870] The equity index of the Standard Portfolio, for example, performs over the time period Dec-2001 to Nov-2011 a monthly return of 0.06% with a respective standard deviation of 4.95%, whereas the corporate bond index yields 0.35%, with a 1.15% standard deviation.

[871] See Featherstone (2011), p. 194.

[872] As we mentioned beforehand, data provider IPD calculates index prices that have physical real estate objects as underlying. See IPD (2012).

model provides valuable answers to the suitability of real estate assets and commodity investments as an inflation proxy hedge. While there is plenty of research evidence supporting the adequacy of these assets in high inflation time periods, our results would not hold in very high inflationary environments. In addition, we obtained inside into the usefulness of managing portfolios with a high allocation into alternative investments. Despite the undisputed advantages of this asset class, our results suggest that they are only suitable for Pension Insurance Funds up to a certain proportion of the asset allocation.

The most convincing performance figures we have obtained belong to the Credit Risk Hedging model, which is based on the Alternative Portfolio of section 5.4 but applies fixed-income derivatives as risk-management tool on the corporate bond allocation. It therefore combines the performance advantages of a SRI-screened underlying portfolio with the benefits derivative overlay structures can offer to handle equity risk as well as corporate default exposure. Using the possibilities circular letter R3/2000 offers in terms of derivative instruments, we have been able to engineer a portfolio that offers satisfactory tail-risk measures while also generating adequate average portfolio values.

The role of the German regulator and the strict regulatory framework imposed on the investment management of Pension Insurance Funds remain an outstanding issue for further discussion. Assuming defined contributions with capital guarantee as the most recent benefit format introduced by the German legislator in 2002, current investment practise by Pension Insurance Funds seems to be the most suitable strategy. So far the results of our simulation study indicate that the performance achieved is sufficient to cover the maximum guaranteed return of currently 1.75% p.a. and to offer pension beneficiaries capital guarantee at nominal terms on their pension contributions. Moreover, even for a moderate inflation environment, the results of the study would be appropriate. A point of debate is hereby doubtlessly the uncommon performance of equity assets during our 10-year observation period discussed beforehand. This has exerted influence on the results of the empirical analysis and on the conclusions of our dissertation with regard to potential modifications of the prevailing regulatory environment for German Pension Insurance Funds in Germany. A risk-return reversal of equity investments versus fixed-income securities could be triggered by significant interventions in financial markets by central bank authorities or Governments in the upcoming years, combined with major disruptions in the international bond markets.

6.1.2 Specific Research Questions

In terms of the specific research questions we defined in our introduction in section 1.3, we have formulated the answers providing evidence both from a strategic asset management perspective as well as from an empirical angle.

A. Should German Pension Insurance Funds invest in Social Responsible Investments (SRIs) as part of their strategic asset management?

A.1 Strategic Considerations

We have discussed in detail the suitability of SRIs for German Pension Insurance Funds from a strategic point of view. While their current weight within the asset mix of occupational pension schemes remains low, there are in general no apparent reasons why pension funds should not increase their involvement in this asset class in the future.

First, Pension Insurance Funds can implement all three most commonly applied SRI screening methods (best-in-class, negative screening and positive screening) to both their corporate bond allocation and their equity funds. The inclusion of corporate fixed-income securities is essential as they represent to date approximately 40% of the overall average portfolio allocation. Second, best-in-class (BiC) methods combined with negative screening exclusion criteria appear as the most suited investment approach for corporate securities (equities, corporate bonds) in this context and are also the most commonly used technique by institutional investors in Europe. Additionally, they enable portfolio managers to select assets that outperform based on a pre-defined set of KPIs (BiC screening method), while the negative screening filter eliminates companies or governments that pursue business activities commonly perceived by society as repulsive and inopportune. Furthermore, exclusion criteria can also act as a shield against criticism or activism activities by external stakeholders for investing in undesired industries. BiC combined with negative screening is also the SRI screening method we have applied in our empirical study for both the equity allocation and the corporate bond assets.[873] Apart from screening methods for equities and corporate bonds, portfolio managers can use specific SRI techniques to invest into government bonds, as we discussed in section 3.2.4, B1 in more detail.[874] Applying SRI screening methods to corporate and government bonds as well as equities covers already around 90% of the total average asset allocation of German Pension Insurance Funds. Our methodology is therefore the first empirical research study that includes SRIs across all three major asset classes.

In addition to presenting a methodology on how SRI screening methods can be implemented across various asset classes, we have discussed a number of drivers that may cause Pension Insurance Funds to increase their involvement in SRIs in the future:

1. An intrinsic motivation to pursue sustainable investments based on ethical beliefs or mission-related motivations by management or major shareholders.
2. Corporate governance aspects, as high governance standards can be a competitive advantage and act as a shield against external criticism.
3. Avoidance of reputational risks and external stakeholder pressure, as Germany's corporations are increasingly getting under pressure to include sustainability considerations in the strategic investment management of their occupational pension schemes.
4. The lawful interpretation of fiduciary duty suggests pension fund managers in Germany might be obliged to consider SRIs as part of their regular portfolio management.
5. The reporting requirements of the AltZertG and the VAG acts force pension managers to disclose their SRI involvement. While this does not represent a requirement to invest in SRIs per se, it is an incentive to do so.
6. Robust research evidence in numerous academic papers claiming that SRI assets perform as well as conventional assets do. More recent empirical analysis show even consistent outperformance of SRI-screened

[873] The equity as well as corporate bond indices we have used all apply BiC with negative screening ex-AGTAFA (ex alcohol, gambling, tobacco, armaments, firearms and adult entertainment).

[874] For government bonds from EMU countries, our positive screening method appears to be the most suitable technique.

investments. These studies cover equities, corporate bonds as well as government securities.

7. The SRI-sector has benefitted in the past years from a significant product innovation and the appearance of a related services industry (i.e. consulting services, rating companies), so that SRI as an investment approach is becoming easier implementable across asset classes and investment strategies for Pension Insurance Funds.
8. SRI investing is already best practise in leading European capital-funded pension systems, e.g. in the UK and the Netherlands. Pension funds in those countries have large proportions of their asset base already invested in SRIs. Besides, growth rates for SRI assets in Europe, especially for the mutual fund industry, indicate that the SRI method will gain more market share in the future. In this context, growth rates for the German sustainable mutual fund industry also look promising. An important aspect of the SRI mutual fund industry in Europe in general and in Germany in particular is its already considerable involvement in fixed-income securities.

A.2 Empirical Evidence

The empirical analysis based on the VEC model and the bootstrap simulation technique is targeted towards providing the quantitative verification of the suitability of SRI assets for the asset management of Pension Insurance Funds. Our empirical results yield hereby consistent evidence that SRI portfolios, as defined in our research study, perform at least as well as Standard Portfolios do. In terms of average values after the 3-year forecasting period, absolute minimum values as well as downside risk measures, the SRI portfolios obtain in general better results than Standard Portfolios. Moreover, for both portfolios, the underlying Buy-and-Hold outright strategies achieve more favourable return distributions than Constant-Mix methods.

Average values for both outright strategies considered in the analysis (Buy-and-Hold, Constant-Mix) reach for the SRI Portfolios 109.75 and 108.82 after 3 years, respectively, versus 108.07 and 107.34 for the Standard Portfolio. The absolute minimum values for the SRI Portfolio are 90.20 and 89.18, in comparison to the 87.89 and 85.82 obtained for the Standard Portfolio. With respect to the standard deviation of portfolio returns, the SRI funds and the Standard Portfolios yield similar results (5.47% and 5.42% against 5.46% and 5.24%). Within downside risk measures, SRI Portfolios have lower downside deviation (0.55% and 0.71%, correspondingly, versus 0.82% and 1.08%) and more risk-averse downside statistics (e.g. Omega of 110.37 and 66.69 against 44.84 and 27.70). In connection with the upside potential of the portfolios, the SRI funds also outperform (Upside Potential Ratio of 16.69 and 11.83 in comparison to 9.43 and 6.68).

An essential limitation to our results is the SRI screening method we have applied in our simulation study. Best-in-class combined with negative screening is the methodology underlying equity assets and corporate bonds for our respective SRI portfolios. For government bonds, on the other hand, the screening filter is based on the fulfilment by a government of a set of internationally recognized standards in terms of governance practises, human rights treaties, labour rights conventions or environmental policies.[875] As discussed in sections 3.2.3, D, a combined strategy of BiC plus negative screening has many benefits for the strategic asset management of pension funds and is also very common in practise. Our index selection attempts to replicate this combined SRI screening methodology for corporate securities (equities, corporate bonds).

The output of SRI screening filters is obviously dependent on the individual criteria determined for the asset selection process. Ultimately, the respective index providers define the underlying SRI methodology. There are differing methodologies and approaches for the same underlying sustainability concept.[876] While we believe that our indices chosen for equities and corporate bonds represent a commonly accepted understanding of BiC with negative screening, other large index providers like FTSE or Dow Jones have slightly different methodologies for the same underlying SRI strategy.

---

875 See section 3.2.4 for more details.

876 See appendix B with the precise definitions of the underlying SRI screening filters for each index used in our simulation study.

B. Are alternative investments a suitable asset class for German Pension Insurance Funds?

B.1 Strategic Considerations

Our conclusions with respect to the suitability of alternative investments as part of the strategic asset management of Pension Insurance Funds are based entirely on economic reasons. Apart from the maximum allocation limits the German regulator has imposed on alternative investments, we do not see any other legal or regulatory reasons why pension fund managers shall be motivated to include alternative assets to their traditional allocation mix. Nonetheless, the high involvement of European pension funds in general, with almost €300bln AuM in the alternative investment space, is a reflection on the importance this asset class is already playing for the pension fund system. The market share in alternative investments by pension funds is also an indication of the potential fit of these assets for Pension Insurance Funds in Germany.

In terms of the two alternative asset categories we have considered in our analysis, hedge funds and commodity assets, there are various economic reasons to include them in the investment portfolio mix. Research studies for hedge fund strategies indicate that large hedge fund firms with a long track record and a high ownership by the fund managers tend to generate alpha returns due to managerial skills. Moreover, hedge funds usually have low correlations to conventional asset classes, what can lead to an overall portfolio risk reduction. The correlation effect is even more pronounced for commodity assets, as demonstrated in numerous research papers. Furthermore, commodities are a suitable inflation hedge for traditional asset portfolios. Consequently, the risk reduction achieved by adding commodity investments into a portfolio can be meaningful. Many academic studies confirm these findings with respect to risk diversification. Overall, there are therefore sufficient and justifiable reasons to consider alternative assets from a strategic asset management standpoint for Pension Insurance Funds. Apart from purely economic benefits alternative assets have in the context of a modern portfolio allocation, they can be used by SRI minded investors to pursue SRI-related objectives. Given the negative external effects associated with alternative investments,[877] a shareholder activism approach, as discussed in section 3.2.3, E, seems a suitable methodology for SRI investors.

From a practitioner's point of view, the product range available to portfolio managers in terms of fund of fund investments for hedge fund strategies as well as the increasing supply of commodities ETFs and mutual funds enable Pension Insurance Funds to access the alternative investment space in a cost-efficient way without requiring any major in-house research capabilities. Additionally, the availability of sustainable alternative assets is growing. Due to the lack of respective historical time series data, nonetheless, we have not been able to include any sustainable alternative investments in our simulation study. As we elaborated in section 3.3.5, sustainability considerations in the alternative investment space is a highly debated and controversial topic, both in academia and amongst practitioners. While empirical evidence is available that suggests European institutional investors in general and pension funds in particular are already committing funds into SRI-structured alternative investment strategies,[878] the suitability of these categories for SRI purposes remain an area within sustainability investing for which clear rules or principles need to be defined. This is undoubtedly an area for future research.

B.2 Empirical Evidence

The Alternative Portfolio invests in our empirical analysis up to 10% of the total asset allocation into alternative investments, with an equal 50% split between hedge fund and commodity investments. The portfolio therefore applies the maximum asset allocation allowed by the German regulator. The portfolio of this third fund can then be compared to the results obtained by the Standard and SRI Portfolios, respectively. It is important to highlight that for the equity, corporate and government bond segments of the Alternative Portfolio, the same underlying sustainable indices are used than for the SRI Portfolio.

---

[877] As discussed in section 3.3.5, hedge funds are less suitable for SRI purposes given their short-term investing horizon, their perceived disruptive effect caused by short selling activeties and their prime focus on absolute financial returns only. Investments in commodities, on the other hand, are heavily criticized by NGOs given their negative impact on environmental pollution, exploitation of workers and price speculation on soft commodities, which can trigger severe shortage of stock

[878] See statistics shown in section 3.3.5.D.

In section 3.3.4 we have demonstrated with a simple sensitivity analysis in the Markowitz portfolio framework that adding commodity and hedge fund assets to corporate and government bonds leads to a beneficial shift of the efficient frontier. This portfolio exercise, which is based entirely on historical time series data only, is a good indicator of the potential effect alternative assets may have on traditional investment portfolios. The results of our stochastic simulation exercise confirm these preliminary findings. In terms of average fund value after the forecasting period, the Alternative Portfolio outperforms both the Standard as well as the SRI Portfolios. Within the two outright strategies, the Alternative Portfolio achieves 109.79 as average portfolio value for the Buy-and-Hold method and 109.28 for the Constant-Mix approach, a small outperformance versus the 109.75 and 108.82 respectively generated by the SRI Portfolio.[879] With respect to portfolio risk measures, the Alternative Portfolio demonstrates an overall more risk-conservative profile. Standard deviation of portfolio returns is with 5.28% for Buy-and-Hold the lowest level of all three portfolios, whereas the downside deviation below initial par value is at 0.51% and hence less risky than the SRI Portfolio with 0.55% (Buy-and-Hold). Also risk measures based on Lower Partial Moments are more favourable for the Alternative Portfolio: Omega values for the fund, for example, are with 131.26 (Buy-and-Hold) as well as 92.84 (Constant-Mix) less risky than for the SRI fund (110.37, 66.69).

C. Should Pension Insurance Funds consider derivative overlays as part of their strategic asset allocation?

C.1 Strategic Considerations

As we discussed in section 4.4.4, German Pension Insurance Funds can use derivative overlay structures as part of their portfolio management. This flexibility is granted by the regulator via circular R3/2000. Given the investment objectives Pension Insurance Funds have, we have considered in our analysis exclusively derivative strategies that are in-line with their predefined investment targets. Hedging strategies, both put option overlays and collars, yield enhancement methods as well as bond-call option approaches seem hereby appropriate risk management tools for Pension Insurance Funds.

---

[879] We compare here the Alternative Portfolio to the SRI Portfolio only, as the latter outperformed the Standard Portfolio, as already alluded in previous section 6.1.2, A.

The German regulator restricts the structural features of the allowed derivatives, in particular with respect to strike levels and maximum sizes. Furthermore, we have imposed additional restrictions on our empirical analysis, as we have applied these derivative overlays to the equity tranches of the overall investment portfolio only.[880] This limitation has various reasons. First, hedging large proportions of a portfolio across different asset classes is in practise challenging, as the counterparty of the trades (in general investment banks) may not be able to offer sizeable derivatives due to their own in-house risk management limitations. For equity underlyings, in particular blue chip names, on the contrary, hedging is more feasible given the high liquidity of the underlying and stock borrow availability in the open market. Therefore hedging the entire equity portfolio seems a realistic proposition to us. Besides, equity investments have historically had higher volatilities than corporate or government bonds, so that their inclusion into the investment portfolio will in general lead to an increase in portfolio risk. During our 10-year observation period, however, these higher probabilities were not compensated by higher realised returns.

While the regulator has worded derivative circular letter R3/2000 carefully to ensure derivative instruments are used with diligence and caution and not as speculative tools, the current regulatory framework allows for sufficient loopholes that could be arbitraged by risk-seeking investors. While outright positions in call options have been restricted in size,[881] collar structures have no *per se* sizing constraints. The major inherent risk of a collar instrument is its short call position at the upper strike, which can in theory lead to unlimited losses. Often, collar positions can also easily be used to enter into levered transactions,[882] increasing even further the risk-profile of the investment. Such highly engineered derivative instruments would nonetheless contradict the investment principles of the VAG. A sizing limitation by the regulator for this derivative type seems appropriate to us to avoid any arbitrage of the prevailing regulation.

---

880 Hedging considerations for the corporate bond sections have been contemplated in section 5.5.4 of our research study as an alternative investment model (Credit Risk Hedging model). See also subsection D in this chapter.

881 See details on table 14 in section 4.4.4.

882 So-called funded collars, in which investors raise financing against the protected put value of the collar. These structures can lead to a highly levered position on the initial investment as the initial equity value of the position can be eliminated completely for small share price decreases on the underlying.

C.2 Empirical Evidence

The results of our quantitative analysis provide satisfactory results for the use of derivative overlays, in particular in comparison to our two outright strategies. For all major performance and risk categories we have contemplated, portfolios with derivative overlays perform better than the corresponding outright methods, justifying thereby their use as a strategic risk management instrument for German Pension Insurance Funds.

In terms of average portfolio values, the Bond-Call Option strategy for the Buy-and-Hold approach in the SRI portfolio obtains the highest average value of all strategies (110.09). The absolute maximum value across all strategies is reached in the Alternative Portfolio using again the Bond-Call Option structure (142.91 for Buy-and-Hold), whereas the collar in the SRI portfolio creates the portfolio with the highest minimum value (92.03 for Buy-and-Hold). The lowest portfolio return volatility (4.68%) is achieved with the 100/115 collar overlay in the Alternative Portfolio scenario.

With reference to downside risk indicators, collar derivatives yield consistently the best results across all portfolios and investment strategies contemplated. The downside deviation below par is for the collar in the Alternative Portfolio with 0.39% the lowest of all values (for Buy-and-Hold strategy), in comparison to the highest measured figure of our simulation study at 1.08% for the outright approach in the Standard Portfolio (Constant-Mix). The best Omega value is hereby also achieved with the collar in the Alternative Portfolio (200.29 versus the lowest Omega of 27.70 for the Standard Portfolio in the Constant-Mix outright scenario). Finally, the value of 23.56 for the Upside Potential Ratio for the collar in the Alternative Portfolio indicates that collar derivatives also offer the highest upside potential of all strategies contemplated in our research study.

D. What alternative asset allocation models may be suitable for Pension Insurance Funds?

D.1 Strategic Considerations

Section 5.5 allowed us to simulate alternative investment scenarios that are not constrained by prevailing German regulation. The objective of these alternative models is to determine whether different asset compositions may lead to investment results that are more suitable for the asset management strategy of Pension Insurance Funds.

One group of alternative models we have considered correspond to portfolios with a high equity exposure. Here, we have simulated the so-called UK and Dutch models, as the respective pension systems are the largest for capital-funded pension plans in Europe. The UK model is thereby the most equity-dominated portfolio of all models considered in our research study, with a total of 55% of the asset allocation invested into equities. The Dutch model, on the other hand, has 30% of AuM in equity securities. Including the standard allocation of 5% for equities we have used in the first section of our empirical analysis, we obtain therefore a scaling sensitivity on equity allocations from 5%-30%-55%.

The Inflation Hedge model in section 5.5.3 pursues a different investment objective: rather than replicating an existing pension fund model, it attempts to allow Pension Insurance Funds to better risk-manage potential high inflationary environments. Based on academic research evidence, we have chosen asset classes that perform well in periods of high inflation. For real estate assets and commodity investments, in particular, empirical evidence indicates adequate inflation hedging qualities. For Pension Insurance Funds that invest to date up to 85% of their asset base in fixed-income securities, a proper inflation risk management is essential. In our view, the effort by the ECB as well as European governments to save the European Monetary Union at any cost may lead to a situation in financial markets in which artificially low interest rates exist alongside inflationary pressure. For long-term investors with a focus in bond securities, this 'yield-trap' could severely deteriorate performance returns in real money terms. Moreover, the Inflation Hedge model also allows us simultaneously to assess the suitability of portfolios with a high exposure to alternative investments.

Furthermore, we have expanded the usage of derivative overlay structures to enable portfolio managers to better manage credit risk on their corporate bond portfolios. The Credit Risk Hedging model provides interesting and far-reaching results in terms of tail-risk management for German Pension Insurance Funds.

As our data indicates, the Credit Risk Hedging portfolio generates the best downside risk measures of all portfolios contemplated.

D.2 Empirical Evidence

The results from the simulation study for the two equity models are rather disappointing: while the riskiness of both equity models is, as anticipated, higher versus the Alternative Portfolio (our reference model for comparison purposes) due to the higher equity exposure, the average portfolio values do not compensate investors for the higher risks incurred.

For the outright strategy of the UK model, the average value is 106.55 after year 3, versus 109.79 for our Alternative Portfolio, whereas the range of extreme values (absolute maximum / minimum) expands from 141.14-89.77 for the reference model to 181.88-70.81 for the UK portfolio.[883] The increased riskiness of the investment strategy is also reflected in the deterioration of the downside risk measures: with a lower Omega value of 3.29 (vs. 131.26 for the reference model), higher downside deviation of 5.47% (vs. 0.51%) and a considerably lower Upside Potential Ratio of 1.48 (vs. 18.13), the results of the UK study consistently underperform the Alternative Portfolio. Contrasting the results of the respective derivative overlay structures does not change the overall conclusion: a higher equity exposure of up to 55%, as replicated in the UK model, and a concurrent increase of the overall riskiness of the portfolio in terms of portfolio volatility is not compensated by higher average returns. The derivative overlays, however, manage to improve considerably the overall risk-return profile of the UK model in contrast to the corresponding outright strategy, highlighting thereby the general suitability of derivatives as risk management instruments. Some selected downside risk measures illustrate the overall improvement: the collar structure has a minimum value of 89.28, and therefore 18.47 points higher than the outright strategy and considerably better downside risk measures (e.g. Omega increases by 8.14 points from 3.29 to 11.43). The highest average portfolio value is generated with the Yield Enhancement method, with an average portfolio value of 109.09 versus 106.55 for the outright approach.

---

[883] For all portfolios, we have contemplated only Buy-and-Hold strategies for this section, as they have been consistently superior to Constant-Mix methods.

The performance of the Dutch model scenario appears more promising. With an average value of 109.30 for the outright investing approach and a value range of 157.36-82.41, the portfolio results obtain better downside risk figures than the UK model (e.g. Omega of 15.54 for the Dutch model versus 3.29 for the UK outright model). More importantly, the Upside Potential Ratio of 4.59 (vs. 1.48 for the UK portfolio) indicates a better investor upside reward for incurring downside risk below the MAR. In contrast to the Alternative Portfolio, nonetheless, the Dutch model clearly underperforms. For the outright strategy, the Dutch model has a lower average value (109.30 vs. 109.79), a higher volatility of portfolio returns (8.22% vs. 5.28%) and worse downside risk measures (Omega of 15.54 vs. 131.26). The inclusion of derivative overlays does not lead to better portfolio results in comparison to the Alternative Portfolio. Using as reference the collar hedging structure for both portfolios as the most successful approach in terms of downside risk mitigation and upside potential, the Dutch portfolio yields an Omega of 108.99 (vs. 200.29), an Upside Potential Ratio of 16.42 (vs. 23.56) and a downside deviation of 0.50% against the 0.39% for the Alternative Portfolio. With respect to return volatility, however the Dutch portfolio slightly outperforms the reference fund (4.67% vs. 4.82%).

With regards to our proposed inflation risk approach, the Inflation Hedge model provides robust results for a moderate inflation environment, based on the average inflation in the European Monetary Union of the last 10 years. With a range of average values of 109.25-110.36, it yields very comparable results to the Alternative Portfolio in section 5.4, with a value range of 109.45-110.01 (Buy-and-Hold). However, comparing downside risk measures, the Alternative Portfolio clearly outperforms (Omega range across Buy-and-Hold strategies of 131.26-200.29 versus 3.72-4.38, respectively). Also when we stress-test the model against high inflationary environments, the results are rather disappointing: in both the 4.01% as well as 5.42% annual inflation scenarios contemplated, Sortino Ratios turn negative and Upside Potential Ratios drop to a range of 0.28-0.33 and 0.14-0.17 from 1.62-1.81 for the base case inflation scenario. We believe that a portfolio invested in physical real estate assets rather than a real estate equity index, as we have used, may lead to better inflation hedge characteristics. After all, real estate has a 25% weight in the Inflation Hedge model.

Future research study may be able to provide better answers to the inflation model than we have obtained so far.

The empirical results for the Credit Risk Hedging model specifications, on the contrary, are promising: it offers the best downside risk measures of all investment strategies contemplated across all portfolios considered in our research study. As table 53 in section 5.5.5 highlights, the Credit Risk Hedging model yields the highest absolute minimum value recorded (95.41 for the collar versus 92.03 for the collar in the SRI Portfolio, the best value recorded for section 5.4),[884] the lowest return volatility (4.57% versus 4.68% for the collar in the Alternative Portfolio in section 5.4), the highest Omega (796.23 versus 200.29), the lowest downside deviation (0.17% against 0.39%), the highest Sortino Ratio (58.17 versus 23.45) and the most attractive upside potential (Upside Potential Ratio of 58.24 versus 23.56). The empirical evidence supports therefore our suggestion to apply fixed-income derivatives to the credit portfolio to optimise the fund's downside risk management. The improved downside risk profile of the value distribution of the portfolio is thereby not negatively impacted by a lower average return, as the 110.52 for the collar are the third highest value recorded in our entire empirical study.

In conclusion, a side-by-side analysis of all alternative models suggests considering for German Pension Insurance Funds the Inflation Hedge model as a partial proxy hedge against inflation and the Credit Risk Hedging portfolio for downside risk protection. An important and necessary observation at this point is that the Credit Risk Hedging portfolio is based on the Alternative Portfolio of section 5.4, with the main difference that the corporate bond segments are risk-managed with a set of fixed-income derivatives. Nonetheless, the underlying equity, corporate and government bond assets have been chosen using SRI screening methodologies, therefore highlighting again the superior performance sustainable investments have been able to generate throughout our research study.

---

[884] The best-performing results for section 5.4 are summarized in section 5.4.7, table 45.

6.2 Criticism

While we restricted the scope of our research study in section 1.5.2 'Delimitations' and defined a number of limitations for the empirical analysis in chapter 5.4.1, there are nonetheless a number of outstanding aspects that either denote additional limitations or weaknesses of our analysis.

In general, the 10-year monthly time-series data we have used as input data for our VEC model can be criticised for being too short for long-term cointegration analysis. While there are numerous research studies based on VECM regressions that have a 10-year or shorter observation period, for some of the indices we have used, no data is available for longer historical time periods. Our chosen time frame has been therefore primarily conditioned by the availability of time series data.

As already alluded to, the performances of equity assets for both the Standard Portfolio as well as all SRI-related funds have been unusual over our 10-year observation period. Despite higher return volatilities, equity assets have yielded lower average returns in comparison to fixed-income securities (both corporate and government bonds). As a consequence, the alternative scenarios with higher equity allocations obtain weaker results in the simulation study versus the more risk-averse portfolios of our conventional funds. While a 10-year historical data range appears sufficiently long to us, in the future the performance of equity assets could reverse back to reflect the higher riskiness of the asset class versus low-risk bond investments. Such a reversal should then lead to higher expected return distributions for equities.

In terms of SRI screening methods for corporate securities (equities, corporate bonds), we have focused our study on the combined approach of BiC with negative screening. In our view, this method is justified given that it is the most popular strategy by institutional investors in practise. Moreover, the target assets included in the portfolio are selected based on a set of quantifiable performance indicators for the BiC method (KPIs), whereas the exclusions imposed by the negative screening filters eliminate companies involved in commonly unacceptable business sectors or activities. But we are aware that a SRI-screened portfolio could also have been selected using alternative techniques, as we discussed in 3.2.3. Applying for government bonds from the EMU a positive screening selection filter seems to us the most appropriate approach, as a BiC combined with negative screening method would not be applicable for European government securities. For a global government bond fund, a negative screening filter may also be recommendable, particularly in combination with other SRI screening techniques. Also, we have relied on time series data of a specific group of data providers, mainly Stoxx and ECPI for the sustainability indices that use their own in-house screening methodologies. Even though data providers may apply similar SRI strategies, the underlying selection criteria may differ from one provider to another.

Another valid criticism could be related to the equity profile of the real estate index we have used for the simulation study. In reality, some pension funds may prefer to invest in real estate developments directly rather than acquiring the equity portion of a real estate company. The imposition on the real estate allocation in our analysis is caused by the unavailability on our side of time series data for a pan-European real estate index that reflects the price evolution of physical real estate objects. We are aware though that data may be available for commercial use that replicates the price performance of real estate buildings.[885]

A further point of weakness of our analysis could be the pricing of the derivative overlay structures based on the commonly used Black-Scholes pricing formula. As is widely known by finance professionals and academics, the pricing method is based on a set of strong assumptions that do not all hold in reality. Also the Black-76 pricing approach for the fixed-income derivatives is a rather simple model that we have used. Its implementation was justified in our view due to the simulation complexities under which our empirical model had to operate. We admit that a professional credit risk management could be realised using different instruments, in particular CDS contracts. Overall, the computational extend of the simulation study, with 10,000 prices per asset class per month over a 3-year observation period, required a set of restrictions to enable us running the model.

[885] See IPD (2012).

6.3 Research Outlook

Due to the comprehensive research topic of this dissertation as well as the complexity of the overall research study, there remain several outstanding issues that have not been covered in this thesis but that have nonetheless the potential to be part of future research.

Within SRIs, for example, new studies could extend the SRI screening methodology to real estate assets. In this context, we would suggest the creation of a real estate index that replicates the performance of sustainable real estate buildings. Such assets could appeal to pension funds that seek to allocate funds into SRI assets. In general, the suitability of sustainable alternative investments for pension funds requires more attention, as it is a controversial area of SRI investing. We discussed in relation to sustainable commodity investments what type of conflicts might arise. Due to the relevance alternative assets are already having in the asset allocation of pension funds, future research studies have to provide more clarification and guidance on how the apparently incompatible areas of SRI and alternative investments can be brought together.

Furthermore, prospective academic studies could extend the derivative overlay structures we have followed to include in addition government bonds, given their weight within the asset allocation of German Pension Insurance Funds. This is particularly relevant in times of distress in the European government bond markets amid the current sovereign debt crisis.

We would also recommend that the performance impact of using more advanced option-pricing methods for equity derivatives should be considered. Based on the econometric nature of our empirical analysis, using a valuation method focused on a time-series technique seems appropriate. A pricing model using GARCH effects, for example, could lead to an improvement in option pricing. The assumption of the Black-Scholes method that stock returns are normally distributed with constant mean and variance has been refuted in academia, as empirical studies have proved that volatility is time-varying and tends to cluster. Advanced option pricing models are able to incorporate nowadays time-varying volatility.[886]

The main issue is that the vast majority of these models do not have a closed-form analytical solution,[887] so that the price can only be determined via a Monte Carlo simulation.[888] The Heston, Nandi pricing method, nevertheless, allows a closed-form GARCH option pricing calculation. It is hereby the first computed option formula available in academic research for a GARCH volatility model that can be estimated purely on the basis of observable data only.[889]

[886] See Douglas Rouah, Vainberg (2007), p. 136.
[887] See for example Duan (1995) for such a model approach.
[888] See Douglas Rouah, Vainberg (2007), p. 136.
[889] See Heston, Nandi (2000), p. 585.

Bibliography

aba (Arbeitsgemeinschaft fuer betriebliche Altersversorgung) (2011), Prozentuale Aufteilung der Deckungsmittel in der betrieblichen Altersversorgung im Jahr 2008 - nach Durchführungswegen, *homepage of aba, URL: http://www.aba-online.de/seiten/betriebsrente/daten_fakten/ 1_Deckungsmittel_bav//Aktualisierungen_0811/1d-Deckungsmittel-bAV-seit1990relativ-2009_03_08_2011__SD_.pdf, accessed on 26-July-2011*

aba (Arbeitsgemeinschaft fuer betriebliche Altersversorgung) (editors, 2009), Kapitalanlage in der betrieblichen Altersversorgung – Grundlagen und Praxis, *Heidelberg, Munich i.a., 2009.*

Agarwal, V., Daniel, N. and Naik, N. (2009), Role of managerial incentives and discretion in hedge fund performance, *in: The Journal of Finance, 2009, vol. 64, no. 5, pp. 2221-2256.*

Ahn, S. (1988), Distribution for residual autocovariances in multivariate autoregressive models with structured parametrization, *in: Biometrika, 1988, vol. 75, no. 3, pp. 590-593.*

Akaike, H. (1976), Canonical correlation analysis of time series and the use of an information criterion, *in: Mathematics in Science and Engineering, 1976, vol. 126, pp. 27-96.*

Akaike, H. (1974), A new look at statistical model identification, *in: IEEE Transactions on Automatic Control, 1974, vol. 19, issue 6, pp. 716-726.*

Akella, S. and A. Patel, A. (1996), An examination of real interest rates in the United States, Canada, France and Germany during the recent floating exchange rate period, *in: Review of Quantitative Finance and Accounting, 1996, vol. 6, pp. 277-292.*

Alexander, C. (2008), Practical financial econometrics, *Chichester, 2008.*

Allianz Global Investors (2010), Doing good by investing well? Pension funds and socially responsible investment: results of an expert survey, *copy of the document available under URL: http://papers.ssrn.com/sol3 / papers.cfm?abstract_id=1607730, accessed on 15-Sep-2012.*

Amenc, N., Goltz, F., Martellini, L. and Milhau, V. (2011), Asset allocation and portfolio construction, *in: Fabozzi, F. and Markowitz, H. (editors, 2011), pp. 159-203.*

Amenc, N. and Le Sourd, V. (2003), Portfolio theory and performance analysis, *Chichester, 2003.*

Anand, P. and Cowton, C. (1993), The ethical investor: exploring dimensions of investment behaviour, *in: Journal of Economic Psychology, 1993, vol. 14, no. 2, pp. 377-385.*

Anson, M., Fabozzi, F. and Jones, F. (2011), Asset classes, alternative investments, investment companies and exchange-traded funds, *in: Fabozzi, F. and Markowitz, H. (editors, 2011), pp. 15-44.*

Aras, G. and Crowther, D. (editors, 2010), A handbook of corporate and social responsibility, *Farnham, Burlington, 2010.*

Asteriou, D. and Hall, S. (2007), Applied econometrics – a modern approach, *revised edition, New York, 2007.*

Baffes, J. and Haniotis, T. (2010), Placing the 2006/2008 commodity price boom into perspective, *in: The World Bank Group, Policy Research Working paper, 2010, no. 5371, pp. 1-40.*

BaFin (Bundesanstalt für Finanzdienstleistungsaufsicht) (2012, a), Liste der Pensionskassen mit Geschäftstätigkeit, *homepage of the BaFin, URL: http://www.bafin.de/SharedDocs/Downloads/DE/Liste/Unternehmen/dl_li_vu _pensionskasse_mit_gesch.html?nn=2696686, accessed on 11-Jun-2012.*

BaFin (Bundesanstalt für Finanzdienstleistungsaufsicht) (2012, b), Einzelangaben zu den Kapitalanlagen der Erstversicherungsunternehmen. Bestand in den einzelnen Versicherungssparten 4. Quartal 2011, *copy of the document available under URL: http://www.bafin.de/SharedDocs /Downloads/DE/Statistik/2011/dl_kapitalanlagen_4q_11_va.pdf?__blob=pu blicationFile&v=2, accessed on 10-Jun-2012.*

BaFin (Bundesanstalt fuer Finanzdienstleistungsaufsicht) (2012, c), Investments, *copy of the document available under URL: http://www.bafin.de/EN/Supervision/InsuranceUndertakingsPensionFunds/I nvestments/investments_node.html, accessed on 19-Jun-2012.*

BaFin (Bundesanstalt fuer Finanzdienstleistungsaufsicht) (2012, d), Statistiken – Kapitalanlagen der Erstversicherer, *homepage of the BaFin, URL: http://www.bafin.de/DE/Aufsicht/VersichererPensionsfonds/Kapital anlagen /kapitalanlagen_node.html, accessed on 20-Jun-2012.*

BaFin (Bundesanstalt fuer Finanzdienstleistungsaufsicht) (2012, e), Solvency II, *homepage of the BaFin, URL: http://www.bafin.de/ DE/Internationales/Regelungsvorhaben/Solvency2/solvency2_node.html, accessed on 20-Jun-2012.*

BaFin (Bundesanstalt fuer Finanzdienstleistungsaufsicht) (2011, a), Anlageverordnung (AnlV) – Verordnung ueber die Anlage des gebundenen Vermoegens von Versicherungsunternehmen, *copy of the document available under URL: http://www.bafin.de/cln_117/nn_722564/ DE/Unternehmen/ VersichererPensionsfonds/Kapitalanlagen/kapitalanlagen __node.html?__nnn=true, accessed on 27-Mar-2012.*

BaFin (Bundesanstalt fuer Finanzdienstleistungsaufsicht) (2011, b), Rundschreiben R4/2011 – Hinweise zur Anlage des gebundenen Vermoegens von Versicherungsunternehmen , *copy of the document available under URL: http://www.bafin.de/cln_117/nn_722564/DE/ Unternehmen/VersichererPensionsfonds/Kapitalanlagen/kapitalanlagen__node.html? __nnn=true, accessed on 28-Mar-2012.*

BaFin (Bundesanstalt fuer Finanzdienstleistungsaufsicht) (2011, c), Anordnung betreffend die Anzeige- und Berichtspflichten der Versicherungsunternehmen ueber ihre Kapitalanlagen, *copy of the document available under*

URL: http://www.bafin.de/SharedDocs/ Aufsichtsrecht /DE /Verfuegung/vf_110621_anzeige_berichtspflichten_ kapitalanlagen_va.html, accessed on 27-Sep-2011.

BaFin (Bundesanstalt fuer Finanzdienstleistungsaufsicht) (2009, a), Kapitalausstattungs-Verordung (KapAusstV) – Verordnung ueber die Kapitalausstattung von Versicherungsunternehmen, *copy of the document available under URL: http://www.bafin.de/SharedDocs/Aufsichtsrecht /DE/Verordnung/KapAusstV_831213_va.html, accessed on 19-Jun-2012.*

BaFin (Bundesanstalt fuer Finanzdienstleistungsaufsicht) (2009, b), Rundschreiben 3/2009 (VA) – Aufsichtsrechtliche Mindestanforderungen an das Risikomanagement (MaRisk VA), *copy of the document available under URL: http://www.bafin.de/ SharedDocs/ Veroeffentlichungen /DE /Rund schreiben/rs_0903_va_marisk.html?nn=2798666, accessed on 15-Jun-2012.*

BaFin (Bundesanstalt für Finanzdienstleistungsaufsicht) (2006), Rundschreiben 1/2006 (VA) - Hinweise zur Bearbeitung von Beschwerden, *homepage of the BaFin, URL: http://www.bafin.de/SharedDocs/ Veroeffentlichungen/DE/Rundschreiben/rs_0601_va_Beschwerdebearbeitung.html, accessed on 18-Jun-2012.*

BaFin (Bundesanstalt fuer Finanzdienstleistungsaufsicht) (2000), Rundschreiben R3/2000 – Derivate Rundschreiben, *copy of the document available under URL: http://www.BaFin.de/cln_228/nn_724174/DE/ Unternehmen/VersichererPensionsfonds/Kapitalanlagen/kapitalanlagen__node.html?__nnn=true, accessed on 19-Apr-2012.*

Baillie, R. and Bollerslev, T. (1989), Common stochastic trends in a system of exchange rates, *in: The Journal of Finance, 1989, vol. 44, no. 1, pp. 167-181.*

Balduzzi, P., Das, S.R., Foresi, S. and Sundaram, R. (1996), A simple approach to three-factor affine term structure models, *in: Journal of Fixed-Income, 1996, vol. 6, no. 3, pp. 43-53.*

Barnhart, S. and Szakmary, A. (1991), Testing the unbiased forward rate hypothesis: evidence on unit roots, cointegration, and stochastic coefficients, *in: Journal of Financial and Quantitative Analysis, 1991, vol. 26, no. 2, pp. 245–267.*

Bauer, R., Koedijk, K. and Otten, R. (2005), International evidence on ethical mutual fund performance and investment style, *in: Journal of Banking & Finance, 2005, vol. 29, pp. 1751-1767.*

Bawa, V. (1976), Admissible portfolios for all individuals, *in: The Journal of Finance, 1976, vol. 31, no. 4, pp. 1169-1183.*

Beal, D., Goyen, M. and Phillips, P. (2005), Why do we invest ethically, *in: Journal of Investing, 2005, vol. 14, no. 3, pp. 66-77.*

Beckstette, F. and Schmidt, A. (2002), Pensionsfonds – Der fuenfte Durchfuehrungsweg der betrieblichen Altersversorgung, *Ulm, 2002.*

Belousova, J. and Dorfleitner, G. (2012), On the diversification benefits of commodities from the perspective of euro investors, *in: Journal of Banking & Finance, 2012, vol. 36, no. 9, pp. 2455-2472.*

Benston, G. and Smith, C. (1976), A transaction cost approach to the theory of financial intermediation, *in: Journal of Finance, 1976, vol. 31, no. 2, pp. 215-231.*

Bertrand, P. and Prigent, J. (2011), Omega performance measure and portfolio insurance, *in: Journal of Banking and Finance, 2011, vol. 35, p. 1811-1823.*

Bertrand, P. and Prigent, J. (2003), Portfolio insurance strategies: a comparison of standard methods when the volatility of the stock is stochastic, *in: International Journal of Business, 2003, vol. 8, no. 4, pp. 462-470.*

Beyer, A. (1998), Modelling money demand in Germany, *in: Journal of Applied Econometrics, 1998, vol. 13, pp. 57-76.*

Binkley, J. (1982), The effect of variable correlation on the efficiency of seemingly unrelated regression in a two-equation model, *in: Journal of the American Statistical Association, 1982, vol. 77, no. 380, pp. 890-895.*

Bird, R., Cunningham, R., Dennis, D. and Tippett, M. (1990), Portfolio insurance: a simulation under different market conditions, *in: Insurance: Mathematics and Economics, 1990, vol. 9, pp. 1-19.*

Bird, P. (1984), Commodities as hedge against inflation, *in: Applied Economics, 1984, vol. 16, no. 6, pp. 855-867.*

Bissels, A. (2009), Betriebliche Altersversorgung und Mitbestimmung. Neuregelungen des BetrAVG unter Berücksichtigung von Mitbestimmungsrechten des Betriebsrates bei Pensionsfonds, *Hamburg, 2009 (dissertation admitted at the University of Bonn, 2009).*

Black, F. (1976), The pricing of commodity contracts, *in: Journal of Financial Economics, 1976, vol. 3, no. 1 and 2, pp. 167-179.*

Black, F. and Scholes M. (1973), The pricing of options and corporate liabilities, *in: Journal of Political Economy, 1973, vol. 81, no. 3, pp. 637-654.*

Board, J., Sutcliffe, C. and Patrinos, E. (2000), The performance of covered calls, in*: The European Journal of Finance, 2000, vol. 6, no. 1, pp. 1-17.*

Bodie, Z. and Rosansky, V. (1980), Risk and return in commodity futures, *in: Financial Analysts Journal, 1980, vol. 36, no. 3, pp. 27-39.*

Bodie, Z. (1976), Common stock as a hedge against inflation, *in: Journal of Finance, 1976, vol. 31, no. 2, pp. 459-470.*

Boersch-Supan, A., Reil-Held, A. and Wilke, C.B. (2003), How to make a defined benefit system sustainable: the "Sustainability Factor" in the German benefit indexation formula, *research paper published by the Mannheim Research Institute for the Economics of Aging, Mannheim, 2003, copy of the document available under URL: http://mea.mpisoc.mpg.de/uploads / user_mea_discussionpapers/ tveu7lm3e66xcza4_DPNr37.pdf, accessed on 23-Jun-2012.*

Bollen, N. (2007), Mutual fund attributes and investor behaviour, *in: Journal of Financial and Quantitative Analysis, 2007, vol. 42, no. 3, pp. 683-708.*

Bolzen, S. and Eder, F. (2012), Bruessel rueckt Pensionskassen zu Leibe, *in: Die Welt (online), 08-Feb-2012, copy of the document available under URL: http://www.welt.de/105963342, accessed on 17-Jun-2012.*

Bonham, C., Gangnes, B. and Zhou, T. (2009), Modelling tourism: a fully identified VECM approach, *in: International Journal of Forecasting, 2009, vol. 25, no. 3, pp. 531-549.*

Bonin, H. (2009), 15 years of pension reform in Germany: old successes and new threats, *in: Geneva Papers on Risk & Insurance, 2009, vol. 34, no. 4, pp. 548-560.*

Boudoukh, J. and Richardson, M. (1993), Stock return and inflation: a long-horizon perspective, *in: The American Economic Review, 1993, vol. 83, no. 5, pp. 1346-1355.*

Bouzoubaa, M. and Osseiran, A. (2010), Exotic options and hybrids – a guide to structuring, pricing and trading, *Chichester, 2010.*

Box, G. and Jenkins, G. (1970), Time series analysis: forecasting and control, *San Francisco, 1970.*

Boyson, N. (2008), Hedge fund performance: a new approach, *in: Financial Analysts Journal, 2008, vol. 64, no. 6, pp. 27-44.*

Braueninger, D. (2010) Betriebliche Altersversorgung: Raum fuer weitere Expansion, *research study published by Deutsche Bank Research, in: Deutschland – Aktuelle Themen, 2010, no. 487, copy of the document available under URL: http://www.dbresearch.de/PROD/DBR_INTERNET _DE-PROD/PROD0000000000259333/Betriebliche+Altersversorgung %3A+Raum+für+weitere+Expansion.PDF, accessed on 03-Apr-2012.*

Braun, M. (2010), Betriebliche Alterssicherung im Spannungsfeld von betrieblicher Altersversorgung und betrieblicher Altersvorsorge, *Aachen, 2010 (dissertation admitted at the University of Bayreuth, 2009).*

Brenner, R. and Kroner, F. (1995), Arbitrage, cointegration, and testing the unbiasedness hypothesis in financial markets, *in: Journal of Financial and Quantitative Analysis, 1995, vol. 30, no. 1, pp. 23-42.*

Breuer, W., Guertler, M. and Schuhmacher, F. (2006), Portfoliomanagement II – Weiterfuehrende Anlagestrategien, *Wiesbaden, 2006.*

Breusch, T. (1978), Testing for autocorrelation in dynamic linear models, *in: Australian Economic Papers, 1978, vol. 17, no. 31, pp. 334-355.*

Briand, R., Urwin, R. and Chia, C. (2011), Integrating ESG into the investment process – from aspiration to effective implementation, research published by MSCI ESG Research, 2011, copy of the document available under URL: http://www.msci.com/products/esg/integrating_esg_into_the_investment_process.html, accessed on 15-Sep-2012.

Brooks, C. (2008), Introductory econometrics for finance, *2nd edition, Cambridge, New York i.a., 2008.*

Brooks, C., Rew, A. and Ritson, S. (2001), A trading strategy based on the lead-lag relationship between the spot index and futures contract for the FTSE 100, *in: International Journal of Forecasting, 2001, vol. 17, no. 1, pp. 31-44.*

Brooks, C. (1997), Linear and non-linear (non-) forecastability of high-frequency exchange rates, *in: Journal of Forecasting, 1997, vol. 16, no. 1, pp. 125-145.*

Brown, R., Durbin, J. and Evans. J. (1975), Techniques for testing the consistency of regression relationships over time, *in: Journal of the Royal Statistical Society, 1975, vol. 37, no. 2, pp. 149-192.*

Browne, S. (1999), Beating a moving target: optimal portfolio strategies for outperforming a stochastic benchmark, *in: Finance and Stochastics, 1999, vol. 3, no. 3, pp. 275-294.*

Browne, S. (1998), The return on investment from proportional portfolio strategies, *in: Advances in Applied Probability, 1998, vol. 30, no. 1, pp. 216-238.*

Brueggemann, R. (2006), Sources of German unemployment: a structural vector error correction analysis, *in: Empirical Economics, 2006, vol. 31, no. 2, pp. 409-431.*

Brueggemann, R., Krolzig, H-M. and Luetkepohl, H. (2002), Comparison of model reduction methods for VAR processes, *in: EUI Working Paper, 2002, ECO No. 2002/19.*

Brueggeman, W., Chen, A. and Thibodeau, T. (1984), Real estate investment funds: performance and portfolio considerations, *in: AREUEA Journal, 1984, vol. 12, no. 3, pp. 333-354.*

Brunnermeier, M. and Nagel, S. (2004), Hedge funds and the technology bubble, *in: Journal of Finance, 2004, vol. 59, no. 5, pp. 2013-2040.*

Bulmahn, T. (2003), Zur Entwicklung der privaten Altersvorsorge in Deutschland, *in: Kölner Zeitschrift für Soziologie und Sozialpsychologie, 2003, vol. 55, no. 1, pp. 29-54.*

Bundesministerium der Finanzen (2011), Alterseinkuenftegesetz (AltEinkG), *homepage of the German Federal Ministry of Finance, URL: http://www.bundesfinanzministerium.de/nn_39812/DE/BMF__Startseite/Service/Glossar/A/008__Alterseinkuenftegesetz.html, accessed on 26-Mar-2011.*

Bundesministerium der Justiz (2011), Gesetz ueber die Zertifizierung von Altersvorsorge- und Basisrentenvertraegen, *homepage of the German Federal Ministry of Justice, URL: http://www.gesetze-im-internet.de/altzertg/index.html, accessed on 26-Mar-2011.*

Bundesministerium fuer Umwelt, Naturschutz und Reaktorsicherheit (2009), Was Investoren wollen. Nachhaltigkeit in der Lageberichterstattung, *Berlin, 2009.*

Bundesministerium fuer Umwelt, Naturschutz und Reaktorsicherheit and Fortis Investments (2008), Occupational pensions and sustainable investments in Germany, *Frankfurt, 2008, copy of the document available under URL: http://www.sd-m.de/files/Hesse_Occupational_pensions_ and_ SRI_in_Germany.pdf, accessed on 15-Aug-2011.*

Bundesministerium fuer Arbeit und Soziales (2008), Situation und Entwicklung der betrieblichen Altersversorgung in Privatwirtschaft und öffentlichem Dienst 2001-2007, *survey conducted by TNS Infratest Sozialforschung, copy of the document available under URL: http://www.bmas.de /DE/Service/Publikationen/Forschungsberichte/Forschungsberichte-Rente/forschungsbericht-f384.html, accessed on 04-Aug-2011.*

Buscher, H. (2002), Angewandte Zeitreihenanalyse, *in: Schroeder, M. (editor, 2002), pp. 131-212.*

Busemeyer, M. (2005), Pension reform in Germany and Austria: system change vs. quantitative retrenchment, *in: West European Politics, 2005, vol. 28, no. 3, pp. 569-591.*

Campbell, J. and Shiller, R. (1987), Cointegration and tests of present value models, *in: Journal of Political Economy, 1987, vol. 95, no. 5, pp. 1062–1088.*

Campen, K. (2009), Betriebliche Altersversorgung, *in: Deutsche Rentenversicherung Bund and PWC (editors, 2009), pp. 153-172.*

Carino, D. and Ziemba, W. (1998), Formulation of the Russell-Yasuda Kasai financial planning model, *in: Operations Research, 1998, vol. 46, no. 4, pp. 433-449.*

Carletti, M. and Weigel, E. (1992), The bond/call option strategy, *in: The Journal of Portfolio Management, 1992, vol. 19, no. 1, pp. 76-83.*

Cerchi, M. and Havenner, A. (1988), Cointegration and stock prices: the random walk on Wall Street revisited, *in: Journal of Economic Dynamics and Control, 1988, vol. 12, no. 2-3, pp. 333–346.*

Cesari, R. and Cremonini, D. (2003), Benchmarking, portfolio insurance and technical analysis: a Monte Carlo comparison of dynamic strategies of asset allocation, *in: Journal of Dynamics & Control, 2003, vol. 27, no. 6, pp. 987-1011.*

Chatfield, C. (2004), The Analysis of Time Series, *6th edition, Boca Raton, London i.a., 2004.*

Chaudhury, A. and Johnson, H. (2008), The efficacy of the Sortino Ratio and other benchmarked performance measures under skewed return distributions, *in: Australian Journal of Management, 2008, vol. 32, no. 3, pp. 485-502.*

Chen, L. (1996), Stochastic mean and stochastic volatility – a three factor model of the term structure of interest rates and its application in derivatives pricing and risk management, *in: Financial Markets, Institutions and Instruments, 1996, vol. 5, no. 1, pp. 1-87.*

Cheung, Y-W. and Lai, K. (1998), Power of the Augmented Dickey-Fuller test with information-based lag selection, *in: Journal of Statistical Computation and Simulation, 1998, vol. 60, no. 1, pp. 57-65.*

Cheung, Y-W. and Lai, K. (1993), Finite sample sizes of Johansen's likelihood ratio tests for cointegration, *in: Oxford Bulletin of Economics and Statistics, 1993, vol. 55, no. 3, pp. 313-328.*

Clapp, J. (2009), Food price volatility and vulnerability in the global south: considering the global economic context, *in: Third World Quarterly, 2009, vol. 30, no. 6, pp. 1183-1196.*

Clare, A., Maras, M. and Thomas, S. (1995), The integration and efficiency of international bond markets, *in: Journal of Business Finance & Accounting, 1995, vol. 22, no. 2, pp. 313-322.*

Clark, G. and Whiteside, N. (editors, 2005), Pension security in the 21st century, *Oxford, 2005.*

Clark, T. and West, K. (2007), Approximately normal tests for equal predictive accuracy in nested models, *in: Journal of Econometrics, 2007, vol. 138, no. 1, pp. 291-311.*

Clotfelter, C. and Rothschild, M. (editors, 1993), Studies of supply and demand in higher education, *Chicago, 1993.*

Cochrane, J. (1994), Permanent and transitory components of GNP and stock prices, *in: Quarterly Journal of Economics, 1994, vol. 109, no. 1, pp. 241-265.*

Conover, M., Jensen, G., Johnson, R. and Mercer, J. (2010), Is now the time to add commodities to your portfolio?, *in: The Journal of Investing, 2010, vol. 19, no. 3, pp. 10-19.*

Copeland, T., Weston, F. and Shastri, K. (2005), Financial theory and corporate policy, *4th edition, Boston, 2005.*

Cowton, C. (1994), The development of ethical investment products, *in: Prindl, A. and Prodhan, B. (editors, 1994), pp. 213-232.*

Cullis, J., Lewis, A. and Winnett, A. (1992), Paying to be good? UK ethical investments, *in: Kyklos, 1992, vol. 45, no. 1, pp. 3-24.*

Culver, S. and Papell, D. (1999), Long-run purchasing power parity with short-run data: evidence with a null hypothesis of stationarity, *in: Journal of International Money and Finance, 1999, vol. 18, no. 5, pp. 751-768.*

Dartanto, T. and Usman (2011), Volatility of world soybean prices, import tariffs and poverty in Indonesia: a CGE-microsimulation analysis, *in: Journal of Applied Economic Research, 2011, vol. 5, no. 2, pp. 139-181.*

Daskaladi, C. and Skiadopoulos, G. (2011), Should Investors Include commodities in their portfolio after all? New evidence, *in: Journal of Banking & Finance, 2011, vol. 35, no. 10, pp. 2606-2626.*

De Gooijer, J. and Hyndman, R. (2006), 25 years of time series forecasting, *in: International Journal of Forecasting, vol. 22, no. 3, pp. 443-473.*

De Groot, S.E. (2010), Der deutsche Pensionsfonds als Instrument der betrieblichen Altersversorgung im Spannungsfeld zwischen Betriebsrenten- und Versicherungsrecht, *Munich, 2010 (dissertation admitted at the University of Bielefeld, 2008).*

DeJong, D. Nankervis, J. Savin, N. and Whiteman, C. (1992), Integration versus trend stationarity in time series, *in: Econometrica, 1992, vol. 60, no. 2, pp. 423-433.*

Del Guercio, D. and Hawkins, J. (1999), The motivation and impact of pension fund activism, *in: Journal of Financial Economics, 1999, vol. 52, no.3, pp. 293-340.*

Derwall, J. and Koedijk, K. (2009), Socially responsible fixed-income funds, *in: Journal of Business Finance & Accounting, 2009, vol. 36, no. 1 and 2, pp. 210-229.*

Deutsche Nationalbibliothek (2012), Otto von Bismarck, *homepage of the German National Library, URL: http://d-nb.info/gnd/11851136X/about/html, accessed on 08-Jun-2012.*

Deutsche Rentenversicherung Bund (2012), Beitragsbemessungsgrenze 2011 und 2012, *homepage of the German Statutory Pension Insurance Scheme, URL: http://www.deutsche-rentenversicherung.de/nn_6480/SharedDocs/de/Inhalt/Servicebereich2/Lexikon/B/beitragsbemessungsgrenze.html, accessed on 09-Jun-2012.*

Deutsche Rentenversicherung Bund (2011), Rentenversicherung in Zahlen 2011. Statistik der Deutschen Lebensversicherung, *copy of the document available under URL: http://www.deutsche-rentenversicherung.de/cae/servlet/contentblob/138218/publicationFile/23658/rv_in_zahlen_2011_pdf.pdf, accessed on 09-Jun-2012.*

Deutsche Rentenversicherung Bund and PWC (PriceWaterHouseCoopers) (editors, 2009), Altersvorsorge: Beraten, Gestalten, Optimieren, *Bonn, 2009.*

Deutsche Rentenversicherung Bund (2005), Altersvorsorge in Deutschland 2005 (AVID 2005), *presentation for the 3. Press Seminar of Deutsche Rentenversicherung Bund on the 20./21.Nov.2007 in Wuerzburg, copy of* *the presentation available under URL: http://www.altersvorsorge-in-deutschland.de/DOWNLOADS/Folien_ Rische.pdf, accessed on 01-May-2011.*

Deutscher Derivate Verband (2009), Studie zum Markt fuer nachhaltige Zertifikate und Exchange Traded Funds in Deutschland, *copy of the document available under URL: http://www.derivateverband.de/DEU/ Publikationen/ Studien, accessed on 29-Sep-2011.*

Dhaene, J., Vanduffel, S., Goovaerts, M., Kaas, R. and Vyncke, D. (2005), Comonotonic approximations for optimal portfolio selection problems, *in: The Journal of Risk and Insurance, 2005, vol. 72, no. 2, pp. 253-300.*

Dichev, I. and Yu, G. (2011), Higher risk, lower returns: what hedge fund investors really earn, *in: Journal of Financial Economics, 2011, vol. 100, no. 2, pp. 248-263.*

Dickey, D. and Fuller, W. (1979), Distribution of the estimators for autoregressive time series with a unit root, *in: Journal of the American Statistical Association, 1979, vol. 74, no. 366, pp. 427-431.*

Dimitrios, T. and Guerard (2004), Naïve, ARIMA, nonparametric, transfer function and VAR models: a comparison of forecasting performance, *in: International Journal of Forecasting, 2004, vol. 20, no. 1, pp. 53-67.*

Ding, B., Shawky, H. and Tian, J. (2009), Liquidity shocks, size and the relative performance of hedge fund strategies, *in: Journal of Banking & Finance, 2009, vol. 33, no. 5, pp. 883-891.*

Dittrich, M. (2009), Motivation, Erfahrungen und Herausforderungen im Management von SRI-Anlagen, *in: Schaefer, H. and Schroeder, M. (editors, 2009), pp. 19-31.*

Doering, D. (2000), Grundlinien der langfristigen Systementwicklung der gesetzlichen Rentenversicherung – Personenkreis, Rentenformel, Finanzierung, *in: Fisch, S. and Haerendel, U. (editors, 2000), pp.169-187.*

Doetsch, P., Hagemann, T, Oecking, S. and Reichenbach, R. (2010), Betriebliche Altersversorgung, *3rd edition, Freiburg, 2010.*

Doornik, J., Hendry, D. and Nielsen, B. (1998), Inference in cointegrating models: UK M1 revisited, *in: Journal of Economic Surveys, 1998, vol. 12, no. 5, pp. 533-572.*

Douglas Rouah, F. and Vainberg, G. (2007), Option pricing models and volatility, *Hoboken, 2007.*

Dow Jones and Credit Suisse (2012, a), Dow Jones Credit Suisse core hedge fund index – index rules, *copy of the document available under URL: http://www.hedgeindex.com/hedgeindex/secure/en/documents.aspx?cy=USD&indexname=CORE, accessed on 10-Oct-2012.*

Dow Jones and Credit Suisse (2012, b), Dow Jones Credit Suisse core hedge fund index – performance update, *copy of the document available under URL: http://www.hedgeindex.com/hedgeindex / documents / HFI_Perfor -*

mance%20Update_DJCS%20Core%20Hedge%20Fund%20Index_Global.pdf, accessed on 19-Oct-2012

Dow Jones and UBS (2012), Dow Jones-UBS commodity index - brochure, *copy of the document available under URL: http://www.djindexes.com /mdsidx/downloads/brochure_info/Dow_Jones_UBS_Commodity_Indices_Brochure.pdf, accessed on 11-Oct-2012.*

Dow Jones and UBS (2011), DJ-UBS CI – the Dow Jones-UBS commodity index handbook, *copy of the document available under URL: http://www.djindexes.com /commodity/, accessed on 10-Oct-2012.*

Dresp, F., Fabian, R., Fath, R., Schwind, J. and Wolf, S. (2011, editors), Pensionskassen - Grundlagen und Praxis, *Heidelberg, Munich i.a., 2011.*

Dresp. F. (2011, a), Arten der Pensionskasse, *in: Dresp, F., Fabian, R., Fath, R., Schwind, J. and Wolf, S. (2011, editors), p. 27 et seq.*

Dresp. F. (2011, b), Leistungen der Pensionskasse, *in: Dresp, F., Fabian, R., Fath, R., Schwind, J. and Wolf, S. (2011, editors), pp. 89-107.*

Dresp. F. (2011, c), Versicherungsaufsichsrecht, *in: Dresp, F., Fabian, R., Fath, R., Schwind, J. and Wolf, S. (2011, editors), pp. 177-185.*

Dreyer, R. and Vischer, A. (2004), Indices for option-based strategies, *in: Risk Waters Group, Barclays Capital (editors, 2004), pp. 10-14.*

Drols, W. (editor, 2004), Handbuch betriebliche Altersversorgung, *Wiesbaden, 2004.*

Drut, B. (2010), Sovereign bonds and socially responsible investment, *in: Journal of Business Ethics, 2010, vol. 92, pp. 131-145.*

Duan, J.C. (1995), The GARCH option pricing model, *in: Mathematical Finance, 1995, vol. 5, no. 1, pp. 13-32.*

Duenn, S. and Fasshauer, S. (2009), Gesamtsystem der Alterssicherung, *in: Deutsche Rentenversicherung Bund and PWC (editors, 2009), pp. 109-118.*

Eberts, E. (2002), Strategische stochastische Investmentmodelle fuer den deutschen Kapitalmarkt, *Karlsruhe, 2002 (dissertation admitted at the University of Mannheim, 2002).*

ECB (European Central Bank) (2012, a), HICP overall index, Euro area, monthly index, seasonally adjusted, not working day adjusted, *data available under URL: http://sdw.ecb.europa.eu/quickview.do?SERIES _KEY=122.ICP.M. U2.S.000000.3.INX, accessed on 04-Jan-2012.*

ECB (European Central Bank) (2012, b), Inflation forecasts, *data available under URL: http://www.ecb.int/stats/prices/indic/forecast/html/table _3_ 2012q1.en.html , accessed on 01-May-2012.*

ECB (European Central Bank) (2012, c), Strategy European Central Bank, *copy of the document available under URL: http://www.ecb.europa.eu /mopo/strategy/html/index.en.html, accessed on 01-May-2012.*

ECB (European Central Bank) (2012, d), Euro area, Euribor 1-year, historical close, *data available under URL: http://sdw.ecb.europa.eu/ quick-view.do?SERIES_KEY=143.FM.M.U2.EUR.RT.MM.EURIBOR1YD_.HSTA, accessed on 03-May-2012.*

ECB (European Central Bank) (2012, e), Key ECB interest rates, *data available under URL: http://www.ecb.int/stats/monetary/rates/html/index. en.html, accessed on 07-Jun-2012.*

ECB (European Central Bank) (2012, f), Long-term interest rate statistics for EU member states, *data available under URL: http://www.ecb.int/ stats/money/long/html/index.en.html, accessed on 13-Jul-2012.*

ECB (European Central Bank) (2011, a), The monetary policy of the ECB, *copy of the document available under URL: http://www.ecb.int/pub/pdf/ other/monetarypolicy2011en.pdf, accessed on 13-Oct-2012.*

ECB (European Central Bank) (2011, b), Price stability: why is it so important for you?, *copy of the document available under URL: http://www.ecb.int/ pub/pdf/other/price_stability_web_2011en.pdf?fa3f37d3d204ba5092c4987 76c4a603f, accessed on 13-Oct-2012.*

Eccles, N. (2011), New values in responsible investment, *in: Vandekerckhove, W., Leys, J., Alm, K., Scholtens, B., Signore, S. and Schaefer, H. (editors, 2011), pp. 19-34.*

ECOreporter (*2011),* Marktdaten nachhaltige Publikumsfonds in Deutschland, *homepage of ECOreporter, URL: http://www.ecoreporter.de/Fonds-Portraits.125.0.html. Secondary source.*

ECPI (2012), About Us, *homepage of ECPI, URL: http://www.ecpigroup. com/ecpi_about_us.asp?IdSEZ=12, accessed on 08-Jul-2012.*

ECPI (2011, a), ECPI and ESG Analysis, *company presentation held on October 2011. Materials can be delivered via email by the author on this thesis upon request.*

ECPI (2011, b), ECPI euro bond index family, *copy of the document available under URL:* http://www.ecpigroup.com/PDF_Indici/ECPI_Euro_Bond_ *INDEX_RULES.pdf, accessed on 07-Jul-2012.*

ECPI (2011, c), ECPI ethical euro corporate bond index, *copy of the document available under URL: http://www.ecpigroup.com/ecpi_indices.asp?IdSEZ =15&IdCAT=3, ac cessed on 29-Sep-2012.*

ECPI (2010), ECPI ethical government bond Index, *copy of the document available under URL: http://www.ecpigroup.com/ecpi_indices.asp?IdSEZ=15&Id CAT=3, accessed on 20-Mar-2012.*

EFAMA (European Fund and Asset Management Association) (2010) Asset management in Europe: facts and figures, *4th annual review, Brussels, 2010. Copy of the document available under URL: http://www.efama.org/ index.php?option=com_docman&task=cat_view&gid=89&Itemid=-99, accessed on 12-Aug-2011.*

Efron, B. and Tibshirani, R. (1986), Bootstrap methods for standard errors, confidence intervals, and other measures of statistical accuracy, *in: Statistical Science, 1986, vol. 1, no. 1, pp. 54-77.*

Efron, B. (1979), Bootstrap methods: another look at the jackknife, *in: The Annals of Statistics, 1979, vol. 7, no. 1, pp. 1-26.*

EIOPIA (European Insurance and Occupational Pensions Authority) (2012), EIOPA's timeline for Solvency II, *homepage of the EIOPIA, URL: https://eiopa.europa.eu/activities/insurance/solvency-ii/index.html, accessed on 20-Jun-2012.*

EIRIS (Ethical Investment Research Services), UKSIF (UK Social Investment Forum) (2006), Responsible investment approaches to non-equity investments, *copy of the document available under URL: http://www.charitysri.org/homearea/documents/Investingresponsibly-non-equityinvestments.pdf, accessed on 28-May-2012.*

Eling, M. (2009), Does hedge fund performance persist? Overview and new empirical evidence, *in: European Financial Management, 2009, vol. 15, no. 2, pp. 362-401.*

Eling, M. and Parnitzke, T. (2007), Dynamic financial analysis: classification, conception and implementation, *in: Risk Management and Insurance Review, 2007, vol. 10, no. 1, pp. 33-50.*

Eling, M. and Schuhmacher, F. (2007), Does the choice of performance measure influence the evaluation of hedge funds?, *in: Journal of Banking and Finance, 2007, vol. 31, no. 9, pp. 2632-2647.*

Elton, E., Gruber, M., Brown, S. and Goetzmann, W. (2011), Modern portfolio theory and investment analysis, *8th edition, Hoboken, 2011.*

Enders, W. (2010), Applied econometric time series, *3rd edition, Hoboken, 2010.*

Engle, R. and Granger, W. (editors, 1991), Long run economic relations, *Oxford, 1991.*

Engle, R. and Granger, W. (1987), Co-integration and error correction: representation, estimation and testing, *in: Econometrica, 1987, vol. 55, no. 2, pp. 251-276.*

Engle, R. (1982), Autoregressive conditional heteroskedasticity with estimates of the variance of United Kingdom inflation, *in: Econometrica, 1982, vol. 50, no. 4, pp. 987-1007.*

Entine, J. (2003), The myth of social investing – a critique of its practise and consequences for corporate social performance research, *in: Organization & Environment, 2003, vol. 20, no. 10, pp. 1-17.*

Erb, C. and Harvey, C. (2006), The strategic and tactical values of commodity futures, *in: Financial Analysts Journal, 2006, vol. 62, no. 2, pp. 69-97.*

Estrada, J. (2008), Mean-semivariance optimization: a heuristic approach, *in: Journal of Applied Finance, 2008, vol. 18, no. 1, pp. 57-72.*

Estrada, J. (2007), Mean-semivariance behaviour: downside risk and capital asset pricing, *in: International Review of Economics and Finance, 2007, vol. 16, no.2, pp. 169-185.*

Etzioni, A. (1991), Reflections on teaching of business ethics, *in: Business Ethics Quarterly, 1991, vol. 1, no. 4, pp. 355-365.*

European Commission (2012), Insurance reforms: putting the European economy back on the path towards sustainable growth, *speech by Michel Barnier on the Insurance Europe Conference on 01-Jun-2012, copy of the document available under URL: http://ec.europa.eu/commission_2010-2014/barnier/headlines/speeches/2012/06/20120601_en.htm, accessed on 10-Jun-2012.*

European Parliament and the Council of the European Union (2009), Directive 2009/138/EC on the taking-up and pursuit of the business of insurance and reinsurance (Solvency II), *in: Official Journal of the European Union, 2009, pp. L 335/1-L 335/155.*

European Parliament and the Council of the European Union (2003), Directive 2003/41/EC on the activities and supervision of institutions for occupational retirement provision, *in: Official Journal of the European Union, 2003, pp. L 235/10-L 235/21.*

Eurosif (European Sustainable Investment Forum) (2011), Corporate pension funds & sustainable investment study, *copy of the document available under URL: http://www.eurosif.org/research/corporate-pension-funds, accessed on 04-May-2012.*

Eurosif (European Sustainable Investment Forum) (2010), European SRI study 2010, *copy of the document available under URL: http://www.eurosif.org/research/eurosif-sri-study/2010, accessed on 12-Aug-2011.*

Eurosif (European Sustainable Investment Forum) (2007), Venture capital for sustainability, *copy of the document available under URL: http://www.eurosif.org/research/venture-capital-for-sustainability, accessed on 04-Jun-2012.*

Eurosif (European Sustainable Investment Forum) (2005), Pension programme - SRI tool kit, *copy of the document available under URL: http://www.eurosif.org/sri-resources/pension-fund-toolkit, accessed on 15-Aug-2011.*

Fabozzi, F. and Markowitz, H. (editors, 2011), The theory and practice of investment management, *2nd edition, Hoboken, 2011.*

Fabozzi, F., Grant, J. and Vardharaj, R. (2011), Common stock portfolio management strategies, *in: Fabozzi, F. and Markowitz, H. (editors, 2011), pp. 229-270.*

Fama, E. and Schwert, G. (1977), Asset returns and inflation, *in: Journal of Financial Economics, 1977, vol. 5, no. 2, pp. 115-146.*

Farinelli, S. and Tibiletti, L. (2008), Sharpe thinking in asset ranking with one-sided measures, *in: European Journal of Operational Research, 2008, vol. 185, no. 3, pp. 1542-1547, quoted after Sortino, F., van der Meer, R. and Plantinga, A. (1999).*

Fath, R. (2011), Finanzierung der Kassenleistungen, *in: Dresp, F., Fabian, R., Fath, R.Schwind, J. and Wolf, S. (2011, editors), pp. 143-174.*

FAZ Institute (Frankfurter Allgemeine Zeitung) (2008), Welchen Nutzen bringen bAV aus Sicht der Unternehmen?, *research study conducted by the FAZ Institute on behalf of Victoria Lebensversicherung, copy of the document available under URL: http://www.ergo.com/de/Presse/Overview/Publikationen/~/media/ERGOcom/PDF/Praesentationen/2010/20101019-Presseworkshop-Leben.ashx, accessed on 13-Jun-2012.*

FAZ (Frankfurter Allgemeine Zeitung) (2008), Gute Leute binden, *in: Frankfurter Allgemeine Zeitung, 22-Mar-2008, no. 69, section ‚Beruf und Chance', p. C4.*

FAZ (Frankfurter Allgemeine Zeitung) (2005), Deutschland rückt ab vom Glauben an die staatliche Rente, *in: Frankfurter Allgemeine Zeitung, 04-May-2005, no. 103, section ‚Wirtschaft', p. 24.*

Featherstone, K (2011), The Greek sovereign debt crisis and EMU: a failing state in a skewed regime, *in: Journal of Common Market Studies, 2011, vol. 49, no. 2, pp. 193-217.*

Feldstein, M. and Siebert, H. (editors, 2002), Social security pension reform in Europe, *Chicago, 2002.*

Firth, M. (1979), The relationship between stock market returns and rates of inflation, *in: Journal of Finance, 1979, vol. 34, no. 3, pp. 743-749.*

Fisch, S. and Haerendel, U. (editors, 2000), Geschichte und Gegenwart der Rentenversicherung in Deutschland. Beiträge zur Entstehung, Entwicklung und vergleichenden Einordnung der Alterssicherung im Sozialstaat, *Berlin, 2000.*

Fishburn, P. (1977), Mean-risk analysis with risk associated with below-target returns, *in: The American Economic Review, 1977, vol. 67, no. 2, pp. 116-126.*

Fisher, I. (1930), The theory of interest, *New York, 1930.*

FNG (Forum Nachhaltige Geldanlagen) (2012), Sustainable investments, *copy of the document available under URL: http://www.forum-ng.org/en/sustainableinvestments/sustainableinvestments.html, accessed on 23-May-2012.*

FNG (Forum Nachhaltige Geldanlagen) (2010), Marktbericht nachhaltige Geldanlagen 2010, *Berlin, 2010. Copy of the document available under*

URL: http://www.forum-ng.org/de/nachhaltige-geldanlagen/ publikationen .html, accessed on 10-Aug-2011.

Foerster, W. and Rechtenwald, S. (2008), Die betriebliche und private Altersvorsorge, *in: Ruland, F. and Ruerup, B. (editors, 2008), pp. 136-172.*

Fomby, T. and Rhodes, G. (editors, 1990), Advances in econometrics series: cointegration, spurious regression and unit roots, *Greenwich, 1990.*

Fong, H. and Vasicek, O. (1991), Fixed-income volatility management, *in: Journal of Portfolio Management, 1991, vol. 17, no. 4, pp. 41-46.*

Franz, E. (2011), Kapitalanlage: Neue Huerden oder erleichterter Weg zu Solvency II, *in: Versicherungswirtschaft, 2011, vol. 66, no. 14, pp. 1027-1032.*

Freedman, D. (1981), Bootstrapping regression models, *in: The Annals of Statistics, 1981, vol. 9, no. 6, pp. 1218-1228.*

Freedman, D. and Peters, S. (1981), Bootstrapping an econometric model: some empirical results, *in: Journal of Business & Economic Statistics, 1984, vol. 2, no. 2, pp. 150-158.*

Frere, E., Reuse, S. and Schmitt, S. (2009), Asset Liability Management bei Pensionskassen – Einfluss aktueller Problemstellungen und Auswahl von geeigneten Assetklassen, *in: Finanz Betrieb, 2009, no. 2, pp. 62-73.*

Frerich, J. and Frey, M. (1993), Sozialpolitik in der Bundesrepublik Deutschland bis zur Herstellung der Deutschen Einheit, *in: Handbuch der Geschichte der Sozialpolitik in Deutschland, vol. 3, Munich, 1993.*

Freshfields (2005), A legal framework for the integration of environmental, social and governance issues into institutional investment, *study produced by the Asset Management Working Group of the UNEP Finance Initiative, copy of the document available under URL: http://www.unepfi.org/ publications/catalogue/index.html, accessed on 13-Aug-2011.*

FSA (Financial Services Authority) (2012), Background to Solvency II, *homepage of the FSA, URL: http://www.fsa.gov.uk/about/what/international/ solvency/background, accessed on 20-Jun-2012.*

FTSE (2011, a), FTSE EPRA/NAREIT developed Europe index – factsheet, *document available under URL: http://www.ftse.com/Indices/FTSE_EPRA_ NAREIT_Global_Real_Estate_Index_Series/factsheets.jsp, accessed on 10-Nov-2011.*

FTSE (2011, b), Ground rules for the management of the FTSE EPRA/NAREIT Global Real Estate index series, *copy of the document available under URL: http://www.ftse.com/Indices/FTSE_EPRA_NAREIT_Global_Real_ Estate_Index_Series/Index_Rules.jsp, accessed on 12-Nov-2011.*

Fuertes, A.-M., Miffre, J. and Rallis, G. (2010), Tactical allocation in commodity futures markets: combining momentum and term structure signals, *in: Journal of Banking & Finance, 2010, vol. 34, no. 10, pp. 2530-2548.*

Funds@Work (2010), The importance of socially responsible investments for institutional investors in Germany, Austria and Switzerland, *copy of the document available under URL: http://www.funds-at-work.com /fileadmin/downloads/SRI-Landscape_English_final_November_2010.pdf, accessed on 29-Sep-2011.*

Fung, H.G., Law, S. and Yau, J. (2010), Socially responsible investment in a global environment, *Cheltenham, 2010.*

Garz, H. and Volk, C. (2011), Responsible investments 2.1 – a top-down multi asset perspective, *research study published by WestLB, Duesseldorf, London, 2011.*

Garz, H. and Volk, C. (2010), Responsible investments 2.0 – Eine Multi Asset-Perspektive, *research study published by WestLB, Düsseldorf, London, 2010.*

Gascoigne, C. (1999), Putting your money where your principles are: ethical investment, *in: The Financial Times, 15 May 1999, S. 5.*

Georgiev, G. (2001), Benefits of commodity investment, *in: The Journal of Alternative Investment, 2001, vol. 4, no. 1, pp. 40-48.*

Gesamtverband der Deutschen Versicherungswirtschaft (2012), Absenkung des Hoechstzinses hat kaum Einfluss auf die Ablaufleistung, *copy of the document available under URL: http://www.gdv.de/2011 /02/lebensversicherung-bleibt-attraktives-vorsorgeprodukt-absenkung-des-hoechstrechnungszinses-hat-kaum-einfluss-auf-die-ablaufleistung/, accessed on 09-Apr-2012.*

Gieg, M. (2008), Betriebliche Altersversorgung in Deutschland und Grossbritannien, *Munich, 2008 (dissertation admitted at the University of Trier, 2008).*

Gillan, S. and Starks, L. (2000), Corporate governance proposals and shareholder activism: the role of institutional investors, *in: Journal of Financial Economics, 2000, vol. 57, no. 2, pp. 275-305.*

Glascock, J., Lu, C. and So, R. (2002), REIT returns and inflation: perverse or reserve causality effects?, *in: Journal of Real Estate Finance and Economics, 2002, vol. 24, no. 3, pp. 301-317.*

Godfrey, L. (1978), Testing for higher order serial correlation in regression equations when the regressors include lagged dependent variables, *in: Econometrica, 1978, vol. 46, no. 6, pp. 1303-1310.*

Gonzalo, J. and Lee, T.H. (1998), Pitfalls in testing for long run relationships, *in: Journal of Econometrics, 1998, vol. 86, no. 1, pp. 129-154.*

Gorton, G. and Rouwenhorst, K. (2004), Facts and fantasies about commodity futures, *in: National Bureau of Economic Research, working paper 10595, Cambridge, 2004.*

Gough, O. and Hick, R. (2009), Employee evaluations of occupational pensions, *in: Employee Relations, 2009, vol. 31, no. 2, pp. 158-167.*

Greene, W. (2012), Econometric analysis, *7th Edition, Harlow, 2012.*

Greer, R. (2000), The nature of commodity index returns, *in: The Journal of Alternative Investments, 2000, vol. 3, no. 1, pp. 45-52.*

Gregory, A., Matatko, J. and Luther, R. (1997), Ethical unit trust financial performance: small company effects and fund size effects, *in: Journal of Business Finance & Accounting, 1997, vol. 24, no. 5, pp. 705-725.*

Griffin, J. and Xu, J. (2009), How smart are the smart guys? A unique view from hedge Fund Stock Holdings, *in: The Review of Financial Studies, 2009, vol. 22, no. 7, pp. 2531-2570.*

Gruber, J. (editor, 1991), Econometric decision models: new methods of modelling and applications, *New York, 1991.*

Guardiancich, I. (2011), Pan-European pension funds: current situation and future prospects, *in: International Social Security Review, 2011, vol. 64, no. 1, pp. 15-36.*

Gultekin, N. (1983), Stock market returns and inflation: evidence from other countries, *in: Journal of Finance, 1983, vol. 38, no. 1, pp. 49-65.*

Haferstock, B. and Hilka, A. (2009), Kapitalanlageorganisation: Optimierung von Mandats- und Managementstrukturen, *in: aba (editors, 2009), pp. 205-225.*

Hales, C. and Gough, O. (2003), Employee evaluations of company occupational pensions: HR implications, *in: Personnel Review, 2003, vol. 32, no. 3, pp. 319-340.*

Hall, A., Anderson, H. and Granger, C.W. (1992), A cointegration analysis of treasury bill yields, *in: The Review of Economics and Statistics, 1992, vol. 74, no. 1, pp. 116-126.*

Hanau, P., Arteaga, M., Rieble, V. and Veit, A. (2006), Entgeltumwandlung, *2nd edition, Koeln, 2006.*

Hannan, E. and Quinn, B. (1979), The determination of the order of an autoregression, *in: Journal of the Royal Statistical Society, 1979, vol. 41, no. 2, pp. 190-195.*

Hansen, B. (2001), The econometrics of structural change: dating breaks in U.S. labour productivity, *in: Journal of Economic Perspectives, 2001, vol. 15, no. 4, pp. 117-128.*

Harlow, W. (1991), Asset allocation in a downside-risk framework, *in: Financial Analysts Journal, 1991, vol. 47, no. 5, pp. 28-40.*

Harmes, A. (2002), The trouble with hedge funds, *in: Review of Policy Research, 2002, vol. 19, no. 2, pp. 156-176.*

Harris, R. and Sollis, R. (2003), Applied time series modelling and forecasting, *Chichester, 2003.*

Harris, R. (1995), Using cointegration analysis in econometric modelling, *Hampstead, 1995*

Hatemi-j, A. and Shukur, G. (1999), The causal nexus of government spending and revenue in Finland: a bootstrap approach, *in: Applied Economics Letters, 1999, vol. 6, no. 10, pp. 641-644.*

Hawley, J. and Williams, A. (2007), Universal owners: challenges and opportunities, *in: Corporate Governance: An International Review, 2007, vol. 15, no. 3, pp. 415-420.*

Heath, D., Jarrow, R. and Morton, A. (1992), Bond pricing and the term structure of interest rates: a new methodology for contingent claim valuations, *in: Econometrica, 1992, vol. 60, no. 1, pp. 77-105.*

Heath, D., Jarrow, R. and Morton, A. (1990), Bond pricing and the term structure of interest rates: a discrete time approximation, *in: Journal of Financial and Quantitative Analysis, 1990, vol. 25, no. 4, pp. 419-440.*

Hedges, J. (2005), Hedges on hedge funds. how to successfully analyse and select an investment, *Hoboken, 2005.*

Hegelich, S. (2004), Can welfare expansion result in disintegration? The integration of East Germany into the German pension system, *in: German Politics, 2004, vol. 13, no. 1, pp. 81-105.*

Hendry, D and Juselius, K. (2001), Explaining cointegration analysis: Part II, *in: The Energy Journal, 2001, vol. 22, no. 1, pp. 75-120.*

Henning, F.-W. (1995), Die Industrialisierung in Deutschland 1800 bis 1914, *Paderborn, 1995.*

Hermann, C. (1990), Die Zeit von 1957-1991, *in: Ruland, F. (editor, 1990), pp. 105-139.*

Hertrich, C. (2011), Strategic asset allocation considerations for German Pension Insurance Funds: theoretical analysis and empirical evidence, *research project proposal for a doctoral thesis under the supervision of Prof. Dr. H. Schaefer at the Department of Corporate Finance, University of Stuttgart, research project no. 04/2011, ISSN 1864 0125, 2011, Stuttgart, 2011.*

Heston, S. and Nandi, S. (2000), A closed-form GARCH option valuation model, *in: The Review of Financial Studies, 2000, vol. 13, no. 3, pp. 585-625.*

Hill, C., Griffiths, W. and Lim, G. (2008), Principles of econometrics, *3rd edition, Hoboken, 2008.*

Hinrichs, K. and Kangas, O. (2003), When is a change big enough to be a system shift? Small system-shifting changes in German and Finnish pension policies, *in: Social Policy & Administration, 2003, vol. 37, no. 6, pp. 573-591.*

Ho, T. and Lee, S. (1986), Term structure movements and pricing interest rate contingent claims, *in: Journal of Finance, 1986, vol. 41, no. 5, pp. 1011-1029.*

Hoag, J. (1980), Towards indices of real estate value and return, *in: Journal of Finance, 1980, vol. 35, no. 2, pp. 569-580.*

Hockerts, H.G. (1980), Sozialpolitische Entscheidungen im Nachkriegsdeutschland. Allierte und deutsche Sozialversicherungspolitik 1945 bis 1957, *Stuttgart, 1980 (habilitation admitted at the University of Bonn, 1977).*

Hoefer, R. and Steinmeyer, H.D. (2004), Private und betriebliche Altersvorsorge zwischen Sicherheit und Selbstverantwortung, *expert opinion for the 65th German Legal Associations's Annual Meeting in Bonn in 2004, Munich, 2004.*

Holbert, D. and Son, M.-S. (1986), Bootstrapping a time series model, *in: Communications in Statistics – Theory and Methods, 1986, vol. 15, no. 12, pp. 3669-3691.*

Huang, B.N. and Yang, C. (1996), Long-run purchasing power parity revisited: a Monte Carlo simulation, *in: Applied Economics, 1996, vol. 28, no. 8, pp. 967-974.*

Hubrich, S. (2007), Die Betriebliche Altersvorsorge im Kontext der Nachhaltigkeit, *presentation at the FNA Graduate Colloquium on the 22nd of February 2007 at the University of Rostock, copy of the document available under URL: http://forschung.deutsche-rentenversicherung.de/ ForschPortalWeb /ressource?key=main_fna_ beitrag_gk2007_hubrich, accessed on 23-Jun-2012.*

Hull, J. (2006), Options, futures and other derivatives, *6th edition, New Jersey, 2006.*

Hull, J. and White, A. (1990), Pricing interest rate derivatives securities, *in: Review of Financial Studies, vol. 3, no. 4, pp. 573-592.*

Hutton, R., D'Antonio, L. and Johnsen, T. (1998), Socially responsible investing: growing issues and new opportunities, *in: Business & Society, 1998, vol. 37, no. 3, pp. 281-305.*

Idowu, S. and Filho, W. (editors, 2009), Professionals' perspectives of corporate social responsibility, *Berlin, Heidelberg, 2009.*

Inrate (2010), Impact and investing for foundations, *company presentation held on September 2010, materials can be delivered via email by the author on this thesis upon request.*

imug (2002), Institutionelle Investoren und ethisch-oekologische Geldanlagen in Deutschland, *imug working paper 11/2002, Hannover, 2002.*

IPD (2012), IPD indices, *homepage of IPD, URL: http://www1.ipd.com /Pages/DNNPage.aspx?DestUrl=http%3a%2f%2fwww.ipd.com%2fsharepoi nt.aspx%3fTabId%3d400, accessed on 20-Oct-2012.*

Jaeger, R. (2003), All about hedge funds. The easy way to get started, *New York, Chicago i.a., 2003.*

Jaffe, J. and Mandelker, G. (1976), The "Fisher Effect" for risky assets: an empirical investigation, *in: Journal of Finance, 1976, vol. 31, no. 2, pp. 447-458.*

Jagannathan, R., Malakhov, A. and Novikov, D. (2010), Do hot hands exist amongst hedge fund managers? An empirical evaluation, *in: The Journal of Finance, 2010, vol. 65, no. 1, pp. 217-255.*

Jarque, C. and Bera, A. (1987), A test for normality of observations and regression residuals, *in: International Statistical Review, 1987, vol. 55, no. 2, pp. 163-172.*

Jensen, G., Johnson, R., Mercer, J. (2002), Tactical asset allocation and commodity futures, *in: The Journal of Portfolio Management, 2002, vol. 28, no. 4, pp. 100-111.*

Jensen, G., Johnson, R. and Mercer, J. (2000), Efficient use of commodity futures in diversified portfolios, *in: The Journal of Futures Markets, 2000, vol. 20, no. 5, pp. 489-506.*

Johansen, S. (1995), Likelihood-based inference in cointegrated vector autoregressive models, *Oxford, 1995.*

Johansen, S. and Juselius, K. (1992), Testing structural hypotheses in a multivariate cointegration analysis of the PPP and the UIP for UK, *in: Journal of Econometrics, 1992, vol. 53, no. 1-3, pp. 211-244.*

Johansen, S. (1991), The power function for the likelihood ratio test for cointegration, *in: Gruber, J. (editor, 1991), pp. 323-335.*

Johansen, S. and Juselius, K. (1990), Maximum likelihood estimation and inference on cointegration – with applications to the demand for money, *in: Oxford Bulletin of Economics and Statistics, 1990, vol. 52, issue 2, pp. 169-210.*

Johansen, S. (1988), Statistical analysis of cointegration vectors, *in: Journal of Economic Dynamics and Control, 1988, vol. 12, no. 2/3, pp. 231-254.*

John, O. (2009), Wertsicherungsstrategien fuer Aktienportfolios, *in: aba (editors, 2009), pp. 123-128.*

JP Morgan Global Research (2010), Impact investments – an emerging asset class, *New York, 2010.*

Judge, W., Gaur, A. and Muller-Kahle, M. (2010), Antecedents of shareholder activism in target firms: evidence from a multi-country study, *in: Corporate Governance: An International Review, 2010, vol. 18, no. 4, pp. 258-273.*

Juselius, K. (2006), The cointegrated VAR model - methodology and applications, *Oxford, New York i.a., 2006.*

Juselius, K. and MacDonald, R. (2004), International parity relationships between the USA and Japan, *in: Japan and the World Economy, 2004, vol. 16, no. 1, pp. 17-34.*

Juselius, K. and MacDonald, R. (2002), Interest rate and price linkages between the USA and Japan: evidence from the post Bretton Woods period, *in: Discussion Paper 00-13, 2002, Department of Economics University of Copenhagen, copy of the document available under URL: www.econ.ku/okokj, accessed on 03-Apr-2012.*

Juselius, K. (1998), A structured VAR for Denmark under changing monetary regimes, *in: Journal of Business & Economic Statistics, 1998, vol. 16, no. 4, pp. 400-411.*

Kahneman, D., Knetsch, J. and Thaler, R. (1991), The endowment effect, loss aversion, and status quo bias, *in: Journal of Economic Perspectives, 1991, vol. 5, no. 1, pp. 193-206, quoted after Kahneman, D. and Tversky, A. (1984).*

Kahneman, D. and Tversky, A. (1984), Choices, values and frames, *in: American Psychologist, 1984, vol. 39, no. 4, pp. 341-350.*

Kaplan, P. and Knowles, J. (2004), Kappa: a generalized downside risk-adjusted performance measure, *in: Journal of Performance Measurement, 2004, vol. 8, pp. 42-54.*

Keating, C. and Shadwick, W. (2002), An introduction to Omega, *London, 2002.*

Kennedy, P. (2003), A guide to econometrics, *5th edition, Malden, Oxford, Victoria, 2003.*

Kerschbaumer, J. and Perreng, M. (2005), Die neue betriebliche Altersvorsorge, *2nd edition, Frankfurt, 2005.*

Kiernan, M. (2007), Universal owners and ESG: leaving money on the table?, *in: Corporate Governance: International Review, 2007, vol. 15, no. 3, pp. 478-485.*

King, S.R. (1986), Monetary Transmission, *in: Journal of Money, Credit and Banking, 1986, vol. 18, no. 3, pp. 290-303.*

Klatt, M. (2003), Die Pensionskasse in der betrieblichen Altersversorgung, *Karlsruhe, 2003.*

Knoepfel, I. (2011), Responsible investment in commodities. The issue at stake and a potential role for institutional investors, *research project sponsored by Schweizerische Eidgenossenschaft, in collaboration with PRI and Global Compact, Zurich, 2011.*

Knoll, M. (2002), Ethical screening in modern financial markets: the conflicting claims underlying socially responsible investment, *in: Business Lawyer, 2002, vol. 57, no. 2, pp. 681-726.*

Kohlmeier, A. (2008), Die Ausweitung des Versichertenkreises der Gesetzlichen Rentenversicherung – Bestimmungsgruende und Verteilungswirkungen, *Frankfurt Main, 2009 (dissertation admitted at the University of Muenster, 2008).*

Kosowski, R., Naik, N. and Teo, M. (2007), Do hedge funds deliver alpha? A bayesian and bootstrap analysis, *in: Journal of Financial Economics, 2007, vol. 84, no. 1, pp. 229-264.*

Kreander, N., Gray, R., Power, D. and Sinclair, C. (2005), Evaluating the performance of ethical and non-ethical funds: a matched pair analysis, *in: Journal of Business Finance & Accounting, 2005, vol. 32, no. 7, pp. 1465-1493.*

Kroner, K. and Sultan, J. (1993), Time varying distributions and dynamic hedging with foreign currency futures, *in: Journal of Financial and Quantitative Analysis, 1993, vol. 28, no. 4, pp. 535–551.*

Krueger, A. (2011), Solvency II bedroht die Betriebsrenten, *in: Financial Times Deutschland (online), 22-Mar-2011, section ‚Versicherungen' copy of the document available under URL: http://www.ftd.de/unternehmen/ versicherungen/:betriebliche-altersvorsorge-solvency-ii-bedroht-betriebsrenten/ 60029272.html, accessed on 05-Jun-2012.*

Krupp, H.J. (2002), Anforderungen an eine gerechte und funktionsfaehige Alterssicherung, *in: Zeitschrift fuer die gesamte Versicherungswissenschaft, 2002, vol. 91, no. 4, pp. 499-512.*

Kugler, P. (2002), Nichtstationaeritaet und Kointegration, *in: Schroeder, M. (editor, 2002), pp. 263-299.*

Kurtz, L. and diBartolomeo, D. (1996), Socially screened portfolios: an attribution analysis of relative performance, *in: The Journal of Investing, 1996, vol. 5, no. 3, pp. 35-41.*

Kwiatkowski, D., Philips, P., Schmidt, P. and Shin Y. (1992), Testing the null hypothesis of stationarity against the alternative of a unit root, *in: Journal of Econometrics, 1992, vol. 54, no. 1-3, pp. 159-178.*

Lamping, W. and Rueb, F. (2010), Introduction: farewell to Bismarck or moving forward back to Bismarck? Transformations of the German Welfare state, *in: German Policy Studies, 2010, vol. 6, no. 1, pp. 43-63.*

Langohr-Plato, U. (2007), Rechtshandbuch betriebliche Altersversorgung, *4th edition, Muenster, 2007.*

Langohr-Plato, U. and Teslau, J. (2003), Die Beitragszusage mit Mindestleistung, *in: Der Betrieb, 2003, no. 12, pp. 661-667.*

Latane, H. and Young, W. (1969), Test of portfolio building rules, *in: The Journal of Finance, 1969, vol. 24, no. 4, pp. 595-612.*

Leggio, K. and Lien, D. (2003), Comparing alternative investment strategies using risk-adjusted performance measures, *in: Journal of Financial Planning, 2003, vol. 16, no. 1, pp. 82-86.*

Leland, H. (1980), Who should buy portfolio insurance?, *in: The Journal of Finance, 1980, vol. 35, no. 2, pp. 581-594.*

Leland, H. and Rubinstein, M. (1976), The evolution of portfolio insurance, *in: Luskin, D. (editor, 1988), pp. 1-7.*

LeSage, J. (1990), A comparison of the forecasting ability of ECM and VAR models, *in: The Review of Economics and Statistics, 1990, vol. 72, no. 4, pp. 664-671.*

Lettau, M. and Ludvigson, S. (2001), Consumption, aggregate wealth, and expected stock returns, *in: The Journal of Finance, 2001, vol. 16, no. 3, pp. 815-850.*

Lewis, A. and Mackenzie, C. (2000), Morals, money, ethical investing and economic psychology, *in: Human Relations, 2000, vol. 53, no. 2, pp. 179-191.*

Lewis, A. and Waerneryd, K. (editors, 1994), Ethics and economic affairs, *London, 1994.*

Lewis, A. and Webley, P. (1994), Social and ethical investing: beliefs, preferences and the willingness to sacrifice financial return, *in: Lewis, A. and Waerneryd, K. (editors, 1994), pp. 171-182.*

Lewis, A. and Cullis, J. (1990), Ethical investments: preferences and morality, *in: Journal of Behavioural Economics, 1990, vol. 19, no. 4, pp. 395-411.*

Lhabitant, F. (2006), Handbook of hedge funds, *Chichester, 2006.*

Lhabitant, F. (2004), Hedge funds – quantitative insights, *Chichester, 2004.*

Libby, R. and Fishburn, P. (1977), Behavioral models of risk taking in business decisions: a survey and evaluation, *in: Journal of Accounting and Research, 1977, vol. 15, no. 2, pp. 272-292.*

Lien, D. (2002), A Note on the relationship between some risk-adjusted performance measures, *in: The Journal of Futures Markets, 2002, vol. 22, no. 5, pp. 483-495, quoted after Sortino, F., van der Meer, R. and Plantinga, A. (1999).*

Liu, Y. and Enders, W. (2003), Out-of-sample forecasts and nonlinear model selection with an example of the term-structure of interest rates, *in: Southern Economic Journal, 2003, vol. 69, no.3, pp. 520-540.*

Ljung, G. (1986), Diagnostic testing of univariate time series models, *in: Biometrika, 1986, vol. 73, no. 3, pp. 725-730.*

Ljung, G. and Box, G. (1979), The likelihood function of stationary autoregressive-moving average models, *in: Biometrika, 1979, vol. 66, no. 2, pp. 265-270.*

Ljung, G. and Box, G. (1978), On a measure of lack of fit in time series models, *in: Biometrika, 1978, vol. 65, no. 2, pp. 297-303.*

Loew, T. (2002), Internationale Entwicklung der Regulierungen zur Foerderung oekologisch-ethischer Finanzdienstleistungen, *Institut fuer oekologische Wirtschaftsforschung, discussion paper no. 56/02, Berlin, 2002.*

Lomnicki, Z. (1961), Tests for departure from normality in case of stochastic processes, *in: Metrika, 1961, vol. 4, no.1, pp. 37-62.*

Longstaff, F. and Schwartz, E. (1992), Interest rate volatility and the term structure: a two-factor general equilibrium model, *in: Journal of Finance, 1992, vol. 47, no. 4, pp. 1259-1282.*

Loretto, W., White, P. and Duncan, C. (2000), Something for nothing?: employees' views of occupational pension schemes, *In: Employee Relations, 2000, vol. 22, no. 3, pp. 260-271.*

Louche, C. (2009), Corporate social responsibility: the investor's perspective, *in: Idowu, S. and Filho, W. (editors, 2009), pp. 211-232.*

Louche, C. and Lydenberg, S. (2006), Socially responsible investment: differences between Europe and United States, *in: Vlerick Leuven Gent Management School Working Paper Series, 2006, no. 2006/22.*

Luetkepohl, H. (2006), New introduction to multiple time series analysis, *Berlin, Heidelberg, New York, 2006.*

Luetkepohl, H. and Kraetzig, M. (editors, 2004), Applied time series econometrics, *Cambridge, New York i.a., 2004.*

Luetkepohl, H. (2004, a), Univariate time series Analysis, *in: Luetkepohl, H. and Kraetzig, M. (editors, 2004), pp. 8-85.*

Luetkepohl, H. (2004, b), Vector autoregressive and vector error correction models, *in: Luetkepohl, H. and Kraetzig, M. (editors, 2004), pp. 86-158.*

Luskin, D. (editor, 1988), Dynamic hedging: a guide to portfolio insurance, *Hoboken, 1988.*

Luther, R. and Matatko, J. (1994), The performance of ethical unit trusts: choosing an appropriate benchmark, *in: British Accounting Review, 1994, vol. 26, no. 1, pp. 77-89.*

Luther, R., Matatko, J. and Corner, D. (1992), The investment performance of UK "ethical" unit trusts, *in: Accounting, Auditing & Accountability Journal, 1992, vol. 5, no. 4, pp. 57-70.*

Mackenzie, C. and Lewis, A. (1999), Morals and markets: the case of ethical investment, *in: Business Ethics Quarterly, 1999, vol. 9, no. 3, pp. 439-452.*

MacKinnon, J. and Haug, A. (1999), Numerical distribution functions of likelihood ratio tests for cointegration, *in: Journal of Applied Econometrics, 1999, vol. 14, no. 5, pp. 563-577.*

MacKinnon, J. (1991), Critical values for co-integration tests, *in: Engle, R. and Granger, C. (editors, 1991), pp. 267-276.*

Maddala, G. and Kim, I.M. (1998), Unit roots, cointegration and structural change, *Cambridge, New York i.a., 1998.*

Maier, S., Peterson, D. and Vander Weide, J. (1977), A Monte-Carlo investigation of characteristics of optimal geometric mean portfolios, *in: Journal of Financial and Quantitative Analysis, 1977, vol. 12, no. 2, pp. 215-233.*

Malkiel, B. (2003), The efficient market hypothesis and its critics, *in: The Journal of Economic Perspectives, 2003, vol. 17, no. 1, pp. 59-82.*

Mallin, C., Saadouni, B. and Briston, R. (1995), The financial performance of ethical investment funds, *in: Journal of Business Finance & Accounting, 1995, vol. 22, no. 4, pp. 483-496.*

Markit (2012, a), Markit indices – index map Iboxx Eurozone index, *copy of the document available under URL: https://products.markit.com/home/ index.jsp #INDICES.INDEXMAP.IndexOverview, accessed on 27-Oct-2012.*

Markit (2012, b), Markit indices – index map Iboxx EUR Corporates index, *copy of the document available under URL: https://products.markit.com/ home/index.jsp#INDICES.INDEXMAP.IndexOverview, accessed on 27-Oct-2012.*

Markit (2007), Markit Iboxx bond indices: content, valuations, processing, distributions, *copy of the document available under URL: https://products. markit.com/home/index.jsp#INDICES.PUBLICATIONS.FactSheets, accessed on 27-Oct-2012.*

Markowitz, H. (1952), Portfolio selection, *in: The Journal of Finance, 1959, vol. 7, no. 1., pp. 77-91.*

Marshall, B., Cahan, R. and Cahan, J. (2008), Can commodity futures be profitably traded with quantitative market timing strategies? *in: Journal of Banking & Finance, 2008, vol. 32, no. 9, pp. 1810-1819.*

Martellini, L., Priaulet, P. and Priaulet, S. (2003), Fixed-income securities – valuation, risk management and portfolio strategies, *Chichester, 2003.*

Masters, M. (2008), Testimony of Michael W. Masters before the Committee on Homeland Security and Government Affairs, *United States Senate, 20-May-2008.*

May, C. (2010), Generation als Argument – Konflikte um die Rentenversicherung in Deutschland, Großbritannien und den Niederlanden, *Frankfurt Main, 2010 (dissertation admitted at the University of Muenster, 2009).*

McCrary, S. (2005), Hedge fund course, *Hoboken, 2005.*

McLachlan, J. and Gardner, J. (2004), A comparison of socially responsible and conventional investors, *in: Journal of Business Ethics, 2004, vol. 52, no. 1, pp. 11-25.*

McPhail, L., Du, X. and Muhammad, A. (2012), Disentangling corn price volatility: the role of global demand, speculation, and energy, *in: Journal of Agricultural and Applied Economics, 2012, vol. 44, no. 3, pp. 401-410.*

Melchiors, H. (2004), Die Pensionsfonds als fuenfter Durchfuehrungsweg in der betrieblichen Alterversorgung, *in: Drols, W. (editor, 2004), pp. 577-605.*

Mercer (2011), Asset allocation survey – European institutional market place overview 2011, *copy of the document available under URL: http://www.mercer.com/articles/1414340, accessed on 20-Apr-2012.*

Mercer (2010), Asset allocation survey – European institutional market place overview 2010, *copy of the document available under URL: http://www.mercer.com/referencecontent.htm?idContent=1376545, accessed on 20-Apr-2012.*

Mercer (2009), Asset allocation survey – European institutional market place overview 2009, *copy of the document available under URL: http://www.mercer.com/referencecontent.htm? idContent=1343460, accessed on 20-Apr-2012.*

Mercer (2008), Asset allocation survey – European institutional market place overview 2008, *copy of the document available under URL: http://www.mercer.com/referencecontent.htm?idContent=1301240, accessed on 20-Apr-2012.*

Mercer (2007), Asset allocation survey – European institutional market place overview 2007, *copy of the document available under URL: http://www.mercer.com/referencecontent.htm?idContent=1260265, accessed on 20-Apr-2012.*

Merten, D. (2000), Rentenversicherung und deutsche Wiedervereinigung, *in: Fisch, S. and Haerendel, U. (editors, 2000), pp. 317-332.*

Merton, R. (1993), Studies of supply and demand in higher education, *in: Clotfelder, C. and Rothschild, M. (editors, 1993), pp. 211-242.*

Merton, R. (1969), Lifetime portfolio selection under uncertainty: the continuous-time case, *in: The Review of Economics and Statistics, 1969, vol. 51, no. 3, pp. 247-257.*

Merton, M. and Modigliani, F. (1961), Dividend policy, growth and the valuation of shares, *in: Journal of Business, 1961, vol. 34, no. 4, pp. 411-433.*

Mills, T. (1998), Recent developments in modelling nonstationary vector autoregressions, *in: Journal of Economic Surveys, 1998, vol. 12, no. 2, pp. 1-34.*

Misterek, R. (2012), CTA-Governance: Risiken erkennen und vermeiden, in: *Der Betrieb, 2012, no. 12, pp. 641-644.*

Moraleda, J. and Vorst, T. (1997), Pricing American interest rate claims with humped volatility models, *in: Journal of Banking & Finance, 1997, vol. 21, no. 8, pp. 1131-1157.*

Neusser, K. (2011), Zeitreihenanalyse in den Wirtschaftswissenschaften, *3rd edition, Wiesbaden, 2011.*

Nicholas, J. (2004), Hedge fund of funds investing, *Princeton, 2012.*

Nielsen, H. (2004), Cointegration analysis in the presence of outliers, *in: Econometrics Journal, 2004, vol. 7, no. 1, pp. 249-271.*

Nilsson, J. (2009), Segmenting socially responsible mutual fund investors, *in: International Journal of Bank Marketing, 2009, vol. 27, no. 1, pp. 5-31.*

OECD (2012), OECD guidelines for multinational enterprises, *copy of the document available under URL: http://www.oecd.org/ document/28/ 0,3746,en _2649_34889_2397532_1_1_1_1,00.html, accessed on 25-May-2012.*

OECD (2010), Pension markets in focus, *copy of the document available under URL: http://www.oecd.org/dataoecd/46/46/45637367.pdf, accessed on 18-Apr-2012.*

Oekom Research (2011), Corporate responsibility review 2011. Taking stock of sustainability performance in corporate management and capital investment, *Munich, 2011.*

Ohanian, L. (1990), Evaluating trends in aggregate time series: a Monte Carlo based forecasting approach, *in: Fomby, T. and Rhodes, G. (editors, 1990), pp. 323-342.*

Ohlms, C. (2006), Aktives Investmentportfolio Management – Optimierung von Portfolios aus derivatebasierten dynamischen Investmentstrategien, *Wiesbaden, 2006 (dissertation admitted at the University of Darmstadt, 2005).*

Osthoff, P. (2008), Socially responsible investment, *Berlin, 2008 (dissertation admitted at the University of Cologne, 2008).*

Pensionssicherungsverein (2011), Fakten & Zahlen, *homepage of the Pensionssicherungsvereins, URL: http://www.psvag.de/framesets/wir2.html, accessed on 28-Feb-2011.*

Perold, A. and Sharpe, W. (1995), Dynamic strategies for asset allocation, *in: Financial Analysts Journal, 1995, vol. 51, no. 1, pp.149-160.*

Pesaran, H. and Timmermann, A. (1992), A simple nonparametric test of predictive performance, *in: Journal of Business and Economic Statistics, 1992, vol. 10, no. 4, pp. 461-465.*

Philips, P. (1998), Impulse response and forecast error variance asymptotics in nonstationary VARs, *in: Journal of Econometrics, 1998, vol. 83, no. 1-2, pp. 21-56.*

Phillips, P. and Perron, P. (1988), Testing for a unit root in time series regression, *in: Biometrika, 1988, vol. 75, no. 2, pp. 335-346.*

Prangenberg, A. and Liesebach, B. (2004), Chancen und Risiken der Auslagerung von Pensionsverpflichtungen fuer Arbeitnehmer und Unternehmen, *research study for the Hans-Boeckler Stiftung, Duesseldorf, 2004, copy of the document available under URL: http://www.boeckler.de/pdf/mbf_ pensionsrueckstellungen _f_2005.pdf, accessed on 12-Jun-2012.*

Preu, F.J. and Richardson, B.J. (2011), German socially responsible investment: barriers and opportunities, *in: German Law Journal, 2011, vol. 12, no. 3, pp. 865-900.*

PRI (Principles for Responsible Investment) (2012), Signatories to the principles for responsible investment, *homepage of PRI, URL: http://www.unpri.org/signatories/, accessed on 25-Jun-2012.*

PRI (Principles for Responsible Investment) (2011), 5 years of SRI – report on progress 2011. An analysis of signatory progress and guidance on implementation, *copy of the document available under URL: http://www.unpri.org/publications/2011_report_on_progress_low_res.pdf, accessed on 20-May-2012.*

PRI (Principles for Responsible Investment) (2010), Report on progress 2010. An analysis of signatory progress and guidance on implementation, *copy of the document available under U RL: http://www.unpri.org /publications/, accessed on 12-Aug-2011.*

Prindl, A. and Prodhan, B. (editors, 1994), ACT guide to ethical conflicts in finance, *Oxford, 1994.*

Quantitative Micro Software (2007), EViews 6 user's guide II, *Irvine, 2007.*

Rajaguru, G. and Pattnayak, S. (2007), Investigation of a lead-lag relationship between spot and futures indices of the Hang Seng stock average, *in: International Journal of Business Studies, 2007, vol. 15, no. 1, pp. 69-82.*

Rao, B. (2007), Cointegration for the applied economist, *2nd edition, Basingstoke, New York, 2007.*

Reilly, F., Johnson, G. and Smith, R. (1970), Inflation, inflation hedges, and common stocks, *in: Financial Analysts Journal, 1970, vol. 26, no. 1, pp. 104-110.*

Reinschmidt, T. (2005), Dynamische Steuerung von Portfoliorisiken, *Wiesbaden, 2006 (dissertation admitted at the University of Erlangen-Nuernberg, 2005).*

Renneboog, L., Ter Horst, J. and Zhang, C. (2010), Socially responsible investment funds, *in: Aras, G. and Crowther, D. (editors, 2010), pp. 395-412.*

Renneboog, L. and Szilagyi, P. (2009), Shareholder activism through the proxy process, *in: CentER Discussion Paper Series no. 2009-65, 2009, ECGI - Finance Working Paper no. 275/2010, copy of the document available under URL: http://ssrn.com/abstract=1460578, accessed on 24-May-2012.*

Renneboog, L., Ter Horst, J. and Zhang, C. (2008), The price of ethics and stakeholder governance: the performance of socially responsible funds, *in: Journal of Corporate Finance, 2008, vol. 14, no. 3, pp. 302-322.*

Rezmer, A. and Drost, F. (2012), Betriebliche Zusatzrenten in Gefahr, *in: Handelsblatt (online), 03-Apr-2012, copy of the document available under URL: http://www.handelsblatt.com/ politik/deutschland/ eu-richtlinie-betriebliche-zusatzrenten-in-gefahr/6471994.html, accessed on 14-Jun-2012.*

Ribhegge, H. (2004), Sozialpolitik, *Munich, 2004.*

Richardson, B. (2009), Keeping ethical investment ethical: regulatory issues for investing in sustainability, *in: Journal of Business Ethics, 2009, vol. 87, no. 4, pp. 555-572.*

Risk Waters Group, Barclays Capital (editors, 2004), Risk guide to indices: strategies and products, *London, 2004.*

Rohde, W.G. and Kuesters, S. (2007), Betriebliche Altersvorsorge, *2nd edition, Berlin, 2007.*

Roll, R. (1973), Evidence on the "growth-optimum" model, *in: The Journal of Finance, 1973, vol. 28, no. 3, pp. 551-566.*

Roth, M. (2009), Private Altersvorsorge: Betriebsrentenrecht und individuelle Vorsorge, *Tuebingen, 2009.*

Roy, D. (1952), Safety first and the holding of assets, *in: Econometrica, 1977, vol. 20, no. 3, pp. 431-449.*

Rudolf, M. and Ziemba, W. (2004), Intertemporal surplus management, *in: Journal of Economic Dynamics & Control, 2004, vol. 28, no. 5, pp. 975-990.*

Ruerup, B. (2002), The German pension system. Status quo and reform options, *in: Feldstein, M. and Siebert, H. (editors, 2002), pp. 137-171.*

Ruland, F. and Ruerup, B. (editors, 2008), Alterssicherung und Besteuerung, *Wiesbaden, 2008.*

Ruland, F. (editor, 1990), Handbuch der gesetzlichen Rentenversicherung. Festschrift aus Anlass des 100jaehrigen Bestehens der gesetzlichen Rentenversicherung, *Neuwied, 1990.*

Sabrowski, K. (2007), Konzepte der Alterssicherung zur Ergaenzung der gesetzlichen Rentenversicherung – Eine Untersuchung unter besonderer Beruecksichtigung der betrieblichen Altersversorgung, *Saarbruecken, 2007.*

Sadka, R. (2010), Liquidity risk and the cross-section of hedge fund returns, *in: Journal of Financial Economics, 2010, vol. 98, no. 1, pp. 54-71.*

Saikkonen, P. and Luetkepohl, H. (2000), Testing for cointegration rank of a VAR process with structural shifts, *in: Journal of Business & Economic Statistics, 2000, vol. 18, no. 4, pp. 451-464.*

Saikkonen, P. and Luetkepohl, H. (1996), Infinite-order cointegrated vector autoregresive processes: estimation and inference, *in: Econometric Theory, 1996, vol. 12, no. 5, pp. 814-844.*

Sandberg, J. (2010), Socially responsible investment and fiduciary duty: putting the Freshfields report into perspective, *in: Journal of Business Ethics, 2011, vol. 101, no. 1, pp. 143-162.*

Sauer, D. (1997), The impact of social-responsibility screens on investment performance: evidence from the Domini 400 Social Index and Domini Equity Mutual Fund, *in: Review of Financial Economics, 1997, vol. 6, no. 2, pp. 137-149.*

Schaefer, H. (2012), Sustainable finance – a conceptual outline, *University of Stuttgart, research project no. 2/2012, , Stuttgart, 2012.*

Schaefer, H., Gromer, C. and Neligran, A. (2012), The demand for sustainable property investments in Germany. An explorative empirical study, *in: Journal of Property Investment & Finance, 2012, vol. 30, no. 1, pp. 5-17.*

Schaefer, H., Gromer, C. and Lucas, D. (2010), Chancen nutzen durch eine Gesetzesreform. Unausgereiztes Potenzial fuer nachhaltige REITS, *in: Betriebswirtschaftliche Blaetter, 2010, vol. 59, no. 1, pp. 35-43.*

Schaefer, H. and Mayer, N. (2010), Nachhaltige Geldanlagen fuer betriebliche Altersvorsorgeeinrichtungen, *research study in cooperation with Wissenschaftsfoerderung der Sparkassen-Finanzgruppe e.V., Stuttgart, 2010.*

Schaefer, H. (2009), Verantwortliches Investieren: Zur wachsenden oekonomischen Relevanz von Corporate Social Responsibility auf den internationalen Finanzmaerkten, *in: Ulshoefer, G. and Bonnet, G. (editors, 2009), pp. 64-80.*

Schaefer, H. and Schroeder, M. (editors, 2009), Nachhaltige Geldanlagen fuer Stiftungen – aktuelle Entwicklungen und Bewertungen, *ZEW Wirtschaftsanalysen, vol. 92, Mannheim, 2009.*

Schaefer, H. and Engelhardt, M. (2008), Ethische Aktienindizes schaffen Markt fuer nachhaltige Geldanlagen. Beurteilung von Firmen nach Sozial-, Umwelt-, Governance –Kriterien, *in: Betriebswirtschaftliche Blaetter, 2008, no. 9, pp. 506-513.*

Schaefer, H. and Lindenmayer, P. (2007, a), Nachhaltige Geldanlagen (II), *in: WISU, 2007, vol. 36, no. 8-9, pp. 1082-1089.*

Schaefer, H. and Lindenmayer, P. (2007, b), Implikationen von CSR-Rating-Systemen auf SRI-basiertes Asset-Management, University of Stuttgart, *research project 01/2007, Stuttgart, 2007.*

Schaefer, H., Zenker, J. and Fernandes, P. (2006), Who is who in corporate social responsibility rating. A survey of internationally established rating systems that measure corporate social responsibility, *research project for the Bertelsmann Foundation, Guetersloh, 2006.*

Schaefer, H. (2005), Wie nachhaltig ist die Geldanlage in Deutschland?, *in: Kreditwesen, 2005, November edition, pp. 16-20.*

Schaefer, H. (2003), Sozial-oekologische Ratings am Kapitalmarkt, *in: Finanz Betrieb, 2003, no. 9, pp. 556-557.*

Schaefer, H. (2001), Triple Bottom Line Investing – Ethik, Rendite und Risiko in der Kapitalanlage, *in: Zeitschrift fuer das gesamte Kreditwesen, 2001, no. 13, pp. 740-744, quoted after Schaefer, H. and Guelle, A. (2000).*

Schaefer, H. and Guelle, A. (2000), Ethische Kapitalanlagen. Struktur des Angebots an ethischen Kapitalanlagen im deutschsprachigen Raum, *University of Siegen, research study 'Ethische Kapitalanlagen', no. 03/2000, Siegen, 2000.*

Schaltegger, S. and Figge, F. (2008), Finance-oriented sustainability management, *Lueneburg, 2008.*

Scherer, H. (1995), Anlagestrategien fuer Schweizer Pensionskassen, *Bern, 1995 (dissertation admitted at the University of Bern, 1995).*

Schmaehl, W. (2007), Die Einfuehrung der Dynamischen Rente im Jahr 1957: Gruende, Ziele und Massnahmen, *in: DRV-Schriften, 2007, vol. 73, pp. 9-28.*

Schmaehl, W. (2005), Private pensions as partial substitute for public pensions in Germany, *in: Clark, G. and Whiteside, N. (editors, 2005), pp. 115-143.*

Schmidt, M.G. (1998), Sozialpolitik in Deutschland – Historische Entwicklung und internationaler Vergleich, *Opladen, 1998.*

Schmidt, S. and Weistroffer, C. (2010), Responsible Investments – Mehr als eine Modeerscheinung, *research study published by Deutsche Bank Research, in: Themen International – Aktuelle Themen, 2010, no. 484. Copy of the document available under URL: http://www.dbresearch.de /PROD/ DBR_INTERNET _DE-PROD/ PROD0000000000257607.PDF, accessed on 12-Aug-2011.*

Schmitz, J.-P. and Laurich, M. (2004), Die Pensionskasse – eine der attraktivsten Durchfuehrungswege der betrieblichen Altersversorgung, *in: Drols, W. (editor, 2004), pp. 541-575.*

Schneeweiss, A. (2010), Finanzierung nachhaltiger Entwicklung – Ein Ueberblick ueber die Situation nachhaltiger Geldanlagen in Deutschland, *research study in cooperation with the Heinrich Boell Stiftung, Berlin, 2010.*

Schneeweiss, T., Karavas, V. and Georgiev, G. (2002), Alternative investments in the institutional portfolio, *Alternative Investment Management Association (AIMA), 2002. Copy of the document available under URL: http://didattica.unibocconi.it/mypage/upload/49203_2010021 5_063949_ALTINVININSTITPORT_SCHNEEWEISKARAVASGEORGIEV. PDF, accessed on 30-May-2012.*

Schoenheit, I. (2005), Markttransparenz im Socially Responsible Investment, *Frankfurt, 2005.*

Scholtens, B. (2010), The environmental performance of Dutch government bond funds, *in: Journal of Business Ethics, 2010, vol. 92, pp. 117-130.*

Scholtens, B. (2006), Finance as a driver of corporate social responsibility, *in: Journal of Business Ethics, 2006, vol. 68, no. 1, pp. 19-33.*

Schroeder, M. (2010), Die Eignung nachhaltiger Geldanlagen fuer die Vermoegensanlage von Stiftungen, *Baden-Baden, 2010 (habilitation admitted at the University of Stuttgart, 2009).*

Schroeder, M. (2007), Is there a difference? The performance characteristics of SRI equity indices, *in: Journal of Business Finance & Accounting, 2007, vol. 34, no. 1, pp. 331-348.*

Schroeder, M. (2004), The performance of socially responsible investments: investment funds and indices, *in: Financial Markets and Portfolio Management, 2004, vol. 18, no. 2, pp. 122-142.*

Schroeder, M. (editor, 2002), Finanzmarktoekonometrie, *Stuttgart, 2002.*

Schroeder, M. (1999), Messung des Marktrisikos von Kapitalanlagen, *in: Finanz Betrieb, 1999, no. 11, pp. 383-388.*

Schumacher-Hummel, I. (2005), Die Rolle von Pensionskassen im Bereich Socially Responsible Investments – Einflussfaktoren eines aktiven Aktionaerstums, *Wiesbaden, 2005 (dissertation admitted at the University of St. Gallen, 2004).*

Schumann, H. (2003), Betriebliche Altersvorsorge, *Bobingen, 2003.*

Schwarz, G. (1978), Estimating the dimension of a model, *in: The Annals of Statistics, 1978, vol. 6, no. 2, pp. 461-464.*

Schwind, J. (2011), Die Deckungsmittel der betrieblichen Alterversorgung 2009, *in: Betriebliche Alterversorgung, 2011, no. 5, pp. 476-477.*

Simeonova, A. (2008), Covered Call Writing – Portfolio Insurance zur Altervorsorge, *Bamberg, 2008 (dissertation admitted at the University of St.Gallen, 2007), quoted after Dreyer, R. and Vischer, A. (2004).*

Sims, C., Stock, J. and Watson, M. (1990), Inference in linear time series models with some unit roots, *in: Econometrica, 1990, vol. 58, no. 1, pp. 113-145.*

Sims, C. (1980), Macroeconomics and reality, *in: Econometrica, 1980, vol. 48, no. 1, pp. 1-40.*

Smimou, K. (2010), Stock market and agricultural futures diversification: An international perspective, *in: The Journal of Alternative Investments, 2010, vol. 12, no. 4, pp. 36-57.*

Skaanes, S. (2005), Einflussfaktoren auf die strategische Asset Allocation Schweizer Pensionskassen, *Bern, Stuttgart, Wien, 2005 (dissertation admitted at the University of Zurich, 2004).*

Sortino, F., van der Meer, R. and Plantinga, A. (1999), The Dutch triangle: a framework to measure upside potential relative to downside risk, *in: Journal of Portfolio Management, 1999, vol. 26, no. 1, pp. 50-58.*

Souza, R. and Neto, A. (1996), A bootstrap simulation study in ARMA (p,q) structures, *in: Journal of Forecasting, 1996, vol. 15, no. 4, pp. 343-353.*

Sparkes, R. and Cowton, C. (2004), The maturing of socially responsible investment: a review of the developing link with corporate social responsibility, *in: Journal of Business Ethics, 2004, vol. 52, no. 1, pp. 45-57.*

Sparkes, R. (2001), Ethical investment: whose ethics, which investment?, *in: Business Ethics: A European Review, 2001, vol. 10, no. 3, pp. 194-205.*

Spencer, D. (1989), Does money matter? The robustness of evidence from vector autoregressions, *in: Journal of Money, Credit and Banking, 1989, vol. 21, no. 4, pp. 442-454.*

Statistisches Bundesamt (2011, a), Bevoelkerungsvorausberechnung-Entwicklung der Bevoelkerung in Deutschland bis 2060, *homepage of the Federal Statistical Office, URL: http://www.destatis.de/jetspeed/portal/ cms/Sites/destatis/Internet/DE/Content/Statistiken/Bevoelkerung/Vorausber echnungBevoelkerung/Tabellen/Content50/Bevoelkerungsvorausberech-nung,templateId=renderPrint.psml, accessed on 14-Mar-2011.*

Statistisches Bundesamt (2011, b), Birth Rate Germany, *homepage of the German Federal Statistical Office, URL: http://www.destatis.de/ jet-speed/portal/cms/Sites/destatis/Internet/DE/Content/Statistiken/Bevoelkeru ng/AktuellGeburtenentwicklung,templateId=renderPrint.psml, accessed on 14-Mar-2011.*

Statistisches Bundesamt (2009), Bevölkerung Deutschlands bis 2060, *12th Coordinated Population Forecast, support material for the press conference on 18th of November 2009 in Berlin, Wiesbaden, 2009, copy of the document available under URL: https://www.destatis.de/DE/ Publikationen/Thematisch/ Bevoelkerung/VorausberechnungBevoelkerung/ BevoelkerungDeutschland2060Presse5124204099004.pdf?__blob=publicationFile, accessed on 04-May-2012.*

Statistisches Bundesamt (2007), Einnahmen und Ausgaben von Rentner- und Pensionaershaushalten – Untersuchungen auf der Grundlage der Ergebnisse der Einkommens- und Verbrauchsstichprobe 2003, *section Wirtschaft und Statistik, no. 6, Wiesbaden, 2007, copy of the document available under URL: https://www.destatis.de/DE/Publikationen/ WirtschaftStatistik/ WirtschaftsrZeitbudget/EinnahmenAusgabenRentner. pdf?__blob= publicationFile, accessed on 06-Feb-2012.*

Statman, M. (2006), Socially responsible indexes, *in: The Journal of Portfolio Management, 2006, vol. 32, no. 3, pp. 10 0-109.*

Statman, M. (2005), Normal investors, then and now, *in: Financial Analysts Journal, 2005, vol. 61, no. 2, pp. 31-37.*

Statman, M. (2000), Socially responsible mutual funds, *in: Financial Analysts Journal, 2000, vol. 56, no. 3, pp. 30–39.*

Steinmeyer, H.-D. and Foersterling J. (1999), Das Rentenreformgesetz 1999, *Karlsruhe, 1999.*

Stephan, T. (1995), Strategische Asset Allocation in Lebensversicherungs-unternehmen, *Karlsruhe, 1995 (dissertation admitted at the University of Mannheim, 1994).*

Stock, J. and Watson, M. (2012), Introduction to econometrics, *3rd edition, Harlow, 2012.*

Stock, J. and Watson, M. (1993), A simple estimator of cointegrating vectors in higher-order integrated systems, *in: Econometrica, 1993, vol. 61, no. 4, pp. 783-820.*

STOXX (2012, a), Company Profile, *homepage of STOXX, URL: http://www.stoxx.com/corporate/company/stoxx.html, accessed on 08-Jul-2012.*

STOXX (2012, b), STOXX equity Index methodology guide, *copy of the document available under URL: http://www.stoxx.com/download/ indices/rulebooks/stoxx_indexguide.pdf, accessed on 10-Jul-2012.*

STOXX (2012, c), Stoxx Europe 600 size indices – factsheet, *copy of the document available under URL: http://www.stoxx.com/download/ indices/factsheets/sxxp_fs.pdf, accessed on 28-Oct-2012.*

STOXX (2012, d), Stoxx Europe Sustainability indices – factsheet, *copy of the document available under URL: http://www.stoxx.com/download/indices/ factsheets/stx_sustainability_fs.pdf, accessed on 20-Oct-2012.*

Sullivan, R. and Mackenzie, C. (2008), Can investor activism play a meaningful role in addressing market failures, *in: Journal of Corporate Citizenship, 2008, vol. 31, autumn edition, pp. 77–88.*

Sun, Z., Wang, A. and Zheng, L. (2012), The road less travelled: strategy distinctiveness and hedge fund performance, *in: The Review of Financial Studies, 2012, vol. 25, no. 1, pp. 96-143.*

Taylor, M. and Tonks, I. (1989), The internationalisation of stock markets and the abolition of U.K. exchange control, *in: Review of Economics and Statistics, 1989, vol. 71, no. 2, pp. 332-336.*

Taylor, S. (2000), Occupational pensions and employee retention: debate and evidence, *in: Employee Relations, 2000, vol. 22, no. 3, pp. 246-259.*

Terry, N. and White P. (1997), The role of pension schemes in recruitment and motivation: some survey evidence, *in: Employee Relations, 1997, vol. 19, no. 2, pp. 160-175.*

The Royal Swedish Academy of Sciences (2003), Time series econometrics: cointegration and autoregressive conditional heteroskedasticity, *scientific background to the Bank of Sweden Prize in Economic Sciences in Memory of Alfred Nobel, 2003, copy of the document available under following URL: http://www.nobelprize.org/nobel_prizes/economics/laureates/2003/ advanced-economicsciences2003.pdf, accessed on 02.12.2011.*

TheCityUK (2011), Financial markets series – commodities trading, *copy of the document available under URL: www.thecityuk.com/assets/Uploads/ Commodities-Trading-2011.pdf, accessed on 01-Jun-2011.*

Thombs, L. and Schucany, W. (1990), Bootstrap prediction intervals for autoregression, *in: Journal of the American Statistical Association, 1985, vol. 85, no. 410, pp. 486-492.*

Thornton, R. (2008), Ethical investments: a case of disjointed thinking, *in: Cambridge Law Journal, 2008, vol. 67, no. 2, pp. 396-422.*

Tiao, G. and Tsay, R. (1989), Model specification in multivariate time series, *in: Journal of the Royal Statistical Society, 1989, vol. 51, no. 2, pp. 157-213.*

Todd, R. (1990), Vector autoregression evidence on monetarism, *in: Quarterly Review, Federal Reserve Bank of Minneapolis, 1990, vol. 14, no. 2, pp. 19-38.*

Towers Watson and Financial Times (2011), Global alternatives survey 2011, *copy of the document available under URL: http://www.towerswatson.com/ assets/pdf/4844/Global-Alternatives-Survey-2011.pdf, accessed on 01-Jun-2012.*

Towers Watson (2010), Nachhaltiges Mitarbeiterengagement braucht neue Erfolgsformel, *in: Towers Watson Global Workforce Study 2010, copy of the document available under URL: http://www.towerswatson.com/ assets/pdf/1455/GlobalWorkfoceStudy2010_ExecutiveSummary_Germany.pdf, accessed on 10-Jun-2012.*

Triodos Bank (2012), About Triodos – what we do, *homepage of Triodos Bank, URL: http://www.triodos.co.uk/en/about-triodos/what-we-do/, accessed on 09-Sep-2012.*

Tsay, R. (2002), Analysis of financial time series – financial econometrics, *New York, 2002.*

Uebelhack, B. (2011), Betriebliche Alterversorgung – Grundlagen und Praxis, *2nd edition, Heidelberg, Munich i.a., 2011.*

UKSIF (UK Social Investment Forum) (2011), The social business initiative: promoting social investment funds, *copy of the document available under URL: http://www.uksif.org/cmsfiles/responses/5388924/UKSIF_response_to_EC_working_paper_on_Promoting_Social_Investment_Funds_14Sept11.pdf, accessed on 28-Sep-2011.*

Ulshoefer, G. and Bonnet, G. (editors, 2009), Corporate Social Responsibility auf dem Finanzmarkt: Nachhaltiges Investment – politische Strategien – ethische Grundlagen, *Wiesbaden, 2009.*

UNCTAD (United Nations Conference on Trade and Development) (2012), Don't blame the physical markets, *in: UNCATD Policy Brief, 2012, no. 25, quoted after Masters, M. (2008).*

UNEP (United Nations Environment Programme) (2009), Fiduciary responsibility – legal and practical aspects of integrating environmental, social and governance issues into institutional investment, *report by the Asset Management Working Group of the UNEP Finance Initiative. Copy of the document available under URL: http://www.unepfi.org/ publications/catalogue/index.html, accessed on 13.Aug-2011.*

UNEP (United Nations Environment Programme) and Mercer (2007), Demystifying responsible investment performance – a review of key academic and research brokers on ESG factors, *copy of the document available un-*

der URL: *http://www.unepfi.org/publications/catalogue /index.html, accessed on 13 Aug 2011.*

UNEP (United Nations Environment Programme) (2006), Linking environmental, social and governance issues to company value, *copy of the document available under URL: http://www.unepfi.org/fileadmin/documents/ show_me_the_money.pdf, accessed on 16-Sep-2012.*

Union Investment (2011), Institutionelle Anleger befuerworten nachhaltige Investments, *news article published on the homepage of Union Investment on 03-Aug-2011. Copy of the document available under URL: http://unternehmen.union-invest-ment.de/Newsletter/Pressemitteilungen/ 9da644ee77900c22cf8def5f05c36e26.0.0/PM_20110801_Nachhaltigkeitsstudie_2011.pdf, accessed on 29-Sep-2011.*

United Nations (2012, a), United Nations global compact - the ten principles, *homepage of the United Nations, URL: www.unglobalcompact.org/ AboutTheGC/TheTenPrinciples/index.html, accessed on 25-May-2012.*

United Nations (2012, b), Millennium development goals, *homepage of the United Nations, URL: http://www.un.org/millenniumgoals/, accessed on 25-May-2012.*

USSIF (US Social Investment Forum) (2011), Socially responsible investing facts, *homepage of USSFI, URL: http://www.ussif.org/resources/ sri-guide/srifacts.cfm, accessed on 12-Aug-2011.*

Van de Velde, E., Vermeir, W. and Corten, F. (2005), Corporate social responsibility and financial performance, *in: Corporate Governance, 2005, vol. 5, no. 3, pp. 129-138.*

Vandekerckhove, W., Leys, J., Alm, K., Scholtens, B., Signore, S. and Schaefer, H. (editors, 2011), Responsible investment in times of turmoil, *Heidelberg, London, New York, 2011.*

VBDO (Dutch Association of Investors for Sustainable Development) (2011), Benchmark responsible investment by pension funds in the Netherlands 2010, *Culemborg, 2011.*

VBL (Versorgungsanstalt des Bundes und der Laender) (2012), Die VBL auf einen Blick, *homepage of the VBL, URL: http://www.vbl.de/de/ wir_ueber_uns/auf_einen_blick/, accessed on 07-Jun-2012.*

Veit, A. (2009), Betriebliche Altersvorsorge, *in: Deutsche Rentenversicherung Bund and PWC (editors, 2009), chapters C-I, pp. 421-477.*

Verband Deutscher Pfandbriefbanken (2012), Fakten und Daten zu Europas fuehrenden Covered Bonds, *in: Der Pfandbrief, 2012, 2011-2012 edition.*

Vigeo (2012), ESG ratings of countries, *homepage of Vigeo, URL: http://www.vigeo.com/csr-rating-agency/en/311-3-1-2-notation-etats, accessed on 22-Sep-2012.*

Vigeo (2010), Green, social and ethical funds in Europe. 2010 review, *copy of the document available under URL: http://www.vigeo.com/csr-rating-*

agency/images/PDF/Publications/Green_Social_and_Ethical_Funds_in_Europe_2010_Vigeo.pdf, accessed on 26-Jun-2012.

Weber, O., Mansfeld, M. and Schirrmann, E. (2011), The financial performance of RI funds after 2000, *in: Vandekerckhove, W., Leys, J., Alm, K., Scholtens, B., Signore, S. and Schaefer, H. (editors, 2011), pp. 75-91.*

Weber, O., Scholz, R. and Michalik, G. (2008), Incorporating sustainability criteria into credit risk management, *in: Business Strategy and the Environment, 2008, vol. 19, no. 1, pp. 39-50.*

Webley, P., Lews, A. and Mackenzie, C. (2001), Commitment among ethical investors: an experimental approach, *in: Journal of Economic Psychology, 2001, vol. 22, no. 1, pp. 27-42, quoted after Lewis, A. and Cullis, J. (1990), Cullis, J., Lewis, A. and Winnett, A. (1992), Lewis, A. and Webley, P. (1994), Mackenzie, C. and Lewis, A. (1999).*

Winker, P. (2002), Vektor Autoregressive Modelle, *in: Schroeder, M. (2002, editor), pp. 213-262.*

Winker, P. (2000), Optimized multivariate lag structure selection, *in: Computational Economics, 2000, vol. 16, no. 1-2, pp. 87-103.*

Winker, P. (1999), Sluggish adjustment of interest rates and credit rationing: an application of unit root testing and error correction modelling, *in: Applied Economics, 1999, vol. 31, no. 3, pp. 267-277.*

Wolf, S. (2011), Steuerliches Umfeld der Pensionskasse, *in: Dresp, F., Fabian, R., Fath, R., Schwind, J. and Wolf, S. (2011, editors), pp. 204-271.*

Wood, D. and Hoff, B. (2007), Handbook on responsible investment across asset classes, *Chestnut Hill, 2007.*

Woodard, J., Egelkraut, T., Garcia, P. and Pennings, J. (2011), Effects of full collateralization in commodity futures investments, *in: Journal of Derivatives & Hedge Funds, 2011, vol. 16, no. 4, pp. 253-266.*

World Economic Forum (2011), Accelerating the transition towards sustainable investing: strategic options for investors, corporations and other key stakeholders, *Geneva, 2011.*

Zellner, A. (1963), Estimators for seemingly unrelated regression equations: some exact finite sample results, *in: Journal of the American Statistical Association, 1963, vol. 58, no. 304, pp. 977-992.*

Zellner, A. (1962), An efficient method of estimating seemingly unrelated regressions and tests for aggregation bias, *in: Journal of the American Statistical Association, 1962, vol. 57, no. 298, pp. 348-368.*

Zhou, T., Gunasekarage, A. and Power, D. (2005), Do real estate assets hedge inflation better than financial assets? Some New Zealand evidence, *in: Briefings in Real Estate Finance, 2005, vol. 5, no. 1, 2, pp. 39-46.*

Zimmermann, H. and Portmann, T. (2000), Anlagepolitik der Pensionskasen aus oekonomischer Sicht, *in: Der Schweizer Treuhaender, 2000, vol. 5, pp. 507-515.*

Appendix A: Reforms of the German Occupational Pension System

A. Overview

The current shape of the occupational pension scheme in Germany is the result of a number of essential reforms of the overall pension system from a regulatory and legal point of view that has been implemented over many decades. Given the already long history of the occupational pension system, we will not discuss all reforms and modifications this pension method has experienced over the more than 180 years since its foundation back in 1832. This section will focus primarily on more recent major reform undertakings that have had a measurable impact in defining today's role of the second pillar of the German pension system.

The most impactful reform packages that will be examined in this context are illustrated in the following timescale:

Figure 69: Major Reforms of the German Occupational Pension Scheme in Historical Context

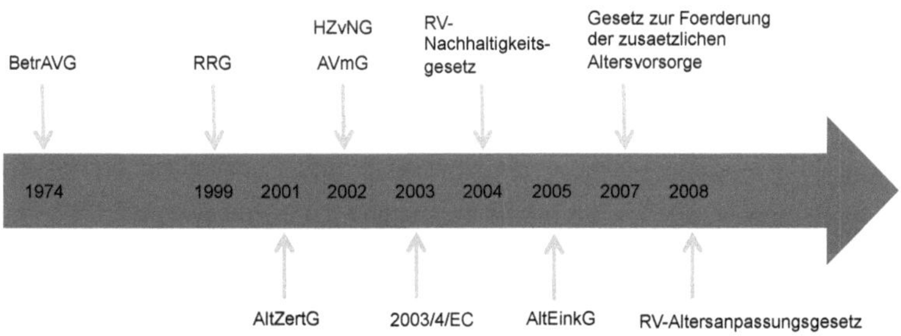

Source: Own figure, on the basis of Hubrich (2007), p.4.

These reforms had as one of the principle objectives to introduce a major shift in the German pension system away from the PAYG public pension scheme to capital funded structures offered and managed by the private sector (occupational and private pension plans). The private sector solution should not only be just a mere additional retirement pension option, but a true substitution.[890]

[890] See Hoefer, Steinmeyer (2004), p. F8.

B. 'Gesetz zur Verbesserung der betrieblichen Altersversorgung' (BetrAVG, 1974)

The BetrAVG defined the statutory regulation of the occupational pension scheme in 1974, a major break-through in the German private pension system. The law outlined the rules under which retirement provisions for employees would become a legal claim, a clear breakout in comparison to the previously dominating perception that occupational pension schemes were entirely at the discretion of the employer. While offering occupational pension plans remained optional under BetrAVG, once certain pension benefits were granted to employees for the purpose of retirement provisions and the insurance of biometric risks, these benefits would transform into legal, enforceable claims.[891]

C. 'Rentenreformgesetz' (RRG, 1999)

The RRG became effective on 01-Jan-1999 and represented the most substantial amendment to the BetrAVG since its introduction in 1974. The reform package came as a reaction to the relatively low degree of acceptance of occupational pension schemes within Germany's workforce at that point in time.[892]

The RRG set the foundation for some fundamental concepts of occupational pension schemes, which in later reforms would become enforceable rights for employees. The main features included the definition of the deferred contribution notion and defined contribution payments as well as clarifications with respects to the contributions of employers to the 'Pensionssicherungsverein' (PSV), the insolvency vehicle for the occupational pension system.[893]

D. 'Altersvorsorgeverträge- Zertifizierungsgesetz' (AltZertG) (2001)

The AltZertG defined the framework for the recognition of adequate capital funded pension plans that would benefit from beneficial taxation treatments. The ruling hereby only referred to occupational or private pension plans for which the respective members pay optional contributions.

The law also determined how the process of "certification of pension plans" had to be accomplished so that the underlying pension agreement would get full

---

891 See Doetsch et al. (2010), p. 31.
892 See Steinmeyer, Foersterling (1999), p. 1 et seq.
893 See Hanau et al. (2006), p. 9. For mode details on the PSV, see Pensionssicherungsverein (2011).

recognition. The German Federal Central Tax Office[894] was put in charge for the realization of the certification procedure.[895]

E. 'Altersvermoegensgesetz' (AVmG) (2002)

Sec. 7 AVmG, which became effective on 01-Jan-2002, introduced the Pension Fund as the fifth alternative of the German occupational pension scheme and is considered one of the major pension reform achievements of recent times. Besides, the Pension Fund was included in Sec. 112 of the Insurance Supervision Act (VAG), reflecting its role as particular form of insurance provider for biometrical risks.[896] Another significant contribution of the AVmG is the implementation (as an enforceable right) of the deferred compensation concept. Rationale for this innovation in 2002 was the expectation by the legislator that this would enable employees to participate in the occupational pension system even for cases where the company was actually not offering any occupational pension plan at all. Further improvements of the AVmG were the introduction of Defined Contributions with Capital Guarantee and the decrease in the minimum requirements for the vesting of pension claims (defined in Sec. 1b Par. 1 Sec. 1 BetrAVG).[897]

F. 'Huettenknappschaftliche-Zusatzversicherungs-Neuregelungsgesetz' (HZvNG) (2002)

The main achievement of the HZvNG was to define that voluntary contributions by employees into their occupational pension plans (either into Pension Funds, Pension Insurance Funds or Direct Insurances) had to be 'ranked' pari-passu from a legal point of view with employer contributions or deferred compensation transfers.[898]

[894] 'Bundeszentralamt fuer Steuern'.
[895] See Bundesministerium der Justiz (2011).
[896] See Schumann (2003), p. 37.
[897] See De Groot (2010), pp. 14-15.
[898] See Schumann (2003), p. 23.

G. European Union Directive 2003/41/EC (2003)[899]

The EU Directive 2003/41/EC focused primarily on the creation of a single European market for pension schemes. The directive defined regulatory minimum standards while still maintaining the peculiarities of each individual domestic market of the European Union. Moreover, the bill outlined the 'principle of prudence' notion for the asset management business of pension schemes. A new and relevant aspect for the German pension market, in particular, was also the disclosure obligation towards pension scheme members. As an overall theme, the directive promoted the expansion of occupational pension schemes for the European market.[900]

H. RV-Nachhaltigkeitsgesetz (2004)

The 'RV-Nachhaltigkeitsgesetz' instituted an innovative 'sustainability factor' into the pension calculation formula. This concept takes into account the ratio of current pensioners to current contributors and adjusts consequently for the intergenerational discrepancy within Germany's population.[901]

The sustainability factor, however, not only contains demographic factors, but also considers employment levels.[902] The "relative number of pensioners to contributors, the so-called system dependency ratio, is the most important long-term determinant of pension financing."[903] The effect of the inclusion is that the pension benefit indexation formula links increases in pension payments to the number of contributors as well as the number of pensioners, which are the two principal factors determining pension financing.[904]

I. 'Alterseinkuenftegesetz' (AltEinkG) (2005)

The AltEinkG redefined the taxation of pension contributions and benefits. It came into effect on 01-Jan-2005. Main driver of the new law was the different taxation basis and methodologies in practise for different pension systems, especially the beneficial tax treatment civil servant employees had been enjoying

[899] See European Parliament and the Council of the European Union (2003), pp. L235/10-L235/21.
[900] See De Groot (2010), p. 16.
[901] See Bonin (2009), p. 552.
[902] Ratio is calculated as number of equivalence pensioners/number of of equivalence contributors = pensioners/(contributors/unemployed). For further details on the formula see Boersch-Supan et al. (2003), p. 16.
[903] Boersch-Supan et al. (2003), p. 15.
[904] See Boersch-Supan et al. (2003), p. 15 et seq.

previously was a point of concern for the German Federal Constitutional Court.[905] With the new regulation, taxation for pension contributions would occur on a deferred basis, i.e. pension contributions would be tax deductible during the qualifying period of the pension schemes, but taxable as soon as benefits would be paid out to pension claimants. An essential aspect of the AltEinkG was to include all forms occupational pension schemes in the new tax treatment.[906] Furthermore, the rule stated that employees could transfer their pension entitlement from one occupational pensions scheme to another when they change company (also called concept of 'portability').[907]

J. 'Gesetz zur Foerderung der zusaetzlichen Altersvorsorge' (2007)

The minimum age to benefit from a vested claim on pension benefits originated from an occupational pension plan was reduced from 30 years of age down to 25 years for all pension claims post 01-Jan-2009.[908]

K. 'RV-Altersanpassungsgesetz' (2008)

The 'RV-Altersanpassungsgesetz' modified at its introduction on 01-Jan-2008 the retirement age of German workers within the statutory pension system. Retirement age would thereby be increased from 65 up to 67 years of age. These changes would come into effect from 01-Jan-2012 onwards. Based on the definition of the law act, the retirement age would be gradually increased from 2012 until 2029. Early retirement from the age of 63 years onwards will still be possible, but at a higher financial haircut than before.[909]

---

[905] See De Groot (2010), p. 18.
[906] See Bundesministerium der Finanzen (2011).
[907] See Hanau et al. (2006), p. 11.
[908] See Doetsch et al. (2010), p. 32.
[909] See Doetsch et al. (2010), p. 10 et seq.

Appendix B: Description Indices

A. Conventional Assets

A.1 Stoxx Europe 600 Index[910]

Provider: Stoxx

Description:

- The Stoxx Europe 600 index is structured as a fixed component number index designed to provide a broad and liquid representation of large, mid and small cap companies in Europe
- The Stoxx Europe 600 Index is derived from the Stoxx Europe Total Market Index (TMI) and is a subset of the Stoxx Global 1800 Index
- The index covers the following countries: Austria, Belgium, Denmark, Finland, France, Germany, Greece, Iceland, Ireland, Italy, Luxembourg, the Netherlands, Norway, Portugal, Spain, Sweden, Switzerland and the United Kingdom
- The index comprises large, mid and small size indices of 200 components each
- The index is divided into 19 supersectors according to ICB (Industry Classification Benchmark)

Price/Return Index: Total return index, dividends reinvested into the index

Currency: EUR

Historical Data Availability: Since 31-Dec-2000

Methodology: Free float market capitalization approach subject to a 20% weighting cap

Review Frequency: Quarterly

Number of Underlyings: 600 stocks

A.2 Iboxx Eurozone Index[911]

Provider: Markit

Description:

- Euro-denominated and Eurozone-currency sovereign debt issued by governments from the Eurozone
- Approximate country split of the index is: 24% Germany, 21% Italy, 21% France, RoW 31%

Average Duration: 6.17yrs

Average Annual Yield: 4.22%

Average Coupon: 3.96%

Price/Return Index: Total return index, coupons reinvested into the index

Currency: EUR

Historical Data Availability: 31-Dec-1998

Methodology:

- Minimum amount outstanding of €2,000m per bond
- Minimum 1 year remaining maturity

---

[910] See STOXX (2012, b) and STOXX (2012, c).
[911] See Markit (2007) and Markit (2012, a).

- The average long-term local currency sovereign debt rating of the country needs to be investment grade
- Individual bonds do not require a rating
- Bond weighting by market capitalisation

Review Frequency: Monthly

Number of Underlyings: 249

A.3 Index: Iboxx EUR Corporates Index[912]

Provider: Markit

Description:

- Investment grade corporate bonds issued in Euro currency
- Industry sector breakdown (in descending oder of relevance): Banks, Utilities, Telecoms, Financial Services, Indsutrials Insurance, Consumer Goods

Average yield: 5.30%

Average coupon: 4.90%

Average duration: 4.79yrs

Price/Return Index: Total return, coupons reinvested into the index

Currency: EUR

Historical Data Availability: 31-Dec-1998

Methodology:

- Minimum amount outstanding of €500m per bond
- Minimum 1 year remaining maturity
- The average long-term local currency sovereign debt rating of the country needs to be investment grade, Individual bonds do not require a rating
- Bond weighting by market capitalisation

Review Frequency: Monthly

Number of Underlyings: 1,286

A.4 Index: FTSE Developed Europe (Real Estate)[913]

Provider: FTSE

Description:

- Index tracks the performance of listed European real estate companies and REITs
- Companies need to generate at least 75% of their EBITDA in real estate business
- Index replicates the total return performance of the stock of the underlying companies

Price/Return Index: Total return index, dividends reinvested into the Index

Currency: EUR

Historical Data Availability: Dec-1989

Methodology:

- Weighting of a particular stock is free-float adjusted

---

[912] See Markit (2007) and Markit (2012, b).

[913] See FTSE (2011, a) and FTSE (2011, b).

- Liquidity screening on an annual basis

Review Frequency: Quarterly

Number of Underlyings: 85 stocks

B. Sustainable Indices

B.1 Stoxx Europe Sustainability ex-AGTAFA Index[914]

Provider: Stoxx

Description:

- The STOXX Europe Sustainability index is designed to provide a representation of sustainability leaders in Europe
- Components are selected according to a systematic corporate sustainability assessment, based on long-term environmental, social and governance criteria. All companies with a positive sustainability rating will be included in the index
- Derived from the Stoxx Europe 600 Index
- Covers the top 20% of components of the STOXX Europe 600 Index in terms of sustainability
- The STOXX Europe Sustainability index ex AGTAFA excludes companies which generate revenues from alcohol, gambling, tobacco, armaments, firearms and adult entertainment (AGTAFA)
- The indices cover Austria, Belgium, Denmark, Finland, France, Germany, Greece, Iceland, Ireland, Italy, Luxembourg, the Netherlands, Norway, Portugal, Spain, Sweden, Switzerland and the United Kingdom

Underlying SRI Methodolody: Best-in-class combined with negative screening

Reference Index: Stoxx Europe 600 index

Price/Return Index: Total return index dividends reinvested into the index

Currency: EUR

Historical Data Availability: 31-Dec-1998

Methodology: Free float market capitalisation

Review Frequency: Quarterly

Number of Underlyings: 200 stocks

B.2 ECPI Euro Ethical Government Bond Index[915]

Provider: ECPI

Description:

- The underlying screening methodology attempt to identify states that follow certain international, social and economic policies and treaties aimed at respecting the environment and the general principles of human rights
- Sovereign screening approach assesses compliance to international standards, treaties and conventions on the following areas:
    - Death penalty, ratification of the main conventions on labor rights, ratification of the main treaties on human rights, ratification of the main treaties on environmental protection, civil liberties and political rights

Underlying SRI Methodolody: Positive screening

---

[914] See STOXX (2012, b) and STOXX (2012, d).

[915] See ECPI (2010) and ECPI (2011, b).

Reference Index: Markit Iboxx Benchmark indices (Iboxx Eurozone index)

Rating Breakdown: 56% AAA, 42% AA, 2% A

Main Countries Represented: 23% Germany, 23% Italy, 20% France, 8% Spain, 6% Belgium, 5% Netherlands

Average Duration: 6.17 years

Average Annual Yield: 3.72%

Average Coupon: 4.30%

Price/Return Index: Total return, as coupons are reinvested into the index

Currency: EUR

Historical Data Availability: 19-Dec-2000

Methodology:

- Capital weighted index by amount outstanding
- Minimum outstanding par amount of €2,000m and a residual life of at least one year
- Includes fixed coupon, zero coupon and step-up structures
- Only investment grade bonds are included publicly issued in the Eurobond and Euro-zone domestic markets

Review Frequency: Monthly

Number of Underlyings: 264

B.3 ECPI Ethical Euro Corporate Bond Index[916]

Provider: ECPI

Description:

- The ECPI Corporate Screening Methodology is a process consisting of two steps:
    - ESG (Environmental, Social and Governance) screening: analysis of issuers along a wide and comprehensive set of indicators grouped in the following macro-categories: environmental strategy; environmental management; products (industry specific); production process (industry specific); community relations; employees and human capital; markets; corp. governance & shareholders
    - Sector screening: exclusion of issuers operating in the following ineligible sectors (the threshold is set in terms of % incidence on annual revenues): military / army; pornography; tobacco; alcohol; gambling; nuclear energy; contraceptives; GMO food production

Underlying SRI Methodolody: Best-in-class combined with negative screening

Reference Index: Markit Iboxx Benchmark indices (Iboxx EUR Corporates index)

Rating Breakdown: 4% AAA, 27% AA, 43% A, 26% BBB

Main Countries Represented: 19% Netherlands, 18% France, 11% UK, 11% US, 8% Italy, 6% Germany

Average Duration: 4.07 years

Average Annual Yield: 4.51%

Average Coupon: 5.15%

---

[916] See ECPI (2011, b) and ECPI (2011, c).

Price/Return Index: Total return, as coupons are reinvested into the index

Currency: EUR

Historical Data Availability: 19-Dec-2000

Methodology:

- Capital weighted index by amount outstanding
- Minimum outstanding par amount of €500m and a residual life of at least one year
- Includes fixed coupon, zero coupon and step-up structures
- Only investment grade bonds are included

Review Frequency: Monthly

Number of Underlyings: 980 bonds

C. Alternative Investments

C.1 DJ Credit Suisse Hedge Fund Index[917]

Provider: Dow Jones, Credit Suisse

Description:

- Index designed to represent the liquid, investable hedge fund universe
- Includes the performance of managed accounts as well as other regulated fund structures
- Index uses as selection pool approximately 8,000 funds and consists only of funds with a minimum of US$50 million under management, a 12-month track record, and audited financial statements
- Underlying funds need to be able to provide daily net asset valuations
- Global investment universe as underlying funds tend to have a broad market focus
- Main investment strategies include: convertible arbitrage, emerging markets, event driven, fixed-income arbitrage, global macro, long/short equity as well as managed futures
- The index does not take into account for any 'survivorship-bias' effect that may occur, as only funds that perform well and have a minimum track record are included in the index composition. This implies that funds that had to close their investment operations due to underperformance or fund withdrawal by clients are not considered. This might distortion the actual performance hedge funds actually obtain

Price/Return Index: Price index

Currency: EUR

Historical Data Availability: 01-Jan-1994

Methodology:

- The index is calculated and rebalanced on a monthly basis, and reflects performance net of all hedge fund component performance fees and expenses
- Asset-weighted hedge fund index and includes only funds

Review Frequency: Quarterly

Underlyings: 40-50 funds

---

[917] See Dow Jones, Credit Suisse (2012, a) and Dow Jones, Credit Suisse (2012, b).

C.2 DJ UBS Commodity Index Total Return[918]

Provider: Dow Jones, UBS

Description:

- Index that provides a broad exposure to the commodities asset class
- Composed of futures contracts on physical commodities
- To measure the importance of a commodity, the index relies on liquidity data or the relative amount of trading activity in a particular commodity. Also production data is used for some assets
- To ensure sufficient diversity, no commodity can represent more than 15% of the index and no related group of commodities (e.g. precious metals or livestock) is allowed to constitute more than 33% of the overall index
- No single commodity can have a weighting of less than 2% of the index
- 2011 commodity weights: 22% petroleum, 19% grains, 18% industrial metals, 14% precious metals, 11% natural gas, 8% softs, 5% livestock, 3% vegetable oils
- The index accounts for the effect of 'rolling' futures contracts, as contracts that approach maturity are sold and new contracts on the same underlying acquired
- Futures rolling can have a price impact: when prices are lower for long-term contracts than short term futures (effect of 'backwardation'), the acquisition of the long term contract would occur at a lower price than the market price of the futures sold. On the opposite, if long-term contracts are trading at a premium to short-dated futures, the rolling into longer-term positions will be realised at a loss ('contango'). This price difference is also called 'roll yield'

Price/Return Index: Total return, as return on the fully collateralized positions in the underlying commodity positions is considered

Currency: EUR

Historical Data Availability: 31-Dec-1990

Methodology:

- Two different indices are constructed:
    - (1) index that takes into account relative liquidity of the underlying commodities,
    - (2) average 5-year production numbers are used to determine the production index of all assets included
- Using a ratio of 2:1, liquidity ratio and production ratio indices are combined into the single index

Review Frequency: Annually

Number of Underlyings: 20 commodities

[918] See Dow Jones, UBS (2011) and Dow Jones, UBS (2012).

Appendix C: Empirical Results

A. 1-Step Ahead Forecasting

Figure 70: 1-Month Ahead Forecast: Standard Portfolio

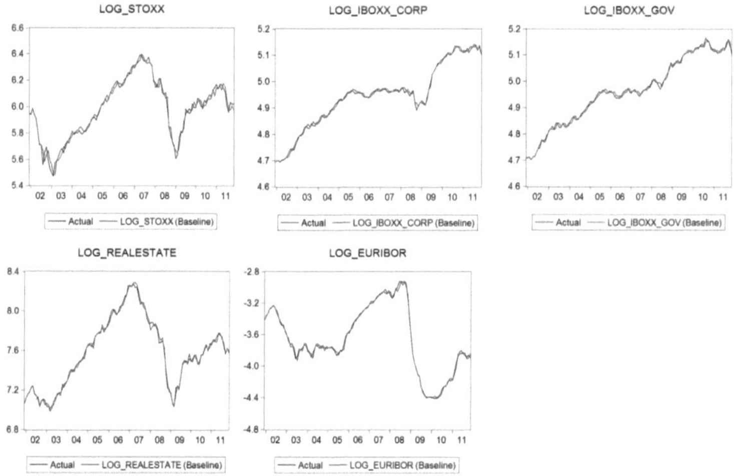

Source: Own figure.

Figure 71: 1-Month Ahead Forecast: SRI Portfolio

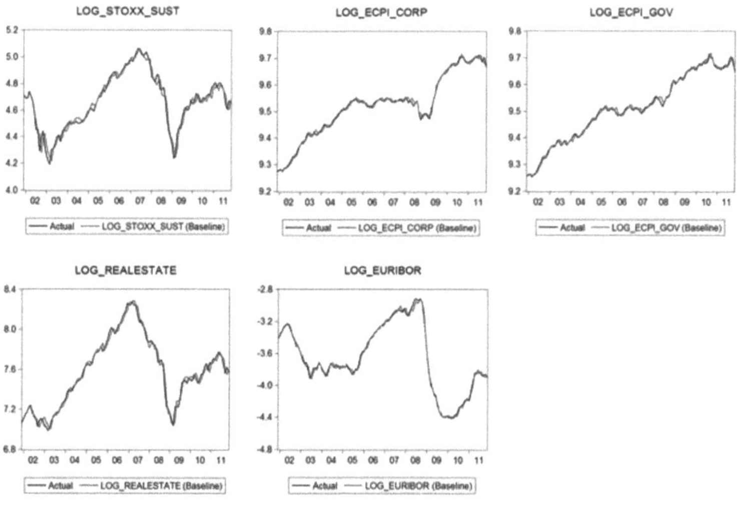

Source: Own figure.

Figure 72: 1-Month Ahead Forecast: Alternative Portfolio

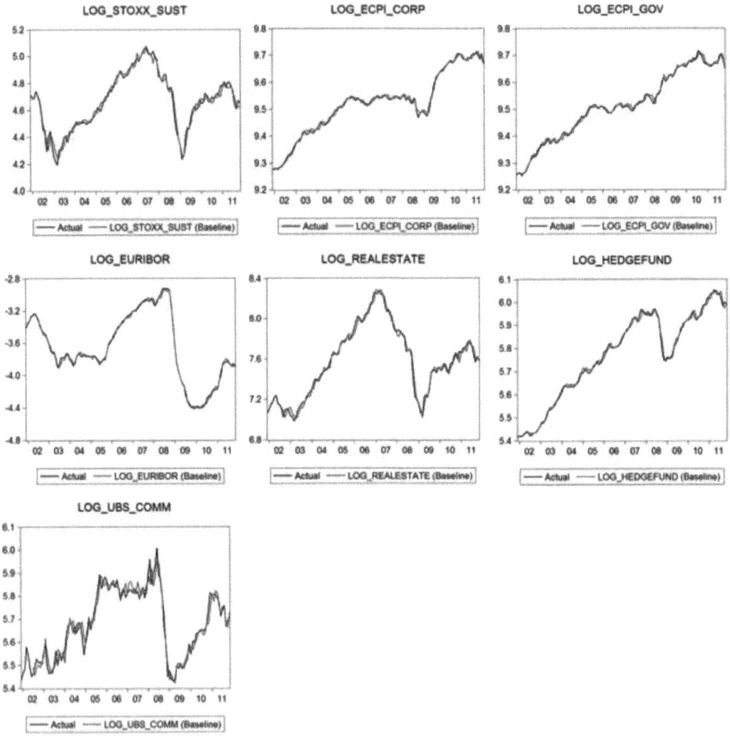

Source: Own figure.

MIX
Papier aus verantwortungsvollen Quellen
Paper from responsible sources
FSC® C105338

If you have any concerns about our products,
you can contact us on
ProductSafety@springernature.com

In case Publisher is established outside the EU,
the EU authorized representative is:
Springer Nature Customer Service Center GmbH
Europaplatz 3, 69115 Heidelberg, Germany

Printed by Libri Plureos GmbH
in Hamburg, Germany